JEWISH

DESTINIES

JEWISH DESTINIES

CITIZENSHIP, STATE,

AND COMMUNITY

IN MODERN FRANCE

PIERRE BIRNBAUM

TRANSLATED BY ARTHUR GOLDHAMMER

HILL AND WANG

A DIVISION OF FARRAR, STRAUS AND GIROUX

NEW YORK

Hill and Wang
A division of Farrar, Straus and Giroux
19 Union Square West, New York 10003

Library of Congress Cataloging-in-Publication Data
Birnbaum, Pierre.
    [Destins juifs. English]
    Jewish destinies : citizenship, state, and community in modern
France / Pierre Birnbaum ; translated by Arthur Goldhammer.—1st
ed.
      p. cm.
    Includes bibliographical references and index.
    ISBN 0-8090-6101-5
    1. Jews—France—Politics and government.   2. Jews—Emancipation—
France.   3. Antisemitism—France.   4. France—Ethnic relations.
    I. Title.
DS135.F83B5713   2000
305.892′4044—dc21   99-16275

CONTENTS

PREFACE TO THE AMERICAN EDITION

The modern history of the Jews of France was shaped by the French Revolution and its universalist message: from the time of the Revolution forward, France has conceived of itself as a progressive nation serving as a beacon to others and rejecting all vestiges of the past. Implicit in the so-called regeneration of the French nation was the idea that the Revolution had brought forth a "new man." Yet, at the same time, it continued the centralizing thrust of the absolute monarchy, crushing the resistance of those who clung to any identity other than that of citizen. The Revolution's liberal phase ended with the victory of the Jacobins, who, led by Maximilien de Robespierre and Louis de Saint-Just, seized power, overcame the Girondin opposition exemplified by men like Honoré-Gabriel Riqueti de Mirabeau, and governed with an iron hand. The Jacobins bitterly fought every effort to preserve the past: in particular, they led a merciless assault on the Catholic Church as well as on groups that championed the interests of a particular province or linguistic minority. As a result, social pluralism suffered a devastating blow, while the prospect of a homogeneous society was embraced. The resulting defeat of cultural pluralism and liberalism was to have a lasting effect on the destiny of the Jews.

The French model of Jewish emancipation therefore led to a rupture with the past and to condemnation of the very idea of a "Jewish community." In the United States and Great Britain, by contrast, renunciation of identity was not an implicit part of Jewish emancipation. In these societies, the state played a less pervasive role than in France. Liberalism and pluralism were fundamental principles that encouraged decentralization along with representation for all social groups and cultural or "ethnic" communities (whereas the word "ethnic" does not exist in the French political vocabulary and is alien to French political tradition). Local politics and organizations of all sorts flourish in these countries. Jews are free to participate in Jewish community life as they see fit and to maintain their own decentralized religious organizations. Like other groups, they may try to pressure politicians and influence decisions through campaigns, lobbying, and other perfectly legitimate activities. In France, however, because of the Revolution's opposition to intermediating structures between the state and its citizens, nothing of the sort exists. But the French model of emancipation has yielded a compensatory benefit: because of its insistence on the equality of all citizens, it created an environment in which Jews as individuals were able to obtain public employment, serve in government, and rise to positions of prestige and prominence. These opportunities had an unexpected consequence, however: as Jews became increasingly visible, anti-Semitism in France attained an extraordinary level of verbal violence. In some ways, one might argue that France was the country that achieved the most radical emancipation of the Jews and, in the late nineteenth century, the most vehement opposition to that emancipation.

In the United States and Great Britain, emancipation did not entail renunciation of one's Jewish identity. Jews long kept faith with their communities and traditions. Where assimilation took place, it was the result of individual decisions rather than state policy. Most Jews thus continued to participate in civil society. They joined private organizations, and many chose careers in the professions or the business world. They did not go into politics or civil-service jobs. These choices were reinforced by the fact that the most prestigious private universities, such as Harvard, Princeton, and Yale in the United States and Oxford and Cambridge in Britain, remained closed to Jews until well into the twentieth century. By contrast, such prestigious French institutions as the Ecole Polytechnique and the Ecole Normale Supérieure accepted qualified Jews from the early nineteenth century. Similarly, Jews in the United States are still excluded from some clubs and wealthy residential communities, whereas in France residence is unrestricted and they have little difficulty in rising to authoritative positions in government. On the other hand, anti-Semitism in the English-speaking countries is mainly social and has generally not taken the form of anti-Jewish political movements. Jewish life in these democratic societies has therefore been relatively tranquil. Jews there have never had to face the dangers that the Jews of France or the Weimar Republic faced when the republican model collapsed. Although they may have to contend with many prejudices in their daily lives and are excluded from certain restricted circles, they have not had to face the bloody pogroms that devastated the Jewish communities of Poland, Russia, and Romania. Relations between American and British Jews and the societies in which they live have been different from relations between French Jews and French society: until recently, the public role of American and British Jews has been limited; they have had relatively little influence on political parties, and their ideological commitment has been moderate, to say the least.

Another important difference deserves mention: France has long been regarded as "the eldest daughter of the Church." French society has been fundamentally Catholic, and its values, traditions, holidays, and rituals have been steeped in Catholicism alone. The emancipation of the Jews must therefore be seen against the background of the struggle between state and church. During the absolute monarchy as well as during the Revolution, the state attempted to exert control over the Church by appointing its priests, monitoring its budget, and revamping its operations so as to undermine its prestige. The state naturally sought to exert similar control over other religions. Under Napoleon, for example, steps were taken to subject Jews to the control of "consistories" set up by the government. By the end of the nineteenth century, however, it was clear that these efforts to control the Church had failed, and the state opted instead for a radical separation of church and state. Religion was to have no presence whatsover in the public sphere: in politics, the schools, the army, the courts, and so on. The state also severed its ties to "the synagogue": the fundamental principle of secularism implied that organized religion had no place in either government or the public schools. In the United States, despite the "wall" that is supposed to separate church and state, public values are deeply influenced by religion and the Bible. The American "civil religion" is based on a plurality of religious identities within a generalized moral consensus upon which American democracy is widely believed to rest. In many ways, the United States sees itself as "the new Israel." The Old Testament is still a force, and social values bear the stamp of Biblical times. To be sure, there were bloody conflicts between Protestants and Catholics in nineteenth-century America, but not, as in France, between Catholics and Jews. (Readers unfamiliar with French history may wish to bear in mind that in France the sixteenth-century Wars of Religion virtually wiped out Protestantism.)

Thus the status of Judaism in the American democracy differs in virtually every respect from the status of Judaism in the French Republic. In America, Judaism has been a part of the cultural landscape since the time of the first European settlements. Jews have existed in France much longer, of course, but before the Revolution Judaism was seen as an alien presence in a society shaped by victorious Catholicism. Later, with the triumph of the Republic and the principle of secularism and emancipation on the universalist model, Judaism was banished from the public sphere along with all other forms of religious expression, though this sphere still bears the impress of its Catholic cultural matrix. In France, then, the fate of the Jews has been caught up in a historical conflict between church and state in which Jews have been mere onlookers. French Jews have proceeded along a chaotic path, which has yielded both brilliant success and dismal failure. It is this path that I hope to retrace in the pages that follow.

Some chapters of this book have appeared in other forms. Chapter 1 was published in *Le Débat*, Jan.–Feb. 1989. Chapter 2 appeared in the *Revue française de sociologie*, July–Dec. 1989. Part of chapter 5 appeared in Zeev Sternhell, ed., *L'Eternel retour: Contre la démocratie, l'idéologie de la décadence* (Paris: Presses de la Fondation Nationale des Sciences Politiques, 1994), and another part was published in *Mille neuf cent* 11 (1993). Chapter 6 appeared in Michel Winock, ed., *Histoire de l'extrême droite en France* (Paris: Editions du Seuil, 1993). To one degree or another, all of these texts have been updated to reflect the current state of debate and to fit with the general argument I am trying to make here.

I want to thank François Azouvi for his rigorous and demanding reading of the entire manuscript. I would also like to thank Lauren Osborne, my editor. She asked a lot of questions and helped me reshape the book for an American audience. It has been a privilege to work with her.

Hill and Wang would like to thank the French Ministry of Culture for its support in the publication of this work.

JEWISH

DESTINIES

INTRODUCTION

With the French Revolution, Jews became full-fledged citizens of France, gained access to public space, and, pursuant to the ideals of the Enlightenment, frequently transformed themselves into ardent advocates of the public weal. Many were tempted to forsake their own values, abandon the Hebrew language, forget ancestral obligations, and reject the laws of their community in favor of the laws of a state defined by the abstract notion of citizenship. Without renouncing their Jewishness, which was an integral part of who they were, Jews did these things in order to pave the way for a "regeneration" capable of freeing them at last from their old collective identity. Public space and private space became separate and distinct entities. Henceforth the nation would be composed exclusively of "citizens" whose private values no longer mattered in the public sphere. Access to public space required total assimilation into a homogeneous nation. This way out of the ghetto was a distinctively French invention, whose absolute, revolutionary character soon made it a model for all the world. It was a very different kind of emancipation from that which took place in democracies such as England, or in authoritarian regimes such as Russia. Even Prussia, so keenly attuned to the statist French model and so ready to import its institutions, hesitated to embrace as radical an idea of emancipation as the French. The French model justly became renowned: the sacrosanct formula "Franco-Judaism" came to symbolize the Jews' marriage with France. As citizens, Jews soon became voters and even garnered the votes of their fellow citizens, which transformed them into full-fledged representatives of the national community. Citizenship also guaranteed them access to the civil service, though not until rather substantial resistance had been overcome, and encouraged many inspired by the emancipatory ideal of Reason to devote body and soul to the search for truth in a variety of academic careers.

Anyone who wishes to ponder the destiny of the Jews of France from the Revolution to the present need not limit himself to a narrowly chronological narrative. A more interpretive approach, one that moves back and forth in time, may offer a better understanding of the issues that French Jews confronted as they made their way in a modernizing society racked by continual social and ideological conflict and sharp reaction against the values of 1789. French Jews were natives of Alsace and Lorraine, of Bayonne, Bordeaux, Avignon, Nîmes, Rouen, and Paris; they were also immigrants from Eastern Europe and, later, from North Africa. The cultures in which they were steeped were in some ways similar to one another but in other ways profoundly different. The bonds of community among Jews were strained as some adopted strategies that risked estrangement from their coreligionists. Nevertheless, most identified with the ideals of the Enlightenment and became loyal citizens of the Republic. They flocked to schools and universities, volunteered to defend France against foreign enemies, and proved to be dutiful citizens prompt to discharge their civic obligations at the ballot box.

To one degree or another, all French Jews, even those who shunned careers in government and chose instead to contribute to the growth of the economy or toil in a variety of professions, remained *fous de la République,* or zealots of the Republic. Although this expression was once reserved exclusively for "state Jews," those who served the public, it can easily be applied to others. Emile Durkheim coined the phrase "functionaries of society" to describe all citizens of the French Republic, but the expression is particularly apt when applied to Jews, whose private values—and, indeed, whose very destinies— seemed permanently bound up with their status as citizens prepared to set aside all particular communal allegiances in order to serve the general public. Readers of this book will encounter people in all walks of life, including scholars, "court Jews," and civil servants as well as spokesmen for a variety of institutions associated with a demanding religious orthodoxy. But since the book is largely concerned with the evolution of the French national and Jewish communal identities, I inevitably focus primarily on men who chose careers in government, politics, the civil service, the military, and teaching—on those, in short, who poured their universalist passion into public service and the pursuit of learning. This exploration of the Jews of France will thus be concerned chiefly with members of the elite who in one way or another allied themselves with the state and who, at the same time, participated most fully in the process of republicanization. As such, they came to symbolize the destiny of all Jews who aspired to become "good citizens" of France. This necessarily entailed a dilution of the collective personality of the Jewish community, and resistance to that dilution set in early and renewed itself repeatedly. Accordingly, I will also examine the arguments of those who sought to restrain the secularization of society because of the threat that secularization posed to Jewish cultural identity. In taking this approach, I do not claim to be recounting the history of all French Jews. The voice of the majority, of those who chose to live their Judaism in silence and in private and who did not participate in crucial public debates, is rarely heard.

Dramatic changes took place in the two centuries that separate the French Revolution from the desecration of a Jewish cemetery in the ancient town of Carpentras, the site of the oldest surviving synagogue in France, which dates from the fourteenth century. Because Carpentras symbolizes the ancientness of the Jewish presence in France, it is easy to overestimate the importance of what happened in Carpentras in May 1990 in relation to earlier assaults on the French model of emancipation, such as the Dreyfus Affair and the persecution of

Jews under the Vichy regime. Nevertheless, it does seem that, in the years since Carpentras, the rules governing Jewish participation in French republican life have changed in ways to which too little attention has thus far been paid. In 1990, a vast majority of the French expressed outrage at what took place in Carpentras. Since then, however, there seems to have been an effort, orchestrated from on high, to redefine French Jews as a community apart. Flying in the face of the universalist tradition of the Enlightenment, the republican state, which had always been an ally of the Jews, appears to want to impose a separate identity on them and to set them apart from their fellow citizens. Jews now find themselves relegated to an imaginary community not by those who once reviled them but by those who were formerly their most zealous defenders. In France in the 1990s, nearly everyone insists on the importance of respecting differences. Many people seem drawn to rediscovering their communal roots. And a muted multiculturalism seems to be emerging for the first time in a public sphere that, according to strict republican ideology, ought to consist of pure, abstract citizens, militant champions of the public good. Yet, despite all this, the logic of Carpentras seems to be one of reifying difference. In the discourse of political leaders and the press, Jews are once again being cast as members of a closed community permanently wedded to cultural practices that amateur ethnographers seem bound and determined to rehash endlessly.

This imposed "communitarization," articulated in phrases resounding with sympathy for the Jewish community, is once again presenting that community as isolated from French society. There can be no doubt, moreover, that this communitarization imposed from above has served to reinforce a tendency toward communitarization stemming from below, actively supported by various religious organizations and other institutions determined to create an authentic and autonomous Jewish community here and now, as well as to restore traditions fallen by the wayside since the republican emancipation. Can we therefore say that Carpentras marked a true turning point because it revealed in a particularly clear way any number of internal conflicts whose effect has been to marginalize Jews within French society? Has it changed the nature of the Jewish community's relation-

ship to the larger nation? Has it altered the contract between the state
and citizens who once set aside their various private allegiances as
the price of participating in the public sphere? Has France's exceptional status as the champion of a "Jacobin" or universalist model
ended with the triumph of an alternative "Girondin" or particularist
model in which communal identities will henceforth be allowed full
expression?

There is ample reason to doubt that any of these questions can be
answered in the affirmative, given the long history of opposition to
such communal expression—opposition that is embodied in the
French state. Nevertheless, the French Revolution and Carpentras
may be taken as symbols that reveal how the destiny of French Jews
has wavered between two extremes: republican assimilation, which
has clearly been compatible with the preservation of Jewish culture
and tradition, and voluntary or involuntary communitarization, which
has just as clearly been incapable of undermining the symbolic importance of citizenship. For two centuries, two hostile rhetorics have
repeatedly clashed: that of the emancipators and their many supporters within the Jewish community, and that of innumerable rabbis hostile to republican homogenization. To complicate the picture still
further, there has also been a durable strain of radical nationalist and
populist rhetoric hostile to the republican integration of the Jews and
determined to promote a very different image of French identity, according to which France is not a community of citizens of different
cultures but a quasi-organic community steeped in a singular cultural
tradition. Over the years, this position has invariably led to outright
rejection of the outsider, whether the Jew or the Protestant, the Italian
or the Arab. Today as in the past, groups and movements of the extreme right continue to vituperate against a Republic which, they argue, cannot be truly French because, in its embrace of Reason, it
inevitably renounces the nation's deeper identity and strikes at the
heart of its culture and religion.

From the Dreyfus Affair to Vichy and beyond, those who reject the
Republic have lashed out against its universalistic practices as well
as against the emancipatory strategies of social assimilation and state
integration adopted by generation after generation of Jews. Paradoxi-

cally, one consequence of this antiuniversalist stance has been to encourage the proponents of communitarization from below, who favor a degree of detachment from the public sphere, withdrawal, and in some cases even a rejection of secular principles. At the time of the French Revolution, enthusiasm and faith in the regeneration of all mankind swept everyone along, and most Jews passionately embraced this path to modernity. The events at Carpentras and their unintended aftermath have signaled a resurgence of the temptation toward communal isolation. Caught between contradictory alternatives, the Jews of France, along with their non-Jewish fellow citizens, face an uncertain future.

PART ONE

Different Roads

to

Emancipation

1

A JACOBIN REGENERATOR:
ABBÉ GRÉGOIRE

Near the end of historian Yosef Yerushalmi's admirable study of Isaac Cardoso, the name of Abbé Henri Grégoire is mentioned for the first time. Yerushalmi remarks that to the author of the *Essai sur la régénération physique, morale et politique des Juifs,* Cardoso's work was already a mere curiosity.[1] As an uncompromising champion of Jewish emancipation under the guidance of a centralized Jacobin state, the abbé was quick to "sound the death knell of the Jewish society that Cardoso had known and celebrated."[2] Indeed, it is hard to imagine a greater contrast than that between Cardoso and Grégoire. Cardoso represented the Jewish *halacha* tradition and its insistence that Jews and non-Jews live separately; rejecting Christianity and fleeing the Spanish Inquisition, he chose to live among fellow Jews in the ghetto of Verona. Grégoire, on the other hand, openly sought to "regenerate" Jews by converting them to Catholicism of a distinctly Jansenist stripe. For Cardoso, the survival of Jewish tradition seemed to require an ingrown, close-knit community. For Grégoire, Jewish emancipation and access to citizenship could come about only if the Jewish community ceased to live apart from the rest of society. This debate would prove crucial, and its terms have remained all but constant ever since. Obviously it raised the more general issue of whether particularist commitments have any place in a modernized society based primarily on universalist, rationalist, and, ultimately, secularist principles. What place might Jews as such occupy in a society that henceforth recognized only "citizens" and vigorously combated all forms of particularist organization, from the guild to the region—a society that sought to confine the expression of religious beliefs to the private sphere? Between Cardoso's radical solution, which questioned the very possibility of an "open society," and universalist assimilation pure and simple, was there room in modern France, with its strong and venerable centralist traditions, for an alternative path to modernization?

Rejecting the Cardoso solution, many French Jews from the end of the eighteenth century to the present have enthusiastically embraced the universalist possibilities opened up by the French Revolution, largely thanks to the efforts of Abbé Grégoire.[3] Faith in the Republic's power to emancipate has seldom flagged. In 1973, an organization whose orientation was fundamentally Zionist solemnly planted trees in a Paris square near the house in which Grégoire died. This odd homage to a man who was at once deeply Catholic and profoundly committed to the assimilation of French Jews was far from an isolated occurrence. In Lunéville, where the abbé delivered his first pro-Jewish sermons, the local Jewish community's admiration is still such that, after a statue of him was destroyed during World War II, members of the community contributed to a fund for replacing it, just as they had contributed to the construction of the original in 1859. In the dark years between the two world wars, when anti-Semitism was on the rise, politician Louis Darquier de Pellepoix delivered a long speech to the municipal council of Paris attacking Léon Blum and the Jews. Amid tumult and shouting, the eldest member of the council, Paul Fleurot, rose in rebuttal: he gravely invoked Grégoire's role in the emancipation of the Jews—an emancipation which in his view had long since been accomplished.[4] A few years earlier, in April 1931, P. Grunebaum-Ballin, the president of the prefectoral council of the Seine and later an eminent member of the Conseil d'Etat, celebrated the hundredth anniversary of the abbé's death with a long lecture to the Cercle d'Etudes Juives and the Société des Etudes Juives. With emotion in his voice, he, too, stressed "Grégoire's constant solicitude for the regeneration of the children of Israel."[5]

Not long before, on the rue Racine in Paris on May 25, 1926, Samuel Schwartzbard murdered Simon Petlyura, the man responsible for horrible pogroms against the Jews of the Ukraine shortly after World War I. This slaying provoked considerable debate around the world, especially among Jews. When Schwartzbard was tried two years later, his lawyer, Henry Torrès, ended a lengthy plea on behalf of the defendant with a reference to Abbé Grégoire, which he hoped would persuade the court to free the accused forthwith. Addressing the jurors, he said "It is not just the voice of Schwartzbard's attorney that you hear, it is also the voice of thousands upon thousands of victims [of anti-Semitic violence]. And besides those voices you also hear the voices of Abbé Grégoire, Mirabeau, Gambetta, and Victor Hugo."[6] Clearly, invoking Grégoire's name had become something of a ritual for French Jews, who believed that he had played a crucial role in setting them free. Go back a few more years: in 1890, Mardochée Vidal-Naquet, president of the Consistoire Israélite of Marseilles, also expressed his view that Grégoire was "the first person to speak out in our behalf." Or take the case of Théodore Reinach, a historian, future deputy, and brother of Joseph and Salomon Reinach, all three of whom would later become active champions of Dreyfus and exemplars of Jewish assimilation. Théodore Reinach, a man with many degrees whose abundant talents won him appointment to any number of eminent positions, published a *History of the Israelites from the Time of the Diaspora to the Present* in 1885; within a short period of time, the book became a standard reference. Commenting on Grégoire's efforts, he noted that "intelligent people regarded the enthusiastic curé's proposed reforms as utopian, but before long those utopias became realities. Grégoire enjoyed the privilege of seeing his dreams fulfilled."[7] In May 1831, when Grégoire died, Adolphe Crémieux, another living symbol of Jewish emancipation, spoke at his graveside about the gratitude felt by "regenerated" Jews, while pupils from Jewish schools, led by their teachers, solemnly filed past.

Crémieux, remembered as the author of the Crémieux Decree, which extended French nationality to the Jews of Algeria, apostrophized the deceased: "Can you hear me, O priest of Jesus Christ? Jews throughout the world will mourn your passing." On another occasion he described Grégoire as "a great citizen, a simple priest who spoke out courageously in favor of emancipation for the Jews and toleration for their religion."[8]

During Grégoire's lifetime, the chorus of Jewish praise was all but unanimous: while traveling through Amsterdam as a senator of the Empire, the abbé was welcomed by all three of the city's synagogues and heard his name included in the verses of a prayer of thanksgiving in Hebrew. He was received just as respectfully in Göttingen, Germany. A short while earlier, on January 23, 1790, the Jews of Bayonne and Bordeaux sent a delegation to thank the celebrated priest and "pay him a deserved tribute of praise and gratitude for the wondrous boons that your efforts have secured for our less fortunate brethren." Furthermore, as Grégoire himself noted in his *Mémoires:* "All the synagogues of France prayed publicly for me and voted to thank me." What uncommon action was it that won for Grégoire the unstinting gratitude of French Jews?

In 1785, the Société Royale des Sciences et des Arts of Metz announced the results of an essay contest on "the most useful and least cumbersome type of wine press" and proclaimed that the topic for 1786 would be how "to ensure the livelihood of bastards and make them more useful to the state." The subject for 1787, however, was rather different in nature. The essayists were asked to respond to the question whether "there are ways to make the Jews of France happier and more useful." Nine contestants responded to this challenge, including Grégoire, who in 1788 was chosen as one of five finalists. Meanwhile, some of the more outrageous contributions were eliminated. The Benedictine monk Chais, for example, had suggested that, "since the Jews are birds of prey, they must be not killed but tamed by having their beaks and claws snipped." And d'Haillecourt, a *procureur* in the Parlement of Metz, argued that the most effective way of dealing with them was simply to deport them all to Guyana. On August 25, 1788, the long-awaited result was announced by a jury that included Pierre-Louis Roederer, later to win fame as a *patriote* member of the Constituent Assembly and senator under Napoleon. Three winners were proclaimed: a lawyer from Nancy by the name of Thiery; Zalkind Hourwitz, who described himself as a "Polish Jew";[9] and Abbé Grégoire. Grégoire, who had delivered his first sermon in favor of Jewish emancipation in 1785, when the first new authorized synagogue was being built in Lorraine, courageously took up the defense of the Jews at a time when they were totally ostracized and exposed to repeated humiliations, to say nothing of being burdened with special taxes, which left them destitute and subject to draconian regulations that limited their movements, confined them to cramped ghettos, prevented them from buying land or becoming farmers, kept them out of most professions, and imposed dress restrictions that set them apart from Christian society. For Grégoire, in his celebrated *Essai sur la régénération physique, morale et politique des Juifs,*[10] which marked a decisive turning point in the history of Jewish emancipation, the solution was clear: with the Age of Enlightenment the time had come to "regenerate" the Jews so that they, too, could become citizens. As a faithful adept of natural-rights philosophy, he was determined to rescue the Jews from vices forced upon them by a Christian society that had lost touch with its original principles. Repudiating the deep-seated anti-Semitism of men like Voltaire and Holbach, Grégoire followed Montesquieu in blaming the climate and social conditions for the real depravity into which, as he saw it, the Jews had fallen. In order to regenerate this depraved people, Grégoire believed, it was enough to bring them Enlightenment and Reason. The need was urgent, moreover, because the abbé claimed to know from personal experience in his native Lorraine that the Jews there had fallen very low indeed.

His description of the Jewish people, to which he wholeheartedly subscribed, was apocalyptic to say the least: "ardent to multiply," Jews "pullulate" in "sad hovels from which foul odors perpetually emanate, and which are apt to spread and even cause epidemics. . . . Would anyone believe that in Metz the synagogue filed papers to bring legal action against several Jews guilty of the abominable crime of wishing to cleanse themselves? Despite the great 'pride' they maintain in their 'debasement,' their 'moral depravity' is total. In short, they have rarely been able to rise to the same level of human dignity as their fellows." Grégoire, soon to become known as an ardent defender of the Jews, nevertheless held that they were "parasitic plants that eat away at the substance of the tree to which they attach themselves." Their usurious ways had reduced "many Christians to begging."

Such was Grégoire's understanding of the issues. His problem was how to bring the precious benefits of Enlightenment to this debased people. To begin with, he recommended "eliminating the argot, the Tudesco-Hebraic-Rabbinical jargon used by German Jews, which is intelligible to no one but themselves and useful only for compounding ignorance or masking dishonesty." Next, he suggested exposing "the myths of the Talmud," that "sewer into which the wildest fantasies of the human mind have been funneled," and eradicating the Jews' "burlesque" religious rituals and traditions, which to him were mere "trifles." He persisted in this judgment of the Jews as late as 1806, when he argued that "their encyclopedia is the Talmud . . . a great work [which] contains flecks of gold scattered throughout a great deal of muck."[11] Berr Isaac Berr, a syndic of the Jews of Lorraine and a proponent of emancipation who arranged for the Jews of Nancy to take the civic oath, was nevertheless quick to reject this idea. In a letter to Grégoire, he wrote: "With a stroke of the pen you condemn some sixty volumes containing 3,047 folio pages written by men the last of whom lived roughly four hundred years after Jesus Christ." To Grégoire's charge that the Jews "shrivel their souls with stupid ideas that weigh down their memory," Berr replied: "This work truly is an encyclopedia, which is filled with enlightened ideas and rare and precious principles."[12]

True to the logic of his Jacobin beliefs, Grégoire demurred. In order to put an end to the Jews' misguided ways and make them at last happy and useful citizens, he was prepared to use the most expeditious means available. Like later Jacobins impatient of particularism in all its forms and ready to apply extreme pressure to eradicate communities based on age-old traditions and values, Abbé Grégoire urged that the Jews be "melded into the mass of the nation" in order to bring about a true "dissolution of [their] communities." In order to "bind them to the state" all the more effectively, he proposed "limiting the number of Jews who may live in each village or town in proportion to its size."[13] The next step was to reshape people's minds. In keeping with the precepts of the *philosophes,* Grégoire argued that the best way to "regenerate" the Jews was through the ineluctable effects of education: "Let us take hold of the generation that has just been born and is now hastening toward puberty" and channel it into state schools. If these children were treated with kindness (*affabilité*), they would, "whether they like it or not, absorb sound ideas that will act as an antidote to the absurdities with which their families fill their minds." The best way to overcome "prejudice" and consolidate the national identity was to instill civic spirit through the teaching of French: this would ensure the regeneration of "savage" France. Grégoire would later make this theme familiar through his well-known "Report on the Need for, and Means of, Abolishing Patois and Universalizing the Use of the French Language." The logic remained the same: Yiddish was just one of the many patois that must be condemned to the guillotine in order to pave the way for the birth of the new man, educated by the Enlightenment and unmoved by "prejudice" or "superstition."[14] Hostile to particularism in all its forms, Grégoire, a consistent Montagnard,[15] was unremitting in his search for ways to unify the nation.

A century later, the anti-Semitic journalist and politician Edouard Drumont noted the vehemence of Grégoire's criticism of the Jews in his *France juive* and then added this comment: "As for the ideas of a man who says, 'Here is the plague, I insist that the entire country be inoculated with it,' I confess that they surpass my understanding."[16] With only slight exaggeration, one might almost say that the diagnoses offered by Abbé Grégoire, the emancipator, and Edouard Drumont, the indefatigable anti-Semite, were virtually identical: they differed only as to their proposed remedies.[17] Grégoire hoped to regenerate the Jews so as to reveal the humanity within them, whereas Drumont wished merely to liquidate them physically or else expel them from French society, which in his view was fundamentally Christian. In reality, Grégoire hoped that by appealing to Reason he might turn the Jews into Catholics, just like other Frenchmen, whereas Drumont rejected the idea that conversion was even possible. Drumont failed to understand that Abbé Grégoire remained a man of the Enlightenment who believed in human nature. He did not know that Grégoire, who was linked to the Jansenist tendency in Catholicism and also influenced by the millenarian doctrines of his time, was interested in the Old Testament. As a "republican Christian,"[18] he looked forward to the conversion of the Jews as proof that a regenerated Church could be reconciled with the Republic. With Enlightenment ideas, he hoped that it might be possible to persuade Jews to throw in their lot with republican Christians so that they would not have to be banished from the sort of organic society that conservatives of every stripe, from Louis de Bonald to Drumont, imagined. "Granting complete freedom to the Jews," he argued, "will mark a major step toward their reform, regeneration, and I daresay conversion."[19] In a later work, the *Histoire des sectes religieuses,* he added: "The large-scale conversion of Jews to Protestantism and Catholicism is one of the most remarkable facts about the nineteenth century. A start has been made. . . . Let us atone for the crimes of our ancestors by redoubling our kindness toward the children of Israel, and, with our prayers, our wishes, and our love, let us hasten the moment when, joined together under the banner of the cross, they [the Jews] will worship together with us at the foot of the same altar."[20] Their conversion was peculiarly compatible with the revolutionary ideal: Grégoire employed "all his moral authority in bolstering the institutions of Christendom, which must live in symbiosis with the revolutionary ideal."[21] The man who assumed leadership of the Constitutional Church[22] was thus by all appearances a Jacobin priest eager to use every available means to persuade the Jews to embrace a Christianity which had itself been "regenerated."

Courageously confronting the hostility both of the Catholic hierarchy, which accused him of transforming his diocese into a "little synagogue," and of revolutionaries such as Camille Desmoulins, who were no less vitriolic, Grégoire, the *"ami des Noirs,"* or "friend of the Blacks," who opposed slavery and racism in all their forms,[23] spoke out on several occasions in revolutionary assemblies in favor of citizenship for the Jews. Thanks to his efforts, a delegation of Alsatian Jews was received by the Assembly on October 14, 1789, and Berr Isaac Berr, the uncontested leader of the group, for the first time took the floor "on behalf of the unhappy descendants of the oldest of all peoples." In December 1789, the Assembly debated the issue of whether non-Catholics could be elected to municipal office. On that occasion, the Comte de Clermont-Tonnerre, who shared Grégoire's views, uttered his famous remark: "We must deny everything to the Jews as Nation, in the sense of a constituted body, and grant them everything as individuals." Despite the support of Robespierre, nothing was done, because opposition in the Assembly remained too strong, and it was not until many subsequent debates had passed that a decree was issued on September 27, 1791, which finally granted emancipation as a logical consequence of the Declaration of the Rights of Man and the Citizen. At a time when many Jews were already present in the ranks of the National Guard in Paris and the revolutionary armies, they were at last granted the right to take the civic oath along with other Frenchmen.

In fact, this forced the revolutionaries to confront a crucial issue: where to draw the dividing line between the public and private spheres. Could Jews enter the public sphere without converting? Could they, in private, simply be French citizens of the Jewish faith? Could they vote (and, within a short time, run) in elections while maintaining a clear allegiance to the Jewish synagogue? In France, a country with a strong state equipped with a powerful bureaucracy and clearly delineated frontiers,[24] the boundary between public and private was defined by three things: the right to vote, access to civil service positions and thus to the machinery of government, and the degree of compatibility between the preservation of communal structures and acceptance of a citizenship that was inevitably based on a more universalist definition. In this specific state context, the meaning of citizenship was multidimensional, and along each axis it could vary from the particular, communal, or local to something more general.[25] In terms of a "sense of belonging," this meaning now shifted from the local and communal toward the broader society. The public-private axis was defined by two different poles: the "civic," which emphasized the nation and its glory, a powerful force in the revolutionary period, and the "civil," which was characterized by a withdrawal into the private realm, in this instance a particular religious community.

As the state acquired even greater power during the revolutionary period, several questions arose. Were the emancipation and "regeneration" of the Jews total and complete? Was their admission into public life without restriction? Did it imply the disappearance of any sense of "civil" commitment to their community? These soon became burning issues as the various participants in the debate were obliged to decide whether or not Jews should be allowed to vote along with other citizens, and whether or not they should be permitted to run for office. For Abbé Grégoire, the solution was simple: the Jews should "be melded, as it were, into the national mass and made citizens throughout the country."[26] In his celebrated *Essai,* the abbé implied that, once the Jews were "regenerated," they should be counted as active citizens identical in every respect to other French citizens. And he was not the only person to take this view: speaking on behalf of his fellow Protestants, Jean-Paul Rabaut-Saint-Etienne, a pastor and deputy from Nîmes, also insisted on equal rights for the Jews: "I am asking that this be done for this Asiatic people [such was his characterization of the Jews] uprooted from their native soil and for almost eighteen centuries banished and persecuted and forced to wander, who would, if incorporated with us by virtue of our laws, adopt our customs and mores."[27] Not everyone was prepared to move so quickly, however. In Bordeaux, when an assembly was convoked to choose deputies for the Estates General, the rules already declared the Jews to be a "constitutive element of the state."[28] In fact, the Jews of that great port city were already highly assimilated and integrated into the local commercial and financial bourgeoisie, which was deeply involved in trade with England, the Netherlands, and colonies such as Martinique and Santo Domingo. As such, they had for centuries enjoyed certain privileges tantamount to provisional citizenship.[29] They now chose four delegates to represent them, one of whom, David Gradis, a member of the city's leading Jewish family, was almost elected to the Estates General. By contrast, in Bayonne, "the Portuguese nation" merely participated in the drafting of *cahiers de doléances,* or lists of grievances to be presented to the king, but played no part in electing deputies to the Estates General. The same was true of other Jewish communities in eastern France. Thus, at this stage of the revolutionary process, Jews seldom enjoyed the right to vote. By a vote of 408 to 403, that right was again denied them on December 24, 1789, when the Constituent Assembly decided not to grant the right to vote in municipal elections to non-Catholics. The Jews of Bordeaux were thereby stripped of one of their former privileges. But on January 24, 1790, the Assembly finally granted Jews of Portuguese, Spanish, and Avignonnais extraction the rights of active citizens. It was not until September 27, 1791, of course, that all Jews became citizens. At that time it was further stipulated that once they had taken the civic oath they were to be granted the right to vote and to run for office. Between December 1791 and April 1792, many Jews in cities such as Paris, Nancy, and Metz took the oath en masse in public ceremonies.[30]

Having achieved this all-important right of access to the public sphere, Jews still needed genuine entrée to the civil service if they wished to exercise the sovereign power of the state. Article Six of the Declaration of the Rights of Man and the Citizen explicitly stated that "the law is the expression of the general will. . . . All citizens, being equal in its eyes, are equally entitled to all public dignities, places, and employments according to their capacities and without distinction other than that of their virtues and talents." Accordingly, meritocratic recruitment for government posts should not have been an issue. On this crucial point, Abbé Grégoire's response at first glance seems quite clear: because "the Jews are children of the state,"[31] there could be no question but that the doors of *lycées* and universities must be opened to them. As one commentator has noted, "As early as 1789, Grégoire championed the regeneration of the Jews through study. . . . Obviously the Jewish population did not turn a deaf ear to his proposals, and during the revolutionary period Jewish prejudices against secular education in the French language waned in the east as well as in the south, where Jews prided themselves on being more civilized."[32] "Let us make them more like us," Grégoire urged, "let us teach them our customs, let us encourage them to develop their talents and virtues, let us bind them to the state by according them hope of public consideration and the right to hold any office in the various classes of society. . . . Of course we do not propose allowing Jews to be prosecutors. The reason for this will be clear. But in admitting them to the bar as lawyers, might we not exempt them from the oath of Catholicism?"[33] Not only were Jews to be offered admission to state schools and universities, they were also to be granted access to most of the positions from which they had once been barred. Nevertheless, what the abbé believed would be "clear" to any astute reader of his text was not just that Jews should still be denied access to the prestigious post of prosecutor but that they should also be barred from any of the *corps d'état,* or central departments of the governmental apparatus, that enjoyed authority of any kind. For Grégoire, one suspects, it was utterly unthinkable that even a converted Jew should aspire to become a high functionary, much less a minister of government, in a society on the road to Enlightenment but still fundamentally committed to Catholicism. His argument was clearly stated, moreover, and largely in tune with the liberal economic theories that would soon hold sway: in order to encourage the Jews to convert, he said, "entice them, lure them with favor, consideration, and self-interest."[34] Here at last we encounter the key word "interest": it was in the Jews' own interest to convert, in the hope of perhaps eventually gaining access to the highest government posts. For Heine, writing at a later date, conversion would be "the price of access to European culture."

Thiery, the lawyer who shared the Metz academy prize with Grégoire, spoke even more plainly on the matter. The Jews, he wrote, "cannot lay claim to dignities and distinctions. Not that the requisite genius, courage, and qualities are not found in all estates. And sooner or later, education, and the new character that it may bestow upon the Jews, may make them capable of such things. But how can they rule over us while professing principles and sentiments that, though foreign to us, are nevertheless an integral part of their law and therefore impossible for them to give up? How can they fill the impressive posts in which our religion displays its grandeur and majesty? How could they simultaneously perform the rites and ceremonies that their religion prescribes? And if such a mixture were possible, would it not be reprehensible? Must we not first and foremost preserve the pre-eminence and power that Christianity now enjoys?"[35] The "impressive posts" of which Thiery speaks are no doubt the same ones that Grégoire had in mind in rejecting the notion that they might be awarded to Jews. By contrast, W. C. Dohm, who at the behest of the philosopher Moses Mendelssohn wrote an important work "on the political reform of the Jews" that was soon translated into French and cited by both Mirabeau and Grégoire, asked whether "our governments cannot admit Jews to public employments at once. Indeed, if they are to enjoy all the rights of the citizen, it would seem that they cannot be barred from aspiring to the glory of serving the state and that, if their applications are supported by the requisite abilities, they must be granted such posts."[36] Clearly, Dohm, whose solution fairly closely reflected Mendelssohn's thinking, was far more favorable to the idea of awarding public posts to Jews than was either Grégoire or Thiery. Yet the issue was so important that, despite his generous intentions, Dohm nevertheless concludes, "In most cases it will be more advantageous to the state if the Jew works not in the chancellery but in a workshop or behind a plow."[37] On this point and others that we will examine later, Mirabeau, who took his inspiration fairly directly from Dohm's work, proved to be far more liberal and open-minded. He stated that the Jews "have shown themselves to advantage in public affairs."[38] And following Mirabeau's lead, the *Courrier de Provence* asked a simple question and answered it: "Do they [the Jews] obey all the laws of the State? [Then] one cannot refuse to grant them all national rights."[39] Despite such favorable pronouncements, French Jews who wished to go into government service would for many years to come be obliged to convert. It was not until the Second Empire and, to an even greater extent, the Third Republic that this obligation was finally lifted, thereby allowing Jews full exercise of both "civil" and "civic" rights.

We come now to the third of the conditions defining the boundary between public and private mentioned above: namely, the degree to which it was acceptable to maintain ties to a community as opposed to allegiance to the nation taken in its most universalistic sense. Gré-goire, both in his Lunéville sermons and in revolutionary debates, vigorously defended the notion that it was possible for the Jews to regenerate themselves and thereby gain access at last to Enlightenment. He did not shrink, however, from the idea of using coercive means if necessary: the "authority of the state" could be employed to "meld" the Jews into the "national mass," to break down communal bonds by "isolating" them as individuals, and to prevent the use of a foreign language. To his way of thinking, "Once the Jew becomes a member of the nation, loyal to the state, . . . his *esprit de corps* will be seen to diminish."[40] It is essential, he added, to "isolate [the Jews], to prevent insofar as possible all communication between them."[41] In his "motion in favor of the Jews" of 1789, Grégoire clung to the same centralist notion of government: "The Jews will share in all the benefits accruing to citizens. Hence there should be no syndic to manage the civil affairs of Jewish communities; there should be no Jewish communities; they should be members of our communities. . . . One great advantage [of this arrangement] is that it then becomes possible to apply the same principles of reform to the nation as a whole, because the nation now has but one character. Let us devise a detailed plan that will make use of all available means."[42]

Grégoire thus revealed himself as a committed Jacobin unwilling to envision a republic tolerant of particularisms of the sort that Mirabeau, in his own essay *Sur la réforme politique des Juifs,* demonstrated his willingness to accept. Among those who debated the destiny of the Jews during the French Revolution, Mirabeau's position was unique. On the one hand were universalistic revolutionaries prepared to transform Jews into human beings and citizens; on the other were Catholic counterrevolutionaries hostile to what they regarded as a "deicide" people and determined either to confine them to ghettos or to expel them from France altogether. Nearly everyone on both sides of the issue rejected the idea of allowing the Jews to maintain their own communal institutions within a society that welcomed them as active citizens. During the debate over the Declaration of the Rights of Man, Mirabeau was one of the few who spoke out clearly against an official religion of any sort.[43] In opposition to both the counterrevolutionaries and Abbé Grégoire, he was never anything less than respectful toward the distinctive rites of Judaism. He denounced criticism of the Jewish religion as "slander," and in regard to its characteristic rituals asked, "What religion does not have them? What kind of reason is that to deny human beings the rights of humanity?"[44] Once again he adopted a point of view similar to that which would later be championed by the Jews of Alsace and Lorraine, who maintained that it was "in order to be better citizens that we are asking to keep our synagogue, our rabbis, and our syndics."[45] By contrast, the Jews of Bordeaux opposed their coreligionists from Alsace, who claimed "to be ruled by their own laws and to constitute a class of citizens separate from all others." This, the Bordeaux Jews alleged, was the product of "ill-considered religious zeal." As for themselves, having already largely rejected the Talmud and redefined Judaism in terms of eighteenth-century rationalism, they looked forward to the day when there would be no more Jewish "nation" and a Jew would therefore be indistinguishable from any other Frenchman. Indeed, the Bordeaux Jews already played an important role in society and controlled substantial businesses.[46] Thus they subscribed to an emancipation of the "atomizing" sort envisioned by Abbé Grégoire, whereas their coreligionists from Alsace, whose views they utterly rejected, found it easier to embrace the ideas of Mirabeau, a liberal hostile to the purely rationalistic tendencies of Jacobinism. The Jews of Paris took an even more uncompromising procentralist Jacobin stance, for they stated in advance their willingness to submit "to a uniform plan of law enforcement and jurisprudence."[47]

Mirabeau followed Dohm's argument every step of the way, and Dohm had of course written his text at the behest of Moses Mendelssohn, the celebrated German Jewish philosopher and adept of the Enlightenment, in response to an appeal from a group of Alsatian Jews, including Cerf Berr. Although both Dohm and Mirabeau claimed to take their inspiration from Mendelssohn, they did not entirely share the philosopher's assimilationist views. In his book *Jerusalem,* which persuaded many Jews to embark upon a process of emancipation that implied a high degree of assimilation, Mendelssohn did, however, call upon his readers "not to create harmony where diversity is obviously the plan and ultimate goal of Providence."[48] And he did call upon Jews in particular to "compromise with the customs and constitution of the country in which you find yourselves, but steadfastly cling to the religion of your fathers."[49] Yet he argued that the Jewish faith was primarily a matter of law, reason, and ethics, and not necessarily linked to strong communal institutions, which he saw no reason to defend in a society that to his mind seemed imbued with the spirit of the Enlightenment. For him, "the true and divine religion has no need of arms or fingers, it is pure spirit and pure heart."[50] If it is true that Abbé Grégoire was using "regeneration" as a pretext when in reality he hoped to convert the Jews to a renewed Catholicism, and if the Jacobins, in their efforts to impose a single standard on all rational minds, hoped to subordinate all religions to a new civic spirit, Mendelssohn for his part did indeed hope to "regenerate" the synagogue as part of a newly enlightened society, but not at the expense of an independent Jewish spirit.

In his book *On the Political Reform of the Jews,* Dohm forthrightly insisted that "granting autonomy to the Jews will have no negative consequences."[51] The government, he added, should "allow each of these small, particular societies to have its own *esprit de corps* and even to persist in its own prejudices so long as these do no harm, but it should strive to inspire in each of its members a greater degree of loyalty to the state. It will attain what should be its main goal when the titles of gentleman, peasant, scholar, artisan, Christian, and Jew are all subordinate to the title of citizen."[52] Dohm, unlike Mendelssohn, many of whose views he shared, and also unlike Grégoire, therefore explicitly accepted the notion that the Jews might, for example, keep their own judges to settle matters of concern only to themselves: "These judges, like those of the higher courts to which the parties could appeal the decision of the Jewish judge, would of course base their judgment on no law other than that of the Jews."[53]

What this shows is that another way was possible. Few people cared to take it, however, in an age wedded to belief in universalism, which measured progress according to a single standard. The alternative path to citizenship would have permitted greater respect for cultural and regional differences than Grégoire and the Jacobins were prepared to allow. In this respect they followed in the footsteps of the absolute monarchy: they persistently used state power in even the most minor matters in order to enforce a universalistic vision of society and a strictly rationalist conception of liberty. Had the revolutionary assemblies subscribed instead to Mirabeau's more liberal view, the many traditions and cultures that were an integral part of the history of French society might have been preserved in a more vital form. Yet such a possibility was scarcely compatible with centralizing tendencies that had originated centuries earlier, as France found its own distinctive path out of a particularly intense form of feudalism. The growth of the state, together with its extremely powerful influence on the social system as a whole, led inevitably to unification, while undermining, even in the early modern period, all attempts by groups within society to organize themselves. If the French state was a force for liberation and emancipation, it did little to encourage liberalism or democracy of the sort found in England and America, where a balance of powers was achieved through pluralism. Thus Mirabeau's strategy for political change had little chance of succeeding in opposition to the statist, centralist policies adopted by the Jacobins, which were in a sense better adapted to the functional realities that existed in France.[54]

In light of this hostility to diversity, the Revolution can in some respects be described as what Arthur Herzberg calls a "totalitarian democracy."[55] As far as the "regeneration" of the Jews was concerned, Herzberg has no doubt that "the Revolution was 'totalitarian.' Almost all those who helped to emancipate the Jews, from Grégoire through Robespierre, had in mind some vision of what they ought to be made to become." Accordingly, some Jewish historians began to point out the cost of the emancipation process, which threatened to erase what was distinctively Jewish about Judaism along with all other forms of particularism. Some of these attacks were more vehement than others, but ultimately they succeeded in raising serious questions about the work of Abbé Grégoire and French Judaism generally, which, as Simon Dubnov has said, achieved total assimilation by dissolving the "Jewish nation." Dubnov deplores the fact that, as a consequence of this type of emancipation, "many Jews went into government service and the professions, but few took an interest in the fate of their people."[56] By contrast, James Darmesteter applauds the fact that, "as of September 28, 1791, there was nothing more to be said about the history of the Jews in France. From then on there was only the history of French Judaism."[57] For the celebrated professor of Orientalism, whose election to the Collège de France was in itself symbolic of the ultimate intellectual distinction that emancipated French Jews could achieve thanks to the efforts of Grégoire and Mirabeau, the French Revolution marked the end of "the material history of the Jewish people, because for the first time Jewish thought was in harmony rather than in conflict with the conscience of mankind."[58]

Thus a debate arose between those who with growing vehemence rejected French-style emancipation, which they accused of destroying the Jews' sense of constituting a people, and those who maintained that, on the contrary, it marked a new "exodus from Egypt," which, though admittedly lacking a collective dimension, guaranteed every citizen the right to practice his or her religion in private. Looked at in this way, Jews were citizens with rights and duties identical to those of all other citizens. They differed from others only in claiming a distinctive religious identity.[59] No longer did they constitute a "Jewish people" that somehow transcended the definition of citizenship. In the new French society, to be an emancipated Jew was simply to be an *israélite*—a French citizen of the Jewish faith. Such was the understanding of the vast majority of French Jews by the end of the eighteenth century. Most remained quite cool, for example, to Zionist ideas for promoting a rebirth of the Jewish people.

Yet few French Jews converted to Catholicism in the nineteenth century, as Abbé Grégoire had hoped they would. Few, in other words, chose "exit" as their option from economist Albert Hirschman's well-known trinity: exit, voice, and loyalty.[60] To be sure, some did choose to pay what Heine called the "price of entry" into bourgeois society.

To mention one lesser-known instance of conversion whose political implications might not have pleased the Jacobin Grégoire, the renowned journalist Gaston Polonais converted on October 30, 1902, at the Church of Saint Thomas in a ceremony attended by François Coppée, Jules Lemaître (who played a leading role in various anti-Semitic movements), Arthur Meyer (a previous convert who shared Polonais's political allegiances), and Generals Gonze and Boisdeffre, known for their hostility to Captain Dreyfus. Father Domenech interrogated the convert:

> "Gaston-Joseph, do you renounce Satan?"
> "I do."
> "Do you renounce Judaic perfidy and Hebraic superstition?"
> "I do."
> "Gaston-Joseph, do you wish to be baptized?"
> "I do."
> Whereupon the bells of Saint Thomas pealed for joy.[61]

This account is especially noteworthy in that historians have turned up relatively few detailed descriptions of conversion ceremonies. Conversion was apparently rare. Attendance at services and frequency of marriage outside the faith are better indicators of the strength of Jewish religious commitment, then as now.[62] Indeed, the religious commitment of all faiths has been affected not so much, as Grégoire had hoped, by conversion as by the secular education offered by republican public schools.[63] In view of this, what basis might exist for a Jewish identity in a France whose guiding principles are universalism, secularism, and social mobility? In a France where traditional allegiances have diminished and people's goals and aspirations have become increasingly individualized? In a France with little tolerance for any form of particularism in a public sphere set aside exclusively for "citizens" defined in universalistic terms? If the efforts of the "regenerators" of 1789 have largely stripped the "Jewish nation" of legitimacy within the "Republic one and indivisible," and if the Jewish religion no longer seems capable of defining, by itself, a specific identity within contemporary France, has emancipation without conversion finally reduced Jewish consciousness to nothing more than "imaginary" identification with a sentimental version of Zionism? If so, the revolutionaries of 1789 would surely be pleased. Yet Grégoire himself would not be entirely satisfied, for he could not help deploring Catholicism's failure. Nor would nineteenth-century *israélites* such as Darmesteter and many others be pleased by the decline of the religious as such.

As enthusiasm for the regenerative ambitions of 1789 recedes into the past along with challenges to the legacy of the process of emancipation launched by the Revolution, we seem now to be moving into a new era. People tired of mere talk have begun to discover the reality of different cultures and traditions that somehow survived the tempests and enthusiasms of the past two centuries and in one way or another adapted to change while holding on to their essential core. It is this reality, even more than the broad revival of religious practice in a variety of forms, that justifies the claim that a Jewish identity persists in France and is flourishing even now. Where this will lead remains to be seen.

2

RESPONDING
TO THE REVOLUTION

In view of the discussion in the previous chapter, the emancipation of the Jews during the French Revolution can be seen as one aspect of a distinctively French way of making the transition from traditional to modern society: the universalistic definition of citizenship favored by the Jacobin state sanctioned individual liberties at the expense of particularistic traditions. The central government, which since the time of the absolute monarchy had been trying to extend its control to all peripheral segments of French society, continued its pursuit of this goal during the Revolution by granting citizenship to all. In this respect it behaved as governments always behave in what political scientists call "strong" states: it sought to stake out a zone of supremacy for itself by defining citizenship in such a way as to exclude all particularistic dimensions. As a result, the emancipation of the Jews implied both access to the state sphere and elimination of the Jewish "nation"—that is, of Jews as a community with their own institutionalized networks of social influence. Accordingly, thinking about the process of Jewish emancipation in revolutionary France should allow us to ask more general questions about how the state, in making the transition from private to public, sought to fill the place once occupied by traditional cultures with a concept of Reason derived directly from Enlightenment philosophy. As a theoretical construct, the importance of Franco-Judaism lies in the fact that it had no historical precedent and could not have existed without a strong, centralized state. It was based on the premise that Jews could be turned into *israélites*, Jewish citizens whose primary allegiance was to France rather than to the Jewish community.

Historical writing about this phenomenon in the twentieth century has been deeply influenced by American authors whose thinking was shaped by the fact that in the United States it is considered perfectly legitimate for citizens to maintain strong ties to highly organized ethnic communities. As a result, much of this writing has been highly critical of Franco-Judaism, blaming the revolutionary emancipation of the Jews for bringing French Jewish history and culture to an end.[1] Emancipation, we are told, inevitably led to a conception of citizenship that excluded any notion of communal solidarity, which in turn put an end to any distinctive Jewish historical consciousness. Toward the end of the nineteenth century, for instance, Théodore Reinach, himself a paragon of universalist, meritocratic Franco-Judaism, wrote that with emancipation "Jewish sensibility will lose its edge and eventually probably wither away entirely." Indeed, the process of assimilation in the nineteenth century was so rapid that it might seem to justify the American historians' rather pessimistic assessment. In their view, which owed a great deal to the theories of economic development of the 1950s, assimilation could be counted on to dissolve traditional communal ties and values. This critical judgment, which has much in common with historian Jacob L. Talmon's interpretation of the French Revolution as a "totalitarian" phenomenon, can also be read as corroboration of revisionist histories of the Revolution that follow the lead of François Furet in attacking the extremist aspirations of the Jacobins. Other historians have gone so far as to portray counterrevolutionary efforts in the Vendée as symbols of legitimate resistance to the Jacobin state. If we wish to reassess the emancipation of the French Jews, therefore, we must also reconsider the significance of the Revolution to the various groups that participated in it.

The origins of contemporary debates about the legitimacy of difference can thus be traced all the way back to the revolutionary events of 1789.[2]

This discussion turns out to be crucial for understanding recent disputes about the possibility of a "pluralist France," whose inception would presumably spell the end of the French model of emancipation. Too little attention has been paid, however, to contrasting views of just what such a pluralist France might look like. Some writers argue that Jacobin state ideology was never fully realized. Up to the end of the nineteenth century, if not beyond, these scholars insist, a variety of local cultures persisted in France, and people in one region were well aware of how they differed from people in other regions. Echoing the arguments of the historian Eugen Weber, many of these commentators emphasize the vast gap that always exists between a universalistic revolutionary ideology and persistent community traditions on which revolutionary discourse apparently exerts little influence.[3] For all the growing talk of universalism in the nineteenth century—especially under the Third Republic, with its commitment to secular education—local solidarities were, it is claimed, largely immune to Jacobin efforts to eliminate them. Indeed, some recent historians of French Judaism argue that, even though the vast majority of French Jews enthusiastically embraced the Republic, with its individualistic notion of citizenship, they nevertheless maintained social ties to other Jews and continued to share certain cultural traditions, so that a minimal degree of community solidarity survived.[4]

Others insist, however, that the power of the revolutionary state cannot be denied, and that it certainly did halt the development of particularistic traditions that had flourished under the Ancien Régime. Nevertheless, the writers in this second group argue that these traditions, though impeded in their growth, were never entirely eradicated. Indeed, the power of the state not only failed to put an end to French Jewish history as such but, in a paradoxical way, has in recent years helped to revive Jewish and other traditions. Michael Graetz, for instance, argues that the French Revolution promoted centralization not just of French society but also of the Jewish community, which emerged from the Revolution stronger and more unified than ever. "How," he asks, "did particularist tendencies persist in an 'open' society hastening toward emancipation and assimilation? How are we to account for this revival of Jewish community spirit, which laid the groundwork for a rebirth of the Jewish nation?"[5]

Indeed, Graetz argues that, until the Revolution granted citizenship to Jews and allowed them to take the civic oath, vote in elections, and run for office, and until Napoleon convoked the Great Sanhedrin and established regulations governing the Jewish community, "particularistic tendencies prevailed within Judaism. These were weakened, and aspirations to unity were reinforced, by the action of the state coupled with the pressure of events."[6] In other words, centralization is not a zero-sum game in which whatever power is gained by the central government is forfeited by local groups and communities. Paradoxically, as French society in general became more centralized during the Revolution, so did certain particularistic groups within that society. These groups were caught up in the broad process of state centralization yet continued to pursue goals of their own. This is a bold thesis and well worth discussing. The questions it raises bear on the history of modern France in general, as well as on the histories of various subcultures and communities. Graetz's thesis also poses a serious challenge to the interpretation of the Revolution as a process leading to emancipation in a rationalist, universalistic mode.

In considering the "unintentional" side effects of emancipation, Graetz tries to show that, in the 1860s, the founders of the Alliance Israélite Universelle—whose goal, influenced by Jacobin ideals, was to "work toward the emancipation and moral advancement of Jews everywhere" by bringing education and modernity to Turkey, Iraq, Tunisia, and other countries—were in fact seen in parts of the world where Jews were still oppressed as advocates of a specifically Jewish politics that would ultimately lead to Zionism, which until recently was regarded as the precise opposite of what these proponents of emancipation in the rationalistic mode stood for.[7] One of the more curious paradoxes of this interpretation is that it portrays the revolutionary consolidation of the centralized state as having strengthened rather than destroyed communal ties by imposing centralized community organization from above. Contrary to what Tocqueville believed, Jacobin policies ultimately reinforced the almost inadvertently regained Jewish identity of the leaders of the Alliance, even though they were among the most assimilated of Jews as well as the most proassimilationist. The historical significance of emancipation was thereby transformed: the most ardent heirs of 1789 unwittingly "initiated a process over which the founders of the Alliance had no control."[8] Thus, Graetz claims, the Jacobin Revolution led, in spite of itself, to Zionism.

We thus have three very different interpretations of the consequences of the French Revolution for Jews. The traditional interpretation holds that the systematic action of the French state emancipated the Jews by destroying the ties that had once bound their community together and given French Jews a distinctive history of their own. But others argue that, for all the talk of unification, neither the official ideology of the Revolution nor the steps taken by revolutionary and imperial governments actually dissolved ethnic and cultural bonds, which persisted throughout the nineteenth century. Finally, still others maintain that, although revolutionary governments did in fact disrupt the unity of the Jewish community, the growing centralization of the French state unintentionally fostered a rebirth of Jewish identity, or so it seemed to Jews in Eastern Europe and in the countries of the Mediterranean, who saw the Revolution and the assimilationist efforts of the Alliance as harbingers of national liberations yet to come.

If we are to grasp the true meaning of the revolutionary process, we must therefore look closely at the intentions of the people who participated in that process. Only then can we say which consequences were intended and which were unintended. At the beginning of the Revolution, the vast majority of Jews of French nationality lived in eastern and southwestern France. A smaller number lived either in Avignon and the Comtat Venaissin or in Paris. Of roughly forty thousand French Jews, twenty thousand lived in Alsace, two thousand in Metz, twenty-five hundred in Bordeaux, and the same number in Saint-Esprit-les-Bayonne. The rest were scattered among small com-

munities from Nancy to Avignon, Carpentras, and Rouen. Here I propose to examine the values to which the Jews of eastern France
subscribed, as well as the values they shared and did not share with
the Jews of southwestern France, for together these two groups constituted the bulk of the Jewish community. What I will argue is that
these two groups responded to a very difficult situation by adopting
strategies that reflected their own distinctive values.[9]

The Sephardic Jews of southwestern France were for the most part
descendants of Marranos, Jews originally from the Iberian Peninsula
who were forcibly converted at the time of the Inquisition but continued to practice Judaism in secret. In the eighteenth century, they
once again began to practice their religion openly. By virtue of
letters-patent granted by the king in 1550 and subsequently renewed,
they enjoyed a highly privileged status that allowed them to take full
part in Christian society. Referred to by their French compatriots as
"Portuguese," these Jews became international traders. Their business activities were facilitated by close contacts with other Marranos
in London and Amsterdam. In economic terms, their success was impressive, and no less an authority than Werner Sombart devoted several pages of his well-known book, *The Jews and Modern Capitalism*,
to their activities.[10] As shipowners, sponsors of colonial expeditions,
and bankers, the Gradis, Raba, and Peixoto clans occupied a prominent place among the opulent families of the Bordeaux bourgeoisie.
They invested a portion of their capital in plantations in Santo
Domingo and Martinique.[11] Moreover, members of these clans regularly married into the other important families. The Jewish community of Bordeaux was in fact officially recognized as a corporation
with numerous subsidiaries. As such, it constituted something akin to
a closed caste.[12]

Because the Jews of Bordeaux shared in the city's economic
growth, which was quite rapid in the eighteenth century, they embraced the customs and values of the larger society as they and their
fellow citizens moved toward modernity. As descendants of men and
women who had been able to practice their religion only in secret,
Bordeaux's Jews had lost contact with certain traditions and had long

since abandoned organized Jewish studies. As a result, they found it that much easier to accept the rationalism and culture of the Enlightenment: "Rejecting the Talmud and Midrash, Sephardim looked upon the Bible as the sole source of divine truth and constructed a Judaism that was compatible with eighteenth-century rationalism. . . . Their de-nationalization of Jewish beliefs helps to explain why they found it so easy to transform themselves into French citizens."[13] Some of them—especially those who, like the Pereires, the d'Eichtals, and the Rodriguèses, became enthusiastic Saint-Simonians and looked to industrialization as the road to progress and emancipation—converted to Catholicism, with an eye to becoming fully integrated members of the society of the future.[14] As one contemporary observer saw it, "Eugène Pereire had no religion. He was neither a Christian nor a Jew. His father, Isaac Pereire, did not favor either religion and preferred to allow his son to make up his own mind upon reaching the age of reason. When Eugène married, however, he was forced to choose and out of gallantry elected to share his wife's religion."[15]

In July 1843, a report on the Jews of Bordeaux was submitted to the prefect. It stated that, "since most members of well-to-do Jewish families receive the same education as Christians, their habits are the same, and so are their career choices and recreational activities. . . . They invariably mingle with Christians, and it would be hard to tell them apart were it not for certain distinctive facial features of the Jews. . . . As for the poorer class of israélites, half of them peddle their wares in the streets. . . . This latter class is still a long way from melting into the Christian population."[16] The Jews of Bordeaux, who were remote from their coreligionists in eastern France not only in terms of distance but also in terms of culture and religious belief, disliked being compared to them. They had "nothing to gain"[17] if others in Bordeaux saw them as similar to the Jews of Alsace and Lorraine, nearly all of whom lived in poverty in constricted, isolated communities. The "Portuguese" had no personal stake in solidarity with their cousins in the east. Solidarity can never be taken for granted, even if certain commentators have lately been too quick to dismiss it as "an anachronistic notion."[18] It is always the result of a deliberate decision by the people involved,[19] a consequence of intentional "identifi-cation" with a social and cultural tradition whose survival depends on resolute personal commitment.[20]

If Bordeaux Jews eschewed solidarity with the Jews of the east, it was because they found themselves in a fortunate position: already emancipated, they had everything to gain by simply working toward even greater participation in the larger society. Still, they might have made a different choice, even in circumstances that favored what Albert Hirschman has called the "exit" option.[21] Bordeaux Jews displayed solidarity with one another in their approach to modernity. By the end of the nineteenth century, that approach had all but put an end to their collective existence as a social and cultural group, although this had not been their intention at the outset. They might have chosen instead to identify with their coreligionists in the east. Even in Bordeaux, defections from the Jewish community and conversions to Catholicism were not undertaken solely for utilitarian reasons. As Yosef Yerushalmi points out, "Contrary to popular belief, these lost Jews were not simply pursuing secular ambitions and advantages. They succumbed to true, genuine despair: they had lost faith in the future of the Jewish people."[22] Nevertheless, if Graetz's attractive hypothesis is correct, the Bordeaux Jews' "exit" from the local Jewish community and refusal to acknowledge religious and social ties to Jews elsewhere in France may also have had another unintended consequence: it may have fostered a broad international solidarity leading ultimately to a revival of Jewish politics, even if such an outcome held little appeal for those Bordeaux Jews who embraced the Saint-Simonian movement and joined the Alliance Israélite Universelle. What had been only latent would then have become manifest.[23]

The situation of the Jews of eastern France at the time was radically different from that of the Jews of Bordeaux, and so was their approach to the revolutionary process. Mired in poverty, the Jews of the east eked out a living in a variety of trades. They were subject to numerous controls: their movements were restricted, for example, and on the eve of the Revolution they were forbidden to reside in Strasbourg. They paid for the privilege of living in France with exorbitant taxes and endured the unremitting hostility of their neighbors. Confined to ghettos in many cities if not banished outright, they lived on the fringes of urban society. Most led precarious rural existences. Eastern Jews, unlike the Jews of Bordeaux, subscribed to a traditional form of Judaism. Rabbis were community leaders whose word was law. A strong collective identity shaped by traditional values ensured that conversions were rare, for individuals were subjected to powerful social controls by a community "wedded to a culture that defined what it meant to be a Jew during each and every hour of the day and night."[24]

The "principal strength" of "this rural and outwardly uncultivated community was its social solidarity," based on "mutual assistance, charity, and a deeply ingrained sense of a common destiny."[25] The community was the "primary group" for nearly all eastern Jews—that is, a resource that could be counted on for "cooperation, assistance, and social intercourse." Communal solidarity arose not only from an exchange of services but also from a sense of "identification," a shared history. It is important to keep these two aspects apart. "At the center of this closely knit network of social exchange stood the synagogue."[26] Indeed, the synagogues and consistories of Alsace enabled Jews to mount a real resistance to assimilation and acculturation in the face of powerful pressures generated by rapid economic change.[27]

As the political sociologist Samuel Popkin has rightly pointed out, peasants are rational actors who make individual choices about their futures. Although subject to "social control" by the villages in which they live, they nevertheless evaluate the options available to them and calculate what course of action might be best. In other words, communities are not like mechanical devices: solidarity, when it exists, is the aggregate result of numerous individual decisions.[28] To be sure, certain types of social organization encourage the types of decisions that tend to create communal solidarity. Nevertheless, solidarity can never be taken for granted. It is never simply a product of powerful social controls that somehow transform independent individuals into mere cogs in a machine. In fact, some eastern Jews did choose to "exit" from their communities and move to Paris in defiance of communal norms and rabbinical edicts. A few actually chose to convert.

Even those who remained within their communities were obliged to make choices, sometimes with dramatic consequences. The vast majority of eastern Jews chose to reinforce the solidarity of the Jewish community, which in turn helped to preserve their identity as Jews. The Jews of eastern France were loyal to their region and locality, yet at the same time fiercely proud of their Judaism.[29]

Yet these choices also had contradictory and unpredictable consequences. Determined to maintain their identity, the Jews of eastern France also chose to serve the state and defend their country, perhaps in order to demonstrate that they could remain Jews and still be loyal Frenchmen.[30] Paradoxically, however, the persistence of this same Jewish culture and tradition may also explain why, at a later date, other Jews from Alsace and Lorraine were virtually the only French Jews to join the Zionist movement. A small but significant number of these eventually chose to emigrate to Israel.[31] By an unforeseeable twist of historical fate, some eastern Jews thereby fulfilled the utopian dreams of certain assimilated Jews in Bordeaux, albeit with a nationalist inflection.

In the 1870s, however, the pace of assimilation picked up in some parts of eastern France, especially in cities such as Metz. Jews entered into social relations with non-Jews as the Jewish population dispersed and shed its traditional costumes.[32] The erstwhile bastion of traditional Judaism seemed threatened by urbanization and industrialization, which afforded individuals greater mobility and new opportunities. Yet the old rituals were not entirely eroded. As in Bordeaux and Bayonne a century earlier, some prominent Jews began to assimilate, but in the east the process of assimilation never went so far, and the Jewish community remained largely intact. Until 1871, moreover, "Jews living in rural parts of eastern France and steeped in a traditional culture maintained linguistic, cultural, religious, and even economic ties with the Ashkenazi Jews of Eastern Europe." Only after Alsace and Lorraine were annexed by Germany in the wake of the Franco-Prussian War did allegiance to France take precedence over religious commitment. Now "exit" meant moving to a different part of France or even emigrating to, say, the United States. The defeat of France and the occupation of the two former

French provinces finally succeeded in breaking down traditional institutions and drove some individual Jews to leave. Those who settled
in Normandy and other parts of France were subsequently exposed to
pressures that pushed them toward assimilation.

As was noted in the previous chapter, Abbé Grégoire, who had
looked upon Jews as homogeneous, had hoped that treating them the
same as other citizens would eventually cause them to cease to exist
as a group. Yet the foregoing discussion shows that the values and
goals of Jews in the southwest of France were very different from the
values and goals of Jews in the east. This diversity is apparent in the
very earliest Jewish petitions to the National Assembly. In a "petition
to the National Assembly" submitted by representatives of the Jews
of "Metz, the three bishoprics, and Alsace and Lorraine" on August 31, 1789, for example, the petitioners state that, because "our
position is different from that of most of the Jews residing in the various provinces of the Empire, we are obliged to present specific demands. . . . So that we may be better citizens, we ask to keep our
synagogue, our rabbis, and our syndics."[33] What the Jews of the east
wanted, in other words, was to preserve institutions that would ensure
the survival of their distinctive traditions. To their way of thinking,
there was no contradiction between the survival of cultural identities
and full adherence to the ideals of the Revolution.

This view of the matter had little in common with the Jacobin ideology of Abbé Grégoire and Robespierre but a great a deal in common with the more liberal view of Mirabeau, who argued that "every
society is composed of small, private societies, each with its own peculiar principles. . . . Let the Christian and the circumcised Jew or
Muslim differ with one another; the great and noble purpose of Government is to see to it that each such division is turned to the advantage of the larger society."[34] Alsatian Jews complained again in 1790
about efforts to weaken their communal ties: "People say that they
would constitute a Jewish colony. Is it therefore impossible to get
used to the idea that the title of citizen is distinct from that of Jew?
Must people see the Jew everywhere and the Citizen nowhere? No,
the colony that would exist in Alsace would be not a Jewish colony
but a colony of citizens. Since Jews are citizens, there should be no

problem if there are more of them in one place than in another . . . just as there is no problem if the Protestants of Languedoc are more numerous and have more money than Protestants in other provinces. This does not mean that there are Protestant colonies, and by the same token there is no reason to believe that there will be Jewish colonies."[35]

The Jews of the southwest presented a very different list of demands. On December 24, 1789, the Assembly revoked their privileges by issuing a broad edict that denied the Jews of France the right to become "active citizens" (that is, citizens with the right to vote). The Jews of Bordeaux protested that they had long been recognized as Jewish subjects of France and as such had participated in the selection of Bordeaux's delegates to the Estates General. "We do not believe that our estate in France would even be subject to discussion," they argued, "were it not for certain demands submitted by the Jews of Alsace, Lorraine, and the three bishoprics, demands that have given rise to a certain confusion in which we find ourselves included. . . . Those demands should be treated as a special case, because the aforementioned Jews wish to live in France under special rules." Expressing the hope that their coreligionists in the east would soon abandon their "ill-considered religious zeal," the Jews of Bordeaux voiced their opposition to the "misguided demands" of eastern Jews who "in any case enjoy almost none of the advantages that we do. . . . In our case it is not so much a matter of obtaining privileges as it is of not losing them."[36]

To speak of "gains" and "losses" at such a dramatic moment in history, when society was being transformed and cultural identities hung in the balance, may seem surprisingly utilitarian. This choice can only be interpreted in the proper context, of course, but the context alone cannot account for the willingness of Bordeaux Jews to reject any notion of cultural solidarity and hence of a shared destiny with the Jews of the east. In any case, they made similar representations on numerous other occasions. On January 28, 1790, the Assembly granted the status of active citizen to the Jews of Bordeaux, the Comtat Venaissin, and Avignon, but to them alone and no others.[37] The Jews of Paris, though less numerous than their Bordeaux brethren, took a similar line. Their petition to the Assembly spoke "of the need for a uniform set of regulations and laws." Consequently, "we renounce, for the public good and for our own benefit, the privilege that was granted to us allowing us to choose our own leaders."[38] Finally, as the Assembly was preparing to conclude its work on September 27, 1791, it voted in favor of emancipation for all French Jews, thereby embracing the assimilationist views of Abbé Grégoire as well as of the Jews of Bordeaux and Paris, who believed that such a step would eventually lead to complete integration of the Jewish community under the auspices of a strong, centralized state.

Confirming Tocqueville's analysis of the logic of centralization, the consolidation of a strong central government turned out to be perfectly compatible with the decision of many Bordeaux Jews to "exit" the Jewish community and try to blend into the society at large over the course of the nineteenth century. Paradoxically, it was the Jews of the east, who so strongly resisted the state's efforts to impose its will on their community, who would later become the most assiduous "state Jews." They found a way to maintain their social and cultural traditions (a modicum of religious practice, marriage within the Jewish community, and so on) while at the same time fully embracing the universalist values of the republican state. As we shall see, many of them became deputies, and an even larger number became judges, prefects, and civil servants who, in addition to their official duties, also served in the Jewish consistories and joined in the work of the Alliance Israélite Universelle. These "state Jews," who loyally supported the efforts of the strong central government to secure the general interest, still managed to keep faith with their own tradition, whereas the "court Jews" of the modern era tended to disappear into the surrounding society. In a strange twist, the centralized state may have allowed particularistic traditions to survive in the private sphere, whereas assimilation would most likely have led to their being swallowed up by the ambient culture.

Curiously, the Napoleonic episode had similar, unexpected consequences. Napoleon, too, was keen to bring the Jewish "nation" under the domination of the French state and assimilate it to the French nation. To that end, he used the power of the state to detach Jews from their religion, estrange them from their customs and traditions, prolong their period of military service, and engage them in exogamous marriages. In 1806, the Assemblée des Notables approved Napoleon's assimilationist program, and in March 1807, the Great Sanhedrin followed suit. Although both groups hesitated on the question of marriage, they agreed that the Jewish religion should be placed under the guidance of a state-controlled Central Consistory, which among other things determined the salaries paid to rabbis. Subsidiary consistories were established in the provinces. In some respects, however, the results of this policy were the opposite of what the emperor had envisioned. The existence of a powerful central Jewish organization endowed with certain powers of enforcement unified the many isolated Jewish communities throughout France and helped them survive. Once again, the logic of the strong state produced unexpected results and ultimately strengthened the bond between Jews and the state, particularly since many state Jews served in both the Central and Regional Consistories.[39]

3

FROM COURT JEWS TO
STATE JEWS

As Werner Sombart long ago pointed out, for once correctly, it was largely because the doors of the state remained closed to Jews in both Germany and France that many "were forced to devote all their efforts to commerce and industry."[1] His psychoanalytic argument that Jews were by nature sexually repressed, hence predisposed to making money, and therefore alien to "Germanness," is another matter.[2] One need not accept this logic to profit from Sombart's chapter on the state. One cannot think of Colbert, Richelieu, Mazarin, Cromwell, or Frederick the Great, Sombart maintains, without also thinking of the role of certain Jews: "To do so would be tantamount to believing that Faust could exist without Mephistopheles. . . . The marriage of the statesman and the Jew is emblematic of the development of capitalism and therefore of the modern state."[3] As a general thesis, which neglects the differences between one type of state and another, this assertion is open to serious question. Nevertheless, Hannah Arendt drew on it indirectly when she argued: "The seventeenth and eighteenth centuries witnessed the slow development of nation-states under the tutelage of absolute monarchs. Individual Jews rose out of deep obscurity into the sometimes glamorous and always influential position of court Jews who financed state affairs and handled the financial transactions of their princes."[4] Leaving aside the almost anti-Semitic character of certain statements in the work of both authors, it is clear that they share a very similar view of the relationship between the Jews, the state, and capitalism.

In Germany until the twentieth century, Jews who did not convert could not hold high government positions. Some were thus forced into the role of "court Jews," while others joined the working class and entered the ranks of the Socialist and, later, Communist Parties.[5] In France, by contrast, we find "state Jews" moving into the place once occupied by "court Jews," while relatively few French Jews joined the ranks of working-class organizations in this period. Adept at negotiating the hierarchy of government, Jews rose quickly to the heights of power under the Second Empire and, even more, the Third Republic.[6] Thus the argument put forward by Sombart and Arendt is applicable in France only to the eighteenth century and the first half of the nineteenth century. After that—*pace* Arendt—state Jews hitched their destiny to the French state.

In the first half of the nineteenth century, it was primarily the wealthy Jews of Bordeaux and Bayonne who "exited" the Jewish community and "joined" the larger society. Hungry for a modernity which they identified with rationality, men like Emile and Isaac Pereire,[7] Olinde Rodrigues, and d'Eichtal converted to the new Christianity, which they saw as a messianic version of Israel's ancient dreams adapted to the needs of modern industrial society.[8] This form of access to modernity came about at a time when France itself was embarked on a slow but steady course of modernization. The process lasted longer than many historians think. Laffitte launched his first experiments with new forms of banking influenced by the ideas of Saint-Simon as early as 1815; Emile and Isaac Pereire, also Saint-Simonians, did not found the Crédit Mobilier until 1852. Although industrialization in France proceeded more slowly than in Great Britain or Germany, most economic historians now agree that it is misleading to regard France as "backward" in this regard. One scholar has even stated, "Among the countries generally agreed to

have industrialized, France was the first to embark on this path."[9] If
any sort of backwardness was perceived at the time, it was surely in
the area of banking, because France's relatively rudimentary banking
system impeded long-term investments of the sort needed for industrialization. In this respect, the large banks failed to encourage industrial development in France.[10]

As it happens, the question of what the proper relationship between big banks and industry ought to be became a subject of controversy among Jewish bankers and eventually led to the stunning crash
of the Crédit Mobilier. The Rothschilds had been among the leading
French bankers since the very beginning of the nineteenth century.
As court Jews who moved to the center of the modern urban economic
system, they constitute what Max Weber called an "ideal type." Like
most German court Jews, they never converted. They remained a part
of the Jewish community; their only "exit" was social, as they rose to
the summit of bourgeois society. James de Rothschild was closely allied with the notoriously reactionary Villèle government in the mid-
1820s. Later, during the July Monarchy, he managed the personal
fortune of King Louis-Philippe and engaged in daily business with
government leaders such as the banker Casimir Périer. In 1840,
James wrote in a letter to one of his friends: "I know all the ministers,
I see them daily, and whenever I observe that any minister's course of
action is contrary to the interests of the government [and, he hardly
needed to add, to his own], I go to the king, whom I see whenever I
wish."[11] That same year, he persuaded Louis-Philippe to dismiss
Adolphe Thiers, his head of government. The next day, *Le Constitu-
tionnel* asked this rhetorical question: "By what right and on what
pretext does this king of finance go about poking his nose into our
business?"[12]

Under the July Monarchy, the Rothschilds were deeply involved in
state loans and in negotiations between the government and other
lenders. As "court Jews," they joined other leading bankers in favor-
ing a prudent approach to investment and were extremely wary of industrial policies that would tie up capital for long periods. In 1833,
however, James de Rothschild found himself persuaded by the arguments of the Pereires, then in his employ, and of d'Eichtal, another

convinced Saint-Simonian, that he would do well to invest in the first French railway line, the Paris–Saint-Germain. Eventually, however, the relationship soured. Because the Pereires, along with Rodriguès, d'Eichtal, and others, saw industrialization in a messianic light, they favored the creation of a new type of bank open to public investment. A titanic struggle began during the Second Empire: the emperor sided with the Pereires (and their partners, the Foulds), supporting the Crédit Mobilier's policy of rapid expansion throughout Europe. He pushed for rapid industrialization in France. Ultimately, the Pereires, symbols of the rational industrial policies promoted by Saint-Simon, went down to defeat. The assimilated Bordeaux Jews, many of them converts who saw all-out industrialization as the source of a new form of social solidarity, fell victim to the financial policies of the Rothschilds, court Jews who maintained close ties to the Jewish community and continued to practice a fairly traditional form of Judaism but who could count on support from other leading bankers, most of whom took a cautious approach to industrialization for fear that overly rapid change might lead to social upheaval.[13] It is scarcely possible to imagine a sharper contrast between two different conceptions of social emancipation, even though both ultimately ran counter to the state-centered approach that would soon give rise to what I am calling "state Jews."

Jules Isaac Mirès was a Jewish banker born in Bordeaux in 1809. One of the founders of the Crédit Mobilier, he later achieved great success through investments in blast furnaces and mines around Marseilles. Like the Pereires, he enjoyed the unstinting support of Napoleon III. In a little-known book entitled *A mes juges,* he pondered the differences between the Rothschilds on the one hand and himself and the Pereires on the other. For Mirès, a banker whose goal was to promote rapid industrialization and who rose rapidly to national celebrity and economic success before losing everything in a stunning collapse that landed him in trouble with the law, "one has to draw a distinction between Northern Jews and Southern Jews. The Jews of Northern Europe, also known as German Jews, are cold and methodical. . . . In Germany, the Jewish race is to this day excluded from the social life of the nation. . . . Hence in Germany the Jews did not in the end link their fortune or wealth to the fortune and future of the state in which they reside. Southern Jews, sometimes character-ized as Portuguese, have imbibed nobler instincts from their Latin roots. The fact that in France they have been granted full rights of cit-izenship has further encouraged them to seek respect by devoting their efforts and wealth to serving the public interest, as if acknowl-edging services received from the French nation with services ren-dered to that nation. . . . The Rothschilds have never been wedded to the interests of France. . . . They oppose doing anything for industry or the state. . . . With the Pereires, on the other hand, the Jews of the South have made the general interest their main goal by seeking to extend the benefits of credit and industry to all."[14]

Despite the almost anti-Semitic tenor of this Jew's account of the two different approaches to emancipation, one could hardly ask for a better description. It is worth recalling that, although James de Roth-schild played a crucial role in French society and lived in a sumptu-ous Parisian residence where he received the cream of bourgeois and aristocratic society, he never became a French citizen, whereas the Pereires, Rodrigues, d'Eichtal, and Mires were all French by birth, and their families had lived in France since before the Revolution. For them it was natural to attempt to assimilate by converting to a ra-tionalized form of Christianity. But French society remained deeply Catholic, and it may have been easier to tolerate a traditional court Jew (like Bleichroder in Germany[15]) than to accept total assimilation and elimination of distinctive traditions.

In this respect, the power of the Rothschilds, though quite real, was nevertheless misleading. They exerted only limited control over the banking system and still less over industry, even though they were among the leading bankers and possessed one of the largest for-tunes in France. Of the thirty-seven people who sat on the board of the Bank of France during the Second Empire, only two were Jews, and they were never both members at the same time: the first was a jeweler named Halphen, and the second was James's son Alphonse de Rothschild, who enjoyed a lengthy tenure.[16] When he died in 1905, his estate, estimated at some 250 million francs, was by far the largest of its day.[17] Yet the Rothschilds were really holdovers from the preindustrial era, from a time before there were steel mills and bank notes.[18] They remained court Jews and never really became capitalists at home in the urbanized, industrialized economy. With the advent of capitalism, their role in banking became increasingly marginal, as the system came to be dominated by Catholics such as Laffitte, Périer, and Davillier, aristocrats such as the Vicomte d'Argout and the Comte de Germiny, and Protestants such as the Mallets, the Hottinguers, and the Schlumbergers, powerful, mutually supportive families[19] that remained aloof from Jewish bankers and were often no less anti-Semitic than their Catholic counterparts.[20] Throughout the nineteenth century, moreover, new banks came into being, banks that offered services geared to the needs of industrial expansion and capitalist growth. These included the Crédit Foncier, the Crédit Agricole, the Comptoir d'Escompte de Paris, and, most important of all, the Société Générale. Jews played no role in these banks, which exerted steadily growing influence on the process of industrialization. Then, in 1863, the Crédit Lyonnais opened its doors, and in 1872 it was joined by the Banque de Paris et des Pays-Bas. Henri Germain, the founder of the Crédit Lyonnais, played a very active role in French industrialization.[21]

Jews, on the other hand, played little or no role in France's industrial expansion.[22] During the second half of the nineteenth century, major investors in industrial ventures included wealthy landowners, both bourgeois and aristocratic. Mechanics and craftsmen, whether Catholic or Protestant, borrowed money from local banks, sometimes with backing from the various national banks mentioned above. Men who had made their money in land or iron now became steel or textile magnates. For example, the de Wendel dynasty, which had amassed a fortune in banking and industry, gained control of mines and steel mills in northeastern France.[23] The Schneiders created an industrial empire around the firm of Le Creusot; Peugeot did the same. In the rapidly growing chemical sector, Saint-Gobain began as a family business that drew support from local factory owners and banks. Péchiney was founded with capital from Lyons investors, and Kullmann drew its capital from the north.[24]

One exception to the rule was the blast furnace at Pompey, which was built in 1850 thanks to the efforts of two Jewish investors from Metz, Mayer Dupont and Myrtil Dreyfus.[25] But most of France's industrial empires were created by members of the provincial bourgeoisie, men who lived far from Paris and the world of high finance. Flavigny began in Elbeuf, Fauchille in Lille, Colcombet in Saint-Etienne, and Berliet near Lyons. All of these businesses depended mainly on local Catholic banks, many of which do not make it into economic histories. Relations between industrialists and their bankers were based on a solid foundation of trust. Local banks in places like Grenoble, Nancy, Tours, Reims, Maubeuge, Château-Thierry, and Bar-le-Duc were vital to France's industrialization. The traditionalist Catholic local bourgeoisie of industrialists and bankers not only shared a common set of values, they also tended to monopolize local elective offices. In Paris, a few court Jews may have risen to positions of misleading prominence, but in the provinces this traditional bourgeoisie remained firmly in control.[26] Among the *conseillers généraux* elected in 1870 whose income exceeded 300,000 francs per year, Alphonse de Rothschild was the only Jew, except Pereire and Fould, who had converted to Christianity. They sat alongside the likes of the Duc de La Rochefoucauld-Doudeauville, the Marquis de Talhouet, the Baron de Graffenried, the Marquis de Vögue, the Marquis de Chasseloup-Laubat, the Prince de Beauvau, and countless other Catholic aristocrats, whose marriage strategies had forged ties with the cream of bourgeois society.[27] The court Jews, whose children generally married the children of other court Jews, had little access to this locally organized upper class, which slowly but steadily monopolized power at the national level as well.[28] This threatened to undermine the traditional separation of powers at a time when the state, faced with the explosive growth of industry all around, seemed to lose some of its confident superiority.

In the eighteenth and nineteenth centuries, Protestants of foreign extraction played a considerable role in the industrialization of France. Dutch immigrants built refineries in Rouen as well as the largest woolen mill in France at Abbeville. Wilkinson from England founded the steel mill at Le Creusot, which became the very symbol of capitalist expansion. Similarly, Oberkampf from Württemberg and

Baron Oscar d'Adelswald from Sweden, with other Protestants from Switzerland and Belgium, helped France to realize its industrial potential, while Jews remained largely on the sidelines.[29] In Mulhouse, a city in eastern France, Koechlin laid the groundwork for a diversified steel industry and, as the head of the Protestant house of Dollfuss-Mieg, created one of the largest firms of its day.[30] Another Protestant from England, by the name of Waddington, joined with German and Swiss investors to create textile and steel mills around Rouen, in competition with the predominantly Catholic local bourgeoisie. It was only after France's defeat in the Franco-Prussian War in 1871 that Jews from Alsace abandoned the textile mills they had built in cities like Mulhouse and Bischwiller[31] and created new businesses in Elbeuf and other places.[32]

Wherever one looks in France, one finds that industrialization at the local level was spearheaded by Catholic capitalists, joined in some places by Protestants. The textile industry of the north, for example, was controlled by bankers and industrialists steeped in traditional Catholicism.[33] In Alsace, the same industry was almost entirely in the hands of Protestant families with local roots, although in the northern part of the province a number of strongly Catholic families dominated; both groups relied entirely on local bankers. To be sure, the small Jewish firm of Herzog-Dreyfus-Lantz began operations in Mulhouse in 1865.[34] And Raphaël Dreyfus, the father of Captain Alfred Dreyfus, founded a cotton mill in the same Protestant-dominated city in 1862.[35] Yet not even brilliant success in their ventures transformed these rare Jewish industrialists into captains of industry. During this period, moreover, young Jews generally avoided careers in the trades and industry and chose instead to go into commercial and white-collar jobs.[36]

Furthermore, the coal mines of northern France, which played such a crucial role in French industrialization generally, were largely in the hands of local bankers with traditional family ties to the business. The Piérard bank played a leading role, as did the Dupont bank, which would be privatized by the socialist government in 1981. These families controlled the blast furnaces, forges, and steel mills of Denain-Anzin, which for a long time required prospective employees to submit proof of baptism and church marriage certificates. One could easily multiply examples to prove beyond the shadow of a doubt that it was the Catholic and, to a lesser extent, Protestant bourgeoisie that guided French industrialization in the nineteenth century. New fortunes were created to rival the traditional and still-substantial fortunes of the landed aristocracy and others.[37] Note, too, that Ancien Régime France had little difficulty adapting to the nineteenth century. At least during the first half of the century, the old aristocracy was well represented among the leaders of industry, alongside and at times in partnership with the new bourgeoisie.[38]

Jews were almost totally excluded from the dominant industrial bourgeoisie. To be sure, the Rothschilds and Pereires and, for a few years, men like Mirès were responsible, virtually by themselves, for covering France and much of Europe with a dense network of railways. These were a key factor in the industrialization process, for they revolutionized the conditions of production and the role of cities.[39] As was noted earlier, however, the Rothschilds were extremely reluctant to invest in manufacturing, and although they did help to finance Denain-Anzin and a few other companies, they never became captains of industry themselves. By contrast, men like the Pereires and Mirès, with backing from Napoleon III, sought to promote a vast policy of urbanization and industrialization as the best way of modernizing France and creating a new social order of the sort envisioned by Saint-Simon.

Ultimately, the Rothschilds' role in high finance diminished as Catholic and Protestant bankers moved fairly quickly to limit their influence at the national level. Meanwhile, the Pereires and Mirès were abruptly and deliberately forced into bankruptcy and driven out of the public eye. Ardent proponents of a new concept of banking in the general interest and open to the public,[40] the Bordeaux Jews failed; the Rothschild family remained a symbol of the power of bankers, and before long became a target of anti-Semitic pamphlets circulated by extremists of both the right and the left, which wrongly painted them as exemplars of ever more merciless capitalist domination. In fact, the Rothschilds had no power in industry, and their influence in banking diminished steadily with the rise of banks such as the Crédit Lyonnais,[41] the Société Générale, and the Banque de Paris et des Pays-Bas. Nevertheless, they became a target of popular wrath throughout the nineteenth and much of the twentieth centuries, so that it was a simple matter for anti-Semites to associate capitalism with the power of Jews. As a result, a peculiarly virulent strain of anti-Semitism developed in France, where for a large segment of public opinion the Rothschild family came to epitomize the very notion of the "fat cat."[42]

The list of anti-Semitic texts devoted to the alleged occult and terrifying power of the Rothschilds goes on and on. From the nineteenth century to this day, writers of every political stripe have demonized the family, which was described as the visible face of a persistent Jewish conspiracy to use capitalism as an instrument for taking over fundamentally Christian France. In 1846, Georges Dairnwaell (who published under the pen name "Satan") produced an *Histoire édifiante et curieuse de Rothschild Ier, roi des Juifs* [*The Strange and Edifying History of Rothschild I, King of the Jews*]. Toussenel and Auguste Chirac, along with Pierre Leroux, Charles Fourier, Jules Guesde, and any number of nineteenth-century French leftist writers, persistently attacked the Rothschilds and likened capitalism to Judaism.[43] The Foulds also became a target. Karl Marx himself singled out Achille Fould as a typical "Jewish financier," and had him in mind when he accused Louis-Philippe's conservative minister François Guizot of "selling the whole French government, piece by piece, along with all of French society, to the Jewish financiers of the Paris stock exchange."[44] Of course, the anti-Semitic message honed by the leading voices of the socialist left and based largely on myth found an attentive audience in populist writers of the extreme right, who shared the left's hostility to capitalism but wanted France to revert to the Catholic nation it had been until the French, industrial, and urban revolutions destroyed what they saw as its former organic unity.

Edouard Drumont, the celebrated author of *La France juive*, of which several million copies were sold, reserved his fiercest passages for Jewish bankers like the Rothschilds, who were also the butt of mockery from the politically highly conservative novelist Honoré de

Balzac.[45] For Emile Zola and countless others, the "banker king" assumed the form of a Jew oppressing the innocent little people of France. Not just the Rothschilds but "Jewry in its entirety" personified the evil power of money. To combat this alleged Jewish power—epitomized, despite his waning influence among bankers, by James de Rothschild—various writers of the mid-nineteenth century called for an alliance of all Frenchmen, from industrial workers to Christian capitalists, who despite class differences could make common cause in order to repel the stateless Jew. This anti-Semitic hatred, which rose steadily in pitch until ultimately it led to tragedy in the era of Vichy, was focused on the Rothschilds and spared the Pereires, who, at least during the Second Empire, when the Crédit Mobilier was at the height of its influence, were at the heart of the nation's economic and political life. Of course, they sprang from a long line of thoroughly assimilated Bordeaux Jews, who took assimilation to the extreme of converting to Catholicism. That James de Rothschild never became French (although his son Alphonse did) further reinforced the anti-Semitic myth of the rootless, cosmopolitan Jew who, as *La Croix* put it, "swooped down on our country" and defiled it.[46] Bizarrely, all the Jews of France, from the poorest to the richest, from the most conservative to the most radical, from the most integrated into society to the most marginal, were portrayed as being like the Rothschilds, financial manipulators whose supposedly unproductive millions sterilized the nation's wealth.[47]

By the mid-nineteenth century, French Jews had been emancipated for more than fifty years, yet they still were not welcome in the councils of government or the upper reaches of the civil service. And they were almost entirely unsuccessful at gaining access to the new bourgeoisie that ultimately seized the reins of power. Assimilation by way of the state was not yet available, and social emancipation seemed to have reached an impasse. Worse yet, the Rothschild myth popularized the image of the Jews as unassimilated yet all-powerful figures who clung to their old faith and community and, by secretly conspiring with coreligionists abroad, sought to gain power over the good people of France. This presaged later forms of exclusionary anti-Semitism. Alleged differences between Jews and Christians that had in fact largely disappeared were nevertheless magnified by extreme Jew-haters who wished to exclude Jews from social and political life.

Thus the social assimilation of Jews in the second half of the nineteenth century remained quite fragile. The Jewish population rose from roughly forty thousand at the time of the Revolution, concentrated mainly in the east (more than twenty-five thousand there) and southwest (twenty-five hundred in Bordeaux alone), to eighty thousand in the census of 1861.[48] By that time there was considerable internal movement within and between regions, and from the countryside to large and middle-sized cities. Industrialization swelled the urban population, and Jews were perhaps even more likely than others to be drawn to the metropolises, especially Paris. As the capital of a highly centralized state, Paris quickly became a magnet to the Jewish population. When the Ecole Rabbinique de France moved from Metz to Paris in 1859, the capital also became the center of Jewish religious life. This had a detrimental impact on the older Jewish communities in the east, which had remained relatively isolated. After German troops occupied Alsace and Lorraine, some fifteen thousand Jews left the region, choosing to retain or acquire French citizenship. Many moved to Paris or its environs, where by 1880 the Jewish population numbered closed to forty-five thousand.[49] In addition, a substantial number of Jews, often of rural origins, emigrated to the United States in order to avoid becoming subjects of a German Reich in which overt anti-Semitism was rampant.[50] Nevertheless, this internal migration was dwarfed by the immigration of Jews from Eastern Europe. Following pogroms in Russia in the 1880s, some eight thousand Russian, Galician, and Romanian Jews moved to Paris; most settled in the Marais, transforming that district into a highly distinctive ethnic enclave. The emergence of this new Jewish community in Paris ran counter to the general decline of ethnic traditions among the Jews of Paris and Bordeaux.

This temporary revival of overtly ethnic aspects of Jewish religious and cultural life was particularly striking because it occurred in an urban neighborhood (in the Marais, also known as Pletz, and later also in Belleville, in the north of Paris) filled with immigrants from the East who, unlike their French coreligionists, were mostly blue-collar workers and artisans. Between 1881 and 1914, perhaps as many as thirty thousand Jewish immigrants came to France from Eastern Europe, far fewer than went to Great Britain and the United States in the same period. Nevertheless, their arrival profoundly altered the nature of the French Jewish population: reversing the trend toward emancipation through greater individualism, the immigrants revived many community-based organizations. They organized their own synagogue and, taking their cue from their countries of origin, formed particularly active trade unions.[51] They also set up mutual-aid societies called *landsmanschaften,* which encouraged new arrivals to settle near others from the same locality and join with them for religious services and funerals. Medical assistance and loans were also provided. In 1913, the Fédération des Sociétés Juives de Paris was set up as an umbrella organization for all these groups. Unlike native-born French Jews, who had been emancipated since the Revolution, many recent immigrants were drawn to extreme left-wing political groups, both Marxist and anarchist. Communist, Bundist, and socialist groups all sprang into existence and began attacking one another in a range of lively newspapers as well as in public rallies. These left-wing groups also clashed with anticommunist immigrant organizations, and both camps maintained turbulent relations with Zionist organizations, most of which originated in immigrant circles even if they sometimes reached out to more assimilated Jews as well. Often relying on Yiddish both in newspapers (such as the *Naye Presse, Parizer Haynt, Unzer Shtime, Die Neye Tsayt,* and *Der Yidisher Arbeiter*) and in public rallies, immigrants threw themselves into the trade-union struggle, sometimes in conjunction with the Confédération Générale du Travail, or CGT, sometimes in their own unions, which were organized by trade and engaged in bitter strikes either by themselves or shoulder to shoulder with non-Jewish workers. One such strike, in the ready-to-wear industry, pitted Jewish workers against the owners of small factories, many of whom were also Jewish.

It is impossible to overemphasize how much the Jewish population had changed since the beginning of the nineteenth century, when more than half of the Jews in Paris were highly assimilated "Portuguese."[52] Henceforth, emancipated Jews and recent immigrants would live in widely separated parts of the capital. In fact, assimilated Jews tended to merge into the rest of the population and disappear as a distinct segment of the Jewish community. Meanwhile, relations between the new immigrants and French-born Jews from Alsace and Lorraine were at once stormy and paternalistic. The immigrants of course lacked French nationality, took a traditional approach to religion, and were often drawn to revolutionary politics.

At a general meeting of the Consistory of Paris in 1913, Edmond de Rothschild disdainfully remarked, "These new immigrants understand nothing of French habits. . . . They keep to themselves, cling to their primitive language, and write in jargon." Striking a similar note, Jules Meyer, another leading figure in the Consistory, which had regulated Jewish affairs since the time of Napoleon, declared: "It is high time that the walls of Paris stop being covered with Hebrew characters. It is time for Paris to stop being inundated with newspapers, books, films, and plays in Yiddish."[53] Furthermore, the Consistory opposed the building of new synagogues in the Marais for the use of immigrants practicing a traditional version of Judaism. As at the time of the French Revolution, solidarity among Jews clearly was not a given, myths to the contrary notwithstanding. On May 1, 1913, the *Archives israélites* ruefully observed, "Jewish solidarity, which in the eyes of those gentlemen [the anti-Semites] is like Nessus' tunic, fell by the wayside on the day when, in equity as well as law, collective responsibility gave way to individual responsibility."[54]

With the arrival in France of Jews steeped in traditional culture and religion, who spoke different languages and shared a profound sense of community, the nature of French anti-Semitism changed dramatically. The Rothschild myth required modification: it was no longer possible to see all Jews as rich and powerful cosmopolitan bankers, since some were obviously poor, exploited workers. A new myth gained popularity. It was drawn directly from *The Protocols of the Elders of Zion*, a work whose French translation was widely read and often met with favorable comment. Jews could well be both opulent capitalists and miserable revolutionaries: according to *The Protocols*, this was their strategy for seizing power. Drumont echoed this line in his works, as did *La Libre Parole*. The widely read Catholic newspaper *La Croix* hammered home the same point, which established a link between the rhetoric of anti-Semitism and the ideology of the extreme right. The most immediate consequence of the presence of Eastern Jewish immigrants on French soil was to demolish the largely mythical image of the court Jew—all but indistinguishable from the *haute bourgeoisie*, mingling freely with the wealthiest aristocrats, frequenting lavish salons, and so on. However integrated into society some Jews might have become, the Jewish "tribe" was henceforth seen as unassimilable. Court Jews and converts found themselves suddenly trapped, even as the triumph of the Third Republic at last made it possible for French Jews, nearly a century after their formal emancipation, to enter the public arena and obtain the government jobs that Abbé Grégoire and the lawyer Thiery had believed should be reserved for Catholics. Despite Sombart's and Arendt's claims to the contrary, Jews in republican France could become state Jews and no longer had to settle for the role, in any case largely exaggerated, of court Jews. Still, Jews had been slow to join the political fray since their emancipation in 1791. Although they could, even under restrictive election rules, participate in local and national elections, it would be nearly a century before careers in politics were truly open to them.

In the 1840s, under the July Monarchy, Max Cerf Berr, Achille Fould, and Adolphe Crémieux were elected deputies. In the provisional government of 1848, Crémieux was named minister of justice, and Michel Goudchaux was named minister of finance. During the Second Empire, Achille Fould, who at the time had yet to convert, became minister of finance and minister of state; in one election or another, Maximilien Koenigswarter, Léopold Javal, Michel Goudchaux, and the three Pereire brothers were elected to the legislature. This political debut was remarkable enough that the editor of *L'Univers israélite*, analyzing the brilliant successes of these Jewish candidates, remarked that "their virtues, patriotism, and intelligence have won the sympathy of the people. They were elected by arch-Catholic voters who knew that these Jews would make noble and worthy representatives of France." Nevertheless, few Jews served in elected office or the civil service before the end of the Second Empire. State Jews—men who would owe their careers to the ultimate victory of the universalistic principles laid down by the French Revolution—were still rare, and success was reserved for court Jews who made their fortunes in commerce and industry. Saint-Simon provided them with a modernizing ideology that justified their withdrawal from politics in favor of industry, which for Saint-Simon stood as a model of progress and rationality.

With the advent of the Third Republic, everything changed. Franco-Judaism, founded on the emancipating message of the French Revolution, could at last be put into practice. Jews were encouraged to assimilate as completely as possible into a society of truly equal citizens. As the organized Jewish community continued to erode, the basic condition of citizenship under the universalistic model was met: Jews suddenly became *israélites,* identical, as far as public life was concerned, to their fellow citizens, and thus able to become part of the "new strata" that Gambetta, in a celebrated speech delivered in Grenoble in September 1872, so earnestly hoped would soon come to power. Jews would be part of a new and ardent generation, of the "new electoral and political personnel" who would experiment with republican government while rejecting what Gambetta in 1881 called "fragmentary autonomy," which could lead to federalism. By contrast, they would work steadfastly to promote "French unity and centrality," with which Jews so passionately identified. Although a few Jews did, as we have seen, serve the state under the July Monarchy (1830–48) and Second Empire (1852–71), it was above all the Third Republic (1877–1940) that gave them the opportunity to rise to the highest levels of government. When the largely Catholic conservative elite pulled back from public service because it was hostile to the new republican regime, Protestant and Jewish elites found their opening. Gambetta could rely on them as loyal allies in his efforts to consolidate the Republic. Indeed, Gambetta's close relationship to the *fous de la République*[55] is all the more significant in view of his great distrust of court Jews, especially the Rothschilds.[56] By contrast, state Jews fully subscribed to the universalistic values of the Republic. Jewish members of the prefectoral corps, judges, and state councilors helped to enforce republican discipline, develop social policy, and establish secular public schools. Thousands of Jewish captains and colonels and even a few generals served in the army in defense of the nation. They distinguished themselves in numerous battles and helped to extend the French Empire.

The old elite were gradually replaced by professional politicians. Recruited from various walks of life, these men became leaders of the new parties on which the republican political system was based. Between 1871 and 1936, fifty-two men who to one degree or another saw themselves as Jews were elected to one of the two houses of the legislature or appointed as ministers of government. Though significant, this number is of course dwarfed by the total of some six thousand deputies elected during this period. But these Jewish officials share certain common characteristics, which deserve analysis. For example, although nearly 15 percent of the deputies of the Third Republic had once served as teachers in primary or secondary schools, only 7 percent of Jewish deputies came from the ranks of educators. Hence they were not as a group typical of what Albert Thibaudet called "the Republic of teachers." There was not a single blue-collar worker among them, despite the fact that 5 percent of all deputies came from that group. Nor was there a single farmer, even though farmers accounted for 10 percent of all deputies. By contrast, 22 percent of the Jewish deputies were industrialists or merchants, compared with only 6 percent of deputies in general. Lawyers were also overrepresented among the Jews (35 percent, as against 25 percent of deputies in general), as were journalists (13 percent as against 5 percent). These figures show that the backgrounds most typical of Gambetta's "new strata" were even more typical of Jewish deputies, who found that, with the advent of the Third Republic, these career choices opened the way to political advancement. On the other hand, agriculture had always been inhospitable to Jews, so it should come as no surprise that we find no farmers among the Jewish deputies even though farmers were still the dominant social group in France by a considerable margin. Nor is it surprising that many Jewish deputies came from backgrounds in commerce and industry, since these had long served Jews as springboards to social advancement.

By and large, Jews who ran for office were not born with silver spoons in their mouths. Most came from solid middle-class backgrounds, and a few were "scholarship boys." Only a small number began their political careers with a clearly defined or articulated idea of politics, and hardly any inherited their seats from their fathers. Whereas some three hundred non-Jewish deputies managed to pass their seats on to their sons, among Jewish deputies we find only one instance of this: three generations of Javals successively represented the *département* of the Yonne. Once elected, however, Jewish deputies were more likely to be re-elected than were their gentile colleagues. Whereas more than a third of the deputies of the Third Republic were elected only once, nearly all Jewish deputies were re-elected at least once to either the Assembly or the Senate. Note, too, that, although only 631 of the 4,892 deputies of the Third Republic became ministers, twenty-three of forty-eight Jewish deputies were named ministers or secretaries of state during the same period. Furthermore, two-thirds of the Jewish ministers and secretaries served in more than one government, whereas the figure for all ministers was less than one-half.

Thus, although the total number of Jewish deputies was actually rather small, what is striking is how important a role they played in government. Quite a few became ministers of the interior, for example, and this was a particularly crucial post at a time when the Republic faced countless crises.[57] And from 1880 to 1884, at an important point in the industrialization of France, which was so heavily dependent on the development of railroads and other forms of transportation, David Raynal served as minister of public works almost continuously.[58] Jews were also influential in a number of political parties, including the Opportunists, the Socialists, and the anarchists.[59] Jews also played significant roles in many of the great crises from the Dreyfus Affair to the Popular Front, including the Boulangist movement,* the affair of the *lois scélérates,* and the

---

*In the late 1880s, General Boulanger drew support from both the extreme right and the extreme left for his nationalist, antiparliamentarian, protofascist movement. Faced with vigorous opposition from the government, he was defeated and sent into exile, where he eventually committed suicide on the grave of his late mistress.

Panama scandal. This gave them considerable visibility and made them prime targets of polemical attack, compounded by the fact that they were frequently involved in policies that had a direct impact on the way people lived: allowing girls access to public education, instituting divorce, separation of church and state, and more recently, abolition of the death penalty, liberalization of abortion laws, and so on. In addition to those Jews who exercised authority directly as ministers of government, others served in the bureaucracy and public universities. Still others taught in the secondary schools or served in lower-level civil-service positions. Many were drawn to science as their means of access to the public sphere.

Jews from 1877 onwards
had complect assimilation

4

The Love of Learning:
Sociologists and Their Roots

In November 1982, Raymond Aron accepted an honorary degree from the Weizmann Institute in Israel. At the time, the country was still reeling from the war in Lebanon and its aftermath. In his acceptance speech, Aron spoke of the responsibilities of intellectuals to their nation's military. What principles should govern this relationship? The ethics of responsibility or the ethics of conviction? The needs of national defense or the defense of universal values? At this difficult juncture in Israel's history, Aron spoke about the Dreyfus Affair, in which an innocent Jewish officer was framed by other officers, found guilty of spying for Germany, and sentenced to a term of prison on Devil's Island:

> Dreyfus was exceptional, a clear-cut case. It was a judicial error, plain and simple. Some people lied, while others told the truth. At some point, to insist in the face of all the facts, all the evidence, that Dreyfus was guilty had the effect not of protecting the general staff but of compromising it still further. Hence, even if the Dreyfusards damaged French national unity and un-

dermined confidence in the country's military leaders, they could not withdraw their allegations or remain silent. . . . Few public issues are as pure and simple as the Dreyfus Affair.[1]

For Aron, the Dreyfus Affair was all but inescapable. He died suddenly in October 1983, just after starting to read Jean-Denis Bredin's book on the case, *L'Affaire*.[2] It was as if the tragedy symbolized his own destiny as a French Jew: having surmounted every hurdle to achieve the highest levels of intellectual honor and public acclaim, he still felt somehow "marginal" in French society. As a boy, just past his tenth birthday, he had found, in a locked chest atop the bookshelves in his father's library, a treasure trove of information about the Affair. As he later recalled, "I plunged into the Dreyfus Affair without recognizing the challenge it posed to Jews and their status in France. It was during [World War I], and my parents shared the same patriotic passions as everyone else. . . . The Dreyfus Affair did not ruffle my sense of myself as a little Frenchman."

To his "surprise," however, his father pointed out that the Affair had proved to be an even sterner test of men and character than World War I, for all its horrors. As a teenager, Aron heard one of his history teachers, a man whose sympathies lay with the right-wing Action Française, attempt to plant doubts about Dreyfus's innocence in the minds of his students: "Even years after the event, this teacher claimed, no one could say for sure whether Dreyfus was guilty or innocent." Armed with detailed knowledge of the case, Aron plunged into a vigorous defense of the captain. "My fellow students were aware that I was Jewish," Aron wrote. "But in the debate with the teacher, neither of us, as far as I can recall, mentioned or at any rate attached much weight to fact that Dreyfus and I were both Jewish. In those days—it was 1920 or 1921—something still remained of the spirit of the Union Sacrée."*[3]

At widely separated intervals in his life, Aron discussed details of the Affair, which he knew intimately. In commenting on Hannah

*The Union Sacrée was the name for the coalition government that ruled France during World War I, when partisan rivalries were put aside in order to save the nation. — TRANS.

Arendt's *Origins of Totalitarianism* in 1954, for example, he spotted many factual errors: "The Affair was ended not as she states by a decision of the Cour d'Appel but by a decision of the Cour de Cassation, all chambers combined." He remarked that "the anti-Semitic crowds that demonstrated against Zola in Paris and against Victor Basch in Rennes were by no means homogeneous," and expressed his view that Arendt's "portrayal of Captain Dreyfus draws heavily on anti-Dreyfusard literature and, to my mind, bears little resemblance to reality." His conclusion was in keeping with his Weberian method of analyzing social facts: "Mrs. Arendt's interpretation of the Dreyfus Affair leaves a French reader with mixed feelings. . . . She goes to seemingly great lengths to avoid seeing the wrenching inner dramas that tore people apart, Dreyfusards out of concern for the truth and conservatives and militarists out of conviction."[4] In 1983, near the end of his life, while working on his memoirs, he wrote, "The Dreyfus Affair attests not only to the virulence of the disease of anti-Semitism but also to the resistance of the French body politic."[5] His approach to the Affair was thus purely rational. As a sociologist, he stressed the intentions of the various actors and sought to understand their underlying motives. He avoided describing the Affair from a Jewish point of view. Nevertheless, in February 1951, in a lecture to B'nai B'rith of France, he stated: "I am personally a Frenchman of Jewish birth or tradition. . . . The idea of total assimilation, which some years ago I thought could be taken for granted, no longer seems quite so certain. Irreparable events have taught us that things could happen even in this community [that is, France], a community to which I have felt more deeply attached than to any other—things that have once again placed the issue squarely on the agenda."[6] To what extent did he succeed in adopting a purely objective attitude toward events that affected him as a Jew? As he observed in speaking of the Nazi threat: "How can I honestly tell you that I am impartial when Hitlerism has always been anti-Semitic?" And later, in 1967, this man who considered himself to be a "nonreligious Jew" (*Juif déjudaïsé*) felt a "burst of Judaism"[7] when General de Gaulle uttered some rather harsh words about Israel. In regard to the Dreyfus Affair, which belonged to the more distant past, he adopted a more rationalistic attitude, and yet he returned to it again and again because it seemed to crystallize tensions that revealed something important about the history of France. Ultimately, however, as an heir to the Enlightenment and to the secular, universalistic Third Republic, he radically rejected the idea that there might be a specifically Jewish way of doing sociology.[8]

Related by marriage to Emile Durkheim, with whom his father had dealings, Aron also had family ties to Marcel Mauss. Both Durkheim and Mauss were contemporaries of the unfortunate Captain Dreyfus and deeply immersed in the Affair. Although Aron by his own admission found Durkheim's sociology uncongenial, he and Durkheim were both assimilated French Jews. As such, they shared a common destiny, as both men discovered when a resurgence of anti-Semitism threatened their basic rights as citizens. Like Durkheim, Aron tried to respond as an impartial observer, making no concessions to his Jewish background, but eventually he was forced to concede that under certain circumstances it was impossible to reconcile a detached, rational approach with the sense of belonging to a certain community, however vague that sense might be. He thus faced the same dilemma as the author of *Les Règles de la méthode sociologique,* who treated what he called "social facts" as "things" independent of any "preconceptions." Indeed, preconceptions were all too likely to become sources of error. Alain Touraine has argued that Durkheim's objective stance was an outgrowth of the Dreyfus Affair: "It was in part because anti-Semites rejected them that Jewish bourgeois intellectuals felt sufficiently distant from their society that they were able to analyze it. It is no accident that French sociology, and for that matter American sociology, were almost totally Jewish."[9] And, true enough, from Durkheim to Lucien Lévy-Bruhl, Marcel Mauss, and Raymond Aron, many sociologists of Jewish descent have been captivated by the Affair. Its consequences posed a challenge not only to the rationalist foundations of the Third Republic but also to the theoretical perspective of thinkers as different in other respects as, say, Durkheim, whose outlook was fundamentally positivist, and Aron, a convinced Weberian for whom values, whether based in reason or not, were paramount.[10]

Durkheim's rationalism clearly differentiated him from such rivals as Gustave Le Bon and Gabriel Tarde. For Le Bon, the behavior of crowds was basically an irrational, mystical phenomenon. In this he followed the lead of Dr. Charcot, the theorist of hypnosis, who, though a republican, was a committed anti-Dreyfusard who made no secret of his anti-Semitic sentiments.[11] Tarde, who had ties to many prominent Catholics,[12] based his explanation of elite influence on a similar psychological phenomenon, imitation; he had little to say about the Affair, however.[13] Durkheim, unlike his rivals, had confidence in the modernization process, which he believed would lead ultimately to greater rationality, justice, and solidarity among increasingly interdependent individuals. In the normal course of things, he argued, coercion would decrease and individuals would be encouraged to develop their talents. Passions, ideologies, and other sources of violence and intolerance would diminish. In his book *De la division du travail social* (1893), published just before the Dreyfus Affair erupted, he retraced the main phases of this process. When he realized the extent of the resurgence of anti-Semitism, he was therefore greatly disillusioned. In his view, anti-Semitism was a pathology of a dysfunctional society. In his scientific work, however, he stuck to his guns. In 1895, the year in which Dreyfus was banished to Devil's Island, he published *Les Règles de la méthode sociologique*, a work that he hoped would serve as the foundation of a rigorous sociology conceived as a value-free science of cause and effect.

Accordingly, he approached the wave of anti-Semitism triggered by the Affair as a sociologist accustomed to dealing with social pathology in its many forms and eager to restore social cohesion as quickly as possible. Early in 1898, he sent his nephew Marcel Mauss a sociological interpretation of the crisis that would shape all his later thinking:

The situation is indeed grave, but in my view anti-Semitism is only a surface manifestation. What is really serious is first of all that such a minor affair—for in itself it doesn't amount to anything—could have stirred up so much trouble. There had to be a deep moral confusion underneath all this for such a minor incident to have been the source of so much turmoil. It also troubles me that what seems to be emerging is a reaction against any number of principles that had seemed firmly established.[14]

On several occasions Durkheim turned to this unexpected rebirth of anti-Semitism, which he saw as a direct attack on the Republic itself. At the height of the Affair, in 1899, he revealed his true patriotic colors when he drew a contrast between, on the one hand, "chronic, traditional" anti-Semitism in Germany and Russia and, on the other hand, anti-Semitism in France, which he characterized as nothing more than an "acute crisis triggered by a temporary set of circumstances." There had been an earlier outbreak of anti-Semitic sentiment in France during the Franco-Prussian War of 1870–71. "Being of Jewish descent myself," he noted, "I was able to observe this closely at the time. Jews were attacked because of France's defeats."

As for the social conflict stemming from the Dreyfus Affair, he had this to say:

When society suffers, it feels the need to blame someone for its sickness, someone on whom it can take out its disappointment. The natural choice for this role is someone already viewed unfavorably by public opinion. These pariahs serve as expiatory victims. What persuades me that this interpretation is correct is the way in which the outcome of the Dreyfus trial was greeted in 1894. There was an explosion of joy in the streets. People celebrated as a success what they should have mourned. Now they knew who to blame for the economic difficulties and moral distress in which they had been living. The sickness came from the Jews. . . . Already things seemed to be improving, and people felt comforted.[15]

What Durkheim offers in this brief paragraph is a sociological theory of the scapegoat. In a society with extensive social division of labor such as that of late-nineteenth-century France, he argued, a crisis as serious as the Dreyfus Affair had to reflect underlying ailments that were not simply economic but also "moral." Anti-Semitism then served a social function: by designating the Jew as adversary, it restored social solidarity, uniting society around hatred of the Jew. Anti-Semitism "is a symptom of the grave moral disorder from which we are suffering. Consequently, the real way to stop it is to put an end to this unhealthy condition." To combat this evil, Durkheim recommended "severe punishment for any citizen who incites other citizens to hatred." Such measures "would remind the public of the odiousness of this crime, which has been forgotten." Furthermore, "all men of good sense . . . should join forces to defeat this public madness."[16] Durkheim here reverts to the familiar vocabulary of crisis, public awareness, and crime. But he also relies on new notions to explain this otherwise incomprehensible disorder: it is, he maintains, a pathological form of the social division of labor. This pathology does not lead to anomie because anti-Semitism fulfills the role ascribed to religion in *Les Formes élémentaires de la vie religieuse:* specifically, it generates a collective "warmth" that rekindles the group spirit. Durkheim here employs words such as "madness" and "hatred" that rarely occur elsewhere in his writing in order to suggest how anti-Semitism stirs up atavistic emotions, feelings that are out of place in an advanced, modern society. This social pathology is all it takes to unleash a tidal wave of insanity and hatred.

From the beginning, Durkheim the sociologist fought against that pathology. His letters reveal a true militant. From correspondence with Henri Hubert, who played an important role in running the journal *L'Année sociologique* and was the friend and closest collaborator of Durkheim's nephew Marcel Mauss, we learn that Durkheim was one of the founders of the Ligue des Droits de l'Homme et du Citoyen (the League of the Rights of Man and the Citizen).[17] In January and February 1898, as echoes of anti-Semitism reverberated throughout France, Durkheim wrote to a number of his collaborators urging them to lodge official protests. He rejected "League for a New Trial" as a name for the future organization, because he wanted the group to be committed not just to proving the captain's innocence but to a "general cause." For him, it was a matter of defending principles, of standing up for universal ethics and for the moral system which it had been his life's work to analyze and which he saw as the basis of national solidarity. His counterproposal was to name the group "League for Respect for Legality and Defense of National Honor": such a choice, he argued, "would bring in the self-styled nationalists." As a proud patriot, he hoped to build a national consensus around respect for the law and for the rights of all citizens. As he confessed to fellow sociologist Célestin Bouglé:

> I was a member of the League before it existed; I belonged before there was a League. During the Zola trial, whose outcome was never in doubt, I wrote to Hubert and urged him to suggest to various people with whom he was in contact the idea of a permanent organization whose purpose would be to demonstrate that we had not given up, to anticipate the effects of the verdict, and to prepare for the future. Reinach had a similar idea. Someone notified Duclaux, to whom I wrote directly, and that is how the charter came to be drawn up two weeks ago this Sunday.

This letter highlights the crucial role that Durkheim played in the creation of the League, a role that most historians have ignored. It also reveals how aware he was of the risk he was taking, given the climate of the time: "True enough, our attitude is quite revolutionary. But who is to blame? This revolt was implicit in the logic of events."[18] The Durkheim we see here has little in common with the usual image of him as a cautious, conservative thinker.

Although Durkheim was "personally convinced of D's innocence," he stressed the need to organize the protest "around the procedural question: Was he found guilty without being given an opportunity to defend himself against the charges?" In numerous letters written in the heat of action in early 1898, he urged timorous colleagues to sign the petition. These were men afraid of incurring the wrath of the minister of education and thereby damaging their careers. Durkheim stressed the need for quick action. "We can't make too much of a fuss, but we mustn't allow ourselves to be scared off, either. . . . All these people are going to do their individual parts, but a bond needs to be forged so that they don't feel isolated. In public, especially, it is important not to back down." At about the same time, Durkheim wrote a similar letter to another contributor to *L'Année sociologique:*

"When this case is finally laid to rest, we will still need to deal with the moral situation that this sad but in itself not terribly significant incident has revealed. We must try to understand the implications of the crisis and do what we can to keep it from happening again, for otherwise we will see it again in a different form. Let us take advantage of the lesson we have been given."[19] Having written so much as a sociologist about the baleful effects of isolation, and having studied the sources of social cohesiveness in societies with substantial division of labor, he hoped that the captain's supporters would be able to mount a truly collective protest, so that afterward they might go on to combat other injustices as well. He compiled lists of likely supporters, wrote letters urging various people to join the group, and personally called on Emile Duclaux, the director of the Institut Pasteur, whose position he deemed insufficiently combative. Legislative elections loomed on the horizon, and in his view there was a danger that afterward "the Affair may be buried. So many people have an interest in seeing it buried." In June 1898, he wrote: "The number of people who are coming over to our side in the D Affair . . . is growing in the provinces. . . . Unfortunately, the power of public opinion is so daunting that people are willing to say what they think only *sotto voce*." All of these quotations are from letters written as part of the editorial labor of putting out *L'Année sociologique*. Yet even in this business correspondence Durkheim frequently made brief allusions to the Affair. Toward the end of 1898, he wrote: "I shall send a telegram tomorrow to add my name to the list of protesters. I would have preferred a less restrained form of protest. [This petition] doesn't fully convey all the things we are committed to." Clearly, this austere and dignified professor, who worried about the need to advance his own and his colleagues' careers in order to establish the new sociology on a firm footing, was nevertheless prepared to throw himself fully into the struggle against injustice. As late as February 1899, he wrote, "If the Affair survives this latest crisis, it must be truly invincible. How craven people have been! I've had it up to here."[20]

The founder of French sociology was not alone in this fight, however. For one thing, his early efforts coincided, as he himself noted, with the still largely isolated initiatives of Joseph Reinach, a state

Jew par excellence[21] and, like Durkheim, a staunch admirer of Gambetta, the man who still stood for the implementation of the ideals of 1789.[22] For another, Durkheim was able to enlist the support of his closest colleagues, Jews and non-Jews alike. Foremost among them was his nephew Marcel Mauss. In a letter to Mauss at the beginning of 1898, Durkheim admitted that he was "not very optimistic. But that is no reason to discourage you from joining the struggle. Indeed, one of the good things about the situation is that it has reawakened the zest for combat, which has been asleep for so long. There is something to do because there is a new battle to fight." He added that "the essential thing is that the elements of this new coalition remain united and do not scatter to the winds."[23] Mauss became a Dreyfusard. In 1898, he wrote to Henri Hubert: "Thinking of my country gives me no pleasure. . . . The moral fog that blankets France makes me forget her beauties." But "when it comes to France," he added, "I feel not disgusted but rebellious."[24] His mother, Rosine Mauss, worried that his work for the Dreyfusards might "hinder his career."[25] But Durkheim repeatedly egged him on: "The indignation that one feels at the sight of such things demands action," he wrote. "Without plunging into the mêlée, I am doing what I can to halt the intellectual and moral reaction that is very clearly setting in. You are evidently unaware of the existence and magnitude of this reaction, but the upcoming elections will show you what I mean."[26] In fact, Mauss's reactions were influenced by his socialist leanings. He shared the reservations if not the animosity of socialist leader Jean Jaurès. Against Durkheim's wishes, Mauss enlisted in the socialist movement and accepted its class analysis of the situation: "Two years after France succumbed to the fever of nationalism, now it is England's turn," he wrote in June 1900. "In France, however, nationalism is complicated by anti-Semitism, and as in Germany it thrives on the thinking of the *petite bourgeoisie* and the reactionary caste. In England it is the work of the military and political aristocracy and of the high financiers who exploit the people. But for this one exception, nationalism is everywhere essentially bourgeois. What we are seeing right now is the ultimate form of the society that the coming social revolution will destroy."[27] Clearly, this class-based socialist analysis was less likely than Durkheim's universalistic moral analysis to inspire total commitment to the Dreyfusard cause. Indeed, Jaurès remained officially aloof from both sides in the Affair, and as late as 1898 he was condemning both camps for prolonging a conflict that in his view only put off the final social confrontation. But Mauss did eventually yield to the urgings of Lucien Herr and agree to join Charles Péguy, who led a contingent of Dreyfusards in a clash with nationalists at Félix Faure's funeral.[28] He nevertheless chose to devote most of his energy in this period to socialism, and in December 1899 participated in the Japy Congress, whose purpose was to unify the socialist movement. His view was that the Socialist Party, which in the end did enlist in the pro-Dreyfus cause in order to save the Republic, must now move toward "its ultimate political and economic goal" by combating the forces of both reaction and anti-Semitism, which for Mauss was simply "the economic doctrine of the *petite bourgeoisie*."[29]

It will come as no surprise that Mauss, given his interpretation of anti-Semitism, was no more than a moderate Dreyfusard. In this respect he differed from Durkheim, for whom the Affair reflected a "suffering" society, a disequilibrium—indeed, a moral disorder that called for an ethical response based on universal values rather than on contested economic categories. Despite such marked differences, it is nevertheless true that, among "this first generation of assimilated Jews in high academic positions, many took political positions that reflected a preference for universal values. . . . This disposition was even stronger among Jews from eastern France." (Durkheim and Mauss both came from the Jewish *petite bourgeoisie* of the East, and Maurice Halbwachs was tied to the same group by marriage.)[30] Another example is the case of Lucien Lévy-Bruhl, a "crypto-Durkheimian" who stood close to the inner circle and who also enlisted in the Dreyfusard cause. Moreover, Durkheim championed Lévy-Bruhl's most important work, *Les Fonctions mentales dans les sociétés primitives*, which was published in the series of *Travaux de l'Année sociologique*. Like Durkheim and Mauss, Lévy-Bruhl was an Alsatian Jew, and like Durkheim, he attended the Ecole Normale Supérieure. Throughout their lives, the two men shared similar intellectual preoccupations, and Lévy-Bruhl at several points gave Durkheim's career a boost. Like the author of *Suicide,* Lévy-Bruhl married well, choosing as his bride a daughter of the Jewish elite.[31] In fact, his wife was a cousin of Captain Dreyfus, and Lévy-Bruhl courageously testified in the captain's behalf during the 1894 trial. On December 27, 1894, he received a letter from Dreyfus addressed to Monsieur Lucien Lévy-Bruhl, Professor of Philosophy at the Lycée Louis le Grand. "Until now," Dreyfus wrote, "I have not had the heart to thank you for your earnest efforts on behalf of an innocent man." He recognized the depth of his predicament: "I understand the rage and anger of a nation that has learned that one of its officers is a traitor." As a loyal military man, he could not believe that a fellow officer was guilty of treason: "Indeed, my conviction is that it was not an officer." Although the Affair was only just beginning, Dreyfus asked, in the course of his long letter, "if there is justice on this earth. Unfortunately, I lack the faith of which martyrs are made. . . . Come what may, my dear Lucien, hold your heads high, all of you, and look the world in the eye. I am not guilty. I am the victim of a terrible fate." This deeply intimate letter speaks volumes about the close relationship between Captain Dreyfus and Lucien Lévy-Bruhl.[32]

According to Charles Andler, a socialist intellectual, it was Lévy-Bruhl who made sure that Lucien Herr "always knew the truth about Alfred Dreyfus." Later, Lévy-Bruhl, the author of *La Mentalité primitive,* joined Dreyfus's brother Mathieu in pleading the captain's case to Waldeck-Rousseau, the head of government. Indefatigable in his efforts to free Dreyfus, Lévy-Bruhl, like Durkheim, joined the Ligue des Droits de l'Homme et du Citoyen. His interest in the Affair continued long after it was over: in 1930, he wrote a lengthy preface to the notebooks of Schwartzkoppen, the German military attaché who had played a key role in the case. Displaying remarkably detailed knowledge of the facts of the case, he seized the opportunity to proclaim his unabashed patriotism: "France has once again become the most human of nations, the champion of justice, where, despite a conspiracy of social forces bent on maintaining an undeserved conviction, truth and justice ultimately won out. The entire nation—and in particular, despite all the resistance, the army—recognized this.

And when the great test came, the Germans discovered that the affair had not sapped their adversaries' moral resolve—far from it."[33]

Times had changed, however, and in both countries the nationalist right was once again on the move. Lévy-Bruhl, convinced of the need to do something to combat the rising tide of anti-Semitism, believed that the kind of protest that had worked in the Dreyfus Affair—the expression of individual moral outrage—was still the best approach. In 1938, a Comité de Vigilance Juif was organized. At a meeting discreetly held in February of that year, Lévy-Bruhl noted, "We are under attack and we are French, true enough, but soon we are going to come under attack as Jews. How should we react?"[34] Once again he became a target of anti-Semitic polemics. In March 1939, the newspaper *L'Action française* described him in these terms: "Like so many members of his generation, especially the Jews (he is a cousin of the traitor Dreyfus), [Lévy-Bruhl] was marked by Germanic philosophy and began his career with a thesis of Kantian inspiration. . . . Soon thereafter he came under the influence of another Jew, Emile Durkheim."[35]

Some of the non-Jewish sociologists and philosophers involved with Durkheim in *L'Année sociologique* also shared his commitment in the Dreyfus Affair. They included François Simiand,[36] Henri Hubert, D. Parodi, and Paul Lapie. On March 16, 1898, Lapie wrote to Célestin Bouglé: "Has M. Durkheim sent you the regulations for the Ligue pour la Défense des Droits du Citoyen? If not, I have a copy for you in case you might like to join. . . . I hesitated before signing up because I was afraid that the League might come under the jurisdiction of the law on associations. But since the purpose of the group is to defend the principles of 1789, I do not believe that it can be treated as a subversive organization."[37]

L'Année sociologique came into being at the height of the Affair, and in the correspondence pertaining to the journal's inception we find editorial concerns (such as the choice of an editor, revisions to articles, encouragement to contributors) mingled with news about Dreyfusard activities.[38] As the sociologist Philippe Besnard observes, "The Dreyfus Affair was a golden opportunity to reinforce the unity of the core group. It strengthened the ties, for example, between Durkheim and Bouglé."[39]

Bouglé, who would become the director of the Ecole Normale Supérieure after World War I, was one of the first members of the Ligue des Droits de l'Homme. Durkheim, pleased that Bouglé had joined the group, wrote him on March 18, 1898. "In a true case of telepathy, we had reached the same point in regard to the unfortunate Affair . . . but persuading people to join will be difficult. What pettiness and cowardice one encounters. . . . But those of us who have joined must stick together all the more. This, at least, may be the moral benefit of the situation."[40] Bouglé gave of himself unstintingly. On January 14, 1898, he joined Paul Lapie and François Simiand (the economist of L'Année sociologique) in signing a "Manifesto of Intellectuals" in the wake of Zola's "J'accuse." The manifesto protested what it called "the mysteries" of the Esterhazy trial and called for a review of the verdict in the Dreyfus case.[41] Clearly, the Durkheimian sociologists were among the most active members of the circle of normaliens that gathered around Lucien Herr and Charles Andler. On December 5, 1898, in an electrified atmosphere, Francis de Pressensé went to Montpellier to plead the case of Dreyfus and Picquart.* A large anti-Dreyfus demonstration took place on the Place de la Comédie. More than five thousand people turned out to cheer the army, attack Zola, and vilify the Jews. A few days later, a group of university students attacked a Dreyfusard professor. Célestin Bouglé joined in drafting an open letter in support of his colleague. Responding to the royalist, Catholic newspaper L'Eclair, which had questioned the "Swiss or German influence by blood or marriage" in the background of certain Dreyfusard professors, Bouglé and several colleagues met the charge head-on: "You insinuate that these 'intellectuals,' who have publicly called for justice in this case, are neither Frenchmen nor patriots. . . . We believe that to prevent the cover-up of an injustice perpetrated by a small number of men is to be good

---

*Colonel Georges Picquart was an anti-Semitic Catholic officer who discovered that Dreyfus was in fact innocent and dared to denounce the general staff for framing him. He was imprisoned as a result.

Frenchmen." Bouglé launched even sharper attacks in several lectures. Speaking in Montpellier in February 1899, he accused republican leaders of passive complicity:

> The republican gentlemen who reason thus are like people who sleep while a riot is raging. You try to rouse them: "Wake up! Danger! People are fighting in the streets!" And they answer: "It's nothing, they're just murdering a Jew." Grumbling, they go back to sleep. What they fail to see is that the murderers who are killing this Jew will not stop at one victim. They have higher ambitions. It's not just Dreyfus they're after, it's the Republic. And, my good republican friends, by the time you deign to wake up, it will be too late. By then your precious France may already have a knife at her throat. . . . If those people really want our scalps, we will defend ourselves. If their gangs take to the streets, they won't find the streets undefended. . . . Republicans of every stripe, consider yourselves forewarned. Will you allow the idea of equality, which is France's badge of honor, to be destroyed by resurrected distinctions of caste, race, and religious creed? That is the question.[42]

On June 4, 1899, the text of a telegram of support from the Montpellier branch of the Ligue des Droits de l'Homme to Madame Dreyfus appeared on the front pages of Montpellier's two leading newspapers, *Le Petit Méridional* and *L'Eclair*. Bouglé was once again among the signers.[43] He had the temerity, moreover, to denounce the vitriolic anti-Semitism of *La Libre Parole*: "Listen to these litanies of hatred," he wrote, "and you might think you were in hell as portrayed by Michelangelo or Rubens, a pit filled with grimacing figures breathing fire from their mouths and nostrils."[44] Durkheim worried about *La Libre Parole*'s attacks on his collaborator,[45] but Bouglé persisted. In a text on the "philosophy of anti-Semitism," he not only alleged that anti-Semitism had become "a French political party," which was more than Durkheim ever claimed, but also attacked Drumont's use of racist arguments: "Suppose that you raving anti-Semites opened the skulls of a hundred Jews. Would you find any proof that Jews are congenitally incapable of loving France? This is a myth."[46] His conclusion was passionate: "If we worked so hard to bring Dreyfus back from Devil's Island, it was because we hoped that a whole host of ideas that we hold sacred would return on the same ship. We were fighting not for just one Frenchman but for France; not for just one citizen but for the Republic; not just for a man but for humankind."[47]

Despite conflicting intellectual allegiances, the Dreyfusards, bound by invisible sympathies, shared a true community of values and became a genuine force for collective action. They found their voice in any number of journals, in whose pages they applied scientific principles to the mysteries of the Affair. In article after article they "demonstrated their civic spirit and showed that science has a social mission."[48] Within this intellectual community, Protestants and Jews were overrepresented.[49] Not all were Durkheimian sociologists: there were philosophers and historians as well.[50] The religious background of the Dreyfusard intellectuals drew sarcastic comment from colleagues such as Hubert Bourgin, who noted that Durkheim was a "Jew, a Jew of illustrious descent." And he was not the only one: "You also have Léon Brunschvicg, professor of philosophy at the Sorbonne, an *israélite* like Durkheim, and Lévy-Bruhl and Henri Berr. And think of Elie Halévy and Louis Eisenmann, who joined up with Lucien Herr: no accident. So you see how the Jewish *normaliens* have taken a leading role in the school's transformation and subversion."[51]

Now, it is true that Henri Berr, the founder of the *Revue de synthèse,* was indeed a Jew from Lorraine, and through his wife he was rather distantly related to both Captain Dreyfus and Emile Durkheim. He was also active in the *normalien* milieu. But as a moderate republican, he "was not part of the avant-garde of the Dreyfusard movement."[52] In a long text written in 1901, he looked back on the Affair. Taking his lead from Fichte, he tried to weigh the motives of everyone involved: "These days it is a natural ambition of every French thinker to seek to restore the country's unity, which has been badly shaken, and thereby to lay the groundwork for the unification of all mankind. Today even more than in Johann Gottlieb Fichte's time, it is the task of philosophy to resolve the current crisis." A "good many French people, good French people," had assailed one another, he noted, and the case had taken a particularly grave turn because "the man found guilty was Jewish." Those who defended the verdict "said that they were acting out of respect for the army, patriotism, and, in many instances, anti-Semitism." For Berr, the explanation for all this lay in the need for belief in a period otherwise marked by uncertainty and lack of passion: "The nation, the army, the flag—these things stood for the eternal need to transcend the individual, for an experiment in religion if you will, despite the sometimes selfish and even violent forms that the expression of that religion sometimes took." Anti-Semitism itself was primarily "an aspect of nationalist passion," which turned vehement because the categorical denial of faith caused people "to rebel and turn fanatical." In order to restore national unity, he argued, it would be enough to "oppose faith with faith."[53] Profoundly nationalist himself, Berr angrily rejected the expression "Jewish people" and expressed his desire to create "a French oeuvre, in the French manner." Although he was probably jeered by his students during this period of nationalistic fervor, he chose to remain aloof from the time of the Dreyfus Affair to the advent of Vichy, and during the Occupation he refused to wear the yellow star.[54]

Another figure in the Affair was Xavier Léon, the cofounder of the *Revue de métaphysique et de morale*. When Célestin Bouglé advised him to intervene with "a discreet campaign," Léon at first tried to avoid confrontation. A thoroughly assimilated Jew, he was even capable of asking his friend whether he had "read in the newspapers the great polemic swirling around poor Dreyfus. If his family is behind it, they'd do better to keep quiet."[55] Related by marriage to an influential jurist, M. Bloch-Laroque, Léon had joined with Elie Halévy to found the review, a spiritualist philosophical journal whose point of view could not have been more alien to Durkheim's sociological perspective.[56] Halévy kept Léon informed of events surrounding the trial in Rennes. This was how he finally came to take a public position in the Affair, when he signed a petition in *L'Aurore* on December 7, 1898 calling for postponement of the Picquart trial. In May 1898, A. Darlu, a highly respected teacher of philosophy at the Lycée Condorcet who had taught many of these Jewish intellectuals in their youth, wrote a celebrated article in Léon's *Revue* in which he attacked Brunetière's critique of individualism (as Durkheim did elsewhere).[57] During the summer of 1899, as Léon was making preparations for the International Congress of Philosophy, several foreign members of the sponsoring committee resigned in protest against the Rennes verdict. Although Léon confessed that he shared their feelings about the verdict, he nevertheless argued that it was wrong to "confuse the military judges with the intellectuals who are battling their efforts and striving to repair their mistakes."[58] Elie Halévy was a well-known historian of English political thought, and Léon supported his candidacy for the Ecole Libre des Sciences Politiques. The two men worked very closely together on the journal. Both were members of "the first generation of emancipated Jews, who felt no need to define themselves as Jews since they identified with the image of the republican."[59]

Elie Halévy and his brother Daniel had been raised as Protestants by their mother. Their father, Ludovic Halévy, had been brought up as a Catholic, but both their grandfather Léon, a follower of Saint-Simon and author of the *Résumé de l'histoire des Juifs anciens,* and their great-grandfather Elie were practicing Jews. The elder Elie even served as cantor of the synagogue on the rue de la Victoire and was himself the son of a rabbi. Eventually, the younger Elie Halévy was moved to write to the Durkheimian Célestin Bouglé: "Even if Dreyfus is guilty, he is the victim of a terrible machination. But I carry a Jewish name even if I am Protestant. Am I the victim of a caste illusion? Answer me quickly, for right now my life is unbearable." Lucien Herr, who was in touch with both Durkheim and Lévy-Bruhl, proved to Halévy's satisfaction that Dreyfus was innocent. He confided this information to Léon on November 24, 1897: "It is a case of apathy in the face of a very powerful clerical organization. It has become impossible for me to doubt Captain Dreyfus's innocence. Your duty is to say so." In a subsequent letter to Bouglé, dated January 1, 1898, Halévy wrote of his "hope that you have not lost interest in the Dreyfus Affair or ceased to be alarmed at how easily France dishes up preposterous lies, because injustice is evil not for those who must bear it but for those who perpetrate it."[60] Yet he refused to commit himself to political activism and, unlike many Dreyfusards, declined to join the Socialist Party. He was active in the Affair, however; it was he who in January 1898 asked Célestin Bouglé to sign the "Manifesto of Intellectuals." In another letter to Bouglé, he expressed his pleasure that "the protest has been going well. We thought we had collected seventy signatures, but on counting we realized that there were a hundred." Later, he would join the Ligue des Droits de l'Homme, along with Bouglé and Durkheim. On March 10, 1898, he wrote to Bouglé: "I am in Paris, thinking about what can be done to champion the cause of Dreyfus in particular and France in general. The League is being organized. . . . Naturally, my father and I will join." Greatly concerned about anti-Semitism, he broached the subject in yet another letter to Bouglé: "I am deeply convinced that militarism, clericalism, and anti-Semitism will become inseparable and that the twentieth century will be a sad disavowal of the nineteenth if we do not respond at once." On January 1, 1899, he wrote another feverish letter to Bouglé, in which he raised a crucial issue: "In Montpellier, are the anti-Semites and the clericals the same, or is the Radical, Radical-Socialist republican party in Montpellier contaminated, as it is in so many other places by anti-Semitism? . . . The Republic is in danger."[61]

His brother Daniel felt "Protestant but remembered his Jewish great-grandfather, who came from Germany."[62] The future author of *La Fin des notables* (1930) was more deeply involved in Dreyfusard activities than was Elie. He contributed to pro-Dreyfus magazines such as *La Conque* and *Le Banquet*. He signed the "Manifesto of Intellectuals" and joined the Ligue des Droits de l'Homme et du Citoyen. He was especially distressed by the wave of anti-Semitism unleashed by the Affair, and by the behavior of Edgar Degas, the painter, a longtime friend of the Halévy family, who suddenly broke off relations in the midst of the crisis. Previously, he wrote, Degas "had always taken great pains not to reveal his anti-Semitic feelings in our presence because of my father's Jewish background." His diary entry for November 18, 1897, states that Dreyfus "has been found guilty of all of Israel's unpunished crimes. . . . The army does not want to exonerate a Jew that it has sentenced." On November 21, he wrote, "The Boulangist movement was the same as the Dreyfus Affair: clericalism and demagoguery. The emotions of the mob dictate the law."[63] He saw Lucien Herr and Xavier Léon regularly. He worked for Dreyfus day in and day out and offered public support to Colonel Picquart. Despite all this, Daniel Halévy's attitude toward Judaism remained complicated. He described Dreyfus's father-in-law, a Monsieur Hadamard, as an "old Jew, broken down, filthy, and disagreeable." When he discussed Judaism with Bernard Lazare, some of his hidden feelings came out: "Oh, how happy I am that I escaped from that hell, that I escaped from Judaism. . . . How tragic your destiny is. You are fulfilling the Biblical prophecy, becoming Christian." Yet, in October 1898, when he ran into a group of nationalists shouting "Death to the Jews" on the avenue de Wagram and saw a priest congratulate one of the demonstrators, he "accosted the man and told him that of all people he, a priest, should not be applauding a fellow who shouts 'Death to the Jews.' The whole group came to his defense. All of a sudden, one young man pointed at me and said, 'Isn't it disgraceful when people shout 'Down with France'? Luckily for me, I spoke sharply to him and the man had no backbone, or I might have taken a beating."[64] To one degree or another, obviously, the Affair affected many intellectuals whose relation to Judaism was distant and little more than symbolic.[65]

In Bordeaux, Durkheim was the target of vehement attacks by both colleagues and the press. He was bitterly disappointed by the academic world's response to the Affair, as he wrote to Marcel Mauss in February 1898: "Let's do what we can and resign ourselves to the rest. I feel like an internal exile. I've almost completely withdrawn from academic life. What I see going on there is just too painful to watch."[66] To Célestin Bouglé he confided that he had

just suffered through the most depressing winter. So many distressing events, and the sense they created of our moral isolation, coupled with the revolting sight of countless acts of cowardice, ultimately sapped my courage or at any rate undermined my resolve. The attitude of people in Bordeaux—and I mean academics—had a big impact. . . . In conditions such as this, you end up withdrawing into yourself and losing faith in action. At bottom I am an optimist, though, and ask for nothing better than to get moving again.

He added that he had organized a section of the Ligue des Droits de l'Homme: "It wasn't easy: the Bordeaux temperament is so indolent." But, under fire from anti-Semites, he found it impossible to do more, and expressed regret at his inability to act as publicly as Bouglé: "I followed your lecture tour and was very happy to see that you did so well. Here we still cannot risk a public lecture."[67] Durkheim in fact became the prime target of the nationalist right.[68] Despite the very tense situation in Bordeaux, where large crowds of anti-Semitic demonstrators converged on the synagogue on more than one occasion, Durkheim was nevertheless an active Dreyfusard who as early as 1896 spoke out in favor of the captain. He helped found the Jeunesse Laïque and, according to a very critical report submitted by the rector of the university, delivered inflammatory speeches at political banquets.[69]

In February 1898, Durkheim joined two colleagues at the University of Bordeaux, O. Hamelin and G. Rodier, to write a letter to the editor of the newspaper *Le Nouvelliste:*

Nobody now denies that there were irregularities in Dreyfus's trial, whatever one may think of the outcome, and it was against these violations of judicial procedure that we felt it was our duty to protest. You criticize us for having done so. This is not an occasion for either anger or surprise. But the phrase "friends of the syndicate" in your brief notice goes too far, because we are totally unaware of the existence of any syndicate, and in any case, when it comes to matters of conscience, we take orders from no one. If, despite these explanations, you wish to continue your polemic . . . We, however, consider the matter closed.

The newspaper's response is worth quoting at length:

So these gentlemen admit that they made a public protest concerning "irregularities" and "violations of judicial procedure" that they claim existed in the Dreyfus trial. Yet they reject the epithet "friends of the syndicate" because they are unaware that any such syndicate exists. These gentlemen know to a scientific certainty what no one has so much as attempted to prove in a court of law and what all our officers and the entire government categorically deny, namely, that irregularities were committed in the trial of Dreyfus. . . . The knowledge these gentlemen possess is as peculiar as their professed ignorance. Their protest against supposed "irregularities" in the Dreyfus trial is a slap at the government, which has stated several times that the case was properly heard, as well as a gesture of support for the cosmopolitans who are using those supposed irregularities as a pretext for waging an abominable campaign against the army. Whether they know it or not, they are therefore indeed "friends of the syndicate" as well as functionaries in rebellion against the government. . . . No one has ever mistaken these gentlemen for socialists or revolutionaries. Hence the secret of their attitude must lie elsewhere. For our part, it is enough to note that they are functionaries who have publicly expressed their sympathy for people who are attacking and insulting the army, people against whom France and its government are forced to defend themselves while foreigners encourage and applaud their actions. If Messieurs Hamelin, Durkheim, and Rodier today find themselves in difficulty, they should complain not to us but to the Dreyfusard papers to which they sent their petition for judicial review of the Dreyfus trial, papers that inscribed their names among the "friends of the syndicate." Have they protested to the editors of those newspapers?[70]

Another scandal, known as the Stapfer Affair, also divided the Bordeaux academic community. In July 1898, Paul Stapfer, dean of the University of Bordeaux's Faculty of Letters, spoke at the funeral of the university's rector, Auguste Couat. Before an audience of prominent local citizens, Stapfer, a liberal Protestant, gave a speech filled with transparent allusions to the Affair that made his support for Captain Dreyfus perfectly clear. He eulogized the late rector in these terms:

> As a man of justice and logic, [Couat] was genuinely horrified by the sectarian violence, confusion, and disarray stirred up by the furious winds of unreason. I must not dwell on this subject, and I will say nothing for fear of saying too much. Since I am not permitted to state outright which side the great soul of this noble "intellectual" was on, let me say simply that the deep wound to his patriotism sapped the wellspring of his existence. Gentlemen, justice is sometimes eclipsed by clouds of passion. If today we no longer know where justice lies, let us always follow in the footsteps of this just man: then we shall be certain of adhering to the truth. That is all I will say.

A scandal erupted. On July 24, 1898, *La Petite Gironde* noted, "A group of professors insisted on shaking General Varaigne's hand and assuring him and the army of their total sympathy." The article continued: "Was this an appropriate occasion to plunge into an affair that has already stirred up too many passions and troubled too many consciences?"[71] Meanwhile, the faculty assembly refused to consider itself bound by Stapfer's declaration, and Léon Bourgeois, the minister of public instruction, suspended the audacious eulogist from his post for six months. On July 26, Durkheim sent a letter to *Le Temps* stating that he shared Dean Stapfer's values. *Le Nouvelliste* published the text of this letter together with a comment of its own: "Monsieur Durkheim evidently wants it to be known that he shares Monsieur Stapfer's opinions on the Dreyfus question. We have no doubt that he is also asking to share the dean's disgrace and that he wrote his letter with that heroic purpose in mind."[72] Seven other professors replied to Durkheim's letter in *Le Temps* and *Le Nouvelliste* and stated their opposition to Stapfer's claims. Durkheim, though he was, as we have seen, isolated and discouraged, showed great courage in this situation. On October 24, 1898, he wrote to his friend and colleague

Camille Jullian, who, much to Durkheim's surprise, had apparently given his support to the seven professors who had criticized Durkheim: "You share none of the values of clericalism, you do not live in a military milieu, and you were quite well informed. You gave me proof of this. . . . Under the circumstances, your attitude seemed inexplicable to me."[73]

Durkheim worked feverishly on his response, which came in the form of a reply to an article by the Catholic writer Ferdinand Brunetière in the March 15, 1898, issue of the *Revue des deux mondes*. Brunetière's piece was a sharp attack on the intellectuals who had mobilized to protest the verdict in the Zola trial.[74] Durkheim's reply obviously meant a lot to a him, and he revised it repeatedly, with advice and encouragement from Bouglé. Despite his "moral exhaustion" and "sense of helplessness," he sent a draft of his reply to the historian Ernest Lavisse, the editor of the *Revue de Paris*, and asked Henri Hubert to urge Lucien Herr to sound out Lavisse about his intentions. Lavisse, who was strangely cautious throughout the Affair, probably declined to publish the article. Ultimately, it appeared in the *Revue bleue*, which counted a number of Dreyfusard intellectuals among its contributors. After lengthy discussions with Salomon Reinach, Durkheim sat down to write: "I see things a little more clearly now. The duplicity is even more horrible than I imagined. The day will come when those who are refusing to join us out of fear of what people may say will blush at the thought of their cowardice, and Lavisse will regret his temporizing and his politics."[75]

"Leaving aside the question of Dreyfus," Durkheim continued, "I want to talk about individualism, which our critics say is dissolving the bonds of society. I want to show that they have been playing with words; that individualism is not selfishness but sympathy and pity [?] between men . . . and, furthermore, that there is no better place for men to come together, that all history, including Christianity, is taking us in this direction."[76]

Clearly, Durkheim intended to base all social solidarity on the individual. Surprisingly, the sociologist who had made his name with the study of collective consciousness, the social causes of suicide (*Le Suicide* was published in 1897), and the primacy of the whole over its parts, who had stressed the distinctive nature of social facts, and who is often portrayed in histories of sociology as taking a "holistic" approach in which society tends to become "reified," was now proposing to treat the individual as the basis of the social bond. In recent years, to be sure, commentators have done much to restore the individual to his rightful place in Durkheim's work from *Le Suicide* to *Les Formes élémentaires de la vie religieuse*.[77] His response to Brunetière, written in the context of the Dreyfus Affair, takes on considerable importance in this light. It can be read as a sociological and philosophical reflection on France by a sociologist who was at once a Dreyfusard, a republican, and an assimilated Jew, a scholar continually vilified by the anti-Semitic press yet determined to answer his attackers without descending to polemic.

He began by asking his readers to "forget the Affair itself." He called instead for a debate about principles: the legitimacy of all authority, including that of the army, rested, he argued, on individual rights. With masterful skill he pointed up the differences between individualism and utilitarianism and argued that the former was perfectly compatible with a cohesive society. The doctrine of individualism, he claimed, could be traced back to Kant and Rousseau and the Declaration of the Rights of Man, and he was merely echoing the "moral catechism" that French schools used as the basis of their civics instruction. Considering "the character of man *in abstracto*," he rejected any selfish "cult of the self"* and instead advocated "averting our eyes from what concerns us personally." All that matters is the individual human being. Hence "no *raison d'état* can excuse an attack on any individual if individual rights take precedence over the state." The "religion of humanity replaces" all other religions and is just as binding on the person: it "rules" each and every one of us. In other words, the sociologist who coined the phrase "collective consciousness" was arguing that, even in highly individualistic modern societies, a normative "constraint" still existed in the form of the "religion of humanity." If this fundamental principle happened

---

*"*Le culte de moi*" was a phrase made famous by the right-wing nationalist writer Maurice Barrès. —TRANS.

to conflict with "the operation of a department of government . . . indispensable to the security of the state," that was unfortunate: it still must not be violated.[78] Now, it so happens that it was during this troubled period in France's history that Durkheim was working out his theory of the state as an "organ of reflection" responsible for "the moral life of the country." As he put it, "The stronger the state, the freer the individual. It is the state that liberates the individual." The state must "bring greater justice to the society that it personifies."[79] But in the Dreyfus Affair, in which the state was a party to the injustice visited upon the individual Dreyfus, Durkheim believed that the actual state, the government of the Third Republic, fell short of this ideal because it failed to act as an instrument of individual liberation.

Durkheim accordingly modified his theory of the state to fit the facts, since the actual state was not, like the ideal state, an organ of clear thinking whose decisions should be binding on everyone: "Every organ of public life, no matter how important, is only an instrument, a means to an end." In other words, in the Dreyfus Affair the state had failed to fulfill its vocation. This debate about the nature of the state was particularly crucial in the development of Durkheim's thinking, since, according to Mauss, his fundamental lectures on this subject, published under the title *Leçons de sociologie: Physique des moeurs et du droit,* apparently received their final revision between November 1898 and June 1900—that is, during the climactic period of the Affair.[80] In these lectures, Durkheim contrasts two types of thinking: one that "remains in the penumbra of the subconscious" and is shaped by various "collective prejudices," and another that emanates from the state, a veritable "organ of reflection" that is alone capable of "preventing unreflective, automatic, blind action." Using a vocabulary that is relatively unusual in his writing, he argues that "the role of the state is not to express or condense the unreflective thought of the crowd but to ponder matters more deeply and add its own thoughts, which will inevitably be different." Is Durkheim thinking here of the passions unleashed by the Affair and of the "crowd," as described by Gustave Le Bon, mobilized in this instance by a specific type of prejudice, anti-Semitism? Did he expect the state to impose rationality on a chaotic situation? If so, he must have been disappointed to discover that the state was slow to act because it tended to follow in the wake of blind prejudice and its ever more vociferous expression. The result, according to Durkheim, was that "nothing is stable."[81]

As Durkheim saw it, the state had temporarily ceased to fulfill its function of ensuring the "moral unity" of the country by giving voice to the "hunger for greater justice" for each and every individual.[82] To his way of thinking, "A cohesive society is possible only if a certain intellectual and moral community exists among its members." Remember that Durkheim, the theorist of the division of labor, had earlier distinguished between community and society: a society exists only where there is extensive and "normal" division of labor. His discussion in this text marks the beginning of a reinterpretation of that earlier theory, a revision that would lead ultimately to his later work on the function of religion. Henceforth, a society must also meet the conditions of a community: the actions of individuals in society have no meaning in the absence of moral unity stemming from acceptance of values promoting respect for individual rights. The "communion of spirits" now pertains to the individual himself, not just rites and prejudices.[83]

What kind of society was Durkheim describing? Was it, implicitly, a society in which a secular civil religion was the sole bond among citizens, a civil religion which, in the public arena, granted respect to all citizens without regard to their class, cultural, or religious background? Along with the founders of the Third Republic and the state Jews of his day, Durkheim fought hard for a secular public-school system capable of shaping the ideals of young French citizens, and his ideas were influential on the teachers responsible for inculcating republican lessons in civics.[84] In 1904, he stated his belief that "the policies adopted over the past few years are preferable to the ones that preceded them, because they have fostered a certain level of ongoing collective action. To be sure, I am far from believing that anticlericalism by itself is enough. Indeed, I am eager for the society to adopt more objective goals. The important thing, however, was not to fall back into the state of moral stagnation in which we had wallowed for so long."[85] Anticlericalism had stirred many people to action. In a time of moral crisis, it had created the level of "intensity" necessary to perpetuate "community" within "society." It was not easy, however, for this specifically French form of what Robert Bellah has called "civil religion" to establish itself.[86]

Although Durkheim intended his reply to Brunetière to remain on the level of pure principle, he nevertheless did not hesitate to venture into the quasi-civil war that raged around the Dreyfus Affair. Abstractions aside, he made it plain, wittingly or unwittingly, that he sided with the republicans who enjoyed the ardent support of Protestants and Jews in their battle with the political forces of Catholicism.[87] Locally as well as nationally, he quickly became the bête noire of the nationalists. Hostile petitions circulated among students in Bordeaux.[88] Leading spokesmen in the nationalist camp attacked his conception of a scientific sociology whose methodology was to be free of any religious notions. Writing in *L'Action française*, Léon Daudet sarcastically attacked Durkheim's *"haute Guldure."** In a similar vein, Pierre Lasserre charged that "Durkheim is controlled, supported, inspired, and guided by the Jewish nationalist community, which lives among us" and is dedicated to "the systematic destruction, elimination, and subjugation of the French people."[89] And Dom Besse, a member of the Action Française, wrote, "Monsieur Durkheim's invasion and conquest of public education has demonstrated the inexhaustible wiliness and bitter tenacity of the Jew bent on acquiring a monopoly. Others of his race have helped and supported him."[90] In 1916, in the middle of World War I, when Durkheim, inspired by his son and several of his students, had joined the war effort by writing patriotic pamphlets attacking Germany and assuming leadership of a committee organized to publish studies and documents related to the war, he was distressed to learn that *La Libre Parole* had attacked him as "a Boche [German] with a fake nose who represents the Kriegsministerium and its swarms of agents throughout France." At a time when Captain Dreyfus, for whom he had given his all, was back in service and participating in General Nivelle's offensive on the Aisne, and when his own son André, in whom he had

* "High culture" with a German accent. —TRANS.

invested all his hopes, was putting his life on the line (he would die in combat), Durkheim once again became the favorite target of the nationalist right, despite the Union Sacrée, which was supposed to have united all the "families of France."

The thoroughly assimilated son of a rabbi, the founder of positivist sociology, an advocate of republican secularism, and a dedicated patriot who defended Dreyfus in the name of the ideals of 1789—Durkheim was all of these things. But he was also the man who, as head of a special commission responsible for looking into the situation of foreign immigrants in the *département* of the Seine, came to the defense of poor Russian Jews living in France. He vigorously denounced hostile measures against these refugees, measures "advocated by a notoriously anti-Semitic party." And he noted how important it was that these Jewish immigrants, who were deeply aware of "everything that Judaism owes to France," were present on French soil. With statistics as impressive in their way as those of *Le Suicide,* he proved how much these refugees had contributed to the war effort and demolished the allegations of the anti-Semites.[91] In March 1916, a senator quoted to his colleagues a newspaper article that claimed that "the membership of the committee includes, along with various functionaries, Jews of foreign descent such as Emile Durkheim, a professor at the Sorbonne." Yet, even as he championed the refugees' cause and sustained the enmity of the anti-Semitic right, he was also voicing sentiments similar to those of many other assimilated Jews, whose support for the immigrants was at best lukewarm. In February 1916, for example, he wrote to Mauss: "Although it is too soon to say if this Russian business will turn out well, I hope it will soon be over. . . . I have never been so 'Jewified' [*enjuivé*]. If this thing continues, I will become exotic Judaism's adviser and tutor. There is of course a great deal of misery there of every kind. Just a moment ago I received a letter from an unfortunate Russian Jew who in all likelihood is being persecuted by the police. They'll sabotage his existence. What misery!"[92]

To be sure, Durkheim did not revert to the Judaism of his forebears. He did nevertheless stand up repeatedly for persecuted Jews in the period between the Dreyfus Affair and World War I. As a universalist sociologist, however, he had mixed feelings about what he was doing and about becoming, as he put it, "Jewified." To his way of thinking, it was the nationalist anti-Semitic movement that had challenged republican principles and thus justified his own commitment to the struggle against injustice. But Durkheim was not blind: "I see poetic justice in the fact that the republican party itself incubated the egg from which nationalism hatched. The idea of revenge and the desire to regain military glory at the expense of an enemy cannot be used to shape a nation's collective consciousness with impunity."[93] Did the fact that republican elites shared in and promoted nationalist sentiment lead to appeasement of the opposition in the Dreyfus Affair? Did this result in the infamous pronouncement that "there is no Dreyfus Affair" when the government sought to end the matter by confirming the captain's sentence? Does it explain why many republican leaders for many years colluded with leading anti-Dreyfusards? It is true that nationalist sentiment in France was on the upswing.[94] As late as 1932, even the celebrated political essayist Albert Thibaudet could speak of "the Talmudic sociology practiced by Durkheim, a rabbi's son," without batting an eye.[95] Was it possible that, in this climate, even those Jews most fully committed to universal, republican values reverted just a bit to their former particularist identity? Can we go so far as to argue that men like Durkheim and Mauss, Lévy-Bruhl and Jules Isaac, "even those most estranged from Judaism, experienced the resurgence of an ancient solidarity in the face of a common ordeal, even if they never specifically acknowledged this in so many words"?[96]

Once again, Durkheim is a case in point. Descended from a long line of rabbis and himself destined for the rabbinate, he did indeed turn his back on Jewish tradition. In the name of the Republic as well as of science and reason, he rejected all preconceived notions. Yet some commentators have seen central values of Judaism reflected in his sociology: the role assigned to justice and charity, for example, or the importance ascribed to teaching and social solidarity or to the sacred, or the ideas of impurity and sacrifice.[97] Such vague parallels and allusions remain unconvincing, however. Other commentators stress the evolution of Durkheim's thinking, which dates from the beginning of the Dreyfus Affair. They cite a letter from Durkheim to one of his critics, S. Deploige, written in 1907: "It was not until 1895 that I had a clear sense of the crucial role that religion plays in social life. For me this came as a revelation. My 1895 lectures marked a watershed in my thinking." That watershed separated the period of *De la division du travail social* from the later period, whose major work was *Les Formes élémentaires de la vie religieuse*, and whose principal thesis was that even in modern societies ritual and the sacred continue to play an important role. From a study of the "social question" Durkheim moved on to a consideration of the moral crisis affecting modern society. This "turning point" actually extended over the half-decade from 1895 to 1900, and it involved "pondering, in a largely implicit way, the Jewish question in the France of his time."[98] Is it too much to suggest that what we see taking shape here—between the lines, as it were—was a theory of the collective consciousness as unified by shared values yet quietly tolerant of beliefs and allegiances that could not be accommodated within the limits of a purely "scientific" and "universalistic" sociology? Did Durkheim move beyond the realm of pure theory to suggest that republican assimilation make room for the recognition of differences? Although it is difficult to prove in any rigorous way that he did, the possibility encourages us to look at the impressive sociological machinery he created in a new light.

Obviously, the period in question coincides with the Dreyfus Affair and the revival of religious passions in a positivist France in the throes of industrialization. Did the climate also influence *Le Suicide*, which Durkheim wrote at the height of the Affair and published in 1897? To what extent is it legitimate to ask

whether *Le Suicide* might not also have been sparked by the dramatic events of the day? Whether it might have been a reflection on the different ethical attitudes required of the military officer and the university professor, a way for Durkheim to convince himself that Dreyfus was not a coward to remain passive in the face of his accusers? And whether it was not also, in a broader sense, a reflection in which Durkheim had quietly been engaged for some time, on the various ways in which Jews were integrated into the France of his time? It might be possible to show that this was one of those times when Jewish culture and tradition once again entered Durkheim's consciousness.[99]

True, Durkheim does comment frequently on why Jews living in tightly integrated communities are relatively immune to suicide. In light of all this, it may indeed be true that Durkheimian sociology was deeply influenced by the Affair. Even more than industrial and commercial crises, antagonism between capital and labor, and the advent of the Machine Age—all sources of passions and ideologies reflecting a pathological division of labor—the Affair symbolized a moral and political breakdown that inhibited the formation of a cohesive society.

Did Durkheim believe that the sharp rise in anti-Semitism was a consequence of what he called *anomie,* a concept that gained central importance in his thinking in 1896?[100] He does not establish any specific link between the two phenomena, although he did hold that anti-Semitism was "the superficial consequence and symptom of a state of social malaise" stemming from "moral distress" and that it therefore expressed a need to strengthen social bonds, if need be by excluding people perceived as "different." In normal circumstances, he argued, such pathological sources of solidarity were unnecessary: holidays and ceremonies alone sufficed to create a "center of warmth providing moral comfort to members of modern societies."[101] Durkheim was a great believer in secular schools, which he hoped would lead to full integration of all citizens in the public arena, but he paid little attention to what happened to religion when it was relegated to the private sphere. Some commentators argue that secularism became the "civil religion" of late-nineteenth-century France, but secularism by itself was not enough to maintain social cohesion, despite the enthusiasm of adherents to the new republican form of civic spirit. Is it possible that anti-Semitism arose as a substitute for the sense of community without which social cohesion is impossible? Would it disappear when *anomie* ceased to exist, when the sacred was reborn and social relations were at last organized in a satisfactory manner, perhaps through some type of corporate body? In any case, according to Durkheim, "The Jews are losing their ethnic characteristics extremely rapidly. Two more generations and it will all be over."[102]

Did the Affair disrupt the expected "normal" evolution toward assimilation based on the wedding of Judaism with the Republic and on the internalization of universalistic norms? In *Les Formes élémentaires de la vie religieuse* (1912), Durkheim would argue for the permanence of the religious as the bedrock upon which the moral unity of society is based. Nowhere in his discussion of modern society, however, did he allude to conflicts between rival faiths or to anti-Semitism, which—as World War I would force even Durkheim to admit—had not disappeared. Did he become, more explicitly than during the Affair, "re-Jewified," as he had wisecracked years earlier while helping Jewish refugees, at a time when some of his remarks came close to Jewish self-hatred (as, for example, when he mentioned the number of "Semites" he had encountered on the square in Le Touquet[103])? Though he fought against anti-Semitism, Durkheim had nevertheless become so estranged from Jewish ritual that, at the height of the Dreyfus Affair, Rosine Mauss commented on it in a letter to her son: "I must confess that I am determined to celebrate Passover as I have always done. The problem is that I would like to invite Emile, but I don't know how to reconcile the requirements of his stomach with the religious requirements of Passover. If he insists on eating bread anywhere but in his room, I don't think I will be able to sit next to him at dinner." Like Mauss, who at around the same time complained of "all the fuss and feasting" that was "absolutely no good" and kept him from his work, Durkheim had abandoned the religious observances of his childhood. Yet he was determined to preserve family harmony and unity, so he went to Epinal for Passover. According to Mauss, he "comes and spends twenty hours on the road and twenty here, twelve of them dressed in evening wear."[104]

He would be buried, however, in the Jewish section of the Montparnasse cemetery, where his tombstone bears an inscription in Hebrew which unfortunately can no longer be made out. Was it true, as an obituary in the *Archives israélites* stated, that, "while no longer a practicing Jew, he remained a Jew at heart"?[105] Or was *L'Univers is-*

raélite correct when it greeted his death with these words: "It pains us to think that this rabbi's son knew nothing of his forefathers' religion, that this sociologist was unable to appreciate the social nature of Judaism, and that this scholar and teacher of Jewish descent no doubt did his share to estrange more than one Jewish intellectual from Judaism"?[106] Some hold to this day that his sociology was responsible for the decline of Jewish learning in France, after all that the previous generation of scholars (such as Salomon Munk, Joseph Derenbourg, and Adolphe Franck) had done to establish Judaic scholarship in the most prestigious institutions of higher learning, including the Collège de France. The secularization of themes once linked to the sacred bears witness, we are told, to the "disappearance of Jewish learning as an intellectual force, yet another victim of the Affair. . . . Durkheimian sociology, drawing together theories developed in the historical branches of knowledge, formulated the new positivist credo."[107] There is no doubt that Durkheim's path diverged totally from that of the scholars who imported "Jewish science" from Germany, where it was flourishing. His republican positivism led him to found a French form of civil religion.

Yet, as we saw earlier, other commentators insist, admittedly without convincing proof, that certain aspects of his sociology actually reflect his earlier religious concerns. He was sometimes described as an "inspired prophet,"[108] a scholar "dressed in black . . . with the air of a mystical rabbi,"[109] a "new Moses for whom the revelations of science take the place of the revelations of religion."[110] But was he still part of the religious order? There is absolutely no basis for such an assertion. Revolted by anti-Semitism, he was not afraid to defend its Jewish victims publicly, sometimes in the name of universal values but sometimes in a more avowedly particularist way. To be sure, he chose to renounce his given name, David, and the transmission of tradition, that cornerstone of Judaism, was of no importance to him. Marie, his daughter, whose first name was hardly Jewish, would raise her sons without religious training of any kind. All three eventually married Catholics, and two converted. His relationship to Judaism was vexed, but no more so than that of Lucien Lévy-Bruhl, who, "though French first and foremost, never ceased to feel Jewish";[111] or

Marcel Mauss, an unreligious man who late in life, shortly after his mother's death, married a Catholic, yet who served several terms as a member of the central committee of the Alliance Israélite Universelle in the period between the two world wars; or Raymond Aron, who felt "less distant from an anti-Semitic Frenchman than from a South Moroccan Jew who speaks no language but Arabic and is barely removed from what looks to me like the Middle Ages or, rather, the impenetrable obscurity of a radically foreign culture" and yet acknowledged being "moved by a sense of continuity and tradition." Aron added, moreover, "If someday I should find myself in the presence of my grandparents or great-grandparents, people who defined themselves as Jews and experienced their Jewishness as a living phenomenon, I would like to be able to look them in the eye without blushing."[112] The tie to Judaism, even when vociferously renounced, had a way of reappearing in a disguised form. This was especially true when anti-Semitism re-emerged in French society, as it did during the Dreyfus Affair, the Occupation, and the Six-Day War in 1967. The sociologists and anthropologists mentioned above maintained a sort of hidden fidelity to their Jewish roots. At times this fidelity found public expression and on occasion resulted in surprising commitments.

PART TWO

THE SCOPE
OF THE
OPPOSITION

5

The Drumont Paradigm

Bitterly disappointed by the failure of the nationalist movement and reduced at the end of his life to a state of utter hopelessness, Edouard Drumont contemplated "the end of France" as he sat down to write his own obituary: "Why is France decadent? Because, after fourteen centuries of effort to establish and shape a nation, she destroyed herself virtually overnight and plainly took pleasure in the process. . . . The elimination of every last vestige of the Christian, conservative, traditional, 'old France' side of France is clearly an event of some magnitude. The patient campaign that led up to this is perhaps the best proof of the political skill of the Jews, at least when it comes to conquest and destruction."[1] He was further disgruntled about the banning of an anti-Semitic play entitled *Decadence*, an action that he took to be irrefutable proof that the Jews had "finally seized control of the Republic."[2] In fact, Drumont had long been insisting that France had begun a fatal downward spiral: "France is compounding her decadence with a vain ostentation, an insane quackery and impudence" typical of the Jew.[3] In article after article he issued the same somber judgment, couched in the rhetoric of death: words such as "deliquescence," "degeneration," "dissolution," "putrefaction," "decomposition," "corruption," "liquidation," "disintegration," "degradation," "destruction," "demolition," "demoralization," "perversion," "annihilation," "enfeebling," "softening," "weakening," and "debasement" recur constantly, as do allusions to the Jews' alleged "undermining," "sapping," and "underhanded destruction" of that once vital "organism," French society. "One has only to touch France's coffin," he wrote,

> to release a stream of rotten flesh, pus, and foul gases, and crawling everywhere are worms named Dreyfus and Reinach grown fat on the flesh of the once-hallowed beauty. . . . Poor France! She is so tired, so exhausted from the endless struggles, from the vast quantities of blood spilled. . . . It almost seems as if she has closed her eyes and has but one thought left in her head, which is to lie down in her grave. And the Jew greets her agony with a jackal's laugh. He himself is joyless, a sort of zombie who lurks among the cadavers because he is in love with Death and hungry for Nothingness, the one thing in which he believes.[4]

For Drumont, all of this was an unshakable certainty, to which he returned again and again toward the end of his life. In April 1914, he summed up his life's work with the statement that *La Libre Parole* "will remain as witness to the Jewish conquest: it has demonstrated the Jew's corrosive effect on all our institutions, the satanic effort that denatured the mentality of the French people and destroyed everything that was disinterested and generous, everything that a nation needs if it is not to end up asphyxiated in the mud."[5]

In the final years of the nineteenth century, many in France shared Drumont's view that the country was embarked on a dizzying downward spiral.[6] The word "decadence" was frequently used by populists, who drew on ideologies of both political extremes, the right as well as the left. At the height of the Dreyfus Affair, for instance, *Le Parti ouvrier* lashed out at the "terrifying decadence" of France and denounced the spreading "gangrene" and consequent "degeneracy of the proletariat." *Le Petit Journal* attacked Colonel Picquart, the very image of the "decadent officer," and described the Dreyfusard camp as crawling with "disgusting vermin." And even Emile Zola assailed France's "national decrepitude and disintegration" in a pamphlet entitled *Lettre à la jeunesse* published in December 1897. Paul Bourget saw the age as one dominated by the "cultivated but tired races." Indeed, it has been argued that in this period "the idea of decadence fascinated not only lesser-known writers but also men such as Taine, Bourget, Baudelaire, Flaubert, and Huysmans," as well as Barrès and Lemaître.[7] For many people, France's decadence implied a transition from the Catholic France of old to "Jewish France," which had allegedly seized power with the triumph of the Opportunists and the consolidation of the Third Republic. So incomprehensible was this dramatic turn of events that many people felt it could only have been achieved by black magic: the Jews, having enlisted Satan in their evil enterprise, had moved one step closer to their ultimate goal of destroying a once-powerful Christian society. Drumont employed his considerable powers of imagination to describe the process that would thus inexorably lead to France's demise. The only other country to have suffered a similarly cruel fate was Poland, a deeply Catholic nation toppled from the heights of glory and reduced to insignificance.

In *La France juive*, Drumont described what had happened to Poland in order to prepare his readers for what lay in store for France. He stressed "the antisocial role of Polish Jews and their contribution to that unfortunate country's destruction."[8] To make the parallel more believable, Drumont later published another book, entitled *Les Juifs contre la France: Une Nouvelle Pologne (The Jews Against France: A New Poland)*. To his way of thinking, the Dreyfus Affair would inevitably deliver France into the hands of Germany, just as Poland had ceased to exist after the Jews sold it out to Russia. For the Jews, "the moment has come to eliminate France, just as they eliminated Poland. . . . It is because French society is in a state of dissolution that the Jews have been able to achieve their abominable goals over the past two years. If France does not wake up soon, the Jews will turn it into another Poland and hand it over to a foreign power."

What is more, the Jews were abetted by schoolteachers under "orders alien to the spirit of the nation" issued by such prominent Protestant educators as Ferdinand Buisson and F. Pecaut, men who according to Drumont were only too happy to strike a fatal blow at Catholic France. As a result, the Jews were within striking distance of their ultimate goal, which was to reduce France to a state of decadence so abject that she would cease to exist as an independent nation.[9]

Drumont repeatedly evoked the example of Catholic Poland to warn his compatriots that they must urgently summon up, from "the instincts of nationality and race, the energy needed to save this country, which once was great, from the fate of unfortunate Poland, which died at the hands of foreigners as we shall die at the hands of foreigners and Jews."[10] His fear was that France would be dominated by a foreign power. The French were "good people," but because they were "becoming ever more dependent on the state," their fiber was being sapped by an unrelenting "parasite," the "Jewish Republic," whose devious purpose was to cut the French people off from their "Gallic soil" and impose an artificial order alien to true French values. This idea of the "Jewish Republic"[11] (which, incidentally, enjoyed an astonishing rebirth in Poland under communist rule, as Polish nationalists sought to throw off the "Jewish Bolsheviks" whose values were alien to the eternal values of Catholic Poland[12]) is an important key to Drumont's thinking. He told a colorful tale to explain how Catholic France was destroyed by the Revolution and delivered into the hands of an alien government run by Jews, thus plunging it into decadence. The Polish nationalists of the communist era became his unwitting disciples. For both Drumont and the Poles, the enemy was the universalistic tradition inaugurated by the French Revolution and carried on, often with tragic consequences, by Bolsheviks who wrapped themselves in the mantle of Enlightenment rationalism. The goal in each case, be it Poland or France, was to save a nation whose true glory lay in Catholicism from lapsing irretrievably into decadence. By getting rid of its last Jews, nationalists argued, Poland would also rid itself of a parasitic state and once again become "entirely Catholic," thereby regaining its lost "energy."[13] The nationalists had learned Drumont's lesson well. The hidden link between the two became clear when Cardinal Glemp, the Polish primate, accepted an invitation from French extreme-rightist Philippe de Villiers to visit him in Puy-du-Fou in February 1990: this gesture linked the struggle of Polish Catholics to that of French "Vendéens"—that is, opponents of the (allegedly) Enlightenment-inspired Reign of Terror. It became even more explicit when Cardinal Glemp resorted to unusually hostile language to attack Jews supposedly out to deprive Poland of its identity by monopolizing the memory of Auschwitz.[14]

Drumont's goal remained constant: to continue the work of revolutionary historian Hippolyte Taine by showing that the Jacobin conquest of power really masked a Jewish conquest whose ultimate purpose was "to destroy everything that constituted old France, all the types impressed upon memory by the genius of Balzac that since his time have slowly vanished from the face of the earth."[15] Drumont was an autodidact whose ambition to become a scholar was thwarted by his father's premature death. Nevertheless, emulating the great historian, he donned a scholar's gown and put in countless hours at the Bibliothèque Nationale amassing what he took to be irrefutable proof of a Jewish plot to destroy France. At a time when the social sciences were flourishing in the work of men as different as Emile Durkheim, Gustave Le Bon, and Gabriel Tarde, and when sociologists and psychologists were pondering the sources of what Durkheim called *anomie* in the hope of gaining a better understanding of mass society (that is, a society of increasingly atomized individuals without shared values), Drumont brought his own unique brand of expertise to bear on the same basic question of social cohesion.

If he repeatedly described his work as an offshoot of Taine's, he also invoked another, equally conservative authority, Frédéric Le Play, whose work Drumont believed lent empirical support to his claims about the destructive effects of the Jews. As early as *La France juive*, Drumont described his work as an "application of the method of Monsieur Le Play,"[16] and much later, deploring yet again the fact that "Paris is no longer Paris but has become cosmopolitan" because "no one can feel at home among all these Jews, wops, and foreigners," he immediately invoked the work of Le Play as confirmation.[17] Drumont's ambition to emulate the rigor of the sociologist is

perhaps nowhere more apparent than in his study of a city in decline.
He treats Fourmies, a small industrial city, as a symbol of Catholic
France: its inhabitants, workers and employers alike, are "good
people" who to their misfortune find themselves subjected to the un-
scrupulous domination of a "Jewish Republic." The local representa-
tive of that Republic is the subprefect, a Jew by the name of Isaac,
who does not hesitate to spill French blood. In fact, Drumont went to
Fourmies accompanied by a disciple of Le Play to lend an air of
scholarly objectivity to his investigation (and apparently he was successful, because to this day some sociologists continue to treat his research as a valid report of conditions in the city). There he witnessed
a bloody clash between police and local demonstrators that "afforded
the doctor an opportunity to listen to his patient's heartbeat."[18] He
studied the city's social structure in detail and examined its people's
customs and values. As Drumont saw it, the good Catholics of Fourmies had fallen under the thumb of Jewish "sorcerers and magnetiz-
ers [hypnotists]," whom he compares to "snakes that exert a kind of
fascination on their prey." These men were out to "debase the healthy
elements in our France."[19] Drumont prided himself on his scientific
objectivity: "Without rancor or hatred, in the spirit of sociology and
psychology, I seek to examine the debased condition into which
France has fallen. . . . My mission as a sociologist is to show people
as they are."[20] Indeed, "what is interesting to the sociologist is to see
how the Jewish crisis repeats itself."[21]

In fact, sociology was not the only instrument that Drumont was
keen to use to explore France's decline. At a turning point in the history of both psychology and psychoanalysis, he also took inspiration
from the work of the celebrated Dr. Charcot, whom he cites as often
as he does Le Play. This was especially true after Charcot delivered a
lecture at the Salpêtrière Hospital on November 15, 1887, a lecture
to which Drumont explicitly refers. In it, the famed physician apparently argued that study of the Jews was indispensable if one hoped to
grasp that "neurosis is the malady of a primitive Semitic race." Not
surprisingly, Drumont remarked, "Charcot is right, and such a study
would be of considerable interest. . . . The scientist's observations are
in agreement with the findings of the sociologist."[22] Charcot repeat-

edly invoked the legend of the wandering Jew to explain certain mental pathologies. During a clinical session at the Salpêtrière in February 1889, Charcot introduced a young Hungarian-born Jew by the name of Klein as a true descendant of the wandering Jew: his Jewish origins, Charcot claimed, predisposed him to episodes of somnambulism and serious nervous pathology.[23] Photographs of "wandering neuropathic" Jews were frequently displayed at the hospital. For Charcot and his collaborators, hysteria was also symptomatic of maladies afflicting "Oriental" women, both Jew and Arab.[24] Thus, even though Charcot was on the most cordial of terms with republican authorities, who appointed him to his prestigious chair and whose hostility to Catholicism he shared, he nevertheless exhibited a kind of medical anti-Semitism that was quickly exploited by the Republic's detractors.

In his pamphlets, Drumont repeatedly referred to the works of Charcot. In *La Dernière Bataille*, for example, he used Charcot's findings about "afflicted families" to describe the Jewish neurosis. To Drumont, Charcot's eerie experiments with hypnosis seemed to provide an explanation of how the Jews had managed to seize power in France while sapping the country's energy: "Psychologists," he wrote, should note that "Dr. Charcot has magnetized, or induced a state of magnetic sleep, in thousands of subjects, and he has asked for and received the approval of the Académie des Sciences."[25] With this august institution vouching for his results, it was clear that Charcot had explained how the Jews were able to reduce "worthy" French Catholics to "impotence" by preying on their "credulousness" and enchanting them with black magic. These occult mysteries proved too much for men of "true heart," who found themselves "stunned" into "submission": "Nowadays the witches' sabbath is held not out on the barren moors but in the corridors of power." And Drumont continued: " 'Where am I?' asks the Christian. 'I'm surrounded by magicians and sorcerers. The things I see going on around me are like the possessions and enchantments described by medieval writers.' . . . The Christian has only to look out the window to see the river of filth flowing past." Hypnosis was thus a crucial element in the nation's "decadence."[26] Drumont was an enthusiastic follower of Charcot's experiments. Suddenly, everything became clear. Jewish domination, otherwise inexplicable, stemmed from a kind of mental illness: "What is most striking to me is the irresistible fascination that those who will perish by the hand of the Jew feel for him. Obviously some sort of hypnosis is involved, some form of enchantment or sorcery."[27]

Drumont even mimicked Charcot's vocabulary: as he saw it, the "Jewish epilepsy"[28] was spreading like wildfire. "The Jews carry everyone along in their anxious movement. . . . The strength of the Jew is to feel his way forward unconsciously, like certain neurotics." In short, "these people's brains are not really like ours."[29] Being "subject to every type of neurosis, always agitated, feverish, and disturbed,"[30] the Jewish brain was different from the Aryan, Catholic brain. Drumont, who was well versed in contemporary scholarship, read many studies of brain size. In the work of men like Taine, Le Bon, and Lombroso, as well as in Dr. Bénédict-Augustin Morel's studies of degeneracy,[31] he found arguments to support his "medical" opinions. To be sure, "one cannot reproach the Jews for not having brains like ours. The brains of Negroes aren't like those of Japanese. The brains of Japanese aren't like those of Slavs. What is certain is that the brains of Jews are not made the same way as our brains."[32] In fact, "leprosy has affected the [Jewish] brain."[33] Drumont was convinced of this: "Neurosis is the implacable malady of the Jews." Like any good scientist, moreover, he went out of his way to provide his readers with comparative statistics concerning the percentage of mentally ill Jews, Protestants, and Catholics. But the strange thing about the Jewish neurosis was that "in the end the Jews have transmitted it to an entire generation." As a result, the French race had been "deceived, perverted, and dazed." Jews had easily managed to "scramble childrens' brains"[34] by inducing schoolteachers to "twist young minds."[35] These teachers, swayed by the dominant Jewish sociology, were, according to Drumont, "the principal artisans of this demoralizing and stupefying propaganda."[36] Like Maurice Barrès, Drumont pointed an accusatory finger at those whose "insane ideas" were being taught to France's children: the culprits were the members of the Ligue de l'Enseignement, who had poisoned the minds of the nation's educators.[37]

In a symbolic way, the madness of a revolutionary like Marat was for Drumont the perfect embodiment of a Jewish neurosis, an epitome of the "heresy of 1789."[38] Over the ensuing century, that heresy had reduced France to a state of decadence. As the Jewish Republic steadily expanded its power, "the mental deterioration and cerebral atrophy" of the French proceeded inexorably: "Today, many Frenchmen unfortunately fit the medical description of the degenerate," Drumont contended. It was easy to link the word *dégénéré* (degenerate) to Maurice Barrès's *déraciné* (uprooted). Jews were driving France toward "a state of absolute indifference, a sort of ataraxia, a general impassiveness, a sickly inertia, a state of prostration that nothing can alter. Death gains a foothold by dulling the senses and inducing a state of asthenia. The social asthenia known as ataraxia penetrates the masses, resulting in degeneration of the race and paralysis of the will."[39] This nightmarish vision of the end of France, couched in pseudo-scientific medical jargon, attests to the profound influence of Charcot's work on Drumont's world-view. The Jews, Drumont insisted, had done all they could to "anesthetize and deaden France, to diminish her in her own eyes in order to ease the task of surrendering her to a foreign power."[40]

In order to justify the myth of "Jewish France" and accredit the notion of an omnipotent "Jewish Republic," Drumont resorted to the language of magic and medicine. He believed that the Jews had come to France from the Orient in order to hypnotize the country and sap its energy: "They might not even have enough strength to hold a tool or lie down in one of our posh Champs-Elysées hotels."[41] And that was not all: "Our beloved, wonderful Paris . . . is tired," he lamented, for it had lost its "energy" and, unlike Algiers, had demonstrated its inability "to fight off Jewish domination."[42] The Jews had even communicated their innumerable diseases to the French: "Hundreds of thousands of Christian bodies are going to rot," he assured his readers.[43] In his characteristic pseudo-scientific manner, Drumont gave a long list of such maladies, with plague at the very top: "The Jew carries the plague but does not succumb to it."[44] French decadence was a direct result of these Jewish diseases: "Gangrene is invading the entire French organism. The country is falling apart, rotting."[45] Indeed, since "France is a female nation, she is accessible and penetrable."[46] Exotic Jewish diseases, mental as well as physical, were spreading like wildfire, causing "mortal lesions"[47] and "rotting [the various strata of society] to the core."[48] After "taking the pulse" of ailing France, Drumont voiced his fear that it might already be too late, because these alleged Jewish diseases had by now done irremediable damage. For Drumont, French Catholics, "contaminated and gangrenous," were in an almost hopeless predicament.[49]

On the subject of Jewish diseases, Drumont was inexhaustible. The result was

disintegration of a sort that has occurred in every country in which the Jews have seized control of the government and the economy. Poland suffered the same fate before disappearing from the roster of nations. Scientists are familiar with a class of parasitic worms that live in different host animals at various stages in their life cycle. Implanted in the most richly nourished parts of the host's body, wherever the river of red blood passes, along with the slower stream of yellow fats and the rich flow of highly digested juices . . . bristling with hooks and terrifying to behold, these creatures eat their fill and for a while become drowsy and numb. But after a brief interlude they begin again, as tenacious as ever. . . . In society, the Jewish nation is a faithful replica of the animal world, of which it is one of the higher orders. Wily, devious, frenetic, and bold, the Jews are quick to sink in their hooks and aesthetically odious, just like the vagabond vampires that prey upon more robust forms of life. . . . [They are] swarming barbarians, microbes, sources of putrefaction which invade decomposing societies. They come to the West from the East, helping one another find their way. Infinitesimally small, infinitely numerous, and infinitely rapid, they multiply at the rate of two hundred generations per day.[50]

The result of this brutal invasion of Aryan and Catholic France by countless disease-bearing animals was social degeneracy. Like other contemporary authors, Drumont used a whole litany of animal metaphors to describe the bestial invasion that was causing France to regress toward animality. Jews put him in mind of various animals from the East—now the orangutan, now the camel, now again the pig, rat, or microbe, that vector of terrifying epidemics that threatened to sap France's "vitality" for good. The "Jewish vermin" spread its "poison" everywhere.[51]

Given this diagnosis, one might be tempted to imagine that Drumont, faced with a country in an advanced and apparently irremediable state of decay, would have succumbed to fatalistic despair. Despite his gloom, however, he still wanted to believe that the French organism, goaded into action by his scathing diatribes, could muster up some of its old energy to fight the Jews and their allies. There was still time for Catholic and Aryan France to awaken from its slumbers and resist the process of decay. "Jews, Jews, Jews!" Drumont warned. "If France still possesses an ounce of virility, we will win."[52] He hoped against hope for the arrival of a "dictator, a strong, patriotic leader who will put an end to Jewish supremacy and cleanse our Augean stables of vice and corruption."[53] France must "cauterize the wound or risk seeing the gangrene spread throughout the entire organism and the country fall apart and rot."[54] What form this indispensable reaction might take was of no great concern to him. Despite his inveterate hostility to the Revolution, he nevertheless saw certain advantages in following its lead: "Anti-Semites will know how to do what is necessary. They will emulate the Jacobins if they have to. . . . They will unflinchingly confiscate property once again. . . . France for Frenchmen!"[55] Tirelessly repeated in the provinces as well as in Paris, this slogan of the nationalist right became the rallying cry for the many "leagues" that formed to combat "Jew decadence."[56] Spurred by leaders such as Charles Maurras and Georges Sorel, men also "haunted by the erosion of energy [and] the perception of decadence at work" in France, a nationalist revival was already under way.[57] The leagues' moment had come.

The Dreyfus Affair is evidence of this: Drumont urged the new mass-based organizations to take the offensive while attempting to orchestrate their protests behind the scenes. Writing in *La Libre Parole*, he was the first to denounce Captain Dreyfus publicly as a symbol of the decadence of France, a country that did not hesitate to entrust a position of such responsibility to a Jew. To anti-Dreyfusards throughout France he issued repeated, vehement calls to action, never failing to mention that in his long career as a professional anti-Semite he had met many other Dreyfuses. It was in *Le Testament d'un antisémite* (1891) that Drumont first used the phrase "Dreyfus Affair," but in connection with another Dreyfus—a businessman involved in trade with South America, and a Catholic to boot. But this fact was of little moment to Drumont, for whom true conversion was impossible for anyone of the Jewish race. Drumont was obsessed with the name Dreyfus.[58] It appears several times in *La France juive* (1886), in which Drumont lashed out at a number of men named Dreyfus, including Ferdinand Dreyfus, a Jewish deputy who later became a friend and colleague of Raymond Poincaré: according to Drumont, this Dreyfus was "a member of the tribe that is infesting France. . . . Why should Dreyfus care about the molestation of a few Christians?"[59] The preparation of this screed consumed ten years of Drumont's life, ten years during which he worked diligently as a clerk at the Hôtel de Ville while doing meticulous research, some of it at the Bibliothèque Nationale, on his breviary of hatred, which became one of the best-selling works of its day. The Austrian anti-Semitic leader Karl Lüger took his inspiration from it, and through Lüger it may have influenced Hitler himself. There was something ominous about Drumont's messianic anti-Semitism. He was an amateur sociologist who knew how to manipulate the facts to paint the portrait he wished to paint. A self-taught historian, he had a way of giving his fantasies about the Jews a specious basis in fact. He even dabbled in the occult, on which he drew in inventing "Dreyfus." He conjured up certain essential features of the "Dreyfus Affair" out of his own imagination, long before anyone had ever heard of Captain Dreyfus.

Indeed, one of his favorite targets was Camille Dreyfus, a nationalist deputy, whose estrangement from Judaism was a source of frequently expressed regret for the *Archives israélites*. Many years before the eruption of the Dreyfus Affair, Drumont attacked Camille Dreyfus in various books as well as in the pages of *La Libre Parole*. The same deputy was also one of the prime targets of *La France juive*. For Drumont, this "poisonous flower of the ghetto" was a prime example of "Jewish constitutional loutishness." Twenty years before the Affair, he complained of the way in which "this Dreyfus settles into his chair in court" and "the Court of Appeals deliberates and changes the law that displeases him."[60] With astonishing prescience, he conjured up the future drama out of his own feverish imagination. Note, moreover, that Camille Dreyfus was the architect of one of the first bills to propose the separation of church and state. To Drumont this was unacceptable. Not only was he a Catholic who had returned to the fold and attended mass regularly, but his book *La France juive* had been warmly received by provincial priests as well as by Catholic newspapers ranging from *La Croix* at the national level to various local weeklies.[61] In fact, Drumont saw himself as carrying on the work of the redoubtable—indeed, almost fanatical—Catholic pamphleteer Louis Veuillot, whom he had known personally.

Camille Dreyfus's proposal to separate church and state thus afforded Drumont a golden opportunity to attack the Third Republic for its supposed willingness to implement a "Jewish plan" to "de-Christianize" France. While the nationalist politician Paul Déroulède railed against the proposed "Judaization" of France in the Chamber of Deputies, Drumont concentrated his fire on Camille Dreyfus, even though the bill also enjoyed the support of numerous other republican deputies.[62] In 1893, he fought a duel with Dreyfus, who also faced the journalist Henri Rochefort. *La Libre Parole*, which frequently lambasted the deputy's "vileness," remarked on "the Jew's abjection" in a front-page article on August 31. The next day's headline announced that the "Drumont-Dreyfus Duel" had taken place, and the accompanying article told in detail how Drumont had severely wounded his opponent.

Thus the name Dreyfus was one with which Drumont was familiar long before the Affair. In May 1892, he published a series of articles in *La Libre Parole* criticizing the army for allowing Jewish officers in its ranks. The names Cahen, Lévy, and Dreyfus were mentioned. Drumont criticized the close relationship that had developed between Théodore Reinach and his fellow Jews in the Twelfth and Thirteenth Artillery Regiments, officers with names such as Lévy and Dreyfus.

In a strange way, this article anticipated the relationship that would later develop between Captain Alfred Dreyfus of the Fourteenth Artillery and Joseph Reinach, Théodore's celebrated brother and the future historian of the Dreyfus Affair as well as a trusted associate of Gambetta, whom he served as chief of staff. The latter Reinach was thus at the center of the Gambettist circle that Drumont detested— detested so much, in fact, that at one point he simply assumed that Gambetta himself must be a Jew. "Many Jews," he wrote, "have followed the lead of the Reinach brothers and had themselves assigned to the general staff, which allows them to slip in among the generals."[63]

To Drumont's mind, this "Jewish France" could only be the result of treason. He came to that conclusion after France's defeat in the Franco-Prussian War, twenty-four years before Dreyfus was convicted. In an article written in August 1870, he pointed to the arrest of German spies in Paris by the people, not by the police. In March 1871, he reiterated his charge that the "soldiers of treason" were Freemasons and Jews. In 1880, along with Henri Rochefort and others, he charged that Colonel Jung, an officer with a German name assigned to the general staff, was a traitor as well as a friend of Gambetta, the inventor of the "Jew Republic."[64] In 1886, he alleged that the Commune had been betrayed by a German-born Jewish officer, Simon Mayer. Thus, well before the Affair, Drumont was convinced that France was being betrayed by German Jews who had infiltrated the general staff of the French army. Patiently he constructed the plot of a drama intended to persuade French Catholics that the country was being sold out by a Republic that had been in the hands of the Jews ever since the Revolution.[65] The various strands of the plot began to run together: on May 23, 1892, Drumont wrote, "On the day [that Jewish officers] take command of the army, France's mobilization plans will be passed to Rothschild, for reasons that must be obvious."

Wherever he looked, Drumont saw France being betrayed by Jews working on Germany's behalf. Take, for example, the shooting of demonstrators that took place at Fourmies, shortly before the Affair began. For Drumont, it was the Jewish subprefect, Isaac, who was responsible for this incident, which was "merely his way of celebrating the emancipation of the Jews in 1791." In his bizarre account of the event, Drumont drew a stark contrast between Father Margerin and Isaac—that is, between Catholic France, symbolized by a priest, and republican France, which in Drumont's view was run by Jews who had infiltrated the bureaucracy. According to Drumont, Isaac had ordered the troops to open fire in order to evaluate the effectiveness of the new Lebel rifle so that he could then pass his observations on to his Prussian friends, who would thus enjoy an advantage in any new confrontation with the French army.[66] Drumont believed that Jewish military officers and civil servants formed a state within the state and that they were bent on promoting German interests in order to prevent France from recapturing the lost provinces of Alsace and Lorraine.

Drumont was fiercely hostile to all Dreyfuses, be they businessmen or state Jews. In April 1894, a few months before the beginning of the Affair, *La Libre Parole* published full details of the "Dreyfus trial," a case involving the international grain dealer Louis Dreyfus. Nothing could dissuade Drumont from his long-held conviction: it was as if the man who combined Catholic anti-Semitism with populist anti-Semitism *needed* the Dreyfus Affair to prove that he was correct, that there really was a conspiracy of Jews who had seized control of the republican government in order to promote the interests of their true fatherland, Germany. By October 29, 1894, the stage was set for *La Libre Parole* to raise the issue that would touch off the powder keg. The paper soon became one of the most widely read in France. On November 8, Drumont congratulated himself on his "prophetic" earlier attacks on Dreyfus and all the other state Jews whose constant goal, according to him, had been to destroy France.

6

THE ERA OF LEAGUES

The early years of the twentieth century resembled not so much the confrontational 1930s as the 1980s and 1990s, a period of deep concern in France about national identity. Although social issues were as contentious then as they are now, leading to some surprising alliances between right- and left-wing populists and to unexpected affinities between rival ideologies, the central issue of the day was who should enjoy the full benefits of citizenship. In a society whose roots lay in Catholicism, was there room for a public space, a distinct political arena to which everyone, regardless of religious creed, could have access? In 1892, following the failure of the Boulangist movement, certain Catholic leaders cautiously and after much deliberation decided to make their peace with the Republic, thus paving the way for a period of stability under the government of Jules Méline (1896–98). Political strategies had changed, and once again anything seemed possible.

In the first few weeks of 1898, however, deep disagreement emerged on a number of fundamental issues. Let us pause a moment to recall some key details of the Dreyfus Affair. In December 1894,

Captain Dreyfus was convicted of spying for Germany by a court-martial that relied on forged documents. He was sentenced to a term of imprisonment on Devil's Island. Subsequently, Colonel Georges Picquart, the newly appointed head of military intelligence, discovered that Dreyfus's handwriting was similar to that of a Major Esterhazy, who had written a note to the German Embassy which French intelligence had intercepted. Picquart informed his superiors of his belief that Dreyfus had been wrongly convicted, but his warnings were dismissed. In November 1897, Mathieu Dreyfus, the captain's brother, also became aware of Esterhazy's guilt. But Esterhazy was tried by a military court and found innocent on January 10, 1898. On January 13 came the thunderclap of Zola's "J'accuse," an article attacking the Esterhazy verdict which appeared in the newspaper *L'Aurore*. Demonstrations erupted throughout France. Eventually, Zola himself was put on trial and convicted. In August 1898, it was discovered that another document had been forged in the case against Dreyfus by Colonel Henry: this became known as the "Henry forgery." On August 31, its author committed suicide. Drumont, the anti-Semitic journalist, launched a fund-raising drive to support Henry's widow. Many contributors sent money along with virulent anti-Semitic remarks, which were collected in a document known as the "Henry Monument." After numerous generals resigned, the Dreyfus case was finally reopened. Despite all the evidence of his innocence, Dreyfus was again found guilty at Rennes on September 9, 1899. He resigned himself to requesting a pardon, which was granted, but it was not until 1906 that his innocence was acknowledged and he was readmitted to the ranks of the army.

Now let us return to the first few months of 1898. On January 14, the day after the publication of "J'accuse," Anatole France and many leading academics published the first "Manifesto of Intellectuals," which insisted on respect for truth, justice, and universal human rights. The pace of events accelerated: in February, nearly two hundred deputies insisted that the government put an end to what they claimed was Jewish domination of a number of government departments. Also in February, Jules Guérin, the head of the Ligue Antisémitique Française, called upon French peasants to follow the lead of their brothers in Galicia, where Jews were being burned alive. In January and February, anti-Semitic riots broke out in both metropolitan France and Algeria, riots of a violence rarely before seen, as local leagues and newspapers fanned the flames. Soon after, Guérin began publishing a new newspaper, *L'Anti-Juif*. In the May legislative elections, the radical right scored a major victory, winning enough seats to constitute an official anti-Semitic caucus in parliament for the first time. This event marked a sort of consecration of the extreme right. In August, Colonel Henry committed suicide; in October, the process leading to revision of the verdict in the Dreyfus trial got under way. To close out this crucial year, a reorganization of the Ligue des Patriotes* was announced on December 29, and on December 31, in response to the "Manifesto of Intellectuals," an anti-Dreyfus petition aimed at perpetuating "the traditions of the French fatherland" was launched and, with it, the Ligue de la Patrie Française. Also in December, *La Libre Parole* organized a fund drive in memory of Colonel Henry, and for the first time Pierre Pujo called for an *action française*, using a phrase that in June 1899 would be adopted as the name of a new political organization. Tragedy seemed to be repeating itself as farce: the abortive coup d'état of February 1889 was followed by yet another attempt to overthrow the government in August 1899, which ended equally ingloriously when the army refused to side with demonstrators at the funeral of Félix Faure. Thanks to the firmness of Waldeck-Rousseau's government and the prefect Lépine, the Republic did not forfeit its authority: many leaders of the leagues were imprisoned, the colorful but ineffective resistance movement was easily subdued, and for a while the success of the leagues was held in check. The protest seemed to have run out of steam.

Appearances were deceiving, however. Even as the leagues passed

---

*The Ligue des Patriotes was founded in 1882 by the republican journalist Paul Déroulède and other former followers of Jules Gambetta. It grew into a huge political organization, which, during the Dreyfus Affair, evolved into a nationalist pressure group. It continued to enjoy the support of prominent members of the Académie Française and the Institut de France. For a time, it enjoyed close ties with anti-Semitic groups and toyed with a putschist strategy. Eventually, however, it was supplanted by an even more extremist nationalist group, the Action Française.

into history, their members continued to participate in a variety of protest movements. Before long, the Action Française, despite its still relatively small membership, began to supplant the leagues at the head of the antirepublican movement. New issues arose, yet it was clear that the fundamental issue of French identity remained unresolved. Among these new issues, the most contentious on the local as well as the national level was the separation of church and state. I will have more to say about this later; it was important because it prolonged the conflict initiated by the Dreyfus Affair, as people on both sides of the issue mobilized to define French identity by specifying who had access to the public sphere. In this respect, the "nationalist revival"[1] was not limited to the parties that now came to the fore in the political scene and ultimately embraced the leagues' main issues. Indeed, the leagues' spirit still hovered in the air as former extremists joined the Action Française without renouncing any of their old ideals, especially anti-Semitism. Symbolizing the change, Paul Déroulède, who had led many a protest between 1888 and 1890 and again in 1898 and 1899, died on January 30, 1914. Thus an agitated period in French history came to a close, and before long the necessities of war would impose a *union sacrée* on Frenchmen of every political stripe. After the war, however, new movements would emerge to carry on the leagues' struggle against republican universalism.

What, then, can we say about these leagues, which for a time spearheaded French political protest? What features of their organization allowed them to become such an effective political force in such a short period of time? Beyond their obvious ideological affinities, how were they related to one another? Most, unlike the Ligue de la Patrie Française, came into being before 1898, in the period between the end of the Boulangist movement, the waning of the Ligue des Patriotes, and the beginning of the Dreyfus Affair. When trouble erupted, they were ready for action. When it came time to prepare for the legislative election campaign, the Union Nationale, led by Abbé Garnier[2] and backed by the Vatican and many bishops, adopted a strategy that emphasized its close working relationship with Jules Guérin's Ligue Antisémitique Française. In fact, the Roanne section of the Ligue Antisémitique was founded by members of the Union

Nationale. In Grenoble, the two groups merged. And everywhere they acted in concert. Similarly, Edouard Dubuc, the head of the Jeunesse Antisémite, belonged to the Union Nationale and made no secret of his links to the Ligue Antisémitique Française. These groups and their many direct affiliates did not hesitate to work hand in hand with other groups viewed as more moderate or as associated with other political camps. In October 1898, for example, Paul Déroulède* presided over a Union Nationale banquet to which members of the Ligue des Patriotes were invited. In the same year, close contacts were established with royalist and Bonapartist groups as well. For a time, the innumerable groups that constituted the radical right seemed headed toward forming a vociferous nationalist "union" whose common denominator was anti-Semitism. Catholicism was the rallying point at the center of this unnatural holy alliance among groups of diverse ideological stripe, an alliance that was formally blessed by such important figures as Maurice Barrès, Jules Lemaître, and, before long, Charles Maurras. It also received enthusiastic daily support from such organs of the press as *La Libre Parole* and *La Croix* and their numerous local counterparts, including newsletters published by a veritable army of committed militants who for the first time were supported by a solid grass-roots organization.

The Union Nationale played a crucial role in unifying this organization. Officially founded in 1893, this Catholic nationalist organization with its ultraconservative social views embraced the new right-wing strategy of dropping opposition to the republican government but without giving up its virulent anti-Semitism.[3] Its general charter of 1897 established a central committee, located in Paris, along with regional, departmental, and local committees. This flexible organizational structure encouraged independent action by local groups, many of which met weekly. Only Catholics could become members. Substantial local committees were soon operating in Lyons,

*Déroulède was the leading spokesman of French nationalists and author of the *Chants du Soldat*. As head of the Ligue des Patriotes, he was an antiparliamentarist, yet he was elected deputy from Charente. On February 23, 1899, during the funeral of President Félix Faure, he attempted to launch a coup d'état, which he hoped the army would support. It failed, and Déroulède was arrested, tried, and convicted.

Rennes, Aix, and Marseilles. By 1898, there were committees in thirty-five *départements* as well as in every Paris *arrondissement* except for the sixth and the sixteenth. By the late 1890s, police estimates of the number of active members ranged as high as 12,500. Although nominally republican, the Union set itself the goals of defending "Catholic citizens" and "re-Christianizing" France. In 1898, only four of twenty-three regional committee chairmen were not clergymen. Various other groups were affiliated with the parent organization: these included the Jeunesse de l'Union Nationale, the Union Nationale Ouvrière, the Ligue de l'Evangile, and the Cercle d'Apologétique Sociale. In 1910, the Cercle's newspaper, *Le Peuple français*, founded in 1893 with backing from *La Croix*, would merge with Drumont's *Libre Parole*, which was widely read by provincial Catholics. As mentioned above, the Union Nationale acted in concert with various anti-Semitic groups and placed its highly effective organization at their disposal. During the 1898 and 1902 legislative elections and the 1900 municipal elections, its local and regional committees played a decisive role. In 1893, Abbé Garnier publicly announced that he was in total agreement with Drumont, and from the first the Union Nationale was consistently anti-Semitic, denouncing the Jewish race on biological grounds and taking the position that the public sphere should be a purely Christian arena from which Jews ought to be banned. In 1896, Abbé Garnier declared that his organization was "an anti-Jewish league." In 1899, the Union circulated a petition attacking Freemasons and gathered seventy thousand signatures. "France for the French! Death to the Jews!" was the group's slogan at meetings held in Paris in April 1900, where participants applauded Jules Guérin, the leader of the Ligue Antisémitique Française. The Union's brand of Catholic populism thus played a role in the broad protest movement that grew out of the Dreyfus Affair. The group relied on all the weapons of mass protest, including demonstrations led by Catholic women under the auspices of the Union Nationaliste des Femmes Françaises, the Cercle Catholique des Dames, and the Ligue Patriotique des Françaises, all of which made no bones about their anti-Semitic sentiment.[4]

Linked to the Union Nationale, Jules Guérin's Ligue Antisémitique

Française was founded in February 1897. It carried on the work of the Ligue Antisémitique de France, founded in 1889 by Edouard Drumont himself, who maintained close ties to Abbé Garnier. In April 1899, the Ligue Antisémitique Française changed its name and became the Grand Occident de France. Jules Guérin had been the friend and lieutenant of the Marquis de Morès, who was famous for leading violent demonstrations of butchers from the La Villette section of Paris. Morès described himself as "Catholic first and foremost," and his seven-pound bronze-headed cane, which he used to good effect in various demonstrations between 1890 and 1897, "was as revered in sacristies as Durandal."* Catholics saw him as "a latter-day Bayard, a second Joan of Arc." He died in 1896, and on June 6, 1897, a huge crowd gathered at the Eglise de la Madeleine for a memorial mass in his honor.[5] In May 1898, around the time he founded his own anti-Semitic newspaper, *L'Anti-Juif*, Guérin managed a campaign in Algiers to elect Drumont, who hoped to become the first anti-Semitic deputy. (Guérin and Drumont would later split, however, owing to personal strains stemming from their rivalry for leadership of the anti-Semitic movement.) According to the prefect Lépine, Guérin's group was the best organized of the leagues and the most difficult for the police to deal with. Its membership included socialists and Blanquists with Boulangist leanings, and some of its slogans alluded to socialism and social struggles while denouncing Jewish monopolies and speculators. Many members were anticlericals, moreover, who rejected the support of the Catholic camp for fear of alienating working-class voters. Yet, despite all this, the League worked hand in glove with the Union Nationale, and many of its leaders were Catholic militants. In July 1898, the police estimated its membership at eleven thousand. There were sections in nearly every *arrondissement* of Paris, including the eleventh, where the Jewish population was substantial. Members of the League included shopkeepers, businessmen, and professionals. There were also many clergymen. Among the leaders were many upper-class Catholics. The League also had sections in fifty-two *départements*. Some of these

---

*The sword that Roland uses at Roncevaux in the *Chanson de Roland*. —TRANS.

were quite large. The Nancy section, for example, had twenty-eight hundred members. A number of provincial leaders were active Catholics (in Poitiers, Toulouse, and Nevers, for example). The organization was still fairly loose, however. Since there was no executive committee, everything depended on the will of the leader. Local sections had little autonomy, and meetings were irregular. The headquarters on the rue Chabrol was well financed, with support from the royalist movement from August 1898 on. There was an in-house telephone system, a rarity at the time, as well as an ultramodern printing operation. Leaders frequently traveled to the provinces by train or automobile. League members, disciplined in almost military fashion and sworn to secrecy, were often violent people spoiling for a fight. They provoked trouble wherever they could and pushed other demonstrators into violent confrontations with police. And they went after Jews wherever and whenever they could.

A closely related organization, the Jeunesse Antisémite et Nationaliste, was created under the double patronage of Drumont and Morès. In the fall of 1896, Edouard Dubuc became its leader. In conjunction with Guérin's followers, he began organizing the first anti-Dreyfusard meetings. The group initially called itself the Jeunesse Antisémitique, but in late 1897 it became the Jeunesse Antisémitique de France, and then, in the summer of 1899 the Jeunesse Antisémite et Nationaliste. In May 1901, it changed its name to the Parti National Antijuif.[6] Like the other leagues, this one was loosely organized and highly decentralized. It had only one plank in its platform: all-out war against the Jews. Its marching song could not have been simpler: "*Chassons les youpins / A grands coups de gourdin*" ("Let's drive out the Yids by clubbing them on the head"). Once again, connections to the Catholic Church should not be overlooked. For instance, the founder of the Caen section was Abbé Masselin, the managing editor of *La Croix du Calvados*. In Lille and Valenciennes, the Chevaliers de la Croix formed the most combative segment of the Jeunesse Antisémitique, and students of the Catholic university in Lille also participated in the movement. In Le Havre, one of the group's most notorious leaders, Flavien Brenier, was a Catholic militant who was secretary of both the Jeunesse Royaliste and the local

Jeunesse Antisémitique. Although founded mostly by Catholic students, the league attracted many office and shop workers. It controlled a number of satellite organizations, such as the Cercle Antisémitique d'Etudes Sociales, the Fédération Antisémitique des Lycées (founded in July 1900), and the Jeunesse Républicaine Nationaliste (founded in 1901). Although relations with Guérin's Ligue Antisémitique were difficult because of competition between the two groups, their goals were identical, and they often shared the same allies, in particular the Ligue des Patriotes. Together these groups participated in violent anti-Dreyfusard demonstrations and spread anti-Semitism in France and Algeria. After Dubuc was elected to the municipal council of Paris in May 1900, the Jeunesse Antisémite et Nationaliste transformed itself into the Parti National Antijuif for the 1902 elections, following which it faded from view. Nevertheless, the organization of the party, with Drumont, Henri Rochefort, and Firmin Faure as honorary chairmen, is interesting because it represented an attempt to create a broad anti-Semitic alliance: over fifty-three groups were represented at the party's first convention. There were a number of violent clashes with members of Drumont's Comité National Antijuif. Dubuc's organization ceased to exist in 1904, and at that time many of its members joined the Ligue des Patriotes. After Déroulèdés return in 1905, Dubuc managed his campaign for election in Charente. Later, he joined the Action Française. His group, a precursor of the Camelots du Roi, claimed to be republican and at times invoked socialism, but its real *raison d'être* was anti-Semitism.

As noted earlier, Drumont indirectly orchestrated the activities of all of these leagues. In 1901, he personally established the Comité National Antijuif, which, after failing to gain a victory in the 1902 elections, was transformed into the Fédération Nationale Antijuive (1903); this sought in vain to become an umbrella organization for all the anti-Semitic groups in France. Its charter is worth examining in detail. For the purpose of establishing "a broad French organization of mutual assistance," it reads, "a league of non-Jewish Frenchmen has been established under the name Fédération Nationale Antijuive." Its goals would be to "combat the pernicious influence of the Judeo-financial oligarchy and its secret conspiracy."

France teemed with rival anti-Semitic groups that had the capacity to mobilize militants; though their numbers were ultimately small, they were nevertheless violent and determined. In Poitou, for example, there was a Ligue Antisémitique du Commerce (1896); in Rennes, a Groupe Antisémitique Nationaliste (1899); in Nantes, a Ligue Patriotique Antisémite; and in Algiers, a Ligue Antijuive (1892). In Paris, the Ligue Radicale Antisémitique (1892) sought to bring Drumont's followers together with ex-Boulangists, and there was also a Groupe des Etudiants Antisémites (1896); its goal was "to get rid of the Jew, whose role in the social body is the same as that of the tapeworm in the human body." There were also weird paramilitary groups such as the Alliance Antijuive, which admitted anyone as a member except "Jews, Jewish renegades, obvious Jew-lovers, and Freemasons." Divided into groups, sections, and "legions," this shadowy organization assigned itself the mission of destroying "the Judeo-Masonic Republic." In order to enable members to recognize one another, it gave out gold-plated medals featuring, on the front, an image of "Edouard Drumont treating the Jew as he deserves" together with the symbol of *La Libre Parole* and, on the back, the symbol of the Alliance Antijuive.[7] The same period saw the formation of a number of Catholic, anti-Masonic leagues, which sometimes joined in anti-Semitic actions. Among the groups organized between 1897 and 1913 were the Comité Antimaçonnique de Paris, the Ligue Française Antimaçonnique, the Conseil Antimaçonnique de France, the Ligue le Franc Catholique, and the Ligue de Défense Nationale Contre la Franc-Maçonnerie, all of which were part of the nationalist movement and overlapped in membership with various anti-Semitic groups. Most of these leagues posed as defenders of France's Catholic identity, and the founders included members of various religious orders.[8]

Together, these rival yet symbiotically related leagues defined the true color of this troubled period in French history. Through demonstrations and publications, they spread anti-Semitic sentiment throughout the country in the hope of solidifying a new imaginary community. They were joined by Bonapartist groups, moreover, whose activities in 1898 and 1899 were similar to those of the leagues. A genuine alliance was forged: Bonapartists sat alongside members of the Jeunesse Antisémite et Nationaliste and the Ligue Antisémitique Française at the convention marking the rebirth of the Ligue des Patriotes. Anti-Semitism proved to be a rallying point. The Jeunesses Plébiscitaires Bonapartistes, another group with some of the characteristics of the leagues, also joined in the national mobilization. Although Prince Victor, the designated successor to Napoleon III, worried about achieving national unity and soon rejected the anti-Semitic excesses of the period and the common nationalist strategy, some Bonapartist groups continued to demonstrate alongside nationalist groups. For example, the Etudiants Plébiscitaires joined forces with the Fédération des Jeunesses Républicaines Patriotes as well as with the Action Française on a number of occasions.[9] The royalists also joined the anti-Semitic movement: after considerable hesitation, the Duc d'Orléans himself raised the Jewish question in terms similar to Drumont and Barrès. The royalist camp then attempted to narrow its differences with the republican Déroulède and, later, Jules Guérin, the head of the Ligue Antisémitique. Royalists hoped to use the mobilization of nationalists to restore the monarchy, and this drove them into the anti-Dreyfusard camp, where they occasionally joined the leagues in violent protest. The Jeunesse Royaliste naturally participated. And the Church as well as the king embraced this tactical alliance with the nationalist and other leagues, especially the new Ligue des Patriotes and the Ligue de la Patrie Française. Once again, the move toward anti-Semitism came primarily in the period following the collapse of the Boulangist movement. In January 1890, for example, the Boulangist Francis Laur waged a particularly violent and radically anti-Semitic campaign that drew praise not only from Drumont but also from the royalist-cum-populist Marquis de Morès and various close friends of the Duc d'Orléans.[10] During the 1902 elections in Meurthe-et-Moselle, the monarchists weighed in on the conservative side in a common struggle against the left. They were joined by the Ligue de la Patrie Française, the Ligue Antisémite, and the Union Catholique.[11] This local example is significant, because it shows that the various leagues shared a common strategy, so that, despite differences of opinion and rivalries, they were led to undertake joint actions.

It has frequently been noted that militants from tl
Semitic leagues often joined royalist groups at some
lives. Once the Action Française was established, it m
the place of the fragmented, unstable leagues, and re
royalists increasingly came together around anti-Semitism as the
defining characteristic of a new French Catholic community, which
would otherwise have been deeply divided. The organization known
as Action Française also emerged out of the Dreyfus era: the movement was launched by an article that Maurras published in *La
Gazette de France* on September 6, 1898. Entitled "The First Blood in
the Dreyfus Affair," it was an apologia for Henry's suicide. As a
spokesman for the Jeunesses Royalistes noted in the same publication some three months later, France was now divided in two: "On
one side, the true France and the army; on the other, the Republic
and the Jews." On December 19, Pierre Pujo called for an *"action
française."* The first Action Française committee was formed in April
1899, at which time Maurice Barrès joined the movement. The real
inception of the new league came at a public rally held on June 20,
1899, and the *Revue d'Action Française* was founded in July. The
Ligue d'Action Française was formally organized at the beginning of
1905. The Institut d'Action Française, a truly innovative development in nationalist politics, was inaugurated in February 1906.
There, future royalist militants studied the theory of nationalism and
regionalism as well as various strands of Catholic thought. Among the
teachers was Dom Besse, who vehemently attacked Jews, Masons,
and Protestants. In December 1911, before an audience of two thousand delegates to the fourth Action Française convention, he lashed
out at Jews and hailed the clergy and the Church. The daily newspaper *Action Française* was founded in 1908, which also saw the debut
of a group that would be much talked about in the 1930s, the
Camelots du Roi, many of whose members were recruited among the
student body of the Catholic university of Paris.[12] Between 1899 and
1906, the Action Française rapidly established itself as the most dynamic organization in a nationalist camp decimated by the elections
of 1902 and 1906. The group accordingly dismissed any thought of
submitting itself to the judgment of the polls.

For Charles Maurras, the theorist of "integral nationalism," the only hope of a nationalist victory after 1899 lay in a movement whose goal was to restore France's Catholic identity. Already there was talk of ridding the nation of Protestants, Jews, and Masons. A battle was soon launched against the "four confederated states" on behalf of the Catholic faith as well as the king. Maurras saw Catholicism as France's "national religion." In August 1900, Henri Vaugeois, the founder of Action Française, who loudly proclaimed his adherence to the Catholic faith, announced that he experienced "an almost physical revulsion at the sight of a Jew." This visceral anti-Semitism became one of the defining characteristics of the new nationalist movement. As Maurras would put it in an article published in *Action Française* on January 4, 1911, "Someday, the time will come to show how much the whole nationalist, monarchist program depends on the anti-Semitic program if it is to move from conception to execution." Take, for example, the rally staged by the Action Française on December 17, 1899. The participation of Edouard Drumont as chairman, assisted by Henri Vaugeois, shows how Drumont's group, which more or less controlled the anti-Semitic leagues, was deeply involved in the nascent royalist movement from the beginning. The audience included many members of the Ligue Antisémitique and the Jeunesse Antisémite. Drumont's arrival was greeted by an ovation and shouts of "Death to the Jews!" Henri Vaugeois hailed Drumont as a "tireless fighter who has raised a cry of alarm against the Jewish peril and the threat it poses to the country. . . . French nationalist sentiment has been revived, and a vast French nationalist movement has been set in motion." Drumont, for his part, emphasized how "the Dreyfus Affair has shown us the Jew in all his horror." This was met with shouts of "*Vive Drumont! Vive Déroulède! Vive Guérin!* Death to the Jews!"

A symbiosis of a sort developed everywhere between the first Action Française groups and the anti-Semitic leagues. In Caen, for example, an Action Française group formed within the Jeunesse Antisémite at the behest of a number of abbés. Abbé Garnier and a number of priests took part in another Action Française rally at which Léon Daudet called upon his audience to defend the Catholic faith and make war on the Jews; the crowd responded with shouts of *"Vive le roi! Vive l'empereur!* Death to the Jews!" Police reports regularly noted the presence of priests at these rallies, which often drew thousands of people. At a rally organized by the student section of the Action Française on January 22, 1908, the main speaker painted an ecstatic portrait of Drumont: "He has unmasked the Jewish enemy. Drumont is a solid fellow. He's not a wishy-washy Catholic but a Catholic through and through. His nationalism was tempered in the flames of his love for his defiled Church." At the end of these public rallies, the crowd often sang the theme song of the Camelots du Roi, "La France bouge" ("France Is On the Move"):

> *Le Juif ayant tout pris,*
> *Tout raflé dans Paris*
>   *Dit à la France:*
> *Tu n'appartiens qu'à nous.*
>   *Obéissance! Tout le monde à genoux!*
> *Non, non, la France bouge. Elle voit rouge.*
>   *Non, non! Assez de trahison . . .*
>   *Juif insolent, tais-toi,*
>   *Voici venir le roi,*
>   *Et notre race*
> *Court au devant de lui:*
>   *Juif, à ta place!*
>   *Notre roi nous conduit!*
>   *Oui, la France aux Français . . .*
>   *Un, deux, la France bouge.*
>   *Elle voit rouge,*
>   *Un, deux,*
> *Les Français sont chez eux!*[13]

("Now that the Jew has taken everything, has picked Paris clean, he says to France, 'You're ours now.' Obey! On your knees! No, no, France is on the move. She sees red. No, no, enough of treason . . . Shut up, insolent Jew! Here comes the king, and ahead of him marches our entire race. Jew, in your place! Our king is leading us! Yes, France for the French . . . One, two, France is on the move. She sees red. One, two. The French have come home!")

True to its principles, the Action Française would soon pour all of its forces into a violent war on Jews, attacking many without letup, sponsoring boycotts of Jewish businesses, and, like countless other anti-Semitic groups, continually issuing lists of Jews to be eliminated from public life. As Eugen Weber has noted, "If the areas of Action Française recruitment were socially heterogeneous, they were almost uniformly Catholic." The movement enjoyed the support of some bishops, "assumptionists," and ultraorthodox clergy. The Catholic military organization Notre Dame des Armées reportedly also acted in its favor. Out of the public eye, however, growing numbers of theologians made no secret of their opposition, which ultimately led to an ambiguous condemnation of the organization by Pope Pius X.[14] The Action Française would forever bear the stamp of the Dreyfus Affair from which it originated, and this explains why Maurras, when found guilty of wartime collaboration by a Lyons court in 1945, exclaimed: "It is Dreyfus's revenge." From a meager beginning, the movement grew quickly, its ranks swelled by former members of other leagues who were drawn to its hierarchical structure and systematic nationalist ideology. Once the group shed its early populist inclinations, its *nationalisme intégral* became profoundly counterrevolutionary.

The Camelots du Roi symbolized this. Many of these young royalists, who were mainly students, had belonged to a group from the seventeenth *arrondissement* that had been formed to sell newspapers at church doors. They were joined by militants of more modest social background, and on November 16, 1908, mounted a highly disciplined operation to sell the *L'Action française*. They subsequently took part in any number of violent clashes with police—for instance, during the so-called Thalamas Affair, named for a Sorbonne professor who attempted to lecture on Joan of Arc in a manner deemed blasphemous by the protesters. They also harassed Jewish professors and attacked republican students. In 1909, it was estimated that there were some sixty-five Camelot groups throughout France. In Paris, some six hundred of them could be mobilized on short notice. In 1910, an elite commando was formed within the group: members were called *commissaires* and carried lead-weighted canes and black-jacks. With military discipline they kept order at demonstrations and served as bodyguards. A similar quasi-military organization existed within the reorganized Ligue des Patriotes, which since the turn of the century had had a *corps de commissaires* of 150 to 500 militants ready and willing to fight. And the one to two thousand members of the Jeunesse Républicaine Plébiscitaire protected and marshaled nationalist demonstrators.[15] The use of force thus became the rule rather than the exception for the Action Française and its allies, who attacked Jews and republicans suspected of collaborating with Jewish interests. Intelligence was provided by Marius Plateau, one of the most active leaders of the Camelots du Roi, and his minions, and links were forged with armed groups in the provinces, in the Jura and Roussillon regions as well as the cites of Nancy, Montpellier, Rouen, Nantes, and Roubaix. In 1911, some 182 groups and sections were scattered throughout France; by 1912, the number had risen to more than 200 and by 1914 to more than 300. In March 1914, 10,000 roy-alists attended the convention of the Paris-area federation of the Ac-tion Française; in May, more than 30,000 people took part in the annual Joan of Arc Day parade that was an Action Française tradi-tion.

In 1898, plans were made for a broad-based league to counter the newly formed Ligue Française pour la Défense des Droits de l'Homme et du Citoyen, which was organized in June of that year and attracted many intellectuals. Three young professors set out to prove that there were just as many intellectuals in the nationalist, anti-Dreyfusard camp. Signatures were gathered. Barrès proposed estab-lishing a new league and even suggested a name. On December 31, an initial list of signatures was published, as an answer to Zola's "J'accuse," which appeared in early January of the same year. The petition was signed by twenty-two members of the Académie Française and leading artists and writers such as Degas, Renoir, Frédéric Mistral, Pierre Louÿs, and Jules Verne. The Ligue de la Pa-trie Française, which grew out of this effort, played an important role in the *fin-de-siècle* nationalist movement.[16] Its organizers deliberately situated it within the republican camp, and they were more concerned with respectability than were the organizers of the anti-Semitic leagues. As moderates, they hoped to attract as broad a membership as possible in order to enhance the League's political effectiveness. Still, on January 3, 1899, Ferdinand Brunetière, a republican who had embraced Catholicism, went so far as to write, "The anti-Semites and followers of Monsieur Déroulède will be welcome among us." Dreyfusards ridiculed the new group as the "Ligue du sabre et du goupillon" (that is, of the army and the Church), but it quickly grew to dominate the nationalist camp while maintaining ties to other leagues more prone to violence. Within a few days of the petition's publication, new members were signing up at the rate of two thousand per day. Many high-school and college students swelled its ranks, as did members of patriotic leagues and veterans of the Franco-Prussian War, along with businessmen, workers, and journalists. Lawyers, artists, writers, and doctors also joined.

By February 1900, the League was firmly established in some thirty *départements*, primarily in the Paris region, along France's eastern border, and in the south. These were for the most part areas either where a Catholic right had survived but had not joined the royalist camp, or had shifted politically from left to right. The League's influence was strongest in the Paris region. In most of the city's *arrondissements*, except the nineteenth and twentieth, it was an active force. In February 1900, the membership stood at almost half a million, an impressive figure given that the very militant Ligue des Patriotes had been able to boast of only fifty to a hundred thousand even in its heyday in the late 1890s and by 1899 had declined to forty-five to sixty thousand. Backed by newspapers that were read by as many as two million people daily, the Ligue de la Patrie Française succeeded in capturing a number of precincts in the municipal elections of 1900. It won these victories at the expense of candidates of the right, whether royalists, Bonapartists, or conservatives. In this respect its political appeal differed from that of Boulangism, which drew votes from the extreme left as well as the right.[17] The working class rejected it. In 1901, membership fell to under two hundred thousand, mostly in the Paris region. The decline proved to be impossible to stop: in 1902, despite a very aggressive campaign, the results of legislative elections were disappointing, although candidates from the League were elected in the first, second, and fifth *arrondissements* of Paris.

In October, Zola was buried. The night before, some thirty deputies and municipal-council members tried to organize a nationalist counterdemonstration led by Barrès, Rochefort, poet François Coppée, and a few others. But there was too little time to get people mobilized, and Barrès would describe the event as "nationalism's funeral." When he himself stood for election in a Paris district a short while later, he was beaten by the candidate of the left-wing coalition: "I was there for the baptism of nationalism, and I am here for its burial."[18] Internal dissension became increasingly apparent. The League was unable to choose between contradictory strategies that appealed to different groups of potential supporters, and eventually this indecisiveness led to its decline. Between 1905 and 1910, the organization abandoned its various activities one after another. Unlike the Ligue des Patriotes, which had become increasingly radicalized in the period leading up to its dissolution in March 1899, the Ligue de la Patrie Française was largely swallowed up by the moderate nationalist right, whose goal was to protect the army and maintain law and order but which had no populist support. Meanwhile, the anti-Semitic leagues, whose membership was declining, stuck with their radically subversive perspective, as did the Action Française. This radicalism was what really distinguished the true *ligueurs* of the period from everyone else.

This difference is particularly clear in the position that the Ligue de la Patrie Française took on the key issue of anti-Semitism. The group's leaders were initially quite cautious: their relations with Jules Guérin's Ligue Antisémitique were anything but cordial. The League's conservatism at first set it apart from Drumont's populist anti-Semitism, as well as from traditional Catholic anti-Semitism. Because the goal of the organization's leaders was to attract as broad a coalition as possible while remaining within a republican framework, they avoided subversive street demonstrations and appeared to eschew the anti-Semitic movement. But their strategy was caught in a web of contradictions. The refusal to engage in illegal acts made it impossible to build a true nationalist party, and little by little the League was forced to confine its efforts to the electoral arena, which transformed it, in Barrès's words, into a "banal antiministerial party." Yet, even as it rejected the strategies of the other leagues and plunged into a variety of political campaigns, the Ligue de la Patrie Française adopted the virulent anti-Semitic language of the extreme right, as though it hoped that it might cover its move into the electoral arena by using the radical rhetoric of the time as a sort of camouflage. It was Jules Lemaître who launched the anti-Masonic campaign in 1899. A short time later, Copin-Albancelli's Ligue Antimaçonnique evolved into the Union Nationale Antimaçonnique, with the *Annales de la patrie française* as its official organ. Also at Lemaître's behest, a central committee was formed in 1900 to manage upcoming election campaigns. Represented on this committee were the Ligue de la Patrie Française and the Ligue des Patriotes, but also Drumont's anti-Semites and Rochefort's "French socialists." To be sure, internal dissension was so strong that the central-committee project eventually collapsed. Still, traces remained at the ideological level. The Ligue de la Patrie Française emulated its ephemeral allies by denouncing the power of Jews and its destructive effects on the national community.

In January and February 1898, anti-Semitic violence erupted in fifty-five cities throughout metropolitan France. These disturbances, which varied in intensity, came in three distinct waves: the first occurred in the third week of January and affected twenty-three cities; the second broke out the following week in nineteen cities; and the third came in the last week of February. During these two months alone, there were sixty-nine riots in all, sometimes several breaking out simultaneously in different places. Other anti-Semitic demonstrations followed later in the year. On October 25, 1898, for example, a large crowd gathered on the Place de la Concorde. The most serious disturbances came in the first wave: in Paris, Marseilles, Nantes, Rouen, Lyons, and Nancy there were riots in the week of January 14–20. On January 23, there were riots in thirteen cities. In the following week, most of the trouble was in eastern France: in Dijon, Saint-Dié, Epinal, and Lunéville, among other places. The third and final wave really affected only two cities, Bar-le-Duc and Dieppe. Thus the anti-Semitic mobilization began in the country's largest cities and spread to the smaller ones. Many of the riots took place in cities with substantial Jewish populations, in eastern France, Paris, and Marseilles. There were also extremely violent incidents in Algeria,[19] whose Jews had been made French citizens by the Crémieux Decree. By May 1897 there were already full-blown riots directed against Jews, involving organizations of anti-Semitic workers joined by socialist militants and local followers of Drumont. The Ligue Radicale Socialiste Antijuive, founded in 1892, became the Ligue Antijuive d'Alger in 1897. Its president, Max Régis, became mayor of Algiers in November 1898. Other anti-Jewish leagues could be found in Constantine, Sétif, and Mostaganem. A network of affiliated organizations aided in mobilizing demonstrations, as did the incendiary local press. In October 1897, 2,000 people demonstrated in Algiers. In the *département* of Algiers alone there were 158 attacks on Jewish property in the month of January 1898, and 17 attacks on individual Jews, one of whom died. In subsequent violence, others would die. Disturbances also erupted in Oran, Constantine, Blida, Sétif, and Mostaganem. The movement was so powerful that, in the May 1898 legislative elections, four anti-Semitic leaders were elected deputies, including Drumont.[20]

Everywhere, the Jewish population was gripped with fear, which seared itself into memory. Although what happened in France cannot be compared to the pogroms that occurred at about the same time in the Russian Empire, physical violence resulting in bodily harm did take place in more than thirty cities in France, as well as in Algeria. Many shops, homes, and synagogues were destroyed. Substantial numbers of people participated in these disturbances: four thousand in Angers and Marseilles, three thousand in Nantes, two thousand in Rouen, a thousand to fifteen hundred each in Saint-Dié, Bar-le-Duc, and Saint-Malo. In seventeen cities, rioting continued for three or more days running. Often the army was involved: in some places soldiers took part in the violence, at times egged on by their superiors, whereas in others the trouble began in the barracks or in a military club or in an eastern border town where numerous troops were stationed. The nationalist implications of the rioting were thus plain to see. Numerous arrests were made, and in some places it took both the police and the army to restore order.

/Although these violent anti-Semitic demonstrations were triggered by the publication of Zola's "J'accuse," they were hardly spontaneous. Usually they followed the distribution of propaganda leaflets, often by Catholic groups. Police reports stress the deep involvement of Catholic school pupils and club members in mobilizing demonstrators. According to the police, moreover, clerical leadership was essential. In Normandy, lists of Jews living in certain cities were distributed at church doors after services. In Nantes, the Catholic bookstore displayed a wide range of anti-Jewish propaganda, and Catholics made up the bulk of the mob of three thousand who screamed "Down with the Jews" on August 28, 1898. The demonstration was instigated by Jules Guérin himself, together with militants of the Ligue Antisémitique. In Saint-Brieuc on August 10, young members of the Cercle Saint-Pierre and students at the Ecole Saint-Charles organized an anti-Jewish demonstration.[21] Although the anti-Semitic leagues were not directly responsible for the riots except in a few cases (including Paris, Marseilles, and Poitiers), they had been active for some time in nearly all the cities involved, handing out leaflets, staging rallies, and so on. Leaders such as Abbé Guérin often delivered inflammatory speeches. For instance, following anti-Semitic protests in Nancy in January 1898, Guérin and other leaders came to the city and held public meetings./A local section of the Ligue Antisémitique was organized, and before long it had signed up twenty-eight hundred members (including five hundred from Lunéville) who would play an important role in subsequent anti-Semitic agitation in the last two months of 1898. In March of that year, the Union Catholique staged a number of rallies at which Jews were harshly attacked./The movement was so powerful that in the May elections Maurice Barrès was defeated by an even more radical candidate backed by the Ligue Antisémitique. That group also staged frequent anti-Semitic banquets (there was one in Nancy in 1900, for example). Members of religious organizations often took part in these events.[22]

A number of historians have called attention to this Catholic involvement in the anti-Semitic protest movement. One also sees signs of it in the drive to collect money to help the widow of Colonel Henry after his suicide and to pay for her lawsuit against Joseph Reinach, a drive launched on December 14, 1898, by *La Libre Parole*. Four hundred clergymen and two hundred self-described Catholics donated funds, in each case citing their loyalty to Catholic France, whose soul was presumably incompatible with a Jewish presence. One heard frequent calls for a new Saint Bartholomew's Day, harking back to the religious violence of the past (against Protestants) and provoking violent attacks on Jews. Many contributors to the fund were militant Catholics or people who made no secret that religion was their motive for contributing: seven hundred nobles fall into this category, along with a number of military men and some two hundred politicians known for their Catholic commitment. This group included François Coppée, Albert de Mun, and Maurice Barrès. Many professors and students at Catholic universities also figured on the lists of contributors, as did pupils at a variety of religious schools. Contributions even came from groups: "thirty Catholics of the fourteenth *arrondissement*," for instance, or "twenty-eight members of a Paris Catholic workers' circle." The Henry fund thus represents "a moment in French Catholic consciousness or of the French Catholic subconscious," one that was highly susceptible to the type of movement promoted by the leagues.[23]

Anti-Semitism penetrated the depths of the countryside and should not be seen as a purely urban phenomenon. Only five of the twenty-two members of the anti-Semitic caucus that was formed in the Chamber of Deputies following the May 1898 elections came from urban precincts. Rural France was thus at the heart of the anti-Semitic nationalist movement that carried the radical right to triumph. Even where nationalist and conservative candidates were defeated, as in Allier, the anti-Semitic movement was a powerful voice that reached even the tiniest villages, such as Ronnet, where an "anti-Semitic festival" lasted several days. Rural anti-Semitism was strongly inflected by local concerns and naturally reflected the distinctive values and interests of the community. The anti-Semitic press also penetrated remote areas, particularly after it began using the language of caricature. *Le Petit Journal*, which filled entire issues with histories of "Jewish France," had a daily circulation of eight hundred thousand, 80 percent of which was outside Paris. The same was true of *La Croix* and its countless local versions, as well as *La Libre Parole*, which sold more than two hundred thousand copies daily. There were anti-Semitic papers everywhere, and the new technology of color printing was used to good effect in satirical cartoons. The local press thus did more to popularize anti-Semitic ideology than the broadsides of the leading anti-Semitic writers, who were mostly Parisians. And the press was abetted in this task by propaganda devices of the most extraordinary variety imaginable: even chocolates became a weapon in the anti-Semitic campaign, and children played at hanging Dreyfus puppets; men smoked cigarettes rolled in paper that recounted the main episodes of the Affair and pronounced Dreyfus guilty; decks of cards depicted Drumont doing battle with Dreyfus; and people throughout the country exchanged vituperatively anti-Semitic postcards. Imagination ran riot in this area; one could even buy kaleidoscopes, board games, and pipes that in one way or another conveyed anti-Semitic messages. By such means was nationalist outrage spread far beyond the big cities, so that by the time of the May elections not a single corner of France remained untouched. Indeed, the conservative right and prominent local leaders took up the cry, and in so doing lent legitimacy to the radical anti-Semitic movement well beyond the milieu reached by the leagues themselves. It was if the moderate right discovered mass politics in the late nineteenth century by way of anti-Semitism, a magical political formula that promised to create a new community united in opposition to Dreyfus/Judas/Satan. The phenomenon was far larger than the leagues themselves, and it resulted in a "nationalization" of nationalist, quasi-Jacobin politics in France that overwhelmed traditional interpersonal ties. Everywhere the same slogan was repeated: "France for the French!"[24]

Some historians view the years preceding World War I as a period of "nationalist revival" in France, linked to both external threats and domestic political considerations. Evidence of such a revival is said to include the re-emergence of the military parade, the dissolution of the Syndicat des Institeurs as an antimilitarist propaganda organization, French reaction to the Agadir incident (in which German and French forces clashed in Morocco), the election of Raymond Poincaré as president following his call for a "national renaissance," and passage of a law requiring three years of compulsory military service.[25] In reality, as we have just seen, the revival of nationalism in this period may have had more to do with the ability to mobilize crowds, as in 1898–99, for the purpose of defending a conception of France as a country with a Catholic identity, and thus excluding not only Jews and Masons but also Protestants from the public sphere. Hence the nationalist public sphere did not coincide with the republican one, a realm of citizens for whom progress and reason counted more than uncompromising loyalty to the France of yesteryear, which derived its values from its position as "eldest daughter of the Church." In many places, moreover, support for the "nationalist revival" came mainly from the traditionalist Catholic camp.[26] Thus the sporadic mobilizations of this period were not devoid of a certain unity, which in some ways set them apart from earlier crises, such as the Boulangist and Panama incidents. These virulently anti-Semitic demonstrations—instigated by militant aggressive leagues, often coordinated at the national level, and often resulting in violence—were thus mainly attempts to re-create an imaginary community of Frenchmen who, whatever social and political differences might separate them, were nevertheless united against their common enemy, the Jew. Demonstrations against the implementation of church-state separation laws and yellow-dog unions (which peaked in 1906) thus drew enthusiastic support from the leagues as well as from the many Catholic organizations that were associated with them. Once again, leading anti-Semitic spokesmen had no hesitation about lending support to the leagues.

For the leagues, the defense of Catholic tradition served to justify an abrupt, noisy entry into the political arena. To be sure, one cannot close one's eyes to the fact that substantial numbers of Catholics did not give in to their demons and rejected the leagues' strategy of exclusion and homogenization.[27] Yet the primary reason for the leagues' explosive growth was their defense of Catholicism against its domestic enemies, above all the Jews. The leagues' identity was further shaped not only by their refusal to accept a political order based on universal principles but also by certain socioeconomic concerns that they shared with the extreme left. In the period between the two world wars, those concerns gave rise to urban-based organizations prepared to do battle if necessary to defend their members' interests and promote nationalist ideals that were more than a little tinged by fascist influences and were now largely indifferent to French cultural identity.

7

The Hidden Face
of the Republican State

Historians of "Franco-French wars" have always been interested in the internal social clashes provoked by the Dreyfus Affair. In general, republicans were more favorable to the banished captain than were conservatives, who worried about preserving order and tradition even at the expense of justice. Scholars have written about the commitments of intellectuals, the influence of rival leagues, the mass demonstrations that took place in both Paris and the provinces, the verbal and physical attacks of each side on the other, and the explosive outpouring of propaganda in the form of articles, pamphlets, plays, books, and so on. In nearly all cases, the primary focus of this work has been the virtual civil war that tore French society apart and threatened to destroy political stability and undermine republican institutions. Scholars working on this period have traditionally paid relatively little attention to the state itself and instead focused mainly on social forces and ideologies shaped by rival elites. They write as though the political machinery of the state were devoid of internal logic, as if all government decisions reflected nothing more than the strategic choices of the people in power. Accordingly, those choices are ultimately interpreted as deriving from the social positions of those who made them—indeed, as a straightforward reflection of the structure of contending social forces.

More recently, however, historians have been rediscovering the complexities of politics and the role played by the state itself. Since the 1970s, historically minded political sociologists have opened up new avenues of research leading to a reinterpretation of Franco-French controversies in terms of institutional conflicts within the government, conflicts of course influenced by external events but nevertheless endowed with a logic of their own. Is the classical sociology of the state a useful instrument for studying such conflicts? In fact, the theory of the "strong" state[1] has drawbacks of its own, which mirror those of the society-centered approach. If one argues that the French state in many ways approximates the ideal type of the strong state, because it is highly differentiated and institutionalized and functions as an independent machine with its own vast "system of roles," then the notorious "Franco-French wars" should have had but little effect on the state apparatus. What I propose, then, is to take a fresh look at how this "strong" state behaved in a context of war between *les deux France*. What were the internal repercussions of extra-governmental conflicts? Although the strong/weak state distinction remains useful, one has to ask how closely the republican state monitored the opinions of those who served it, and how effectively it protected them from the hateful ideologies at loose in society during the Dreyfus era and later. This is particularly important for the study of the Dreyfus era, because the Third Republic had yet to consolidate its power or set its institutions upon a firm foundation. To what extent did divisions within the state hinder the functioning of the government and cast doubt on the very principles of republican administration?

Indeed, the Dreyfus Affair involved the apparatus of the state—the army and the courts—in a fundamental way. These institutions were concerned with order, rules, and, to a certain extent, meritocracy. The state was deeply engaged in the process of institutionalizing itself: it was establishing competitive examinations for civil-service position, recruiting new officials via elite educational institutions (the so-called *grandes écoles*), bolstering the main branches of the administration (*les grands corps*), and seeking to free the political and administrative elite from the influence of big money. Republican elites were drawn from a wide variety of social backgrounds, and many conservative functionaries left over from imperial times now quit the government of their own accord, because, with the influx of new officials, they no longer felt at home. A series of administrative purges also tended to eliminate officials who did not subscribe to republican values.[2] One might think, then, that, whenever a new Franco-French conflict erupted, such a republicanized state would automatically rally around Marianne to defend the Republic, or at the very least give within its own councils only muted expression to the furious hatreds that were rampant in civil society. Yet, in contrast to the predictions of the strong-state model, outside ideological conflicts did find echoes inside the councils of government. The boundary between the bureaucracy and the rest of the world was porous, and the ideological predilections of some bureaucrats were strong enough to threaten the solidarity of certain *corps*. Thus even a "strong" state is vulnerable to external passions "imported" from the society it governs.

Here I propose to consider the paradoxical fate of the state Jews, "fanatics of the Republic" who rose to the highest ranks of the bureaucracy despite ostracism, at times tainted with anti-Semitism, throughout their careers. Such ostracism is surprising precisely because it occurred within a regime supposedly committed to the universalist values of the Republic.[3] Some state Jews continued to hold important positions during the Dreyfus Affair, thus drawing the wrath of anti-Semitic rabble-rousers. The *Semaine religieuse du diocèse de Nevers*, for example, published the following attack on these "Jewish invaders":

> The Jews are everywhere. The Ministry of Finance employs twenty-seven of them in high positions; the Ministry of the Interior has more than thirty Jewish prefects and subprefects; the Ministry of Justice has ten Jewish *conseillers* on the Paris Court of Appeals, nine Jews on the Conseil d'Etat, and countless Jews in all the courts and tribunals of France; at the Ministry of Agri-

culture there are eleven Jews, and at the Ministry of Public Works, thirty; the headquarters of the Post and Telegraph Office employs twenty-four, and the Ministry of Public Instruction has hired thirty, to say nothing of the Jews scattered throughout institutions under that ministry's tutelage. Everywhere they want to be heard and are determined to act. Is it surprising, then, that the Dreyfus Affair has taken on such proportions?[4]

In fact, there were relatively few state Jews, but in the context of the Dreyfus Affair myths took on a life of their own. Drumont claimed that there were two million Jews in France in the 1890s, whereas the actual number was around eighty thousand. He also wildly exaggerated the number of state Jews. Following his lead, any number of pamphlets listed the names and home addresses of high government officials who were assumed to be Jewish. Accordingly, many people believed that Jews were everywhere in government and that, like the convicted captain, they were using their high positions to betray the interests of France. Thus, according to one police report, "the public is highly agitated. The curé of Saint-Martin has issued a call for murder because he believes that the presiding judge of the Cour de Cassation, Monsieur Loew, is Jewish and intends to control the course of the Dreyfus Affair." To this the curé allegedly added, that "Someday they [i.e., the Jews] will have to be exterminated."[5] In fact, Loew, a high magistrate who did play some role in the Affair, was not Jewish at all. As presiding judge of the *chambre criminelle* of the Cour de Cassation, he bore the full brunt of anti-Semitic violence, however: during the review of Dreyfus's conviction, Drumont and Rochefort both referred to him as "the Jew Levy." Later, Judge Loew complained bitterly of the "hatred that honest and conscientious performance of his duties had aroused. . . . It is not necessary to have a French name or share the religion of the majority to be devoted to France."[6] Drumont, bent on amassing ammunition against state Jews, was not above distorting the facts in his attacks on the "Jewish Republic": in his eyes, not only was Gambetta Jewish, but so were any number of prefects (such as Vel-Durant and Schnerb), magistrates, and military officers, who of course could not respond to the attacks.

During the Dreyfus Affair, these distortions became more and more blatant. It was alleged that Jews, some of whom had changed their names in order to conceal their identities, were running the government. Besides infiltrating the general staff so as to furnish intelligence to France's enemies, they were also out to capture every government post they could, in keeping with their strategy to subvert France. Just a few months before the Affair began, *La Libre Parole* launched a no-holds-barred attack on four different Jews in the same issue: one, Léon Cohn, was a prefect, an "eternal Jew, born, like everyone of his race, a fraud and a peddler"; another, Isaïe Levaillant, was a "Jew who, thanks to his agents, holds France's secrets in his hands. You can imagine what a fellow like this can do with today's laws"; the third was "the Jew Isaac, who ordered working women to be shot without warning"; and the fourth was "the Jew Vel-Durand, who has kicked out the sisters [i.e., nuns] whom everyone admired. . . . Catholics have only themselves to blame."[7]

The Dreyfus Affair exacerbated these anti-Semitic attacks on state Jews who had succeeded in obtaining positions in government thanks to republican meritocracy. Indeed, meritocratic recruitment itself was attacked as an artificial device that gave outsiders an unfair advantage and destroyed *le pays réel*, the real France. The case of Isaïe Levaillant is an excellent one for assessing the influence of the Affair on the future of the state Jews. Destined in youth to become a rabbi, Levaillant entered the government after joining Gambetta in the fight to establish the Third Republic. His career seemed assured.[8] Starting in 1879, he served first as subprefect and then as prefect, and in 1885 was named director of the Sûreté Générale in the Ministry of the Interior, which *La Libre Parole* described as "an important post from the standpoint of espionage and one that the Jews are determined to see occupied by one of their own." Levaillant in fact succeeded Schnerb at the Sûreté Générale, and the anti-Semitic press had always mistaken Schnerb for a Jew. Drumont was livid at the thought that this crucial post was about to be occupied by "another" Jew. A few years later, when the discovery of the famous *bordereau*, or list of secret documents, revealed a breach of security that would ultimately be blamed on Captain Dreyfus, Drumont would repeat and elaborate on his allegations concerning Jewish control of the Sûreté Générale.[9] By contrast, *Le Pays* saw nothing inappropriate in Levaillant's appointment: "Monsieur Brisson, who apparently realizes that the Republic is once again in great danger, believes that he is obliged without delay to call upon men who served him so effectively in difficult circumstances. The choice of Monsieur Levaillant is a tribute to his obstinacy as a policeman."[10] When Levaillant was forced out in 1888, *La Cocarde* issued this warning: "Monsieur Floquet has retired the sinister operator and German informer who headed up the Sûreté. . . . Other informers sent to spy on our best generals will soon be shown the door as well."[11] Levaillant, who was soon thereafter appointed treasurer of the Loire *département*, continued to be persecuted by *La Libre Parole*. In March 1893, the paper wrote: "Yes, it has come to this: thirty-eight million Frenchmen are governed by a few thousand Jews. All by himself, Isaïe Levaillant is now more powerful than fifty deputies."[12]

Then, in January 1895, Levaillant was abruptly dismissed from his treasurer's post as the result of a murky case of corruption involving the Schwob brothers. He was accused of accepting a bribe in exchange for intervening with magistrates looking into the matter. Evidence in the case was circulated behind Levaillant's back. Excerpts from subpoenaed private correspondence were published in the press to discredit him. Despite the vitriolic attacks, however, the investigation concluded that Levaillant had done nothing wrong, a finding that provoked charges of corruption in the courts from the anti-Semitic press. But nothing came of these allegations, and Levaillant, the mentor of Prefect Lépine, wrote a long justification of his actions in which he gave details of a plot to discredit him. "Did they go after me because I had been a political operative?" he asked. "Yes, that and my origins no doubt provide the explanation of my downfall. In the course of my career I was often forced to stand in the way of enemies of the Republic. . . . Hence I am not surprised by the implacable hatred of my adversaries. But can I expect no justice from those I have served and fought alongside?"[13] In the midst of the Dreyfus Affair, Paul de Cassagnac, writing in *L'Autorité*, remembered that, when Levaillant was appointed head of the Sûreté Générale, "the Jews of

France screamed with joy." And that was not all. "Their ideal," he added, "is to control the French police, to use informers, and thus to be in a position to spy easily on us wretched Christians. Levaillant made the most of the opportunity." What is more, he had associated himself with Schwob, "a Jew who gave off a foul odor, the stench of his race. . . . He shielded [Schwob] and his partners from the courts. . . . When will Levaillant be arrested, and when will the judges who sold out to Jewry be removed from their positions?"[14] Meanwhile, in *L'Intransigeant*, Henri Rochefort charged that "Levaillant the Jewish spy won't hesitate to ruin the reputations of these low-born Christians" and that his long tenure as head of the police had most likely given him a hold over so many politicians that he would never be convicted.[15] Interestingly, Levaillant's accusers—Drumont, Cassagnac, and Rochefort—would later become leaders of the anti-Dreyfusard camp, where they would use the same types of arguments in attacking the courts, for example. Once the anti-Semites had sunk their teeth into a victim, be it Levaillant or Dreyfus, they would not let go. On February 16, 1895, *La Libre Parole* alleged that "nobody knows where this obscure, miserable Jew came from. Probably some Bavarian village. His background will always be as mysterious as the backgrounds of most others of his ilk. . . . He proved to be a zealous secularizer, always ready to follow Kahal's orders," before being named to the Sûreté Générale, "a key post, of incomparable importance in the world of espionage, as the Jews know perfectly well. . . . As the high sheriff of France," he had access to "secret information that he could use to blackmail his enemies. . . . Levaillant is only one link in the chain that shackles us, one of a thousand tentacles of the horrible octopus that has been sucking our blood for so many years." That same day, *L'Autorité* added yet another allegation: "The current regime is not above using Jews to persecute Catholics. . . . And God knows, there are plenty of Jewish prefects and subprefects."

On February 11, 1895, Denis, a deputy from the Landes, invoked the "Levaillant Affair and the wretched Dreyfus Affair" as grounds for calling upon the government to explain "the facts that led to the removal of a treasurer [Levaillant] and the measures that the government intends to take in order to put a halt to Jewish dominance of various departments of the bureaucracy."[16] Increasingly, there was a tendency to link Levaillant's fate to that of Dreyfus, who was also accused of being a German-born spy, even though his family, like Levaillant's, had chosen to leave Alsace after the defeat of 1870 so as not to live under German rule. Thus these two state Jews, both natives of Mulhouse, became successive incarnations of the "Jewish Republic." Linked to Dreyfus by the anti-Dreyfusards, Levaillant became the managing editor of *L'Univers israélite* in 1896, and in that capacity he tried to warn French Jews about the dangers of anti-Semitism and urge them to organize in order to stop it. On April 30, 1897, he asked what, "in the face of the impending clash, are the Jews of France doing? Are they prepared to stand up against the enemy and repel his attacks? Have they armed themselves to defend their rights, their security, and their honor? . . . The time has come to prepare for battle. Are the Jews of France ready to unite, join together, and organize?"[17] As an old policeman, he knew the need to organize against the powerful anti-Semitic and anti-Dreyfusard movement. In June 1898, he argued that "we were too inclined to lull ourselves to sleep, to think that the rights that were granted us by the French Revolution were secure forever. . . . The Dreyfus Affair awoke us from our complacent certainties and forced us to fight."[18] Levaillant was a man of action as well as words: in 1894, he became secretary of a committee of defense against anti-Semitism, a group discreetly established by the Jewish Consistory, of which he was an active member, to do battle in every way possible against the anti-Semitism that the Affair had unleashed.[19] In 1903, as this former high government official neared the end of his long and diligent struggle, he wrote: "Some will say that Jews ought to keep quiet about the Affair for fear of reawakening the old hatreds that it stirred up against them. . . . If they were to keep quiet, their enemies would not. And so long as anti-Semites can, with impunity, attach the epithet 'traitor' to the name Dreyfus and raise insulting doubts about the French patriotism of their enemies, they will continue to wield their most murderous weapon. They must be deprived of that weapon; it must be broken in two while still in their hands."[20] *La Libre Parole* unwittingly confirmed the importance of Levaillant's role when it published a rumor that, "as soon as the court-martial in Rennes reaches a verdict, Monsieur Viguié, the head of the Sûreté Générale, will reportedly be replaced by . . . Isaïe Levaillant. This information is plausible in the present situation. What did you expect? With Levaillant at the helm of the Sûreté and Grümbach as his right-hand man and Dreyfus in military intelligence alongside the 'divine Picquart,' France will have the public servants she deserves."[21]

Many other state Jews were caught up in the turbulence of the Dreyfus Affair. Levaillant's own son-in-law, Fernand Torrès, served as a subprefect in those troubled times, and according to his personnel file "stood courageously in the breach during the Dreyfus Affair in defense of justice and truth." Yet, at the age of forty-seven, this functionary with an unblemished record "still holds a post that should be that of a beginner."[22] Jews in the prefectoral corps saw their careers derailed. For instance, the personnel file of Lucien Aaron, a *conseiller de préfecture* who was born in Nancy, reveals this comment from 1896: "There is no legal connection between Monsieur Aaron and Captain Dreyfus, but there are family connections that argue against his posting in the Vaucluse. Monsieur Aaron is an intelligent, energetic, and devoted civil servant. He has had a difficult time in recent years because of being Jewish."[23] Similarly, in 1898, Eugène Weill, the subprefect of Meaux, was "suspected of sympathies and friendships in the cosmopolitan gang that is working toward the destruction of France. . . . He is suspected of Dreyfusard leanings." In publishing this text, *L'Indépendant de Seine-et-Marne* called upon "our new subprefect to publicly repudiate any friendships or connections he may have with the big German bankers whose money is supporting the traitor's proponents."[24] In a period of violent anti-Semitic attacks, many Jews in the prefectoral corps became targets of hostile campaigns. In Verdun, for example, according to *L'Est républicain* of January 28, 1898, the home of Monsieur Cahen, the subprefect, was plastered with signs that read, "Death to the Jews! Shame on Zola! Long live the army!"[25]

Jewish magistrates with unblemished records often became targets of various anti-Semitic maneuvers that hindered their work and endangered their careers—proof, if proof were needed, that the republican state, "strong" though it may have been, was not entirely immune to turmoil in the surrounding society. Take, for example, the case of Judge Eugène Dreyfus. Born in Mulhouse, he began his career in 1893 as an assistant prosecutor. A graduate of the Faculty of Law in Paris and an expert on the law of nationality, on which he published an authoritative reference, Dreyfus was a convinced republican who suffered the misfortune of having the same last name as the alleged traitor. In a report dated January 3, 1905, the *premier président* of the Cour d'Appel of Rouen noted:

> When denied a promotion during the Dreyfus Affair because of his name and because he was Jewish, [Judge Dreyfus] returned to his work with even greater diligence and devotion than before. Rather than indulge in recriminations against the government, he gave himself unstintingly to his duties. . . . I shall never forget the firmness he displayed in enforcing the law of 1901 on the congregations at a time when precedents were of little use as a guide. In Monsieur Dreyfus all the characteristics of the republican magistrate are evident.

In 1906, moreover, the *procureur général* of the Cour d'Appel of Rouen wrote that Dreyfus was "an exceptionally gifted magistrate who, as the chancellery has been informed on several occasions, deserves promotion to the post of *avocat général*. Gives excellent summations in civil cases and authoritative charges to the jury in criminal cases. Very firm republican on whom the government can absolutely rely. Has been systematically excluded from promotion for several years solely on account of his name. Deserves compensation." Eventually he got what he deserved: despite his name, he would end his career as *premier président* of the Cour d'Appel of Paris.[26] In 1895, at the height of the Affair, the Alsatian-born judge Oscar Dalmbert met with a similar mishap. His personnel file contains the following notation: "An objection to the position of *président* arises from Monsieur Dalmbert's religion. Monsieur Dalmbert is Jewish. Is it appropriate to appoint him to a court in which one of his coreligionists, Monsieur Dreyfus, is already an assistant prosecutor, and in a city where Jews are involved in a substantial number of cases? This situation might prove embarrassing for Monsieur Dalmbert's independence and impartiality."[27]

The story of a relatively low-ranking magistrate, Paul Bertulus, shows how anti-Semitic pressures from outside the institution could also affect the careers of Jewish officials.[28] His superior wrote, "He demonstrated courage and energy as a *juge d'instruction* [prosecuting magistrate] in incidents related to the Dreyfus Affair when such matters were entrusted to him." On his own initiative, he ordered the arrest of Esterhazy, who was taken to the Santé prison by police on July 12, 1898. Shortly thereafter, he investigated Colonel Picquart's charges against General du Paty de Clam. But Judge Bertulus was Jewish, and anti-Semites went on the offensive against him: "Everybody knows that he is with the Dreyfus syndicate." In April 1899, during the Henry Affair, Quesnay de Beaurepaire pointed a finger at him and accused him of frequenting "exotic company and seeing German Jews in the most intimate of circumstances." To the end of his career he was the target of numerous insults and threats from other magistrates. *La Libre Parole* attacked him constantly, as it attacked other Versailles jurists such as Judge Worms, who allegedly "licked his chops . . . when the Comte de Vezin, a former artillery captain who tendered his resignation during the Dreyfus Affair, appeared before him." The article continued: "No matter how debased we have become, can we permit Frenchmen who were arrested as Catholics, and because they were Catholics, to be judged, to be held up to ridicule in court and tossed into prison, by a Jew?"[29] *L'Intransigeant* also waged a vigorous anti-Semitic campaign against Judge Abram in Uzès. According to Henri Rochefort:

[Abram] is openly protected by all the red and black robes among the Jew-loving defenders of Dreyfus. As a coreligionist of Rothschild and Zadoc-Kahn, he knows full well that he can get away with anything and that all he has to do is whistle for the minister of justice to prostrate himself at his feet and lick the floor with his tongue. . . . The auto-da-fés for which we blame the Inquisition are today being organized by Huguenots and Hebrews against their political and religious enemies, but with one difference: since the price of wood has gone up so much, they have replaced the stake with the guillotine.[30]

In Toul, the prosecutor Léon Sommer became the target of anti-Semitic attacks growing out of the Affair. According to *La Moselle*, "His home was festooned with highly suggestive graffiti regarding this compatriot of Dreyfus." There were also posters that read, "Down with the Jews! Down with Zola! Long live the army!" A native of Bas-Rhin, Sommer met with such hostility that in June 1900 his doctor, a member of the Ligue des Droits de l'Homme, wrote to the group's president, Ludovic Trarieux: "During his illness, the prosecutor seemed preoccupied with the difficulties he had encountered in his career of public service owing to the actions of certain politicians (a long and ignoble campaign in the press, the unforgivable attitude of the nationalist mayor, etc.)." He hoped that Trarieux would quickly intervene to obtain a new post for Sommer.[31]

The anti-Semitic campaigns against state Jews grew worse as the Dreyfus Affair proceeded. One by one, the most prestigious departments of the bureaucracy were affected. On December 28, 1898, for example, *La Libre Parole* accused the Conseil d'Etat of being "Jewified": "The Conseil d'Etat will soon be in the same situation as the *chambre criminelle* of the Cour de Cassation: it will be entirely in the service of Israel. . . . Trarieux got several corrupt judges appointed to the *chambre criminelle* in anticipation of the review of the Dreyfus trial that has long been in the works. Now the same operation is being directed at the Conseil d'Etat." The myth that Jews controlled the bureaucracy took hold at the time of the Dreyfus Affair and proved difficult to combat. It was applied to any number of institutions, including the army. As late as 1907, *La Libre Parole* charged that "Monsieur Clemenceau could not have re-entered public life without the protection of the Jews he served so assiduously at the time of the Dreyfus Affair. . . . But Jewry, as always, exacts a high price. . . . The Grümbach who recently received a splendid promotion is none other than the cousin of Alfred Dreyfus. As bureau chief, he was responsible for keeping an eye on espionage along our borders. What is he going to keep an eye on now that he is deputy chief of the central administration?"[32] The myth of the "Jewish Republic," reinforced by the kinds of fantasy that ran riot during the Dreyfus Affair, became firmly rooted in the imagination of the nationalist right. These episodes lend some credence to those who argue that even at this late date, and at a time when the Republic was itself in peril, some republicans betrayed their own ideals and set "the Republic against freedom."[33]

8

MILITARY PASSION THWARTED

Throughout the Dreyfus Affair, no minister of defense or other top military official ever expressed a moment of doubt about the captain's guilt. General Mercier stated simply, "Captain Dreyfus has committed an act of treason." General Billot proclaimed, "In [his] soul and conscience as a soldier and head of the army, Dreyfus is guilty, Dreyfus is a traitor." Later, General Cavaignac said that he remained "convinced of Dreyfus's guilt," as did General Zurlinden, who stated, "Detailed study of court records in the Dreyfus case has convinced me of his guilt." And General Chanoine remarked, "While respectful of the court's decision, I nevertheless have a right to my opinion, which is the same as that of my predecessors." Much later, on the eve of World War II, Generals Godfroy and Weygand also refused to believe in the captain's innocence. Nearly the only top military official to express any doubt about the verdict was the future Marshal Lyautey, who as early as 1895 wrote, "What makes me even more skeptical is that I think I see signs of pressure from so-called public opinion, or, rather, from the street, the mob. . . . The mob is screaming for the Jew's death because he is Jewish, and nowadays it is anti-Semitism that pulls the strings."[1] A few generals were shocked by the way the captain was treated, but on the whole most high-ranking officers remained anti-Dreyfusards. Though eager to preserve respect for the army in the midst of a violent Franco-French conflict, many military officials lent their enormous prestige to the anti-Dreyfusard camp, thereby encouraging nationalists and anti-Semites to mobilize against the Republic, which was slow to come to the aid of one of its most loyal defenders.

On November 3, 1894, Drumont alleged that "Jews like Dreyfus are probably just spies who take their orders from Jewish financiers. They are pawns in a vast conspiracy." On the same day, *La Vérité* asserted, "This is not the first time in history that a Jew is guilty of treason. Unfortunately, this one is an officer in the French army. He had convinced people that his Jewish skin covered a French soul." *La Libre Parole* interpreted things the same way: "At the Ministry of War he was shunned by his comrades. His pronounced Jewishness, which made him seem like a foreigner disguised as a Frenchman, had something to do with this aversion." Meanwhile, *Le Petit Journal* drew the conclusion that "a purge of the army is necessary if we are to get rid of this leprosy, which is more dangerous than any epidemic, scourge, or cataclysm. . . . No, Captain Dreyfus cannot be and is not French." In fact, Drumont had been systematically persecuting Jewish officers in the French army for years. As if in rehearsal for the Dreyfus Affair, his newspaper, *La Libre Parole*, had published an incendiary series of articles on "Jews in the army" two years earlier:

The army was protected from Jewish influence longer than the rest of society. It owed this immunity to its traditional spirit and to the very nature of its mission. Why did the yids join its ranks? Gambling on the bond market beats gambling one's life in the trenches. . . . The vast majority of military men feel an instinctive revulsion for the sons of Israel. . . . No sooner did Jews gain a foothold in the army than they sought to gain influence. Already masters of finance and the bureaucracy and able to dictate their judgments to the courts, they will at last gain control of all of France once they seize control of the army. Rothschild will then be informed of all our mobilization plans. . . . Guess for what purpose![2]

He went on to attack by name a number of Jewish officers who had graduated from the Ecole Polytechnique, including Cahens and Dreyfuses. Two years before the Affair, in other words, every detail was already in place. Drumont's newspaper was already pointing an accusatory finger at Joseph Reinach, whom Drumont held responsible for "the invasion of the army by Jews." Drumont thus honed his ample arsenal of anti-Semitic insults on his favorite target, a key political figure who would play a considerable role in Dreyfus's defense and who would ultimately become the focal point of unusually intense anti-Semitic hatred. A few days later, on May 29, 1892, *La Libre Parole* published on its front page a letter from Captain Crémieu-Foa to its editor, Edouard Drumont: "By insulting the three hundred French officers of the Jewish faith who are on active duty, you have insulted me personally. I call upon you to cease this odious campaign and warn you that if you do not heed my letter I shall be obliged to insist upon satisfaction by arms." Drumont published his reply in the same issue: "If the Jewish officers of the French army are wounded by our articles, let them choose by lot as many delegates as they wish, and we shall oppose them with an equal number of French swords. As for you, if, as a Jew, you are challenging me, you will find me ready." A duel was now inevitable, and Crémieu-Foa faced Edouard Drumont on June 1, 1892. At the Jewish officer's side, serving as his second, was Major Ferdinand Esterhazy, who would later betray France and allow Captain Alfred Dreyfus to be tried and convicted in his place. Later, in January 1898, after Esterhazy had won an unexpected acquittal, Drumont wrote: "At the time I took off my shirt in the Saint-Germain forest in order to fight Crémieu-Foa, I would have been greatly astonished had anyone told me that my opponent's second would one day come and ask me to defend him against a monstrous machination organized against him by Jews."[3] Drumont, who scored a hit with his sword, accused his opponent of fending off the blade with his hand. Crémieu-Foa denied this but admitted that he might have made an instinctive move to defend himself.

On June 20, Crémieu-Foa next faced Paul de Lamase, the author of the offending articles and assistant editor of *La Libre Parole*. The circumstances of this duel, agreed upon in advance by both parties, were quite a bit more dangerous than was customary at the time: each man was to fire four shots at a distance of twenty-five paces.[4] In the event, however, neither participant was seriously wounded. The Marquis de Morès, who was also on the staff of *La Libre Parole*, then cast about for a pretext to challenge Captain Crémieu-Foa yet again. The two men were supposed to meet the following day, but Crémieu-Foa's commanding officer issued orders forbidding him to fight and confined him to quarters, and his second, Captain Armand Mayer, was dispatched with the news. Despite an agreement between the two opponents in the previous duel that nothing was to be published about it, an account had appeared in the press, and Morès blamed Mayer, who had had no part in what had happened but took offense at the insult and issued yet another challenge. Although Mayer was a fencing instructor at the Ecole Polytechnique, his arm was injured and he was in no condition to fight. The duel was supposed to be fought with swords of normal weight, but Morès, who was quite a strong man, used an extra-heavy sword and succeeded in piercing his opponent's lung. The tip severed his spinal cord, and Mayer died virtually on the spot. An outpouring of emotion followed, especially after Morès described the contest as "the beginning of a civil war."

Mayer, who was born in Lorraine, had studied at the Ecole de Guerre and the Ecole Polytechnique before being named an instructor at the latter. His brother was related by marriage to Captain Mannheim, another professor at the Ecole Polytechnique. Mayer was thus typical of the Jewish officers from eastern France who had chosen a career in the military in order to defend their fatherland. In many respects, Captain Mayer shared the life and values of Captain Dreyfus. Most of the press was hostile to Morès. *Les Débats* expressed its regret at the "revival of hatreds that one had thought forever laid to rest." *Le Siècle* condemned "the results of Drumont and Morès's antipatriotic campaign to revive the wars of religion." For *L'Estaffette*, "The army must be protected against the buccaneers of the gutter press. . . . France has suffered a mortal blow. This country is done for," *Le Temps* wrote, "It is unthinkable that questions of race and religion should be raised in the press and that the members of the French family should be divided into two warring camps." *Le Radical* protested "against a return to the wars of religion. . . . A Frenchman, an officer, was forced into a duel for no good reason. Although he had dedicated his life to his country, he died because the gang that signs itself 'Morès and friends' needed a body." Camille Dreyfus, who himself had faced Morès with pistols two years earlier, delivered a forceful speech to the Chamber of Deputies: "I ask you, Mr. War Minister, if there are two types of sword in the French army: the one worn by our comrades on active duty and the one that we will proudly wear whenever the country calls on us? Is it French, or is it something else?" To which Freycinet, the minister of war, replied:

The honorable Monsieur Dreyfus asks if the minister of war is prepared to adopt language that would have the effect of establishing categories within the army and of setting French swords against Jewish swords. Gentlemen, in the army we recognize neither Jews, nor Protestants, nor Catholics [applause]. We recognize only French officers, with no consideration of background [further applause]. To those officers who feel wounded by polemical attacks of which we deeply disapprove [applause], by passions belonging to another era [Hear, hear!], by prejudices long ago laid to rest by the French Revolution, I say, You are invulnerable to these blanket insults, which in no way impugn either your courage as soldiers or your integrity as private citizens. Rise above these attacks, for you have the support of the government, of the chambers, and of the public at large, which makes no distinction between you and your comrades-at-arms. . . . To stir up citizen against citizen is always a bad thing, but to set officer against officer is a crime against the nation [sustained applause].

Meanwhile, General Saussier, the military governor of Paris, advised "all officers under his command to remain calm and collected and confident in the belief that public outrage will thwart every misguided criminal attempt to sow dissension in the ranks of the nation's active defenders." The *Archives israélites* expressed pleasure at this unanimous expression of support "for Judaism, which has been so odiously attacked by the gutter press, support that will bring consolation and comfort while reminding Jews that France remains steadfastly committed to its generous and liberal traditions."

Captain Mayer was given a grandiose burial. Military honors were provided by an infantry company and a platoon of students from the Ecole Polytechnique, which had closed for a week of mourning. A huge crowd gathered: some journalists put its size as high as a hundred thousand, though the actual number was probably much less. Each of the major newspapers (*Le Radical, Le Matin, L'Echo de Paris, Le National, La République française, La Nation*, etc.) sent a wreath. The pallbearers included the two student commandants of the Ecole Polytechnique and two instructor captains. Drums rolled and bugles sounded. Many deputies, senators, and military officers joined the entire student body of the Ecole Polytechnique. General Borius, commandant of the Ecole, marched behind the hearse in full-dress uniform. Jewish officers and government officials were also represented: among them were General Sée, Senator Millaud, and Deputies Camille Dreyfus, Joseph Reinach, David Raynal, and Alfred Naquet. Zadoc Kahn, the Grand Rabbi of France, spoke at the Montparnasse cemetery:

At the sight of this coffin we are gripped by pain. It contains the lifeless remains of a noble young man, a man in every way worthy of belonging to the admirable corps of French officers who represent righteousness, loyalty, honor, scorn for danger, and habitual sacrifice. . . . What a loss for the army, which in the person of Captain Mayer has lost one of its best-educated, most courageous officers. What a loss for France. . . . What a loss for French Judaism . . . We are left with at least one consolation in our unspeakable sorrow. The cruel lesson of this universally deplored event has been understood: I can attest to the widespread sorrow and unanimous regret that have manifested themselves from one end of our country to the other. The soul of France has shown itself to be intact, with all its native generosity and passion for justice. . . . All hearts, without exception, were afflicted by his death. A cry of pain went forth from every mouth. Never has our national conscience spoken with so strong a voice. . . . Gentlemen, this funeral has an eloquence all its own, for it has been conducted, as it were, by France herself.

Then General Borius spoke:

It is with deep sadness that I come to bid Captain Mayer a final farewell in the name of the Ecole Polytechnique and in the name of his comrades in the Corps of Engineers, of which he was one of the brightest officers. . . . He enjoyed the most brilliant gifts. A bright future lay ahead of him. His death is a great loss for the Corps of Engineers, a great loss for the army. Farewell, Captain Mayer. Farewell, my friend.[5]

French Jews were reassured by these and other official statements from the Ministry of the Army and the director of the Ecole Polytechnique as well as by the reaction of the press. The Central Consistory discussed the matter of Mayer's death internally and expressed regret at "intolerant polemics unworthy of our time and place. . . . Since the fatal duel that cost the life of a Jewish officer, a favorable reaction has occurred, calm heads have made noticeable progress, and we have every reason to believe that the attacks on us will soon give way to more wholesome and balanced judgments."[6]

Morès was placed on trial. The prosecutor accused him of having "laid down a trail of blood. Put an end to it. Tomorrow, public wrath may smash your presses and break your swords. . . . What Frenchman would not answer yes if called upon to oppose these men, who have unleashed this terrible war upon their country, a war reminiscent of our old wars of religion, which did so much harm to our fatherland?"[7]

Morès was defended by none other than Edgar Demange, who would later serve as an attorney for, of all people, Captain Dreyfus. In the end, the marquis was acquitted.

Not long thereafter, fate seemed to turn against the Jewish officers who had had the audacity to stand up to Drumont and his friends. Captain Crémieu-Foa was killed in action in Dahomey (now Benin, in West Africa), and another *polytechnicien*, Navy Lieutenant Alphonse Valabrègue, was also killed there in another battle. Other Jewish officers died elsewhere in Africa, and in Tonkin, Captain Oppenheim met his death in July of the same year. The *Archives israélites* offered this comment: "The insulted Jews responded to these outrageous charges by redoubling their devotion to our common fatherland." A ceremony in honor of Crémieu-Foa, Valabrègue, and Oppenheim was held at the synagogue on the rue de la Victoire and attended by many of their comrades. In his eulogy, Rabbi Zadoc Kahn noted, "The tiny African expeditionary force is the noble and living image of the *grande armée* that is France's pride and honor." And *L'Univers israélite* published the following poem in honor of Crémieu-Foa:

> *Il a croisé le fer pour l'honneur de sa race,*
> *Pour le nom d'Israël il a donné son sang;*
> *Voyez-vous l'auréole autour de ce front blanc?*
> *Français, découvrez-vous. . . . c'est un martyr qui passe.*
>
> *Au mépris des trois mots de ta devise, ô France!*
> *Qui s'imposent au monde en dogmes triomphants,*
> *Quelques louches esprits (sont-ils bien tes enfants?)*
> *Voudraient ressusciter les siècles d'ignorance.*
>
> *Honte à deux qui, semant la haine et la discorde,*
> *Espéraient conquérir la palme des vainqueurs!*
> *Non! le dégout enfin a soulevé les coeurs . . .*
> *C'est vraiment trop de fiel et leur fange déborde.*[8]

(He crossed swords for the honor of his race, for the name of Israel he shed his blood. Do you see the halo that encircles his pale brow? Bare your heads, Frenchmen, a martyr is passing. Contemptuous of the three words of your motto, O France! words that lay your triumphant dogmas before the world, a few dubious minds [can they be your children?] would like to revive centuries of ignorance. Shame upon those who, sowing hatred and discord, hoped to win the conqueror's palm. No! Good people have finally turned away in disgust. Choking with bile, they spew filth everywhere.)

The Jews of France had long since made citizenship an integral part of their existence, and instinctively they looked to the army, which they revered in spite of everything. Like other citizens, they were entitled to serve and, if they had the talent, to rise through the ranks. Jews who had attended Saint-Cyr, Polytechnique, and other *grandes écoles* had little by little climbed to the highest ranks of the military, despite the continued presence of anti-Semitism. Under the Empire, many became colonels, but none rose as high as general: with the Church still highly influential, promoting a Jewish officer to the very highest ranks was unthinkable. Lieutenant-Colonel Abraham Lévy never made it to general. Lieutenant-Colonel Léopold Sée, who refused to attend mass, was at first denied promotion to colonel, which would have placed him in a position of command. In 1870, however, Sée became the first Jew to achieve the rank of brigadier general in the French army, and with the advent of the Republic other Jewish officers were also promoted to prestigious posts, especially after 1880, when a competitive examination was established for admission to the Ecole Supérieure de Guerre. As meritocratic promotion became the norm in the 1890s, the proportion of Jewish officers rose rapidly. Many of these men were from Alsace and Lorraine, and therefore eager to demonstrate their patriotic attachment to France. For them, the return to France of the two provinces lost during the Franco-Prussian War was an urgent and sacred duty. Revanchism was the focal point of all their hopes, especially since many of these Jewish officers had already fought the Germans in 1870. Included in this group were Colonels Gabriel Brisac, Jules Moch, and Isidore Ausher, and Captains Abraham Samuel, Léon Francfort, and Victor Mannheim. During the siege of Paris, Mannheim had commanded an artillery battery at the Ecole Polytechnique. Many of these same officers would later fight in World War I, and some received battlefield promotions to the rank of general, such as Jules Heymann, Georges Alexandre, Lucien Lévy, Gédéon Geismar, and Camille Lévi. Lévi, who hailed from the Bas-Rhin, told his officers, "If you pronounce the word *boche* [a pejorative term for German], you'll sense how abject it is: it's a mark of infamy."[9]

Meanwhile, by the end of the nineteenth century, the army already had any number of Jewish captains and colonels, and even a few generals, such as Samuel Naquet-Laroque. Republican meritocracy had opened up the military hierarchy to the "new strata" of society. Jewish officers were more likely than their non-Jewish comrades to be graduates of the *grandes écoles*, especially Polytechnique. In 1890, eight were admitted to Polytechnique and six to Saint-Cyr; in 1891, another eight were admitted to Polytechnique and five to Saint-Cyr; in 1892, nine Jewish applicants made it into Polytechnique and five into Saint-Cyr, including one Edouard Dreyfus. Within a few days of the beginning of the Dreyfus Affair, the list of 210 successful applicants to Polytechnique was published: of these, eleven were Jewish, and one bore the name Dreyfus. The exacerbation of anti-Semitic feeling as a result of the Affair did nothing to slow the influx of Jewish officer candidates. In September 1898, ten Jews were admitted to Polytechnique. In September 1899, after the decision to grant Dreyfus a pardon had been made, another nine Jews were admitted. Indeed, for Jews, the attractiveness of the most prestigious military institutions grew steadily. In February 1895, with the shock of Dreyfus's conviction still fresh in mind, several Jewish officers graduated as usual from the Ecole Supérieure de Guerre and were commissioned captains of infantry. And again, in October 1898, in the midst of a terrible year that saw virtual pogroms throughout France, numerous Jewish candidates applied to Polytechnique, and nine were fortunate enough to be admitted to the Ecole Spéciale Militaire at Saint-Cyr; others were selected in 1899.[10]

This was the background against which the fate of Alfred Dreyfus was played out. Like so many of his fellow Jewish officers, Dreyfus was born in the east of France, in Mulhouse, and steeped in a patriotism born of the defeat of 1870–71, the determination to reconquer France's lost provinces, and the decision to leave Alsace voluntarily

in order to remain French. He began his studies at the Ecole Polytechnique in November 1878, willingly submitting himself to the
harsh constraints of a discipline that he loved. His severe military
training transformed his appearance, as several biographers have
noted, and by the end of his schooling he had the proud, muscular,
self-confident look of an officer.[11] Like many of his classmates, Dreyfus chose the artillery, a key branch of the army that was then in the
throes of reorganization. He therefore entered the Ecole d'Application de l'Artillerie at Fontainebleau and, upon completion of his
training, served with the Thirty-first Artillery Regiment in Le Mans
before moving on to a Paris-based cavalry unit of the same regiment.
Despite good evaluations from his superiors, he apparently remained
somewhat aloof from his comrades. After being assigned to the
Twenty-first Artillery Regiment in Bourges, he spent the winter
preparing for the entrance examination to the Ecole de Guerre. He
wrote long, tender letters to Lucie Hadamard, who was the grand-
daughter of Captain Hatsfeld, who graduated from Polytechnique in
1835, and the sister of Captain Paul Hadamard, whom Dreyfus had
met at Polytechnique. On April 18, 1890, Alfred Dreyfus and Lucie
Hadamard were married in a civil ceremony. On April 20, Dreyfus
learned that he had been admitted to the Ecole de Guerre, and the
day after that he celebrated his marriage to Lucie Hadamard in a religious ceremony held at the synagogue on the rue de la Victoire with
Grand Rabbi Zadoc Kahn in attendance. The ceremony was symbolic
of Dreyfus's fate. On the one hand, he was a state Jew whose passionate devotion to the army, frequently displayed throughout his trial, ir-
ritated some of his supporters. On the other hand, in his private life
he faithfully observed the religious traditions of his family. In his
mind, these two dimensions of his being were perfectly compatible in
a Republic that triumphantly upheld the emancipatory ideals of the
French Revolution. At the Ecole de Guerre he worked on improving
military transportation in eastern France and on several possible sce-
narios for conflict with the German army occupying the lost provinces
of which he was a native. His personnel file contains the following
evaluation: "Rides a horse quite well; very good officer; quick mind;

grasps issues quite well; works easily and consistently. Well suited for staff duty."

In 1892, while Drumont was waging his campaign against Jewish officers, Dreyfus was completing his studies. He finished ninth in a class of eighty-one, a rank high enough to earn him a place as a *stagiaire*, or intern, on the army's general staff. An incident from this period reveals what kind of man he was. During his final examinations, General Pierre Bonnefond, a member of the jury, apparently stated that he did not want any Jews on the general staff, a remark explicitly aimed at Dreyfus and another Jewish officer by the name of Picard. As a result, Dreyfus's grade was deliberately lowered. He nevertheless did brilliantly on his exams. The next day, he boldly asked to see General Lebelin de Dionne, who assured him that the army took no account of religion. Dreyfus was reassured: he could count on republican meritocracy in pursuing a military career. Despite the vehemence of the anti-Semitic attacks he would endure during the Affair, he remained confident that the army of the Republic ultimately would not discriminate against a man because of his religion. During the ceremony attending his degradation, he shouted, "Soldiers, they are stripping the rank from an innocent man! Soldiers, they are dishonoring an innocent man! Long live France! Long live the army!" Less than ten years after his rehabilitation, he was back on active duty. Twenty years after his degradation, he took part in several World War I offensives, was deemed "an excellent superior officer," and received a promotion to the rank of lieutenant-colonel. On a battlefield near Verdun, he encountered his son, Lieutenant Pierre Dreyfus, who like his father had joined the fight to liberate the lost provinces.

During the Dreyfus Affair, of course, the nationalist camp backed the army's version of events, and as a result the army was associated in the popular mind with the anti-Semites and anti-Dreyfusards. Despite this, however, many Jewish officers apparently enjoyed relatively unproblematic careers, although some were not promoted as quickly as might have been expected. For example, Sylvain Dreyfus graduated from Polytechnique, became a captain in 1891, was assigned to the staff of the Corps of Engineers in 1894, and became a lieutenant-colonel in 1910. Similarly, Emile Dreyfus was promoted to lieutenant-colonel in the infantry in 1896; Paul Dreyfus, a graduate of both Polytechnique and the Ecole de Guerre, was promoted to captain in 1892 and assigned to the staff of the Thirty-second Infantry Division in the midst of Drumont's campaign against Jewish officers. He was promoted to squadron leader in 1897, lieutenant-colonel in 1907, and colonel in 1912, and he fought in World War I. In 1896, however, in the midst of the Dreyfus Affair, Paul Dreyfus sought and obtained a ministerial decision allowing him to change his last name from Dreyfus to Deslaurens.[12] His case was an exception, though. Looking back on the Affair long after the events, *L'Univers israélite* wrote: "For many Jewish officers the Dreyfus Affair was a trying moral dilemma, and if we were obliged on several occasions to deplore certain failures of nerve, the example set by those who, like General Weiller, refused to renounce or hide their Jewish origins is all the more remarkable."[13] In January 1895, when Dreyfus was stripped of his rank, several other Jewish officers were promoted to lieutenant, captain, or major. A few months later, in November 1895, others were promoted to lieutenant-colonel and even colonel; in July 1895, Colonel Samuel Naquet-Laroque was promoted to general. Toward the end of 1898, a terrible year that saw a groundswell of anti-Semitism in France, the War Ministry promoted several Jewish graduates of Polytechnique to the rank of sublieutenant of artillery. Of course these promotions should not be allowed to hide the fact that other Jewish officers who deserved promotions did not receive them. Some who should have been elevated to the highest ranks, including general, were not promoted until after 1905, when the Affair was more or less settled. Nevertheless, there appears to have been no major impediment during this period to decorating Jewish officers with the various grades of the Légion d'Honneur.[14]

Initially, therefore, the army seems to have been relatively immune to the effects of the anti-Semitic mobilization in the surrounding society. In January 1898, as violence flared in many French cities, Captain Seligmann of the First Artillery Regiment in Lille died suddenly of a ruptured aneurysm. He was buried with military honors in a ceremony attended by Grand Rabbi Emile Cahen, who was at the time leading protests against anti-Semitic violence and seeking ways to limit its spread. Among the mourners was a delegation of officers representing all branches of the army and led by Seligmann's battalion commander. Six artillerymen served as pallbearers, and three large wreaths, each carried by two artillerymen, were presented as gifts from the deceased's fellow officers. The hearse that carried the captain's body across the city was followed by the Grand Rabbi and then by the officers of the battalion led by their commander. Such a public ceremony was dramatic proof of the solidarity that existed among officers despite cultural and religious differences. At the height of the tempest, the "Holy Ark" (that is, the army) honored one of its own in the presence of the Grand Rabbi—and all this in a region where populist, anti-Semitic feeling had been running high ever since the beginnings of the Boulangist movement. At the synagogue on the rue de la Victoire, Grand Rabbi Zadoc Kahn led his congregation in celebrating the departure of Jews called up for military service. As if to underscore Jewish confidence in the army, the same rabbi also organized, "at the behest of former students of Polytechnique who belong to our congregation," a May 1894 service to celebrate the hundredth anniversary of the founding of that prestigious institution. Participants included numerous Jewish officers, generals, colonels, and teachers at the Ecole.[15]

Yet things were not as simple as they might appear. Outside the army, the anti-Semites were on the prowl. Not only did the nationalist press keep up its unrelenting attacks on Jewish officers, but there were almost daily demonstrations in the streets. In June 1893, for example, when a few Jewish candidates emerged from the examining room after taking the admission test for the military academy at Saint-Cyr, "a hundred students massed around the gate greeted them with shouts of 'Down with the Jews! To Palestine!' Then they sang an anti-Semitic song composed for the occasion."[16] In the Chamber of Deputies, a bill filed by Deputy Pontbriand went down to defeat, but not before garnering seventy-three votes. It stipulated that, "in order to be eligible for employment by the French government, or for a commission as an officer in the army or navy, or for election to an elective body, one must be French or the child of parents naturalized French for at least three generations." For the *Archives israélites*, "It is once again the murky affair of Captain Dreyfus that has given rise to the suspicions that cloud the current political climate."[17] Anti-Semitism was also spread by the nationalist papers, assisted by *La Croix*. On November 9, 1894, for example, *La Croix* published the following text: "Among the more noteworthy posts held by Jewish officers, Major Heumann is director of studies at the Ecole Spéciale Militaire of Saint-Cyr. There are more than a thousand commanders of infantry battalions, many of whom we know to be remarkable officers, studious men raised in the great military traditions. But they are not the ones chosen to train officers worthy of Turenne, Desaix, Bosquet, and Canrobert. It has to be a Jew."[18] In 1899, J.-M. Villefranche published a virulent nationalist pamphlet containing the following attack on Jewish officers: "Since they are intelligent and gifted, especially in mathematics, they have invaded our military schools. . . . Within twenty years, France will have at least a hundred Jewish colonels and generals. The country's defense will be in the hands of a general staff without a country."[19]

Ultimately, anti-Semitism destroyed the internal cohesion of the army to the point where seven Jews who graduated from Polytechnique in 1900 chose to resign from the army "because it become clear that they would inevitably meet with disappointment in their military careers." Other Jewish officers also opted for civilian life in the highly charged climate of the time.[20] Research has shown that between 1894 and 1906 five of sixteen noncommissioned officers with the last name Bloch resigned from the army, as did four of sixteen with the name Blum, sixteen of thirty-three with the name Lévy, and so on. For comparison, in the same period only eight of thirty Duponts quit.* General Justin Dennery, whose promotions had come more slowly than expected throughout his career, wrote to Captain André Boris: "I note with regret that not many [Jews] are entering

---

* Dupont is the French equivalent of Smith, whereas the others are all "Jewish" names. —TRANS.

Saint-Cyr or X [Polytechnique] lately. This is a mistake, because it plays into the hands of our enemies."[21] There were any number of anti-Semitic incidents. One led to the death of a cavalryman by the name of Bernard. In another case, eleven Jewish students at the Ecole de Fontainebleau were subjected to humiliations of various sorts. Somewhat later, General André, by then minister of war, noted in an official report to the Chamber that Jewish officers in some battalions had been interrogated as to their private religious beliefs: "One was confined to quarters until he produced his baptismal certificate. . . . One officer stated that he did not want Jews in the school. I transferred him. The school commander protested and asked to be relieved of his duties. In another school, an examiner gave a grade of fourteen to a Jewish candidate. The colonel who was chair of the jury said, 'I do not want to admit Jews. I give him a grade of two.'" General André also dealt at length with the case of Captain Picard. When a fellow officer in Orléans refused to return his salute, Picard made a point of it, and the other officer replied, "I don't salute Jews." Captain Picard sent his seconds, but the officer said, "I will not duel with a Jew." General André recounted what happened next:

> Captain Picard was assigned to the staff of an infantry division. There he was confined to quarters. The commanding general of the division drafted and sent to General Galliffet, the minister of war, a report stating that ugly rumors were circulating about the officer in question, whose morality was in doubt and who could not be trusted with national-defense secrets. The supporting evidence included the allegation that Captain Picard had refused to fight a duel with another officer, whom he had insulted. . . . Here is an officer who had charges against him for a year, charges that took a year to refute, and nothing less than a formal refutation was required to clear his name.

General André also told the deputies about a Lieutenant Gluck who was wrongly suspected of being Jewish because of his name and found himself confined to quarters by his regimental commander. As the *Archives israélites* pointed out, "Were it not for this frame of mind,

the Dreyfus Affair could never have gotten started. Those who persecute our coreligionists do not need secret files or confessions. A name
is enough to hinder their advancement."[22] Lieutenant-Colonel Weiss,
a native of the Bas-Rhin and a graduate of Saint-Cyr as well as the
brother of a *polytechnicien*, witnessed the degradation of Dreyfus and
became "indignant at the attitude of most of the Protestants, who
sided with the Jews."(He therefore chose to abjure his faith and convert to Catholicism. At the time of the Affair, he ran into a German officer who asked him why there was such hatred for Jewish officers in
the French army. Weiss responded: "How many Jewish officers are
there in the German army?" The German answered, "Oh, you know,
with us, such a thing is impossible," whereupon Weiss triumphantly
replied, "Well, then?"[23]

Still other instances of anti-Semitic behavior helped bring Franco-
French conflict into the bosom of the republican state. In Grenoble, a
number of officers thought that the base should cancel its subscription to *Le Figaro* when that paper took up the Dreyfusard cause; they
proposed a change to *La Libre Parole*. On December 15, 1897, these
officers signed a statement that was published in the officers' club
newsletter: "In view of the ignoble campaign that *Le Figaro* is waging
on behalf of Jews and traitors, we, the undersigned officers, demand
that our subscription be canceled at once." A Jewish colonel by the
name of Léon Francfort was outraged by this and lodged a vigorous
complaint. General Faure-Biguet, the base commander, informed his
superior, General Zédé, that, though he "shared the outrage of the
Grenoble garrison," he was not sure that such a decision would be legal. General Zédé then wrote to the Ministry of War, ending his letter
with the following remark: "These gentlemen wish to make a loud
public statement by canceling their subscription. I think they are
right. . . . I approve of the views of these officers." Meanwhile,
Colonel Francfort, whose personnel file noted that he was "impatient
with the predicament in which he sometimes finds himself on account
of his Jewish ancestry," tried in vain to maneuver his adversaries into
a duel.[24] In officers' messes across France, anti-Semitism grew increasingly overt in this period, and some anti-Dreyfusard officers
went so far as to dream of a "Saint Bartholomew's Day for the

Jews."*[25] Some personnel files reveal traces of this overt anti-Semitism: in 1899, at the height of the Affair, an inspector general's report on a Major Bloch noted that he was "highly intelligent, very hardworking . . . appreciated by those who employ him. Along with the qualities, however, he also shares the defects of his race. He is rather vulgar, never doubts himself for a moment, and shows off a lot."[26] To fan the flames throughout the Affair, *La Libre Parole* regularly published vitriolic attacks on Jewish officers, who were identified by name, just as in 1892. On November 2, 1894, the paper aimed its fire at seven officers named Dreyfus, five of whom were serving in the artillery. On November 4, it railed against the Blochs and Cahens who occupied choice positions on the general staff or at military-training schools. On November 6, Drumont described his 1892 articles as "in some ways prophetic." On November 8 and 10, *La Libre Parole* continued its offensive against Jewish officers, concluding thus: "If one looks among the corporals, the mechanics, the gunners, and the other modest and brave soldiers of the line, one finds not a single Jew." *La Libre Parole* would remain faithful to its vocation: in November 1898, it launched yet another offensive against Jewish army officers, once again identifying them by name.[27]

A second example is worth recounting in detail. It involves Colonel Edmond Mayer. Born in Nancy into a family with deep roots in eastern France, Mayer was the son of a *polytechnicien* with very traditional Jewish values. He was accepted by both the Ecole Normale Supérieure and the Ecole Polytechnique but chose to attend the latter "for the sake of *la revanche*"—that is, because he hoped to help France recapture its lost provinces. A friend of Joffre and Foch, the famous World War I generals, he would also become an authority on warfare whose writings were among those that Charles de Gaulle most respected. It was from Mayer that de Gaulle learned of the importance of aviation, and in conversations between the two world wars, the two men regularly discussed the advantages of various military strategies and the use of new types of weapons. This brilliant officer was nevertheless summarily retired from the army in May 1899 be-

* That is, a massacre. —TRANS.

cause of articles he published about the Dreyfus Affair, and it took
nothing less than the full support of the Ligue des Droits de l'Homme
et du Citoyen to have him restored to the ranks. His career suffered
as a result, and during World War I he served only in the rank of
colonel; two of his sons, also officers, died in the conflict. In a personal letter dated December 25, 1894, he wrote, "The Dreyfus Affair
has kept me in a fever for several days. I had hoped, in spite of everything, for a unanimous acquittal. Hence the guilty verdict momentar-
ily threw me for a loop. . . . Can it be that the court-martial reached a
verdict contrary to its conscience and failed to scout out its religion
sufficiently? But that would be more criminal than treason itself:
complicity on the part of seven individuals would be terrible." Later,
in February 1898, he wrote, "It makes no difference to me personally
if Dreyfus is guilty. What does bother me is to have doubts that he
is. . . . In this whole business there is such a jumble of interests, such
a tangle of lies, such an accumulation of contradictions, that I cannot find any clear thread." Mayer had himself encountered anti-
Semitism: in 1890, General Mathieu, chief of artillery at the Ministry
of War, had refused to appoint him as instructor at Saint-Cyr "because he was afraid of being attacked by Edouard Drumont." In his
private diary, Mayer linked the anti-Semitic campaign against Dreyfus to his failure to obtain the post he wanted. As proof of the profes-
sionalism of Jewish officers, who made a point in military matters of
forgetting that they were Jewish, he recounted an incident from 1892
that had put him into private correspondence with Captain Dreyfus.
The subject was a cousin of Dreyfus's whose application for a leave
Mayer had turned down. In his letter, Mayer noted that Dreyfus's
cousin was "obliged as a Jew to set a good example, since his coreligionists are the target of a certain hostility. . . . Since he is serving in
a battery commanded by a Jew, he should have felt obliged to be especially diligent about not placing his commander in a difficult position." Captain Dreyfus's response was direct: "I totally agree with
you. I am sorry that you have not been more satisfied with my cousin's
behavior. As you say, he should be setting an example. Under the
present circumstances, we have to show that we are as good as the
others, if not better." Despite this contact with Dreyfus, Mayer "took

no part in the campaign for a review of the verdict," and it was only after the Court of Appeals published its revelations about the so-called Henry forgery that Mayer expressed shock at "the impudence with which they piled lies upon lies." He then published an article in *Le Figaro* in which he stated that the depositions of certain generals contained falsehoods, and somewhat later he published additional articles critical of France's military strategy. After Deputy Lasies rose in the Chamber to accuse him of slandering the army, Mayer was removed from active duty. On June 11, 1899, Emile Boutmy, who had been his teacher and remained his friend, wrote him on the letterhead of the Ecole Libre des Sciences Politiques, the institution he so brilliantly headed:

> I have just learned of the deplorable manner in which you have been treated. . . . I now recognize the inexhaustible rage of anti-Semitism. It seems that one must bow one's head, but when one does it falls on a bosom swollen with silent resentment and mounting anger. When the Cour de Cassation, despite its initial resistance, was obliged to recognize the truth and proclaim it out loud, I had no idea that my joy would soon be so tarnished. . . . You should know at least that all decent people are with you and share your suffering in this ordeal. . . . Oh, dear friend, what times we live in! It is comforting to think that death is near and that soon it will close my eyes and spare me the unbearable sight of men and things.[28]

The dismissal of Colonel Mayer came just a few months after *La Libre Parole* launched its drive to aid the widow of Colonel Henry. Henry had of course committed suicide after his role in fabricating evidence against Dreyfus was discovered. When Joseph Reinach published an account of Henry's part in covering up Esterhazy's treason, Henry's widow threatened to sue for slander, and Drumont's newspaper set itself the mission of drumming up support for the suit. Bear in mind that Henry was an officer who had risen through the ranks, not a brilliant graduate of Polytechnique or one of the other top military schools. Dreyfus and Henry thus stand as symbols of two radically different types of army career.[29] Did Henry's zeal in pursuing Dreyfus reflect the frustration of others like him, officers risen through the ranks who looked on with mounting irritation as men like Dreyfus, many of them Jewish, rose rapidly to staff positions owing to their intellectual abilities? In any case, as Pierre Quillard observed after studying the eighteen lists of contributors to the fund established by *La Libre Parole*, "The 'pretorian' army by itself accounted for more than a tenth of the names." Indeed, it may have accounted for more than that if one allows for those who were associated with the military in one way or another. Stephen Wilson suggests that as many as a third of the signers had military connections, whereas this group accounted for no more than 3 percent of the total active population.[30] The high proportion of military contributors is all the more striking since Freycinet, the minister of war, had explicitly forbidden members of the armed forces to contribute to the fund.

An examination of the long lists of names making up the so-called Henry Monument shows that the army did indeed occupy an important place. Among those on active duty who dared to make a public contribution, we find five generals, nine colonels and lieutenant-colonels, twelve majors, and fifty-four captains, including witnesses who testified against Dreyfus in the Rennes trials, along with sixty-five lieutenants including the future General Weygand. Although these men were officers on active duty, they were not afraid to disclose their vehement anti-Semitic sentiments by offering support to Henry's widow. An even larger number of contributors were soldiers in the reserve: among them were thirty generals, including General Mercier, the former minister of war, fifty-six colonels and lieutenant-colonels, seventy-six majors, 129 captains, and so on. Among those who did not sign their full names but indicated only their ranks and initials, we find ten additional generals, forty-three colonels and lieutenant-colonels, thirty-seven majors, and 293 captains, together with an indeterminate number of captains who signed as a group. A long list of commissioned and noncommissioned officers contained thousands of additional names with no indication of rank. Countless soldiers from the ranks also contributed, some signing only as "soldiers of Christ" while others indicated simply that they were veterans of this or that celebrated battle. Still others signed as "future dragoon," "future cuirassier," or "future soldier of France."

Other lists contained the names of numerous graduates of Polytechnique, and some of these names were accompanied by notations such as "a *polytechnicien* contemporary of Dreyfus's" or "a *polytechnicien* from Dreyfus's class." There were also numerous graduates of France's military academy at Saint-Cyr, including a "group of Saint-Cyrians" and "a Saint-Cyrian anti-Semite." And there were many students from various other military schools. An impressively large number of contributors signed simply as the father, mother, brother, sister, or daughter of an officer, and there were also groups of people with family ties to the military (such as "the wives of officers of the Magnac-Laval garrison"). One also finds a substantial number of sons and grandsons of officers, and even one group of "five orphaned sons and daughters of officers." Some officers' wives described themselves as such; others added details such as "the wife of a general officer in the east and mother of two officers" or "the wives and daughters of cuirassiers." Some officers' valets also signed: thus we find "two batmen of Captain Marchand" and "two former army employees." At the other end of the social hierarchy, many nobles gave their titles and ranks. Among them were Georges de Grandmaison, deputy from Ille-et-Vilaine, Lieutenant-Colonel du Halgouet, and the Comte de Chassy, the Comte des Isnards, the Comte de Villechaise, Max de Saint-Pastou, and many others. Numerous sons, daughters, brothers, wives, and mothers of noble officers sent money to *La Libre Parole*. All this signaled a fairly broad rejection of Jews by the military.

Often that rejection was bluntly expressed, but it was not so much the generals and colonels as the captains, lieutenants, and privates who were likely to go in for public anti-Semitic diatribes. Some of the choicer phrases that accompanied contributions to the Henry fund are worth mentioning. There was "a captain who advises the wretch Dreyfus never to return to France." And there was another "captain from the east who teaches his men about the morality of kikes." There was also the "artillery lieutenant who would like to see all the kikes boiled in oil." And another artillery lieutenant who simply wanted to add his voice to the chorus of those who shouted "France to the French!" And the "poor officer who would give a year's pension to see all the kikes kicked out of France." And the cavalry officer who bellowed, "After the Jews! Attack! Charge! Death to traitors! Long live France for the French!" And the "group of hussar officers who cannot understand why Jews are allowed on the general staff." And the "deeply anti-Dreyfusard reserve officer who asks for nothing more than a chance to massacre the filthy kikes." And then there was the "group of officers impatiently awaiting the order to try out our new explosives and cannons on the hundred thousand Jews who are poisoning the country." And the "group of officers who are hoping for the extermination of the Jews." And the "officer who is of a mind to shoot the Dreyfusard ringleaders and chase the yids out of France. This is the way to save the country." And the "noncom who wants to contribute to the purchase of the most powerful of disinfectants to clean out all the places in France contaminated by the presence of the weasel Dreyfus, the rattlesnake Picquart, the rat Reinach, and the skunk Zola." And another "noncom who gives free boxing lessons to anybody who wants to fight the filthy kikes." And a "group of noncoms from a regiment in the southwest who would be happy to sweep France clean of Jews." And, finally, the "republican guardsman who knows how to cook and would be only too happy to make a Reinach stew to poison all the kikes and Dreyfusards." Such a sampling only scratches the surface.

This verbal violence, which was accompanied by a good deal of physical violence as well, tells us something about the origins of the leagues and other anti-Semitic nationalist movements whose legacy would ultimately pass to the Action Française. Yet these movements clearly failed: the Republic was able to defend its institutions and, in the end, to fight off the dissenters who seized on the Dreyfus Affair and anti-Semitism as a means to their ultimate goal, which was to get rid of the Republic itself. Secure in its strength and certain of its legitimacy, the Republic would eventually rehabilitate Dreyfus at the very moment it decided to enforce the separation of church and state, thereby delineating all the more clearly the boundaries of the public sphere in which all citizens were welcome to participate. Despite brief flare-ups, this antirepublican nationalism was ultimately absorbed into a broad patriotic front against Germany, thus heralding the reconciliation of the families of France that Maurice Barrès would extol during World War I. Yet, even though the war helped to integrate Jews who fought alongside other Frenchmen in defense of the nation, there were still outbreaks of anti-Semitism within the ranks, though relatively muted in comparison with what had gone before.[31]

Of course, national mobilization for war always tends to damp down ideological differences. Nevertheless, Drumont went right on denouncing Jewish officers in the pages of *La Libre Parole*, which continued to publish a regular column on the subject. In 1905, when Mardochée Valabrègue was promoted to general and named director of the Ecole Supérieure de Guerre, Drumont commented bitterly that the new general was "Dreyfus's cousin."[32] By contrast, the *Archives israélites* expressed joy at the news: "Oh, bitter irony! Once upon a time, orders were given that [Jewish] officers should be excluded from the Ecole Supérieure de Guerre, and one of the main objectives of the Dreyfus Affair was to make the glaring injustice of this apparent to all. Now the honor of directing that famous school has been bestowed on a Jewish general. Ten years separate the Dreyfus Affair from the appointment of General Valabrègue, an abyss! What a reverse for the anti-Semites and the naïve Catholics who docilely dogged their steps!"[33] *La Libre Parole* stubbornly persisted, however, and in January 1913 it was still asking, "Which side of the border would Dreyfus be on in case of a dustup?" With unconcealed regret, Drumont's paper was obliged to admit: "The anti-Jewish idea came close to triumph during the Dreyfus Affair. It might have triumphed if among our generals there had been one with a little determination and a little nerve. But none of our leaders stepped forward to answer the call from Paris, which cried out with virtually one voice, 'Down with the Jews!' "[34] It would not be long, though, before a military leader of stature would step forward with resolution enough to impose a regime embodying the "anti-Jewish idea," and thereby to secure for Drumont a posthumous victory.

9

JEWS, ITALIANS, AND ARABS:
PUBLIC VIOLENCE AND PRIVATE VIOLENCE

Shortly before the end of the nineteenth century, France experienced outbreaks of both powerful xenophobia and virulent anti-Semitism. Each implied rejection of outsiders, but in a distinct form, and both developed against a background of rising nationalism and dangerous economic crisis. The "foreigner" was both a contentious public issue and a pretext for numerous demonstrations. The Jewish population, which at this point consisted mainly of French citizens, was put on notice by the charges against Captain Dreyfus. Emancipated by the Revolution, Jews had ostensibly enjoyed the same rights as other French citizens ever since. Patriotic, they had suffered, along with their compatriots, deep humiliation at France's defeat in the Franco-Prussian War. Many had lost no time in making up their minds to evacuate the eastern provinces now occupied by Germany, and most of those who left settled in or around Paris. Thus the rejection of outsiders affected Jewish citizens of France who were eligible to vote in elections and run for office, as well as foreigners, whose numbers were rising rapidly despite an acute and worsening crisis of unemployment.

Between 1866 and 1891, the number of foreign-born persons, most of them workers, residing in France increased from 653,036 to 1,130,211. Of these, 43 percent were Belgian and 24 percent Italian (the number of Italians tripled between 1872 and 1891). Most of the immigrants were young unmarried males. The bulk of the Italian contingent found employment in either chemicals, mining, metals, or construction. Highly concentrated in certain specific areas, such as the southeast, the Lyons region, and the area around Grenoble, these Italians met with periodic open hostility, mainly from French workers worried about competition for jobs but also influenced by nationalism in one form or another (including Boulangism). The nationalist movements were tinged with populism, which allowed for easy mixing of the extreme left and extreme right. In a time of harsh economic and political competition between Italy and France, anti-Italian feeling manifested classic symptoms of xenophobia: fear of treason and espionage, fantasies of invasion, sexual fear of seduction and abandonment of vulnerable girls by predatory males, nervousness about Southern indolence leading to various types of perversion, charges of unfairness to French co-workers, undue compliance with unreasonable demands by employers, and so on. In an effort not to lose touch with the rank-and-file, most unions and working-class political organizations echoed these xenophobic sentiments and, despite their internationalist principles, chose to champion the interests of French workers to the exclusion of others. In May 1882, Jules Guesde alluded to the success of socialists in the United States in repelling the "yellow hordes" from American shores: "In our view they've done the right thing. . . . We would be insulting our proletariat if we were to suggest even for a moment that in similar circumstances we would hesitate to do the same thing."[1] As Michelle Perrot points out, "French workers tended toward nationalism in their relations with immigrants. . . . Clashes with foreign workers had in very concrete ways laid the groundwork for a crystallization of nationalist sentiment."[2] Xenophobic feeling in this period was directed toward Belgian workers but even more toward Italians, who faced an extremely hostile and well-organized opposition.)

From brawls to riots, and from nationalist marches to anti-immigrant strikes, Italian immigrants faced constant hostility, which at times took a dramatic turn. The list of incidents is long: of eighty-nine antiforeign confrontations recorded between 1867 and 1893, sixty-seven involved Italians—mainly construction workers, longshoremen, and miners, these being trades in which violence was endemic. On June 18, 1881, during a parade of troops returning from Tunisia, which the French had just occupied, trouble erupted in Marseilles. In an episode that was quickly dubbed the "Marseillian vespers," a mob of several thousand swooped down on a group of Italian laborers and chased them across the city. Bodies were thrown into the bay. A few days later, on June 24, French longshoremen managed to persuade the authorities to send the Italians home after a series of violent attacks carried out by mobs of French workers carrying the tricolor and shouting, "*Vive la France!*" On February 13, 1882, Italian construction workers in Uzès and Alès were attacked, and many were seriously wounded. A few were savagely beaten to death. During that same year, there were also stabbings.

But it was in August 1893 that there occurred at Aigues-Mortes a veritable massacre, a French-style pogrom whose victims were Italian immigrants. After a series of violent incidents, the authorities had agreed to provide an armed escort for a group of Italian workers who wished to leave the area with their families. According to a report filed by the captain of the *gendarmerie*, a gang of assailants "armed with clubs, revolvers, and rifles" attacked the convoy, while a mob of six hundred bludgeoned the wounded with clubs and rocks. "The hostility of the French workers . . . was so ferocious that any Italian who became separated from the group was systematically slaughtered." The official death toll of eight Italians was certainly far short of the actual number killed. A *London Times* dispatch mentioned fifty killed and more than 150 wounded. The hospital at Aigues-Mortes could not handle all the wounded, and many were sent to Nîmes and Marseilles. And the violence did not end there: on the night of June 24, 1894, thousands of people, upon learning that President Carnot's assassin, the anarchist Caserio, had an Italian-sounding name, set upon a group of Italian immigrants in Lyons, forcing them to run for their lives; pogroms were just barely avoided in Arles in

1896, near Arles in 1897, at the Solvay factory a short time later, and in Aubagne in 1899. In Lorraine in 1905, signs were posted on the walls of one steel mill: "Down with the Italboches!" and "Down with the bears!" A "Gaul" asked the mayor to "hasten the exit" of a "black bear escaped from a Milan zoo" and ended with the familiar cry, "France for the French and not for the foreigner!" Many Italians were expelled from the country. Everywhere there were protests against the Italian "invasion," to use a word from the title of a popular anti-immigrant pamphlet by Louis Bertrand. Italian workers were accused of polluting France with their decadent ways. One Lorraine newspaper described "filthy old ladies with wrinkled skin and sparse hair. . . . Animals killed by disease . . . find their burial place in the stomachs of Italians. . . . Such diabolical cooking may still get by in Italy, but things are different in Lorraine, where the Italians' chronic filth and deplorable life-style poses a serious threat of contamination to the native population."[3]

In the years just before the turn of the twentieth century, Belgian, Spanish, and Gypsy workers were also victims of lynchings and beatings. Foreigners were legally barred from access to certain professions, and various groups urged the authorities to limit the number of foreign workers. Derogatory names such as "wop," "Bedouin," "Zulu," and "dago" were applied to them. Antiforeign sentiment ran high. It was against this background that the Dreyfus Affair erupted, fanning the flames of an anti-Semitism already exacerbated by financial disasters such as the Union Générale crash and the Panama scandal. The atmosphere was further poisoned by populist demonstrations in which socialists joined with radicals of the extreme right to denounce the Rothschilds, the Opportunists (who had allegedly sold out to the Jews), and the government of the corrupt.

But can we really compare xenophobic hostility toward Italian immigrants to anti-Semitism, which affected mainly French citizens? To be sure, there were some Jewish immigrants from Eastern Europe, and although there were fewer of them than Italians, they, too, were often scorned and mistreated. A well-known incident took place in August 1892 at the Gare de Lyon, for example. But Jewish immigrants were not the target of murderous attacks.[4] Anti-Italian feeling, though marginal in political terms, often led to murder, whereas anti-Semitism, which had long been a controversial issue for the French, did not lead to killings despite the existence of large and unruly anti-Semitic crowds, and despite the fact that the nationalist leagues and anti-Semitic press openly called for "death to the Jews." Although Jews were accused of spying for Germany, just as Italians were accused of spying for Italy, the consequences within France were very different. The Italian immigrants lived mainly in border regions, in Marseilles, Nice, and the smaller cities of the southeast. Most were unskilled laborers who competed directly with French workers, and on both sides were men accustomed to settling their personal and collective quarrels with violence.

At the time of the Dreyfus Affair, by contrast, most Jews were French citizens. Early immigrants had been assimilated, and between 1881 and 1896 Jewish immigration slowed to a trickle. Only seven or eight thousand Jews sought refuge in France from pogroms in Russia and Austria-Hungary. French Jews had pursued integration through the schools since the beginning of the nineteenth century. They had entered the liberal professions and achieved elective office on both the national and the local level. Others joined the judicial and military elites. They were deeply involved in building the Third Republic. Although many continued to honor Jewish traditions privately, they also adopted the values of the surrounding society. Two-thirds of them lived in the Paris region and melted into the population of the big city (apart from the Marais quarter, which remained something of a ghetto). Their communal presence was further diminished by the fact that many were self-employed as tradesmen, merchants, doctors, and lawyers. By this time, few Jews lived in small border towns where they would have been more exposed, as the Italians were. And although there were still substantial numbers of Jews in Alsace and Lorraine, they supported the return of the lost provinces to France and were thus in harmony with their neighbors.

Jewish professionals, tradesmen, merchants, teachers, and students did compete with other Frenchmen, who made no secret of their desire to exclude Jews from coveted jobs. Yet these competitors were less prone to violence than were men put out of work or driven from their farms by industrialization. To rid themselves of unwanted competition, they tended to rely more on concerted political action, such as that sponsored by the leagues. And unlike the workers, they were opposed by a republican state determined to perpetuate its own power and limit the unpredictable consequences of anti-Semitic and antirepublican agitation. Although Italian immigrants were often protected by the police and the bureaucracy, as at Aigues-Mortes, the authorities in many small rural towns were outnumbered and hard-pressed to control heavily armed, violence-prone demonstrators. By contrast, the huge mobs that shouted "Death to the Jews!" contented themselves with marching in the streets, breaking windows, and damaging property; they did not resort to firearms. Surprisingly, then, the mass anti-Semitism of the late nineteenth century, encouraged by a venomous press and by leagues that recruited thousands of hot-headed anti-Semites, caused relatively few deaths. With the exception of a few Jews slain in riots in Algeria, one has to go all the way back to 1832 to find a case in which two Jews died in political violence inside metropolitan France.

One final difference between anti-Italian xenophobia and anti-Semitism is rather surprising at first sight: when French workers attacked Italian immigrants, they often shouted "Death to the Cristos!" The Italians were still deeply religious, whereas French workers, particularly in the south and southeast, had largely turned their backs on religion. The clash of values was particularly symbolic at a time of intense struggle over the separation of church and state, but it remained purely social and never became political. By contrast, the vast majority of Jews approved of the secularization of the public sphere. Thus the hatred directed against them by many Catholic groups with support from professionals, students, and merchants was almost always reinforced by antipathy to the republican government and its policy of secularization. The clash was primarily about the public sphere, and the issue was one of national politics. The level of direct, personal animosity was probably lower, however. Hence it was easier for the police, themselves in the throes of reorganization, to control. So, whereas displaced workers felt compelled to attack their Italian immigrant competitors directly, the mobs of anti-Semites

Social for Italians — political for Jews

seemed content to wait until they had gained control of the government to achieve their ends. The republican state withstood their pressure, but when the Republic itself was dissolved by Vichy, extermination of the Jews at last became possible with the help of a state apparatus hijacked by nationalist ideologues.

More recently, between January 1980 and the end of 1994, twenty-six people of North African ancestry were killed in racist incidents in France and 351 were injured. Most of these incidents took place either in the Paris region or in the south and southeast. As the Commission Nationale Consultative des Droits de l'Homme has observed, "Unlike anti-Semitism, which is not reflected in these comprehensive statistics, these racist incidents often pose a grave physical threat to individual victims. The North African population has consistently been one of the primary targets."[5] Beyond the constant racist threats (160 reported in 1994) and anti-Muslim tracts, pamphlets, and graffiti, to say nothing of vandalism against mosques, racist violence has gone from an already high level in 1981 to an even greater number of incidents in 1993. This increase is related to the rise of the "skinhead" movement, as well as to the growth of nationalist organizations and the prevalence of xenophobic violence in Eastern Europe. Persons of North African descent have been the primary target of this racist violence.

On November 16, 1983, three legionnaires threw a young North African out the window of a train traveling from Bordeaux to Ventimiglia. He died instantly. On August 20, 1984, in Haubourdin, another North African was killed by a sympathizer of the National Front. The machine-gunning of a bar in Chateaubriant in that same year killed two Turks and left two others wounded. In May and June 1986, there was a series of bombings in southeastern France. A group calling itself the Commandos de France Contre l'Invasion Maghrébine took credit. A member of this group was killed when a bomb went off in his car. On March 6, June 5, and November 30, bars frequented by North Africans were attacked in Le Petit-Quevilly and Caen, leaving one person dead and five wounded. On December 19, 1988, a dormitory owned by Sonacotra (a private company dedicated to housing foreign workers throughout France) was blown up in

Cagnes-sur-Mer, killing one person and injuring two others. On January 28, 1989, a young French citizen of North African descent was killed in a bar in Montataire. On May 8, an attempt was made to kill a young Tunisian, who was seriously wounded in the incident. In 1993, seven soldiers severely beat three North Africans and sent six high-school students of North African descent to the hospital. In April, another immigrant adolescent was killed by the police at Wattrelos, and a seventeen-year-old Zairean died of a gunshot wound inflicted inside a Paris police station. On September 26, two young North Africans were savagely beaten, then doused with gasoline and set on fire by skinheads. They suffered severe burns about the face and hands. On February 5, 1994, a Moroccan garbage collector was fatally wounded by gunshots fired from a passing car. On the warm summer night of July 13, 1994, seven members of a heavy-metal band, including one of Asian descent, decided to "beat up some blacks or Arabs." They deliberately threw Diera Idrissa, a Malian aged thirty-five, into the Canal Saint-Martin in Paris, where he drowned. In Ault, in the Amiens region, on August 6 of that year, Abederraman Rabah, the son of a *harki* (that is, an Algerian who had worked for the French during the war), was beaten up after a dance by a gang of French youths and then tossed over a cliff; he died instantly. Shortly thereafter, during a police interrogation in Manosque, a policeman (himself the son of a *harki*) killed a young Algerian with a shot fired at point-blank range. Then, in November, a young Turk fatally stabbed Stéphane Di Vincenzo, an adolescent born in Haute-Loire. On Sunday, February 5, 1995, a young man of Berber descent killed a young *beur*, or second-generation Arab, with a rifle shot after a friendly soccer game. On May 7, a French citizen of Tunisian descent drowned in Le Havre after being attacked by a gang of skinheads that included a youth of Portuguese descent. The picture is clear: from the nineteenth century to the present, immigrants and the children of immigrants, whether from Italy or Africa, have been obliged to contend with a high level of "private" violence, at times perpetrated by immigrants themselves.

This "private" violence at the grass roots has also called forth defensive measures by the authorities. In the late 1930s, Italian and

Spanish immigrants were stripped of their French citizenship papers.[6] The same thing happened in the 1940s to recently naturalized Jews, and even to some who had long enjoyed French citizenship. More recently, North Africans have been summarily deported. Thus public—or, more properly, state-sponsored—violence has also been directed against immigrants, but it has been violence of a different kind from public anti-Semitic violence. Leaving aside extreme situations in which the Republic itself was erased from the scene, Jews, most of whom had been citizens of France for many generations, did not have to fear deportation and were never physically violated as a result of xenophobic policies carried out by law-enforcement authorities. Because of their close ties to the state, these Jews chiefly feared the "reactive" public violence of extremist movements determined to redefine France's national identity in terms of certain exclusionary cultural or ethnic criteria. Recent anti-Semitic actions by the extreme right have been no more serious. Bombings and physical assaults on Jews remain rare. By contrast, incidents of vandalism against Jewish property are numerous, as are threats, insults, and acts of intimidation. Since the 1980s, anti-Semitic violence has almost always been associated with international terrorism, from the bombing of the synagogue on the rue Copernic to the bombing of a Jewish restaurant on the rue des Rosiers.[7] Apart from upsurges linked to international events such as the Gulf War, anti-Semitic violence has been on the decline; most incidents have involved vandalism against Jewish cemeteries and synagogues. The numbers of acts of intimidation, anti-Semitic pamphlets, and instances of anti-Semitic graffiti have been on the rise, however. Once again, the areas most affected have been the Paris region and the south and southeast. Concern in Jewish circles has been rising, not only because of actual incidents but also as a result of the publicity given to revisionist works about the Holocaust, allegations in the nationalist press, ambiguous comments made by certain public figures, epithets shouted at certain sporting events, and fears that anti-Semitism in Eastern Europe might spread to France.

Polls show that 89 percent of the French believe that racism is "fairly or extremely widespread" in France today, and that 68 percent have personally witnessed racist remarks. Two out of three French admit to being "somewhat" or "a little" racist, and the same proportion concede that they have either "rarely, occasionally, or frequently" made racist remarks or exhibited racist attitudes. For 48 percent, such attitudes are entirely justifiable, and nearly 70 percent believe that "there are too many Arabs in France." *Beurs* are regarded as "relatively unpleasant" by 54 percent, and just under 20 percent feel hostility toward Jews. With attitudes such as these so widespread, one has to fear that in a more highly charged political climate more violent forms of rejection might manifest themselves.[8] Among those who feel close to the National Front or who "often" vote for it or other extreme-right-wing candidates, 80 percent subscribe to racist, anti-Semitic values. An even larger segment of the population embraces "ethnocentric" views: half of those who score high on one measure of ethnocentrism have never voted for the National Front. Ethnocentrism is apparent in both the moderate right and on the left of the political spectrum, though its consequences are different. It is especially prevalent on the extreme left, which draws much of its support from relatively disadvantaged groups. If "anti-immigrant racism and anti-Semitism are prejudices of the same nature, which originate in the same milieux and are fostered by the same factors,"[9] it is nevertheless also true that anti-Jewish prejudices are less likely to be acted on in France, whereas the inhibitions against acting out racist prejudices are far less powerful.

Still, the decline of the schools and the army as powerful institutions of socialization, and the diminished influence of such powerful agencies of social control as the Church and the Communist Party, may well encourage an exclusionary populism directed against both foreigners and Jews. France nevertheless remains a relatively protected exception, since—paradoxically, in light of the foregoing— 80 percent of the French nowadays stress the importance of human rights and 73 percent believe that a teacher who expresses racist views in the classroom should be fired. Hence now, as in the past—as always, except during the Vichy years—public anti-Semitic violence remains unlikely. Anti-Semitism is still symbolic, a sort of absolute protest against the presence of Jews within the nation. When it is directed against cemeteries and synagogues, it is tantamount to a call to arms aimed at eliminating Jews from the public sphere by political means.[10] By contrast, racism and xenophobia always issue in extreme violence exacerbated by unremitting hatred of outsiders.

PART THREE

THE UNKNOWN PRESENT

10

ON SECULARISM

On January 15, 1994, French leftists turned out in large numbers to march from the Place de la République in Paris to the Place de la Nation. These two sites are long-standing symbols of the left, to which it habitually returns whenever it wants to make a show of force and reaffirm its identity. In this case, the immediate cause for alarm was an unanticipated threat to the public schools. Even when the right-wing government retreated in the face of the massive protest, the left was not appeased. Among the slogans shouted by the thousands of anticlerical demonstrators bent on preserving open public education were these: "Freedom means secular schools!" "Priests go home!" "Down with the clergy!" "No to segregation! Yes to the nation's schools!" "No to the Americanization of the French school system!" "Republican schools: neither chadors nor crucifixes!"[1] It was the sudden and unexpected modification of the old Falloux Law, in December 1993, that had reignited the school wars in France by threatening to undermine the principle of secular education that had reigned in France ever since the Third Republic, when religion was relegated to the private sphere. Religious teaching had then been excluded from the public schools, which were assigned the mission of shaping the minds of citizens in a nation that saw itself as the embodiment of the Enlightenment faith in reason alone. But in 1993, after a right-wing victory at the polls, the law had been changed so as to benefit private schools, most of them religious. This provoked an immediate mobilization in defense of secular education, as demonstrators poured into the streets all across France.

The Church had greeted the new law with undisguised enthusiasm, for it had hoped that it would lead to an expansion of private education in a country where 95 percent of private schools were Church-affiliated. Protestants openly worried about increased Catholic influence, and Muslims worried even more that, in the face of rising xenophobic sentiment, local governments would steer funds away from their schools. By contrast, neither the rabbis of France nor the Jewish Consistory adopted a clear position. The reason for this hesitation was that Jewish attitudes toward secular education had evolved considerably in recent years. Grand Rabbi Joseph Sitruck had made it known as early as November 16, 1993, that he was opposed to "aggressive secularism."[2] He hoped that young Jews would be allowed to wear yarmulkes in public schools if they wished, and he made no secret of his hope that Jews, following the same strategy as Catholics, might develop their own system of private schools. By contrast, another Jewish organization, the Comité Représentatif des Institutions Juives en France, or CRIF, criticized the Grand Rabbi's position on the grounds that "private education should be developed, but this must be done in accordance with republican principles. There is no fundamentalist secularism. . . . No one denies the fundamental importance of Jewish education, but neither can anyone in the Jewish community accept the notion that a unified, secular Republic today constitutes a danger to freedom of religious expression, for history has demonstrated the contrary: the Republic is in fact the guarantor of religious freedom."[3]

The change in the Falloux Law came at a time when Jewish schools were expanding at the unprecedented rate of 5 to 10 percent annually. In the late 1980s, it was estimated that, out of a hundred thousand Jewish children of school age, seventeen thousand were attending Jewish schools.[4] Before World War II, there were only two Jewish schools in all of France, but by 1994, Jewish schools were educating more than twenty thousand students. The system of Ozar-Hatorah schools was growing steadily. Two new Jewish technical high schools were established, essentially independent of the secular-educational authorities. This rapid expansion, which was temporarily slowed when regional officials balked at financing a new Jewish school under construction in Paris's nineteenth *arrondissement*, had not been without problems, now exacerbated by an impending shortage of funds.[5] When the government repeatedly refused to provide financial aid for the construction of a Lubavitcher *lycée*, the community bridled and chose to raise the money itself, thereby ensuring full control of the curriculum. While the extreme right railed against this "rapidly growing fundamentalist community," the socialists and communists justified their refusal to subsidize the new religious school as a defense of the principle of secular education. The ecologists also refused to approve the subsidy, and their spokesman, Guy Konopnicki, stated that, though "some people may want to return to the ghetto voluntarily, they can't make me vote to build its walls with public funds." Everyone had his own interpretation of "secular." After the grant was denied, the head of the Union Intercommunitaire for the Paris region made his feelings plain: "I am a republican and therefore in favor of secularism. But when secularism denies a minority its freedom of expression, I wonder if we don't need to rethink it. If we don't, it will become more and more difficult for minority cultures and religions to make themselves heard."[6]

The Falloux Law was already quite favorable to the Catholic schools, and for Jews and other religious minorities the implications of changing it were contradictory. The new law might have encouraged the construction of additional Jewish schools, but more likely it would have slowed such construction, because, with the grant of more discretionary powers to local governments, the bulk of available funds would most likely be funneled to the Catholic schools. When some local governments did provide financial aid to Jewish schools, they stirred up strong anti-Semitic reactions. In Aix-les-Bains, for example, a famous yeshiva had been in existence since 1945. Over the years it added a kindergarten, a primary school, and a seminary for girls, which together served more than five hundred students. All male students of these institutions wore the yarmulke both inside the classroom and out. But when the municipal council met in November 1989 to vote on renting city land for a new Jewish school, one local official stated that some of his constituents were "worried": "Even if we have no problems with the fully integrated Jews, we may have trouble with the fundamentalists." This anti-Semitic statement provoked a vigorous debate. Although the mayor strongly condemned the comment, he publicly worried that the new school might be the occasion of a "religious war."[7]

The change in the law might also have done further damage to the public schools, thus shutting off one of the key traditional routes by which Jews had joined modern society. Since the early nineteenth century, in fact, French Jews had availed themselves of the meritocratic standards of the public schools to climb the rungs of the social hierarchy. Many had started in public kindergartens, attended public *lycées*, and worked their way up as far as the Ecole Normale Supérieure, the Ecole Polytechnique, and other prestigious institutions. So a great deal was at stake. Faced with the contradictory implications of the new law, Jews remained noticeably silent. Although they were not happy to see the Falloux Law replaced, Jewish leaders did nothing to encourage their followers to participate in the huge January 15 demonstration in support of the republican public schools.

If we want to understand the attitude of these Jewish leaders, we must look back at the positions of earlier Jewish leaders with respect to the Falloux Law. Adopted on March 15, 1850, this fundamental law restructured the relationship between church and state by encouraging the growth of private schools, mostly of Catholic inspiration. Although religious fundamentalists thought it adequate at the time, the left regarded the law as reactionary and steadfastly opposed it. Not the least paradoxical aspect of the current situation is that the left has now mobilized to defend the Falloux Law rather than attack it. In its original form, the law granted the Church full freedom to teach whatever it pleased in the primary and secondary schools. In both public and private schools, religious instruction was made mandatory. Schools were not allowed to be neutral. Teachers had to subscribe to one of the recognized religions, and parents could not refuse to allow their children to receive religious instruction. Most important of all, local authorities (municipal or departmental) could subsidize religious instruction if they chose, although the amount of such subsidies could not exceed 10 percent of the (national) public subsidy.[8]

This aggressive measure was clearly part of a strategy to halt the de-Christianization of French society. Thiers, the very conservative prime minister, proclaimed to the Assembly, "There is but one remedy, to entrust primary education entirely and unreservedly to the Church. I want to make the influence of the clergy all-powerful, and I want the priest's work to be effective." In response, Adolphe Crémieux, a highly placed Jewish official who also played a key role in the Consistory and the Alliance Israélite Universelle, argued that religious education should take place outside the schools: "Then Catholics will not lord it over Protestants and Jews. Then instruction will be free." He invoked the revolutionary tradition against the proposed law and, looking back on his childhood, recalled:

There was secular education, and then religion added morality to that education. . . . In my day, in the imperial *lycée* in Paris, there was only one Jewish family, my family, my brothers and cousins. It was obvious that we didn't count for much against the mass of Catholics. The number of Protestants was infinitesimal. I don't think there were any more of them than there were of us. That is how it was in the imperial *lycée:* six Jews, about as many Protestants, and all the rest Catholics. And you think that the Catholics weren't in charge of moral and religious education in the *lycée*! . . . Which brings me to the law. If the Church is queen in the public schools, I understand why Monsieur de Montalembert wants this law, but he ought to understand why I don't want it. I am a citizen, just as he is. . . . He represents the

Catholic principle; I represent another principle, which was thirty-five hundred years old at a time when yours did not yet exist—you who are interrupting me.[9]

In a similar vein, *L'Univers israélite* then denounced "the occult tendencies of a Church that claims a monopoly on the truth" and argued that "the legislature has routed freedom of conscience." The paper also pointed out that Jewish teachers, "whose only fault was to have been born into our religion," had lost their jobs.[10] Similarly, the *Archives israélites* wrote, "The consequences of the new law on teaching have unfortunately already been felt by our religion. Everywhere religious equality has been shaken. Everywhere religious minorities, especially our own, have been excluded or are about to be excluded from the benefits of public education."[11] Shortly thereafter, the paper remarked, "The arrogance of some of the Catholic clergy in France knows no limits. . . . Secondary teaching will be closed to Jews. Never have such shameless ideas been put forward. It would be easy to think that one was in the Middle Ages." The editors repeatedly attacked the "baleful influence of the clerical party," which had succeeded in eliminating Jewish teachers from the schools.[12] Clearly, then, many Jewish leaders condemned the Falloux Law at the time it was adopted, whereas to many intransigent Catholics it seemed woefully inadequate. If Jewish leaders in recent years have preferred to keep quiet on the subject, the reason is that they are caught between two contradictory positions: on the one hand, the development of Jewish private schools is threatened by competition with Catholic schools for scarce local subsidies; on the other hand, the vast majority of Jewish students still attend public schools, despite the difficulties those schools have faced in recent years.

Militant secularism really became established only during the Third Republic, to the great satisfaction of most Jewish leaders at the time, who knew how vital the public schools were to young Jews who wished to become teachers at the high-school and college level, or even to aspire to that pinnacle of French educational success, the Collège de France.[13] Some state Jews were close associates of the vehemently anticlerical founders of the Third Republic and as such played an important role in establishing the system of secular education on which republican meritocracy—to say nothing of their own success in the state bureaucracy—was based. They approved of Jules Ferry's statement: "It is important to the Republic, to civil society, and to all who believe deeply in the tradition of 1789 that control and governance of the schools not be in the hands of ministers of a religion who, on matters that we hold dear and that form the basis of society, hold opinions so profoundly different from ours."[14] According to one public-school textbook of the period, "Catholics, Protestants, Jews, and freethinkers all have the same rights. All can attend government schools and enjoy access to all employments. . . . Their opinions are nobody's business but their own." State Jews joined Protestants in support of the secularization policy. In 1885, Deputy David Raynal announced his support for "a policy of secularization designed to strenuously resist proclerical efforts and to lay the groundwork for the separation of church and state." His colleague Ferdinand Dreyfus sought to "establish free, public, secular education on a firm foundation." In October 1892, a bill to that end was submitted to the Chamber by another Jewish deputy, Camille Dreyfus, provoking an angry reaction from other deputies, who accused him of "wanting to de-Christianize France, perhaps in order to Judaize it." Although backed by Alfred Naquet, among others, this bill was rejected by Gambetta with support from Joseph Reinach and David Raynal, who favored a more gradual approach.[15] Although many state Jews favored the secularization of education because they did not believe that republican integration would lead to assimilation of a sort that would rob Jews of their cultural identity, some Jewish leaders opposed the complete separation of church and state.[16] But the Jewish community was once again divided. For instance, Adolphe Franck, vice-president of the Consistory, said, "There is one law which governs all men regardless of time, origin, or nationality," and that was the universal law that defined a secularized society. Franck, the author of an elementary-school textbook that was published in 1868, was a proponent of "moral spiritualism" who insisted on clearly separating citizenship from religion.[17]

The Jewish press made no secret of its opposition. Though hostile to the Falloux Law, it was no more favorable to secularization of the school system, which would have deprived religious schools of public funding. In 1871, the *Archives israélites* accepted the idea of free, compulsory public education but frankly stated, "We would be upset if, on the pretext of secularization, the idea of God were banished from the schools."[18] The paper would never waver from this position. During the crucial debates of 1905–6, the same paper remarked, "What is particularly strange and peculiar is that it is religious minorities such as Protestants and Jews, who bear no responsibility for the conflicts stirred up by Rome that have inspired Monsieur Combes's proposal, who stand to be most deeply affected by a bill that seems to be aimed more at Catholics or, rather, clericals." On the pretext of sapping the political power of the Church, the paper added, "the Combes bill will make life singularly difficult for Protestants and Catholics and turn the most devoted democrats among them against the republican regime." What is more, H. Prague, the editor-in-chief of the *Archives*, attacked the "cowardice of the Consistory" in regard to "a proposal that would sacrifice the future of our community."[19] When Isaïe Levaillant, one of the best-known state Jews of the period, became the editor-in-chief of the *L' Univers israélite*, he, too, wondered whether, "by legislating too exclusively in favor of Catholics and seeking primarily to ward off, in an election year, the formidable challenge to the republican government that the Church threatened to mount, [that government] had not lost sight of the rights and interests of dissident religions, from whom there was nothing to fear because they had supported the separation of church and state from the beginning."[20] He worried all the more because, like Prague, he regretted the silence of the Consistory and other Jewish leaders: "After separation, our communities will find themselves in a precarious situation. . . . Such misunderstandings could have been avoided if Jewish representatives had followed the lead of their Protestant counterparts and, instead of watching the debate on separation haughtily from afar, with a detachment that could easily be mistaken for indifference . . . they had taken steps to ensure . . . that they would not be caught off guard."[21] Levaillant would often have occasion to repeat his denunciation of the Consistory's timidity: "We find it truly humiliating to compare the energy and diligence of the Protestant authorities since the issue of separation was first raised in the Chambers with the indifference and apathy of the Jewish representatives," especially since the institutions on which Jewish life depended, most notably religious schools, would henceforth be faced with the all-but-insurmountable difficulty of financing their own operations. By contrast, private Catholic associations could count on inheriting the legacy of the public institutions they were about to replace. "It is essential," Levaillant added, "not to lose sight of the fact that the situation in which Judaism will find itself after separation is not at all the same as that of Catholicism. . . . In short, the Catholic Church will remain the Church. Although there is a Jewish religion in France and a Jewish cult, there is no Jewish church. It is the state that has bound the Jewish community together as a unit. It is quite clear that, once the hand of the state is removed, that unit will fall apart. Once separation occurs, there will still be Jews in France but French Judaism will no longer exist."[22] Then as now, this was indeed the crux of the matter, and Levaillant, who was well informed about the state's activities in general, asked the pertinent question: "Must we resign ourselves as Jews in France to a situation like that which exists in most countries where religion is independent of the state, such as Switzerland and parts of Germany? . . . If the centralization of Jewish authority in France has had the unfortunate effect of sapping Judaism's will and draining its energy, it is important to note that it also fostered a certain community of feeling and aspiration that it would be good to perpetuate. . . . Is it not desirable that the rabbinate not be at the mercy of local influences of every sort? Having enjoyed full independence thanks to government supervision, should it be reduced to a precarious situation?"[23]

Thus, in the late nineteenth century, the role of the state turns out to have been just as vital as it is today. If the state withdrew, leaving local authorities to manage their own budgets, it threatened to undermine a Judaism that had flourished in its shadow, even if the tutelage of that same state was sometimes burdensome, as numerous rabbis did not fail to point out. This contradiction is no less acute today than it was in the past, as we shall see shortly. Levaillant, while expressing regret at the new policy of separation, conceded that "this reform might renovate and regenerate French Judaism" by forcing it to forgo state aid and face up to the enormous challenge of full autonomy.[24] In the same spirit, H. Prague, the editor-in-chief of the *Archives israélites*, who had been just as hostile to separation, came around to thinking of it as an "unexpected stroke of luck. . . . Should we count on the possibility that separation, which will leave a big hole in [Jewish] community budgets, will, though the stimulus of unavoidable necessity, reawaken a dormant zeal, an interest in the needs and affairs of the community that had all but disappeared? It is a question of reviving the idea of duty to the synagogue, of galvanizing a Jewish soul grown rusty from disuse, and of revitalizing our tradition."[25] This was indeed the fundamental issue: in order to revitalize that "Jewish soul grown rusty" from years of reliance on the state without developing a new dependence on local authorities that were likely to prove more generous to Catholic institutions, Jews would henceforth have to rely on their own sense of "duty" and personal commitment. At the turn of the twentieth century, Prague was optimistic: "Unlike the Catholic peasant, who though still attached to the Church feels estranged from the priest, the Jew honors and esteems his rabbis. Among us there are no rabbi-baiters."[26]

Today, things have changed to some extent. Not only are there many Jews in France who are indeed "rabbi-baiters," but some of them reject the old norms of Franco-Judaism that constrained rabbis to respect the republican principle of separation of the public and private spheres. Because of this, rabbis were extremely reluctant to intervene in public political debate. In recent years, however, many rabbis have adopted a very different strategy, opting for a strong public presence in order to weld Jews into a unified community with themselves as its official spokesmen. Such a strategy attests to the depth of the changes that have taken place in the thinking of many French Jews, and it has given rise to intense debate within the Jewish community. With decisive backing from Grand Rabbi Joseph Sitruck, some French Jews have begun openly to question the fundamental republican principle of secular education, which large numbers of both Protestants and Jews had traditionally supported. At about the same time, Monsignor Vilnet, president of the bishops' conference in Lourdes, stated that "the time seems ripe to redefine the institutional framework of secular education." Cardinal Lustiger also declared that it was essential to "redefine the conditions of the separation of church and state." In November 1989, Grand Rabbi Sitruck observed that there was "a dangerous tendency to argue that secularism is the motor of society and that religion should remain a strictly private matter." He offered the following advice to public-school teachers: "Be open to the religious diversity of the young. If a student wears a cross in your presence, or a shawl or a yarmulke, accept that student for what he or she is." Furthermore, in order to combat "the dilution of Jewish values" caused by assimilation, the Grand Rabbi expressed his wish that young Jews be allowed to wear the yarmulke in the public schools and that school schedules be adjusted so that Jewish students did not have to attend school on the Sabbath.*[27]

The rabbi's public statement was especially pertinent because it was made only a short time after an administrative court in Nice upheld the expulsion of a Jewish student from a *lycée* for failure to attend Saturday-morning classes.[28] This episode impelled the Consistory to ask the Conseil d'Etat to rescind a February 1991 order concerning school-attendance requirements. In the view of the Jewish body, the school attendance order constituted an infringement of religious freedom because it allowed for absolutely no exceptions. By contrast, the attorney representing the government argued that the Consistory's request should be rejected on the grounds that "the law of the Republic takes precedence over the precepts of religion." In the government's view, pupils unwilling to abide by that law were free to attend religious schools instead. But "if one chooses to participate in the educational community, then one must abide by its rules." In a brief that was widely commented on, the government attorney argued that suspension of Saturday classes was unacceptable and that the request reflected "a new and very real problem concerning what attitude the state should adopt vis-à-vis communities that are increasingly likely to express their identity through intensification of

---

* Saturday classes are the norm in France. —TRANS.

religious sentiment." If the Conseil approved the Consistory's request, there was a danger of "moving toward an 'à la carte' school system in which every student would be free to pick and choose his or
her own rules and schedule." *Le Monde* embraced this view of the
matter entirely: "In an irony of history, the public schools used to be
seen as both the instrument and the symbol of emancipation and integration of the Protestant and Jewish minorities. Today, however, the
Republic is faced with a very different challenge, a challenge to the
rules governing communal life and religious observance. This raises
the threat of a 'self-service' school. . . . How can the schools avoid becoming enmeshed in a series of special rules and requirements without encouraging a proliferation of separate community schools?"[29]
Rejecting the arguments of the government attorney, the Conseil
d'Etat on April 14, 1995, issued two new orders which opened the
way for observant Jewish students to be authorized not to attend Saturday classes provided that such exceptions did not disrupt the educational process. School principals were asked to judge the effects of
such absences on a case-by-case basis. Although the Conseil upheld
the expulsion of the student from the Lycée Masséna in Nice on the
grounds that all students of advanced mathematics were required to
attend Saturday-morning classes, the high court took a different view
with respect to the chador, or shawl, worn by some Islamic girls,
holding that it was not "in itself" a visible sign of religion. Students
wearing the shawl could be expelled from school only if in so doing
they "disrupted" the educational process.[30] Thus did the Republic
begin, apparently, the difficult process of reinterpreting the law of
separation of church and state.

The case before the Conseil d'Etat therefore constituted a challenge to the republican conception of citizenship, based as it was on
strict separation of the public and private spheres. It also implied rejection of an idea of assimilation whose roots can be traced all the
way back to the French Revolution. And, finally, it reflected a wish on
the part of the Jewish community to reaffirm an identity that many
had thought on the decline. Taken together, these things point to a
profound change in the thinking of French Jews. Another sign of such
a change was the inauguration of an annual Torah Day in Novem-

ber 1989, an event, entirely orchestrated by the rabbinate, that drew some thirty thousand people to Le Bourget in its first year. The occasion was thoroughly religious, and the atmosphere was warm, intimate, and emotional, not uninfluenced by a certain blending of high tech with popular sentimentality that has become quite familiar in this age of wholesale "religious revival."[31] The election of Benny Cohen, a very conservative Jewish bureaucrat, as president of the Paris Consistory in January 1990 gave Orthodox Jews greater influence over the definition of Jewishness in France. Despite support from Grand Rabbi Sitruck, who congratulated the new president on his success in constructing a dozen new synagogues in a relatively short period of time, Benny Cohen was defeated in the November 1993 Consistory elections by a more moderate rival, Moïse Cohen. Le Monde, which had published a full-page article on February 23, 1980, on "the mood of French Jews" stressing growing "tensions between religious and secular" members of the community, now published a long article under the arresting title of "Cohen versus Cohen": "The Jewish community in the Paris region is sitting on a volcano. Never in the entire history of the Consistory since Napoleon has an election campaign been so bitterly fought with so many negative attacks. . . . A populist base, not very familiar with the history of the community, practicing, active, evolving toward a prickly orthodoxy."[32]

To be sure, French society in general has been undergoing a religious revival of sorts in recent years. One reason for this has been the diminished influence of the republican tradition and of institutions of republican socialization such as the public schools; another has been the decline of overarching ideologies such as Marxism, which once exerted a powerful hold on a significant portion of the Jewish intelligentsia. A case in point is the transformation of Benny Lévy, Jean-Paul Sartre's erstwhile private secretary, who moved seamlessly from militant Maoism to the very Orthodox yeshiva headed by Rav Abitbol of Strasbourg—a symbol of the rapidly shifting French cultural landscape.[33] Since 1975, the number of Jewish study groups has increased rapidly: there are now nearly five hundred, serving some ten thousand regular students. Since 1967, several advanced degrees in

Jewish studies have been approved by academic authorities, along with a curriculum in Jewish culture. The number of university-level teachers of Jewish studies has shot up rapidly, as has the number of theses dealing with some aspect of Jewish culture or history. But the most astonishing increase has been in the number of Jewish private schools and the rapid expansion of some of the best known, such as the Ecole Yavné, which was forced to move from the rue Claude-Bernard to the Porte d'Italie to make room for the influx of new students.

In addition to the twenty thousand children attending Jewish schools, ten thousand or more attend one of the 250 "Talmud Torah" schools offering Jewish subjects to supplement the public-school curriculum. There are also Jewish camps and youth groups, so "it would appear that three-quarters of Jewish children have received some type of Jewish education by the time they reach age nineteen."[34] This finding invalidates the notion, widely accepted since 1980, that Jewish education in France has remained particularly "impoverished" since the Revolution.[35] Many Jewish schools do not receive state subsidies and are therefore exempt from state controls: this is the case, for example, with 80 percent of the schools run by the Lubavitchers. Furthermore, six to thirteen hours of instruction per week are devoted to Jewish subjects, whereas religious instruction in Catholic schools occupies only an hour and a half. Clearly, then, the rabbinical call for a re-examination of the republican "contract" has been widely heeded. It would seem that French Jews want to be recognized as a community.

The rapid expansion of Lubavitcher communities in French cities is another important aspect of the public dimension of Judaism today. The Lubavitchers have imported from the United States pressure-group tactics alien to French Jacobin tradition. They have made the Jewish community visible in a new way, quite different from the dialogue that used to be carried on between the state and citizens of various confessions. The Lubavitchers have done the same thing in Paris as in New York, lighting Chanukah candles in public places and carrying signs saying "We want the Messiah now!" Most important of all, they have devoted a great deal of effort to building their own school system. That system has expanded with remarkable rapidity, to the point where more than 10 percent of all students in Jewish private schools now attend a Lubavitcher institution. On the north side of Paris, strict orthodoxy is the norm. Rigorous dress codes are enforced. Men and women study and pray separately. And strict traditional codes of behavior are constantly inculcated in all students. The study of French, on the other hand, is virtually "clandestine," so that "a striking feature of Lubavitcher culture in France is the question of French literacy. The situation is quite different from that which exists in the United States: in France, the Lubavitchers see themselves as a force in opposition, especially since the country is alleged to suffer from a cultural Jacobinism that leaves little room for the expression of minority views."[36]

This brings us to a crucial point: more and more people are rejecting the idea of unity implicit in the revolutionary tradition of 1789, which recognizes only identical citizens subscribing to the same principles of rationality and stripped of their distinguishing characteristics so as to participate in the public sphere in a universalistic mode. Since the Lubavitchers have little interest in French political traditions per se, they feel no compunctions about adopting such a position, at odds though it may be with traditional Franco-Judaism. Yet we find similar positions beginning to be expressed in more institutionalized sectors of the Jewish educational system. Thus Colette Kessler, the longtime head of an important traditional Jewish school, argues: "France has become the prime example of a fraudulent secularism, good in principle but bad in practice. Secularism, which is often antireligious, is perceived by Jews today as an impediment to the expression of their identity. What we need to work for is a form of secularism that allows and encourages religious pluralism, as in the English-speaking countries."[37] Invariably it is the American model that is invoked, with the implication that, if France were to adopt it, Jews would be able to recover their sense of identity by rejecting the Jacobin model compounded by the educational policies of the Third Republic. Such invocations of the "right to be different," which recent socialist governments have legitimized and institutionalized with their "Girondin" policies on cultural difference, reflect a reaction against the French-style strong-state model. As Grand Rabbi Sitruck puts it, "I think it would be deplorable if a country as broad-minded as France were to close its doors to people simply because they want to be different."[38] On this point he agrees, though in more moderate terms, with another rabbi, not part of the Consistory, who forthrightly states: "France cannot cancel out her minorities. We have our own ethos, which is a plus for the country, and that is why the Hebrew principle of *Dina de malhuta dina* (the law of the kingdom is the law) does not apply to France. What Napoleon failed to understand was that Jews do not compromise." The revival of community institutions—which the Sephardics, who today constitute the majority of French Jews, ardently desired—has thus led to a change in rabbinical values: many rabbis now reject the separation of church and state, reject the autonomy of the political and the confinement of religion to the private sphere, and favor a substantial public role for religious and cultural communities. Thus Grand Rabbi Sitruck recently declared himself to be "the Grand Rabbi of all the Jews, even those who do not practice," and maintained, "In Judaism there is no distinction between the religious and the political. Such dichotomies have gone out of fashion. Listen to the nuns, the bishops, and the leaders of Islam. And so, too, in Judaism this dichotomy no longer exists." Controversies among Jewish intellectuals about the consequences of the French Revolution (was it liberating or the opposite?) have also had an impact. Speaking of the French Revolution, Grand Rabbi Goldmann said, "I do not see why I should celebrate an event that made de-Judaization possible by destroying the Jews."[39] Implicit in this view is the idea that Judaism is one of many forms of difference that can legitimately be expressed within the universalist public sphere.

Paradoxically, a series of controversies over the Islamic chador, and hence over the place of Islam in French society, gave rise to attacks on the image, inherited from the nineteenth century, of the assimilated republican Jew at the very moment when many *beurs*, or second-generation Muslims, were looking to the Jewish model as a way of achieving their own integration. In October 1989, three young Muslim girls were expelled from a school in Creil for wearing the chador, triggering a huge national debate in which Jews vigorously participated. The government seemed unsure of how to deal with the demand that students should be allowed to express their religious affiliation within the walls of the public schools. The ensuing controversy was reminiscent of the great educational debates of the Third Republic. The Conseil d'Etat held that students should be entirely free "to express and demonstrate their religious beliefs within educational institutions," provided they "refrain from wearing any visible symbol, clothing, or other accoutrement tending to promote a religious belief." However, "the wearing by students of signs intended to manifest their affiliation with a religion is not in itself incompatible with the principle of secularism." But the text goes on to make the somewhat contradictory statement that such dress does constitute "an act of proselytism or propaganda." Although the girls in question were accordingly readmitted to the school that had expelled them, they chose not to return, precipitating an endless series of debates about the limits of secularism in France today. Speeches were made in the Assembly, demonstrators took to the streets, and so on. Overnight, France seemed to have been thrust back into the "school wars" of the Third Republic.

No sooner had that furor died down than another controversy over a chador erupted at yet another public school, this time in Nantua. Once again several girls were expelled, and angry words flew back and forth. There was a new element, however: an imam of foreign nationality who headed up the local Islamic community insisted, "Islamic law takes precedence over the law of the state." He was quickly deported. Yet his statement was at bottom not very different from the position espoused in recent years by various rabbis who have denied the applicability to France of the dictum *Dina de malhuta dina.* Long ago, in the nineteenth century, rabbis opposed to secularism had taken a similar stance. In 1892, Rabbi Stora was forced to resign after saying that "the teaching of French is useless and harmful." "Have I failed the state," he asked, "by placing religious morality above secular morality?"[40] Even in those days, when many state Jews were helping to implement the government's secularization policies, most rabbis had their doubts, to put it mildly. For instance, Grand Rabbi Zadoc Kahn was sorry to see religious instruction eliminated from the public-school curriculum. And in 1880, Grand Rabbi Isidor voiced criticisms of the secular schools on the grounds that they promoted mixed marriages.[41]

Thus many rabbis were and are reluctant to embrace secularization. When Rabbi Sitruck criticized secular intolerance during the chador crisis, he found himself in agreement with Rabbi Alain Goldmann, who said, "Those who refuse to allow Muslim children to wear the chador or Jewish children to wear the yarmulke are intolerant. Nowadays, it is not religious people who are intolerant but secular people."[42] He thus seemed to be defending the chador on the grounds that free expression of religious differences should be allowed in the public schools, which in his mind meant that he was also defending the yarmulke. In fact, the wearing of yarmulkes in *lycées* is widely tolerated. Even after the Creil incident, despite countless condemnations of both the chador and the yarmulke, young Jews continued to wear the skullcap without being reprimanded, because they "played the republican game" and did not challenge the values of modernity that were embodied in the public-school curriculum.[43] But for perhaps the first time since the Sanhedrin and the association of French Judaism with the state, rabbis publicly joined those who challenged secularism and thus found themselves siding with many Catholic bishops and Muslim leaders and intellectuals. These rabbis—some affiliated with the Consistory, others not—spoke out publicly. They took a position radically different from that of many Jewish intellectuals, who continued to support a rationalist secularism. Even in private they rejected the attitudes of these secular Jews toward Judaism and supported the Muslim position on the chador. In fact, the rabbis sought to make themselves the sole legitimate representatives of the Jews of France in the public sphere by challenging such secular Jewish institutions as the CRIF, these being the only Jewish groups previously recognized by the state.

At this point, a new quarrel broke out among Jews themselves. Alain Finkielkraut, a Jewish intellectual and author of *Le Juif imaginaire* (1980), denounced the "holy alliance of clergies,"[44] and in a direct attack on Grand Rabbi Sitruck he added: "The secular schools have been an instrument of emancipation, and the Jews are deeply indebted to them. By defending the chador and the yarmulke in the same breath, these religious dignitaries have behaved as though they were heading up some syndicate or corporation. Their attitude toward the unfortunate young girls as well as toward the schools has been one of irresponsibility and indifference. Once again, identity has been more important than message."[45] A few months later, Régis Debray, the contemporary herald of the republican idea, and four Jewish intellectuals—Finkielkraut, Elisabeth Badinter, Catherine Kintzler, and Elisabeth de Fontenay, all specialists in Enlightenment thought—signed an incendiary text in favor of secularism and consequently opposed to allowing the expelled students back into school: "*Monsieur le ministre*," they wrote, "only time will tell whether the year of the Bicentennial [of the French Revolution] will have been the Munich of the republican school."[46] Driving the point home, they went on to say: "To allow fundamentalist demonstrations (regardless of whether the fundamentalism is Catholic, Jewish, or Muslim) in the schools (which are the only shared public spaces we have left) is to trigger a chain reaction of the worst kinds of xenophobia. By rejecting this differentialist logic, we wish to indicate our solidarity with all who oppose the communitarian fundamentalism of their own group."[47]

Led by Finkielkraut, these Jewish intellectuals set off an astonishing national polemic that brought forth a daily outpouring of venom in the press. The editor-in-chief of *Le Nouvel Observateur* was moved to write, "Democracy . . . is not a fleabag of sectarianisms or a Club Méditérranée where well-meaning hosts lead well-meaning citizens in fun and games. It has its own temples, where people are obliged to remove their hats, yarmulkes, and chadors. . . . For once, it is the forbidden act that sets us free."[48] This is not the place to rehearse this great public debate, which raged for weeks between the secularist camp, in all its diversity, and those who favored allowing the expression of religious differences in the public schools. Obviously, such a radical declaration in favor of secularism inevitably called forth an equally radical response from the Jewish community. As a result, the chador affair caused profound dissension among Jews. Ugly epithets were bandied about: "proud Jews" denounced "submissive Jews,"

"Jews" denounced "Jew Jews," "assimilated Jews" denounced "clerical Jews" and vice versa. In France, where consensus had long reigned in the Jewish community, this vehement "war of the Jews" was something new.

Then another article ignited the powder keg once again. Its authors also favored preserving the classic idea of republican citizenship based on the separation of public and private spheres, with religion relegated to the private. Dominique Schnapper and Chantal Benayoun vigorously attacked those who advocated a public presence for the Jewish community. The authors charged that such people were "counterrevolutionaries" seeking to abolish the tradition of 1789 and expressed regret that "some young Jews feel closer to the 'counterrevolutionary' position than to the 'republican' one."[49] In a particularly dramatic editorial, Les Nouveaux Cahiers, the official organ of the Alliance Israélite Universelle, asserted that the rise in France of a Jewish fundamentalism threatened "the cultural identity of French Jews" and raised the specter of a "double schism." This fundamentalism, the writer of the editorial alleged,

> is turning its back on French society . . . and trying to establish an unbreachable barrier between Jews and other members of society. . . . This movement, if it spreads, could lead to a double schism: inevitably, Jews of every stripe would be marginalized and eventually repudiated by "civil society." . . . The "real" Jews would be those who cut themselves off. . . . Equally serious would be the schism within the Jewish community. . . . A schism would develop between the good Jews and the bad, leading to reciprocal expulsions and perhaps excommunications. . . . Surely there is still time to stop this splitting of the Jewish "community" . . .

the editorial concluded, but to do so would require French Jews to acknowledge their "attachment to the Republic."[50] In a subsequent issue, Les Nouveaux Cahiers went on to offer a forceful analysis of the "risks of ghettoization."[51]

Now that French Jewish identity is increasingly being shaped by the revival of religious practice, a number of combative secular Jewish organizations have also appeared on the scene. Their membership is small, however: at most a few thousand people. Among the newer groups we find Liberté du Judaïsme (Freedom of Judaism) (1987), the Association pour un Judaïsme Humaniste et Laïque (Association for a Humanist and Secular Judaism) (1989), the Centre Juif Laïque (Lay Jewish Center) (1989), the Association des Etudiants Laïques (Association of Secular Students) (1991), and Rencontre Progressiste Juive (Jewish Progressive Encounter) (1990), in addition to such older organizations as the Cercle Bernard Lazare and the Cercle Gaston Crémieux. All of these groups have participated in organizing public meetings such as the 1992 "Judéoscope," circulating petitions, and so on. Similar organizations exist in the United States, Belgium, and Israel, but in France to date one finds no "lay rabbis" or "secular" Bar Mitzvahs, weddings, and funerals, things that do exist in these other countries. In this respect, at any rate, a certain French exceptionalism persists.[52]

The election of a new Grand Rabbi of France on June 19, 1994, added fuel to the fire, and perhaps for the first time in French history dissension within the Jewish community became a genuine national issue. *Le Monde*, in a marked departure from custom, ran the story of this "battle" on page one with two additional pages inside. The story was one of slander, defamatory articles, and anonymous threats. The Jewish press took sides. *L'Actualité juive*, for example, called upon the Jewish community to unite behind Grand Rabbi Joseph Sitruck, who it alleged had been "odiously persecuted," whereas *L'Information juive* noted that "things have gotten out of hand on what used to be called Jew Street." Sitruck, the incumbent, found himself in the unaccustomed situation of facing a rival for his post, Gilles Bernheim, an Alsatian-born rabbi who had been trained as a philosopher and was serving as rabbi to the Jewish students of Paris. Bernheim wasted no time in cutting straight to the heart of the matter: "Jews have successfully integrated into French society. I think they should serve as models, for the Muslim community in particular. If one wants to integrate—which means not to assimilate but to live in harmony as a practicing Jew without challenging the republican model—then a certain discretion is required. If the rules of Jewish orthodoxy are to be respected, our relation to the republican model will require a great deal of tact."[53] Furthermore, "knowledge of the Torah and of the various other texts that form the basis of Jewish life and thought has become extremely rare nowadays. . . . It is a very good thing that our children can be trained in these arduous disciplines just as rigorously as they are trained in the disciplines studied by all students. But we must take care to ensure that our efforts are not compromised by a rhetoric of contempt or conquest."[54] In the election, 217 rabbis and other community leaders were eligible to vote, and the campaign was a bitter one. To oversimplify somewhat, Ashkenazi Jews and some Franco-Judaic institutions such as the CRIF and the Fonds Social Juif Unifié apparently leaned toward Rabbi Bernheim, whereas Sephardim generally supported Rabbi Sitruck's identity politics and rejection of the republican model of strict division between public and private spheres. To be sure, Bernheim also had Sephardic supporters who were radical critics of the republican social contract. Nevertheless, this controversy, following as it did on the heels of dissension within the Consistory, demonstrates that many French Jews find themselves deeply troubled as the twentieth century draws to a close. The CRIF, noting the emergence of a "popular-based religious enthusiasm that is quite strong, not to say all-consuming," seized the occasion to defend "the framework of the secular state" and suggested that there would be great "risk" in "selecting a leader whose mandate extended beyond the strict limits of religion."[55] Despite this opposition, Grand Rabbi Sitruck scored a quick and stunning victory. Two days later, a new Grand Rabbi of Paris was also elected, and for the first time he, too, was a Sephardic, and a relatively militant one at that.[56] These two elections may mark a turning point in the history of Judaism in France, suggesting as they do a desire on the part of many French Jews to re-establish a Jewish community both inside and outside the political arena. Meanwhile, Gaullist leaders have been calling for a stricter secularism: Edouard Balladur, prime minister at the time of the rabbinical elections, made a point of stating that secularism was the "cement of the republican pact."[57] He did this in a speech to the CRIF, which of course needed no convincing. And shortly thereafter, Jean Kahn, the new president of the Consistory, expressed his regret that "religion has exceeded its prerogatives and clearly thrown all constraint to the winds." He went on to say, "The law of my country is the law, as our texts say. The Jewish community will not violate this rule. It remains deeply attached to the principle of secularism and to the republican schools. This principle is one of the foundations of French society, to which we adhere totally."[58]

11

IDENTITY
AND PUBLIC SPACE

In the recent British and American debates about new forms of communitarianism and multiculturalism, the distinct historical pathways by which various Western nations have achieved a democratic mode of government have seldom been taken into account.[1] Historical sociology has been strangely absent from these controversies between "communitarians" and "libertarians," even though the discipline has flourished of late in the English-speaking world. What is equally strange is that another great debate of recent years, concerning citizenship, has also been carried on in isolation from comparative research on state-building and the public sphere. It has stubbornly remained on the plane of normative philosophy, where John Rawls chose to stake out his position. Even those communitarians who reject the individualist contractualism of Rawls's *Theory of Justice* somewhat willfully ignore what historical sociology might contribute to their arguments in the way of information about the evolution of citizenship and its relation to various types of communal bond. It is as if the revival of political philosophy, coupled with the relative decline of the social sciences, has forced scholars to think about the social bond as something purely abstract, without any sociological dimension whatsoever. Furthermore, although Rawls, in responding to his communitarian critics in *Political Liberalism*, attempted to introduce a modicum of multiculturalism into his conception of society, he nevertheless left it out of his "overlapping consensus," thus leaving the political sphere somewhat disembodied. He had nothing at all to say on the nature of politics or the state and never for a moment considered the idea that, in exploring the relationship between citizenship and community, one might want to look at what kind of state or public sphere goes with what type of society.[2]

A similar critique can be made of the communitarian side of the debate. Take, for example, the contributors to a book on the work of Charles Taylor.[3] Few if any of them consider the sociopolitical dimension, for they prefer to confine the argument to the realm of the ethical. For them, the debate over multiculturalism seems to turn on normative issues, such as the legitimacy of "affirmative discrimination," as if the terms in which such issues are posed were the same in all democratic societies. To simplify matters, suffice it to say that it is not at all clear that the debate takes the same form in countries with "strong" states as in countries with "weak" ones.[4] Or in countries where universal values dominate, as opposed to countries in which citizenship is easily compatible with membership in various types of community. This oversight is particularly problematic since Taylor actually bases his defense of communitarian principles on the very special case of Catholic, Francophone Quebec, whose culture is threatened by the fact that it is surrounded by a Protestant, Anglophone majority. In other words, Taylor's argument depends on a community with a very specific history, a community that has itself not been particularly tolerant of internal cultural differences. In attempting to hold their own against a fairly strong Canadian state, the Québecois have forced minorities within the province to conform to Québecois community values. If we are to examine the place of community identity in the public sphere today, it would therefore seem incumbent on us to take the historical sociology of each nation into account.[5]

Turning now to the destiny of the Jews of France, we are thus led to consider the possibility and consequences of a "communitarian" revival in a society not well prepared historically to deal with its effects. Indeed, ever since the Revolution, French society has rejected any form of community organization that might rival the state for its citizens' allegiance. In recent years, certain once-divisive issues have become less important than they used to be. There is fairly general agreement about the rules of the political game, and a broad institutional consensus has replaced the prejudices, hatreds, and fantasies of yesteryear. In the past, there were times when state force was the only way to maintain order in a society on the verge of explosion. Lately, however, some state power has been shifted to a highly diversified civil society. Whereas citizens once owed all their allegiance to the state, now allegiances to specific subgroups within society have raised questions about this state-centered notion of citizenship: the "civil" is increasingly encroaching on the domain of the "civic." Hence, in France, where "multiculturalism" runs counter to a long historical tradition, the issue is particularly complicated.

This new set of issues will provide the backdrop to our investigation of the fate of French Jews. For many historians, Franco-Judaism is a perfect example of republican assimilation, which welcomed Jews who gave their loyalty to the republican state and gradually worked free of community ties. To be sure, this characterization is greatly oversimplified, and in recent years it has been rejected by other scholars, who have shown that certain cultural ties, networks of sociability, and Jewish values survived. But until recently even historians who take this revisionist view of assimilation have never contended that French Jews constituted a distinct community within French society before 1945.

The first signs of change began to appear just after World War II. During that war, the state (meaning both political leaders and bureaucratic officials) largely betrayed its loyal Jews. It generally left them to fend for themselves, and unhesitatingly handed some over to the German police, thereby willingly contributing to the process of extermination. Fortunately for the Jews, there were many people in France willing to help them escape the wrath of a state that had forgotten its history and lost its reason. Everything changed as a result: salvation came almost invariably from society rather than from the state. Jews, like other groups within civil society, subsequently chose to organize themselves. Like disappointed lovers, they abandoned the state they had once adored. With the formation of the Comité Représentatif des Institutions Juives en France, or CRIF, in 1944, and later of other Jewish institutions, such as the Fonds Social Juif Unifié, or FSJU, as well as the arrival of large numbers of North African Jews in the wake of decolonization, the idea that the Jews might constitute a distinctive community within France began to take shape. This notion, so at odds with the functional conception of the modern nation-state, gradually took hold at a time when the state's claim to be the sole legitimate repository of power was also beginning to be questioned.

A series of events that changed the way the Jews of France saw themselves further reinforced this new idea. One such defining moment came during the Six-Day War in 1967, when General de Gaulle characterized the Jews as "an elite people, sure of themselves and domineering." This deeply shocked many French Jews, and a few even spoke out publicly for the first time to denounce what they considered to be an anti-Semitic statement by a French head of state. For the man who stood as the very symbol of the strong, liberating state, and who had dared virtually single-handedly to oppose Vichy, to make such a statement about Jews forced many to confront the fact that once again they were being set apart from their fellow citizens, accused of a dual allegiance, and described as a "people" characterized, in terms reminiscent of old anti-Semitic myths, as "domineering." René Cassin, long a faithful comrade of de Gaulle's, protested that France was now "identifying itself with injustice" and betraying Abbé Grégoire's emancipatory ideal; Raymond Aron, who was one of the first to join de Gaulle's Free French movement in London, alleged, "General de Gaulle has knowingly, deliberately, inaugurated a new era in Jewish history and perhaps in the history of anti-Semitism." He added: "We all know this style and these adjectives. They belong to Drumont, to Maurras." To make matters worse, Georges Gorse, the minister of information and the general's press secretary, announced on December 6, 1967, that "the head of state did not mean to suggest that Jewish Frenchmen are foreign nationals." Thus, by reviving the specter of dual allegiance, the Six-Day War marked an important moment in the resurgence of Jewish community feeling.

Thereafter, the same sense of exclusion and condemnation would recur periodically. When de Gaulle suddenly resigned in April 1969 after backing the losing side in a referendum, some blamed his defeat on the Jews, who allegedly had voted against him as retribution for his having imposed an embargo on arms for Israel in 1967. After certain missiles mysteriously disappeared from Cherbourg and turned up in Israel, France took umbrage and threatened an armed reprisal. When President Pompidou was later asked why France was maintaining its embargo on Mirage jets for which Israel had already paid, his response could hardly have been more aggressive: "The number you have reached is no longer in service." During Pompidou's visit to Chicago in February 1970, American Jews staged a protest demonstration, and the president's angry reaction nearly turned the demonstration into a riot. In France, a climate of mutual suspicion prevailed between the government and the Jews, some of whom were accused of being incapable of supporting France's pro-Arab foreign policy and hence, implicitly, of treason. Then, on November 23, 1971, President Pompidou granted a pardon to the former *milicien* Paul Touvier, who had killed both resistance fighters and Jews during the Occupation. In the president's mind, it was important to "draw a veil over that period, to forget a time when the French didn't love one another." From then until 1994, the Touvier pardon would continue to reawaken memories of the Vichy years and foster among Jews a sense of a shared historical destiny. The "Vichy syndrome" exacerbated this feeling of difference.[6] Here, memory undeniably contributed to shaping history in the making by changing the way in which people in France looked at one another.

France's pro-Arab tilt would continue unabated. In the 1973 war, France openly backed the Arabs and even increased its military aid. Later, under the presidency of Valéry Giscard d'Estaing, that aid was increased still more. France sold Iraq a nuclear reactor and agreed to abide by the Arab boycott of Israel. A Jewish graduate of the Ecole

Nationale d'Administration was denied a job with a nationalized French oil company out of fear that the Arabs might not approve. The golden age of the state Jew, whose presence was desired in the highest councils of government and whose loyalty went unquestioned, seemed but a distant memory. Indeed, this episode was perceived by many as spelling an end to the dream that had once animated so many "fanatics of the Republic." What a strange reversal of fortune in the once-passionate love affair between the Republic and the Jews! Now it was the officials of the Republic itself who were repeating the traditional accusations of the anti-Semitic right. The malaise grew worse on March 9, 1980, when Giscard, on a state visit to Jordan, peered at Israeli territory through binoculars, as if Israel were the very embodiment of otherness. Stung to the quick, the Jews of France and their leaders reacted as one, once again openly confronting the president of the Republic. The conflict quickly achieved a fever pitch not seen since the end of World War II. When the rue Copernic synagogue was bombed in October 1980, killing several people, Prime Minister Raymond Barre's strange statement added further fuel to the fire: "This odious attack, aimed at Jews attending synagogue . . . hurt innocent French people who happened to be crossing rue Copernic." The "Jewish" victims were thus distinguished from the "French" victims, and the word "innocent" applied only to the latter. As the newspaper *Libération* put it, "Naturally Jews are not innocent Frenchmen. And if they are not innocent but are French, then they must be guilty—guilty of being Jews." On October 7, 1980, more than three hundred thousand people of all political persuasions marched from the Place de la République to the Place de la Nation along the traditional left-wing parade route. Despite this appeal to republican unity in the face of terrorist violence, the wound to Jewish sensibility remained raw.[7]

A "community" that Jews themselves had long considered to be largely "imaginary" slowly began to take shape, although many French Jews still refused to consider themselves part of it. The CRIF ostensibly represented this community vis-à-vis the government, many of whose ministers consulted the Jewish organization and heeded its public statements. President François Mitterrand did not hesitate to use communitarian rhetoric in one of his speeches: on August 9, 1982, after a terrorist attack on the Goldenberg restaurant killed six people, he hastened to the spot and said, "I have always been, and I remain, a friend of the Jewish community in France. Fanaticism such as this, fanaticism of any kind, will find me among its enemies." When Yassir Arafat made an official visit to France in May 1989, the president responded to CRIF protests with a letter: "As Passover draws to a close and on the eve of the day commemorating the deportation of French Jews [during World War II], I wish to express my personal sympathy to the Jewish community of France and to let it know how much I appreciate its contribution to the national community. . . . The cruelty and cowardice of the past remain firmly fixed in our memory when we conduct the foreign policy of France." Shortly thereafter, the president acknowledged that he had "noted the anger of the Jewish community." Thus the existence of a Jewish "community" was officially recognized in public statements by the chief of state, even though the possibility that that community might organize as a particularist pressure group operating in the public arena remained alien to the principles of the nation-state as it had been constructed in France. Paradoxically, the state itself thus accelerated the organization of a community that in many ways was still largely "imaginary" and in which only an exceedingly small number of Jews actively participated. If the *israélites* of the nineteenth century could have witnessed the magnitude of this change, they would have been dumbfounded—and they would have condemned it.

Several factors appear to have reinforced this evolution, which flew in the face of Jacobin tradition by positing a "community" intermediate between the state and its citizens, who were thus encouraged to worry about their "civil" status at the expense, presumably, of their "civic" vision. Let me briefly mention just two of these: first, decentralization, which somewhat diminished the importance of the central government, and second, the challenge to secular schooling that stemmed in part from the arrival in France of a large number of North African Jews eager to preserve their distinctive cultural traditions. This challenge to the universalist principle of "one culture for all" had the unintended consequence of encouraging the "differentialist" racism of Jean-Marie Le Pen's radical-right National Front. Meanwhile, the government, which under the socialists had for a time experimented with state intervention in the economy, had reverted, especially at the ideological level, to the free market, liberalism, and pluralism—in short, to civil society. This return to "Girondin" principles coincided with a rebirth of regional sensibilities: in areas like Brittany and Corsica, regional dialects were granted semiofficial status and included in state-sanctioned curricula as well as approved for use in certain public documents. As decentralization proceeded, it encouraged local particularisms that the nation-state had for centuries consistently combated. Now the state itself was facilitating the revival of regional identities by questioning the wisdom of extreme centralization.[8] By thus legitimating the particularist affiliations of its citizens, the state contributed to an "Americanization" of French society fundamentally at odds with its own history. This sudden change in the relation between center and periphery was of central concern to Jews: long dependent on the state, in keeping with the conception of Franco-Judaism inherited from the Revolution, they now saw the possibility of organizing themselves as other religious and cultural groups were doing and of openly returning to their own values and traditions. Still, the shift toward greater decentralization, which may in any case be temporary and subject to inherent limitations, does not affect Jews in the same way as it affects Bretons, Corsicans, and Basques, because the Jews of France do not occupy any particular portion of the territory. Hence the partial return to a "regionalized" France, of the sort that existed before the revolutionary consolidation of the centralized state emancipated the Jews by imposing a universalist definition of citizenship, may have helped strengthen "communal" sentiment among Jews, but at the same time it threatened to highlight their special "landless" status, which they of course shared with Muslims, whether foreign-born or native French.

Thus the latter-day triumph of "Girondin" thinking has to some extent delegitimized the French Revolution. In addition, some historians have been taking a revisionist approach of late to the history of the Revolution. Among other things, the resistance of the Vendée has been portrayed as resistance to a revolutionary state embodying em-

bryonic totalitarian tendencies. This has further confused the status
of the "landless Jews" who are now being asked, or in some cases
asking themselves, to reconstruct some semblance of communal existence. It should be clear by now why French Jews have reacted in
exceedingly contradictory ways to these historical transformations,
which are shaping their destiny. Some have tried to accentuate the return to diaspora tradition, whose legitimacy now often goes unquestioned. To that end, they have tried to reconstruct Jewish culture and
community by establishing Jewish schools and study centers in the
hope of bringing about a renaissance of Jewish textual scholarship.
Others, however, look upon these efforts, which in the current French
political climate have become almost acceptable, as a threat to universalist values, and have therefore tried to block them. Thus
changes affecting the society as a whole have had repercussions on
the Jewish milieu.

As we saw in the preceding chapter, the question of secularism
continues to be a troublesome one for French Judaism. Take one incident that occurred in March 1994. Pierre Lellouche, a deputy of the
right-wing Rassemblement pour la République, or RPR, wrote to
Charles Pasqua, minister of the interior and as such responsible for
religious matters, to ask him to allow Jewish voters to vote in the second round of the upcoming cantonal elections on a date other than
March 27, the first day of Passover; or, if another date was not possible, perhaps Jewish voters could be allowed to cast absentee ballots.
Since Orthodox Jews were not permitted to drive cars or write on a religious holiday, they would effectively be deprived of their vote if the
minister took no action, or so Lellouche argued. Lellouche, speaking
in the name of "the grass-roots community," was a dynamic young
foreign-policy adviser to RPR leader Jacques Chirac, and he had easily been elected deputy in a Val-d'Oise district that includes Sarcelles, a town with a substantial Jewish vote (see below); he saw
himself as a disinterested party, especially since he was not running
in the cantonal elections. Raising the level of the debate, he described himself as a "deputy of the Republic serving not a single
community but a principle of secularism which . . . should respect
the rights of minorities, including Jews and other groups," because

France was "a multiconfessional Republic." Grand Rabbi Joseph Sitruck immediately published a statement in *La Tribune juive*: "It is my duty to urge Jews not to vote on this particularly important day in the Jewish calendar." Hammering the point home a few days later, he added: "I am in no way antisecular. But we must agree about what the content of secularism is. It is also an opportunity for each religion to find its place. Is secularism simply absolute neutrality? No. Would Christians think it acceptable if the elections were held on Easter Sunday? Like them, I would be shocked if such a thing were to take place."[9]

To be sure, such exceptions are difficult to reconcile with the logic of French history. They threaten to disrupt a republican equilibrium that took a long time to establish. No party shaped by the legacy of Jacobinism could accept such a change readily, the socialists no more than the Gaullists. Interior Minister Pasqua accordingly emerged from a meeting of the Council of Ministers to say this: "French law is not designed or made for any religion. . . . It is impossible to create exceptions. If an exception were to be made, moreover, it might have unfortunate consequences." Did he mean that a new religious war might erupt, or that such a step would play into the hands of the National Front? It is hard to say. Nevertheless, the questions he raised are serious ones, because they take us to the heart of changes that are occurring in France today. Although the country remains a unified, secular republic, it has witnessed in recent years a proliferation of religious beliefs, often outside official institutions and linked to the memories and traditions of groups determined to preserve what they consider to be their authentic heritage. The issue is not just one of "fundamentalism" in its various forms. It is broader than that, and deserves to be taken seriously by opinion-makers, including leading national newspapers that have been all too inclined to take a condescending attitude toward Jewish "exoticism." Indeed, in Italy, where secularism is more limited than in France, the government nevertheless had no difficulty acceding to the request of Jews who wished to vote in the March 1994 elections by keeping polling places open for two additional days so that the voting period would not entirely overlap the Jewish holiday.

Note, too, that guaranteeing every citizen's right to vote while respecting individual religious beliefs can only reinforce republican universalism, especially since the Jewish community at any rate rarely votes as a bloc. Apart from a few exceptions such as the city of Sarcelles, no decisive Jewish bloc vote has been discerned to date, not even in Toulouse or Strasbourg, much less in a national presidential election.[10] Although French Jews, whether religious or not, are more likely than non-Jews to vote for candidates of the center and center left, and although 85 percent of them voted for Mitterrand in the second round of the 1988 presidential election, as a general rule their partisan preferences show little community influence. Jews do, however, vote more regularly than the average citizen, but this simply reflects their deep desire for integration and their drive to be even more civic-minded than their fellow citizens. The only evidence of a Jewish bloc vote pertains to isolated cases such as Sarcelles, a town with a substantial population of recent Sephardic immigrants where traditional ties remain strong and the community has adopted a defensive posture. "Here, the ethnicization of voluntary associations has been the result of a convergence of two forces: the separatist tendencies of North African Jews with a strong sense of tradition and the importation of the American model under which people are identified with the communities to which they belong."[11]

In Strasbourg, by contrast, the behavior of Jewish voters is more likely to be determined by class interest than by religion. The Jewish vote is in fact hard to predict, although Jacques Médecin, at one time a fixture on the political scene as the perennial mayor of Nice, thought he had it figured out. His reasoning, however, was as peculiar as it was specious: "Your community," he told the Jews of Nice, "represents 4 percent of the electorate. The National Front represents 24 percent. The difference is 20 percent. In Nice, 50 percent of the Jews have always abstained, and of the other 50 percent, 25 percent are against me."[12] Despite this tortured logic, the fact is that nearly all Jews vote not as Jews but as citizens of France: "All other things being equal, association with Judaism in either its secular or its religious form is not a determinative predictor of political behavior in France in the late 1980s."[13] Unfortunately, this clear and definitive finding has had little impact. In the 1995 presidential elections, the specter of a "Jewish vote" that could make the difference for one candidate or another was revived yet again. Various candidates made statements that were obviously designed to woo the Jewish voter. Commentators earnestly weighed the possible influence of certain Jewish advisers to socialist candidate Lionel Jospin, while RPR leader Jacques Chirac received the endorsement of leaders of the Lubavitcher movement. Meanwhile, Charles Pasqua, who at the time was backing another RPR candidate, Edouard Balladur, against his party's leader, had a staffer at the Ministry of the Interior, which he headed, prepare, on ministry stationery, an official "message to the Jewish community of France on the occasion of the Passover holiday." This move provoked an angry reaction from Marceau Long, chairman of the national campaign-monitoring commission, who charged that this "message to the Jewish community has the character of an official intervention in the election campaign. Because it discusses the results of the Interior Ministry's initiatives over the past two years, this message departs from those traditionally sent by the minister to religious communities on the occasion of religious holidays."[14] Though the national press continues to use homogenizing language—which allows it to say, for example, that "the center of gravity of the Jewish community has recently shifted to the right"[15]— the official pronouncements of institutions such as the CRIF contradict this: "In accordance with its charter and tradition, the CRIF will not endorse any candidate in the upcoming elections. It may be useful, nevertheless, to point out that we have always warned against parties of exclusion and those who might be tempted to enter into alliances with them. True to the ethics and values of both Judaism and the Republic, the CRIF calls upon each and every one of you to do his civic duty by going to the polls."[16]

Thus, when it comes to politics, at any rate, many Jews continue to believe in the assimilationist model and to reject any notion of a religiously based community. By contrast, many Muslims still feel tied to religious communities and reject the republican model of citizenship. Doubts about republican assimilation have arisen in both groups at a time when France has been experiencing a major upsurge in extreme-right-wing sentiment, as in the late 1800s and again in the 1930s. The National Front, whose rhetoric often has anti-Semitic overtones, has been drawing 10 to 15 percent of the vote nationally and as much as 30 percent in some localities, including big cities.[17] Much of the party's appeal has been based on its hostility to the presence of Islam in a country it sees as Christian. The Front's rhetoric of hate has been built on a clever inversion of antiracist rhetoric: Muslims are accused of not respecting the "Christian identity" of French society. In a strange twist, the renewed emphasis on cultural identity, the rediscovery of the relativism of values, and the relegitimization of particularist communities as the building blocks of a "pluralist France" have led, logically yet paradoxically, to the National Front's efforts to portray itself as the embodiment and champion of "Christian cultural values." In this it must fend off the challenge of traditionalist Philippe de Villiers, who makes a similar claim.

The return to religion and the blurring of the line between the religious and the political have caused difficulties for the republican model of citizenship based on universal principles. In the current tense political climate, leaders of various religions are expressing growing hostility to the separation of church and state. The National Front has been trying to position itself as the defender of beleaguered Christianity, and as such it has systematically and clearly stated its opposition to the Jewish and Islamic traditions, which are in its eyes alien to the true national traditions of France. Once again there is a vigorous effort to cast Jews and Muslims as "anti-France." Both groups are portrayed as unified and homogeneous. For the National Front, the Muslim minority is the primary target, and by attacking that target the party has attracted a growing minority of voters, particularly at the local level. At the same time, the Front has also attacked the Jewish minority as a group no less alien to Christian France than the Muslim minority. For the Front, the only genuine organic community in France is thus the Christian community, which is said to be the true repository of French national values, and for reasons that are almost genetic. As Front leader Jean-Marie Le Pen puts it, "I also have the right to demand that I not be held suspect and persecuted just because I am French and Catholic. Down with anti-French racism!" Instinctively adopting the vocabulary of Maurice Barrès and Edouard Drumont, National Front supporters have begun to shout the old slogan, "France for the French."[18] Once again they have declared war on "the Jewish Republic," and they like to contrast the "biological" identity of France with the "cosmopolitanism" of Jews tied to the capitalist, revolutionary, and Masonic "internationals." More than that, they have heaped abuse of the grossest sort on France's best-known Jewish officials and politicians. As the Front sees it, the "French community," which consists exclusively of Christians, should also be insisting on its "right to be different." In response to "anti-French racism," the Front sees itself as the advocate of "French France." In a truly democratic country, it argues, the vast majority would be able to impose its own "national" values on cultural minorities.[19] This perverse message seems to have some appeal beyond the already ample ranks of the extreme right. Some politicians of the moderate right seem to have picked it up recently, as was evident in an anti-Semitic outburst directed at the quiet, isolated Orthodox Jewish community of Aix-les-Bains in November 1989.

Thus identity politics, to which many Jews themselves subscribe, may, if pushed to an extreme, lead to cultural clashes along any number of fronts. To make matters worse for French Jews, some Muslims, including both recent immigrants and those born on French soil, apparently share some of these anti-Semitic sentiments.[20] Nevertheless, during the Gulf War, both the Jewish and the Muslim communities in France refrained from taking a public position on French policy.[21] Still, in 1995, an official national commission on human rights noted "the animosity of part of the North African population toward the Jewish community" but expressed satisfaction that "vandalism by young North Africans against synagogues" was "not really very serious."[22] Such thinking, by emphasizing community identities, weakens the republican idea of citizenship, substituting the civil for the civic. Those who regret, with good reason, the way in which state action contributed to the disappearance of Jewish culture in France and who favor a return to community traditions are thus embarking, at a particularly delicate moment in French history, on a path whose outcome is uncertain. Will fratricidal battles erupt once again? Will there be a resumption of Franco-French warfare as various groups seek to rediscover their own values? And at a time when the state has suffered a loss of both power and legitimacy, might there be a risk of renewed intolerance and, ultimately, exclusion?

To be sure, the idea of a "right to be different" has lost favor since the 1980s. For instance, the Long Commission's report on what should be required of those who wish to obtain French nationality was dismissive of multiculturalism. In 1992, the Haut Conseil à l'Intégration stated, "The logic of equality dictates that foreigners or people of foreign descent who wish to live on our soil should not seek to do so in communities based on ethnic or national origin which would negotiate to obtain their own enclaves governed by their own distinct laws."[23] According to the Commission, the idea of the French melting-pot, with assimilation promoted and fostered by the state, is not compatible with the American notion of multiculturalism, nor is the American idea of "affirmative action."[24] But is the effort to preserve a universalist public sphere doomed to fail in the face of community passions on all sides? Will identity politics, which has affected even the Jews of France, reshape the public sphere without reviving the bitter conflicts of the past?

12

CARPENTRAS, OR THE TOPPLING
OF CLERMONT-TONNERRE

The Comte de Clermont-Tonnerre would scarcely have believed his eyes. Abbé Grégoire would have been aghast. Once their surprise had dissipated, neither man would have hidden his anger at the public rebirth of a "Jewish nation," of the very nation whose disappearance was the price that Jews were obliged to pay, in the halcyon days of the Revolution, for admission to the rights of citizenship. The Jacobin Revolution had no doubt about the matter whatsoever: it wanted assimilation, not community, and equality meant that all citizens must be virtually identical. It was the Revolution that invited the Jews of Carpentras—known as the "Jerusalem of the Comtat Venaissin" because of its rich Judaic cultural and religious heritage—to abandon the Jewish quarter that had been their home since time immemorial. If Carpentras has lately become a symbol of the relationship between France and its Jews, this is because the very name serves as a reminder of how deeply rooted Judaism is in French soil. From Carpentras—along with Avignon, Tarascon, Bédarrides, and Nîmes—came generation after generation of Jews who, along with others from Alsace and Lorraine, made Franco-Judaism a living reality. Many of the state Jews who distinguished themselves as officials of the Third Republic also came from the city. And it was to Carpentras that Dreyfus went to recuperate after the Rennes trial of 1899 led at last to his being set free. Carpentras has always symbolized the central role of Jews in French history. Yet there were times when the Jews became enmeshed in Franco-French warfare, impelled by circumstances to become the allies and instruments of republican forces in their battles against reactionaries and clericals. For those who disliked republican ideals, certain Jews became the very embodiment of the universalist political morality they fought so hard to defeat. Colorful Jewish personalities became the focus of public attention because they spearheaded the forces of change: from Adolphe Crémieux to Alfred Naquet, Joseph Reinach, Léon Blum, and Pierre Mendès-France, assimilated French Jews symbolized the vigor of republican hopes and so became the target of vehement anti-Semitic attacks and jeers.

Now that French passions have subsided and France has come to some sort of consensus about its government, however, Jews are being attacked not for acting in a certain way but simply for being members of a community. At the same time, their numbers at the highest levels of government have diminished (notwithstanding such important figures as Simone Veil, a noted and popular leader of the liberal right, and Robert Badinter, a former justice minister). Consequently, attacks on the "Jewish Republic" are less common than they once were; such a fantasy could have originated only in a time of near civil war. The republican state, long the passionate concern of the Jews who chose to serve it, has at last been recognized as legitimate by nearly everyone. Political anti-Semitism as such seems to be on the wane everywhere but in the pages of the extreme-right-wing press, which remains quite active. Paradoxically, the diminished level of national conflict has given rise to a more collective perception of Jews, to a sort of reification of the Jewish "community" or "nation." To be sure, the legitimacy of this community is taken for granted, but its customs are seen as so peculiar that it is set apart from the larger community of citizens, who are treated as individuals; the Jews, assigned whether they like it or not to a "community," have in some ways reverted to their prerevolutionary status. And this Jewish "community" is also set apart from other so-called communities. For both the Republic and its adversaries, Jews now exist almost solely in the form of a "community."

Then, in May 1990, came the thunderclap from Carpentras: a Jewish cemetery was desecrated, and a body was exhumed and treated in a most degrading way. The event symbolized the revival of the old idea of the "Jewish community" and thus represented a challenge to a certain idea of the Republic. Various factors had contributed to the new communitarization of French Jews: decentralization, challenges to the authority of the state, the "cohabitation" of a right-wing government with a left-wing president, the decline of political commitment, and the concomitant rise of identity politics. Now, for both the government and the media, Jews were no longer individuals but members of a community. The Grand Rabbi of France declared, "Henceforth time shall be divided into a before Carpentras and an after Carpentras." What could this mean, if not that Carpentras was the first occasion when the Jewish community as such played a public political role? Carpentras thus marked a triumph of collective identification. Some see danger in this: they think that, if nothing is done to prevent it, such identification may eventually impose the idea of a still largely imaginary community on Jews who persist in thinking of themselves as individuals, thus cutting them off from their fellow citizens. What makes this process even more worrisome to many observers is that it also serves the interests of certain Jewish leaders who would like to see the "Jewish community" play a stronger political role. Thus an "imaginary community" is being molded into a real community by forces both inside it and outside, even though it lacks any solid foundation as a community. Carpentras was the occasion when the "national community" came together to express its "solidarity" with what everyone suddenly seemed to think was a smaller "community" within it, the Jewish community. This process of forging a collective identity could already be glimpsed on earlier occasions, after the bombing of the synagogue on the rue Copernic in 1980, for example, or of the Goldenberg restaurant in 1982, but with Carpentras it began to accelerate rapidly.

Signs of this process can be seen in official speeches made at the time. Shocked by the profanation of the dead, French President François Mitterrand offered his "fraternal solidarity" to the "Jewish community of Carpentras, one of the oldest in France, and to the families" of the victims. Similarly, Jacques Chirac let it be known that his "thoughts, full of sadness, are with the families and the Jewish community." The Gaullist *Lettre de la nation* wrote, "All of France came together after Carpentras, as huge numbers of people of every stripe joined the Jewish community. . . . France offers its solidarity and sympathy to an aggrieved community." Valéry Giscard d'Estaing likewise expressed his "respect and affection for the Jewish community of France." And the Communist Party released a formal statement noting how "millions of good men and women . . . are solemnly demonstrating their solidarity with the Jewish community." To be sure, Grand Rabbi Joseph Sitruck issued a warning in his very first statement after the event: "If there is anyone naïve enough to believe that only the Jewish community is affected by this, I would like to disabuse them." But shortly thereafter he noted "how good it is to feel all of France at our side." And then he offered "thanks to the people of France, thanks to France." And Freddy Haddad, president of the Association Culturelle Israélite of Carpentras, said, "In targeting this city and this cemetery, the vandals meant to assault the entire Jewish community." These internal pronouncements carried little weight, however, compared with the rhetoric from outside, which took the theme of "community" as its leitmotif. Thus SOS-Racisme, an organization known for its support of the "right to be different," called upon French moral and religious leaders to join it in expressing total "solidarity with the Jewish community of France."[1]

The press also got into the act, thereby reinforcing the universal perception that the Jews of France formed a community. A review of articles appearing in *Le Monde* shows just how powerful that perception was. The May 13–14 issue of the paper reported on "numerous demonstrations of solidarity with the Jewish community of France." The text went on to note, "The Jewish community is organizing a demonstration in Paris which the parties of the left plan to join." The next day, a front-page headline proclaimed, "The left and the right have come together to demonstrate with the Jewish community," while an article on an inside page echoed the sentiment: "Left and right unite alongside the Jewish community." In other words, all of France was now marching shoulder to shoulder with "the Jewish community." *La Croix*, too, thought the news worth a headline: "First outrage, now solemn mourning with the Jewish community in Carpentras." *L'Humanité* reported, "The Jewish community, amply represented at the scene of the tragedy, conducted itself with dignity." *Témoignage chrétien* also expressed its emotion: "We want to turn now to the members of the Jewish community to tell them how sorry we are." And in *Le Figaro–Magazine*, Jean d'Ormesson wondered "how anyone could not feel solidarity with the Jewish community after such a cruel and abominable act."[2]

Thus a chorus of voices reassured the Jews of France while at the same time setting them apart from their fellow citizens. The press also devoted considerable space to the "reactions of the Jewish community." *Libération*, for example, reported, "Further anti-Semitic acts have heightened the fears of the Jewish community. Two thousand applications for permission to emigrate to Israel were filed this week." An editorial in *La Croix* confirmed this story: "Some Jews are afraid. Parents are contemplating packing their bags and leaving France because their children have been traumatized by the profanation at Carpentras. Leaving France! Yes, just as Jews left Germany in the 1930s when it went Nazi. Their reaction is excessive, irrational, even dangerous."[3] A headline in *Le Monde* stated that Jews at the synagogue on the rue de la Victoire had said that they "would feel safer in Israel." The article went on to say that the issue of French anti-Semitism was "one of the Israeli government's primary preoccupations" and that Israeli intelligence had reportedly set up a special unit to monitor anti-Semitism in other countries.[4] Obviously, the idea that the Jewish community was reacting to Carpentras in a certain way served to substantiate an unconfirmed report that linked this event to quite another historical moment.

The press, moreover, was only too eager to dwell on the distinctive culture and traditions of the "Jewish community." For perhaps the first time in French history, readers of the major newspapers were treated to virtually ethnographic descriptions of various Jewish rituals. *La Croix* ran a detailed article on the prayers said at Carpentras on the day of national mourning, which coincided with "*lag b'omer*, usually a happy occasion that ends the period of mourning following Passover." The assembled mourners chanted "the Kaddish, the prayer for the dead, which was repeated in Hebrew by the Jewish community. The mournful rhythm of this prayer, punctuated by amen, preceded the final, more hopeful chant, Ani Maa Nin [sic]." As *Témoignage chrétien* observed, "The Catholic community openly joined in the tribute, as the priest officiating at the service declared that 'we are very close culturally and fraternally to the Jewish community.' " The weekly went on to comment that "the faithful sang 'Birkat Kohanim' (another prayer for the dead) before chanting the Sh'ma Israel." *Libération* was careful to inform its readers that Jacques Chaban-Delmas wore a gray yarmulke and François Léotard a white one, and commented that "the ceremony ended with Ani Maanim, a hopeful prayer, and the Kaddish, a prayer of sanctification for the dead." *Le Quotidien de Paris* also noted that nearly all the political and civic leaders present at Carpentras wore yarmulkes. André Lajoinie went bare-headed, and Minister of the Interior Pierre Joxe wore "a dark felt hat" that was featured in so many news photographs it will surely go down in history. The newspapers also published countless photographs of another ceremony that was held a few days later at the synagogue on the rue de la Victoire. This occasion, "organized by the Jewish community of France," was attended by virtually every French political leader, and once again the press was careful to note the color of every yarmulke.[5]

The huge demonstration that took place on May 14 along the traditional left-wing parade route from the Place de la République to the Place de la Bastille was held not at the behest of any left-wing party or trade union but "under the aegis of the Conseil Représentatif des Institutions Juives de France." Hundreds of thousands of people marched. President Mitterrand took part, the first time since the Liberation that a head of state had marched in a public demonstration in France. *Le Quotidien de Paris* reported, "Around him, dozens of people chanted Shalom Aleichem, which means 'peace and love' in Hebrew"[6] (Actually the words mean "peace be with you.") For *Le Monde*, this demonstration attested to the "need to be with the Jews, Jewish oneself, out of solidarity, . . . and, for Jews, an occasion to assert an identity."[7] "For Jews"—*"pour les Juifs"*—*Le Monde* wrote; in French, the use of a capital "J" suggests the Jewish nation or people, whereas the adjective "Jewish" is spelled with a small letter, *juif,* suggesting nothing more than adherence to the Jewish faith. Such a description of a public demonstration "by the Jewish people" would surely have caused Clermont-Tonnerre to turn over in his grave, but to the nation that gathered "in solidarity with the Jews" it further confirmed the existence of a collective Jewish identity. Near the end of this impressive demonstration, and not long before the start of services at the synagogue on the rue de la Victoire, the sound of the great bell of Notre-Dame resounded through Paris, seemingly announcing the Jewish service to the other nation, the French, of which it remained the symbol.

The province also got into the act: more than six thousand people protested against anti-Semitism in Marseilles, five thousand apiece in Quimper, Lyons, and Caen, several thousand in Aix, four thousand in Clermont-Ferrand, three thousand in Amiens, two thousand in Montauban, and one thousand in Mulhouse. Long, silent columns snaked through the streets of Metz and Thionville, Nancy and Bordeaux, Strasbourg, Dreux, and Rouen, Saint-Nazaire, Villeurbanne, and Drancy. "France stunned by the shock of anti-Semitism," headlined *Libération*; one poll reported that 62 percent of French citizens believed that the vandalism at Carpentras was the principal problem confronting French society. Meanwhile, Joan of Arc Day celebrations provided an opportunity for a thousand nationalists in Marseilles and six thousand in Lyons to buck the national consensus and proclaim their own nationalist faith with the usual rallying cry, "France for the French," along with a few Nazi slogans. But for the time being, their shouts went unheeded. Militants of the Action Française vied for symbolic mastery of the capital by flying their colors from the tower of Notre-Dame. The all-but-unanimous condemnation of anti-Semitism and public expression of solidarity with the "Jewish community" increased the isolation of the National Front, even though that party had for some years been attracting the votes of a growing proportion of the electorate despite its leader's penchant for anti-Semitic puns.

In this respect, this temporary alliance against anti-Semitism, this harbinger of a common republican front from which only the National Front would be excluded, was by dint of its very unanimity "a demonstration unprecedented in the annals of [French] history," so scarred by division. Traditionally, the battle against anti-Semitism was a weapon in the ideological arsenal of the left in its battle against a right portrayed as purely and simply "reactionary," all but divorced from the good people of France and the republican order. Yet a question remains: "If everyone speaks in unison, where is the danger? But it is there, palpable, perceptible. We know it. Sometimes we even see it."[8]

One has only to recall the endless, albeit incomplete, list of similar anti-Semitic attacks preceding the one at Carpentras, some just as horrifying as the desecration that triggered this unprecedented outpouring of solidarity.[9] Without going back any further than 1980, one can easily compile a long list: August 29, 1980, seventy-two Jewish gravestones overturned in Forbach (Moselle); April 25, 1981, eighty tombstones vandalized and covered with anti-Semitic graffiti in Bagneux (Hauts-de-Seine); June 20, 1981, thirty-odd Jewish monuments overturned and vandalized in Delme (Moselle); September 1984, seventy gravestones smashed in Gerstheim (Bas-Rhin); November 28, 1984, sixty-four gravestones smashed with hammers in Nice; April 28, 1986, twenty-one Jewish gravestones vandalized in Belfort; April 26, 1988, ninety gravestones destroyed in Weiterswiller (Bas-Rhin); May 24, 1988, some sixty steles overturned in Sarre-Union (Bas-Rhin); March 6, 1989, more than twenty Jewish tombstones overturned and smashed in Eleu, near Liévin; April 20, 1990, Nazi graffiti painted on the Bordeaux synagogue; May 1, 1990, anti-Semitic slogans painted on shops in Avignon, including the words *Juden raus* (Jews, get out); May 4, 1990, twenty-two Jewish gravestones destroyed in Wissembourg (Bas-Rhin); May 9 or 10, thirty-seven Jewish headstones destroyed in Carpentras and the body of Félix Germont desecrated; May 12, stars of David painted on stores in Quimper, anti-Semitic slogans painted on walls in Nevers and on the synagogue of Haguenau (Bas-Rhin); shortly thereafter, a group of adolescents are arrested while attempting to gain entry into the Jewish cemetery at Préville near Nancy; May 14, 1990, thirty-two Jewish gravestones destroyed in Clichy-sous-Bois, near Paris, swastikas painted on the headstones; and, according to some, an arson attack on the synagogue of Clichy. In reaction, a protest demonstration is organized by Jewish authorities, trade unions, an antiracist group, and other organizations. In Nice, on the same day, anti-Semitic slogans are painted on shops owned by Jews, and someone attempts to desecrate a headstone in a Jewish cemetery in Lyons. On August 28, 1990, twelve Jewish graves are desecrated in two cemeteries in the Eure. On September 17, 1990, forty-three Jewish headstones are smashed in a cemetery near Colmar. In October 1990, there is an arson attack on the synagogue of Epinay-sous-Sénart. On January 18, 1991, three Molotov cocktails are tossed at a synagogue in Vénissieux, near Lyons. On November 24, 1991, anti-Semitic slogans are painted on a building owned by a Jewish organization in Strasbourg. A few days later, two swastikas are painted on a synagogue and a school in Colmar. On March 14, 1992, arson at the synagogue of La Courneuve; March 20, 1992, neo-Nazi graffiti on the entrance of the Bayonne synagogue, including, in red paint, the words "Jews to the ovens." August 1992, pro-Nazi stickers are affixed to the mailboxes of officials of Jewish organizations in Villepinte; posters asserting that "Hitler was right" are glued to windows of Jewish shops in the Sentier quarter of Paris. August 28, 1992, 193 Jewish headstones are vandalized in Herrlisheim (Haut-Rhin); a thousand people turn out for a prayer vigil. August 31, the synagogue in Saint-Avold (Moselle) is burned. On September 12, anti-Semitic slogans and swastikas are painted on headstones in a Lyons cemetery. Among the slogans: "Adolf Hitler is our father" and "Death to the Jews!" Again, more than a thousand people turn out for a prayer vigil. On September 24, Jewish graves are desecrated in the cemetery of Freyming-Merlebach (Moselle). Swastikas and anti-Semitic slogans are painted. On December 2, anti-Semitic slogans are painted on a building owned by the synagogue of Strasbourg; rooms are vandalized, and the rabbi's office is destroyed. Early January 1993, Jewish cemeteries at Cronenbourg and Schitigheim in Alsace are vandalized; Molotov cocktails are tossed at synagogues in Villepinte (Seine-Saint-Denis) and Chelles; a protest demonstration is held in Paris. February 21, 1993, vandalism at the synagogue and Jewish Community Center of Mulhouse. On May 2, vandalism at the Jewish cemetery in Febersheim. May 8, fifteen gravestones vandalized at a Jewish cemetery in Frauenberg (Moselle). Shortly thereafter, attempted arson at a synagogue in Epinay-sur-Seine. June 14, 1993, nearly a hundred Jewish tombstones are desecrated in the cemetery of Haut-Vernet near Perpignan. Most of these stones marked the graves of Jews who had died in the Rivesaltes concentration camp during World War II; a memorial to the victims of deportation was also destroyed. July 1, 1993, twenty Jewish headstones are overturned in the cemetery at Mertzwiller. July 18 and 28, 1993, gravestones are desecrated in the Jewish cemetery of La Madeleine at Evreux (Eure). August 16, 1993, the Alsatian delegate of the CRIF is attacked by a man he had caught in the act of painting anti-Semitic slogans. On September 9, 1993, the synagogue in Amiens is covered with neo-Nazi graffiti and its gates are broken down. September 11, Jewish graves at the cemetery of Saint-Cyr-l'Ecole (Yvelines) are vandaized. October 8, a memorial plaque honoring the victims of the deportation is covered with swastikas. November 3, 1993, thirty gravestones are destroyed at the Jewish cemetery of Puttelange-aux-Lacs (Moselle). December 18, 1993, attempted arson at a bookstore in Avignon founded by a Jewish family; a star of David is painted on the store window. March 2, 1994, a Molotov cocktail is thrown at a synagogue in Aulnay-sous-Bois (Seine-Saint-Denis), starting a fire. April 26, 1994, twenty gravestones are desecrated at the Jewish cemetery in Merville, along with 26 steles at another Jewish cemetery in Struth. Many of these steles were in memory of people deported by the Germans during World War II. May 20, 1994, a plaque honoring seven Jews shot by *miliciens* led by Paul Touvier in Rilleux-le-Pape is torn down and smashed. On August 15, 1994, anti-Semitic graffiti are painted on the walls of the synagogue in Altkirch (Haut-Rhin). December 26, 1994, a dangerous arson attack on a prayer hall frequently used by more than two hundred Jewish worshipers in the suburbs of Lyons: a car loaded with four bottles of propane gas is set on fire next to the building, but the fire is put out before the gas explodes.

Carpentras was thus one of a long series of anti-Semitic incidents.[10] The list would be even longer if we were to include incidents not involving acts of violence. Anti-Semitism has been constantly in the public eye. Shortly before the Carpentras episode, for example, an angry clash occurred in Nice between the city's mayor, Jacques Médecin, and three Jewish municipal-council members. When Médecin decided to form an alliance with the local National Front in the next municipal election, the three Jewish officials tried to talk him into changing his mind. The mayor's reply brought the incident to national media attention: "I don't know any Jew who would turn down a gift that was offered to him, even if he had qualms about it." The three Jewish councilors immediately resigned, and the mayor's anti-Semitic remark was denounced by a spokesman for the government as well as by the executive office of the Socialist Party, the secretaries general of the RPR and CDS (Centre des Démocrates Sociaux), the Ligue des Droits de l'Homme, the MRAP (Mouvement contre le Racisme et l'Antisémitisme et pour la Paix), the CRIF, etc. The press covered the story extensively.

It would be easy to compile a long list of other anti-Semitic public statements and actions. On May 2, 1990, anti-Semitic tracts were handed out and posted on walls in Limoges. These contained the following statement: "We must get rid of that greatest of scourges, the Jew." On May 15, the faculty council of the Université Jean-Moulin in Lyons unanimously voted to remove two extreme-right-wing professors for teaching revisionist views about the Holocaust. On May 27, 1990, a teacher at a technical college in Nancy was suspended for proposing that a student write a thesis about the Carpentras incident with a very dubious slant. In September 1990, pamphlets denying the existence of Nazi gas chambers were distributed in Nancy. In April 1991, Jean Brière, a former spokesman for an ecology party, published an article on the "war-mongering of Israel and the Zionist lobby." The Greens expressed regret about the content of the article and maintained that they had "never tolerated anti-Semitism." The affair attracted nationwide attention when some members of the party protested and sanctions imposed on Brière were disavowed by the party's national convention. In May 1991, an anti-Semitic missal was distributed in the Vaucluse. In that same month, the founder of the National Front in Aveyron was sentenced for circulating *The Protocols of the Elders of Zion*. On December 10, 1991, Pierre Chrétien, an RPR member and deputy mayor of Sarcelles, was suspended for saying, "As for the Jews, you have to go after them with blackjacks, the way the Germans did." In June 1992, a court sentenced several "negationists" for denying the existence of Nazi gas chambers. In July 1992, the secretary general of *Le Figaro*'s editorial board, who was also the secretary of the Association pour Défendre la Mémoire du Maréchal Pétain, reportedly stated that there was nothing about Vichy, including the Jewish statute, that he could not accept responsibility for. In August 1992, the CRIF denounced anti-Semitic statements by National Front leader Jean-Marie Le Pen. On July 15, 1993, socialist politician Bernard Tapie, who was also the owner of a Marseilles soccer team, made a statement in connection with an investigation of an alleged bribe paid to certain players for another team to lose a game so that Tapie's team could win a championship. Tapie wanted to suggest that the investigators were pressuring one of his stars to turn state's evidence against him. "They're treating this man [Eydelie] the way they did during the war when the Jews were rounded up. They're saying some will give names and others will be sent away. They're looking to make a trade. You want to save your family? Give me ten names. That's what they want to do with Eydelie. That's the way they're treating everybody" thought to be involved in the scandal. Nazi-hunter Serge Klarsfeld disputed this comparison. For one thing, he pointed out that Jews who were arrested were given no such choice. For another, it distressed him that Tapie was spreading the slander that some Jews had betrayed others to save their own skins. Klarsfeld succeeded in extracting an apology from Tapie, who acknowledged that he had "misspoken." In late July and early August 1993, anti-Semitic pamphlets were circulated in and around Paris. These included a reproduction of the cover of *The Protocols of the Elders of Zion*, denounced the "Jewish peril," and lashed out at certain political leaders, journalists, and others. At the same time, the media reported that fights had broken out among students at the Lycée Joliot-Curie in Nanterre when Islamic militants distributed copies of *The Protocols*. On November 21, 1993, a teacher at a *lycée* in Castres was indicted for inciting racial hatred after distributing tracts to his students accusing President Mitterrand of being "in the pay of the Jews."

The foregoing compilations are far from exhaustive. One would have to include countless anti-Semitic statements made by the leaders of the National Front; articles published in that party's various press organs; numerous incidents precipitated by extreme-right-wing student demonstrations, the trial of Paul Touvier (the former *milicien* mentioned earlier), and the investigation of René Bousquet;* various statements by Holocaust negationists; and so on. Clearly, the Carpentras episode occurred in a period when expressions of anti-Semitism were by no means rare in France. Various published surveys suggest that the public was well aware of this. Yet it was also a time when, according to former Prime Minister Edouard Balladur, "For the first time in the history of the Republic, a veritable war is being waged against anti-Semitism."[11] There was nothing manipulated or contrived about the reporting of these many incidents, and Jews frequently spoke out in public to condemn them. Yet only Carpentras triggered the nationwide mobilization described above, bringing people of all parties except the extreme right together in unanimous denunciation.

What set Carpentras apart from so many similar or even more destructive incidents of graveyard vandalism was of course the fact that the body of Félix Germont was dug up and impaled on an umbrella. People were dumbfounded at the thought that such violence could be visited on a corpse, particularly since the attackers placed a star of David next to the body so that there could be no mistaking their intentions. An editorial in *Le Point* described the attack as "racist, anti-Semitic barbarity" that could only have been committed by "psychopaths." *La Tribune de l'expansion* alluded to satanic evil. Jean

---

*An important official of the Vichy regime who was to have been tried for crimes against humanity but was assassinated by a deranged gunman before he could be brought to trial. —TRANS.

Kahn, at the time president of the CRIF, remarked, "Not even the Germans went after bodies in their graves," and the president of the Carpentras synagogue echoed this sentiment by noting, "Not even during the war were such shocking things seen in Carpentras." Many commentators, including Father Michel Riquet, did not hesitate to compare Carpentras to Auschwitz. Jacques Berque was of the opinion that Carpentras represented "the height of anti-Semitism, for such things were unheard of at the time of the Dreyfus Affair and even, as far as I know, in the time of the Nazis." A headline in *The Guardian* proclaimed "Kristallnacht in Carpentras." President Mitterrand condemned the authors of this "particularly abject" crime, who, he said, had carried out their attack "in darkness, in a cowardly manner, against the dead." Cardinal Lustiger ordered "contemplative communities to observe a day of penitence and fasting to ask God to prevent our countrymen from giving in to morbid fantasies and hatreds" and expressed the fear that the incident might betoken the return of "an aggressive paganism." Archbishop Raymond Bouchez of Avignon called the crime an "offense against God," and *La Croix* termed it "blasphemy," adding, "The object of the attack was not human life but the essence of man himself." Georges Balandier opined, "The desecration of the Carpentras cemetery strikes at the very root of civilization because it repudiates one of mankind's essential responsibilities, which is to honor the dead." No detail of the crime was too horrible for the press to report. *Le Monde* described "the worst of the abominations. . . . The legs of Monsieur Germont's corpse were spread apart and the point of an umbrella was shoved into his anus. A star of David was placed next to the body." *Libération* and *Le Figaro* also published full details of the way in which the dignity of the dead Jew had been violated. "France stunned by anti-Semitic shock," headlined *Libération*.[12]

The psychological implications of an attack on a dead Jew thus transformed Carpentras into a historic event that has left an indelible mark on the national consciousness. In the wake of the massive national reaction, some commentators suggested that the response might have been manipulated. Indeed, many political leaders were quick to level a finger of blame at the National Front, with prominent socialists leading the charge. On May 19, Jean d'Ormesson published a cautionary note in *Le Figaro–Magazine:* "It strikes me as inappropriate that the leaders of a country that prides itself on having rehabilitated Captain Dreyfus have allowed themselves to make charges of criminal actions before any serious investigation has been conducted. . . . There are plenty of reasons to be suspicious, from the Reichstag fire to the Katyn massacre to the bombing of the Copernic synagogue. . . . It is quite possible that we are dealing here with a political provocation coming from a wholly unsuspected quarter." In the same issue, Louis Pauwels lashed out at what he called a "witch-hunt in which rumor is substituted for proof." More suspicious still was Alain Griotteray, who wrote of a "brainwashing apparatus suddenly gone amok" and hinted at "irregularities" and "misrepresentations." In a similar vein, *Aspects de la France* thought it saw the culprit in "a socialist government in trouble, trying to regain its popularity by joining the antiracist bandwagon. . . . The only thing the politicians are interested in is scoring points against Le Pen, whose poll numbers are rising steadily."

The National Front's own press soon claimed that it had proof of a deliberate hoax. *National-Hebdo* and *Présent* condemned the way in which the incident had been used to attack Le Pen and blamed the attack on either Muslim fundamentalists or the Israeli Mossad. The one thing both papers were certain of was that the socialists were somehow involved, led by Minister of the Interior Pierre Joxe, who had been the first official to rush to the scene. Joxe's remarks blaming people who promoted "racist hatred" were widely interpreted as a thinly veiled attack on the National Front. "The whole thing seems to have been trumped up," according to *National-Hebdo*, which claimed that the crime had actually been committed on the night of May 8–9 and not the following night, as had originally been alleged. "Le Pen appeared on [the television program] *L'Heure de vérité* [on May 9]. That night, supposedly, you had Carpentras. Carpentras was the centerpiece of a whole cabal that was organized expressly to put an end to Le Pen's string of successes." Le Pen himself immediately accused "professional antiracists" of having deliberately trumped up "a hoax like the one at Timişoara,* a "macabre setup" organized by "professional provocateurs." Another Lepenist paper, *Le Choc du mois*, published a long, detailed article purporting to unmask the "slander machine" known as Carpentras. Making a case that would often be repeated later on, the paper wrote that Le Pen had

> appeared on *L'Heure de vérité* on the night of May 9, when the desecration had already taken place on the previous night but was not discovered until ten the following morning. He was asked a provocative question: "Do you think that Jews have too much power in France today?" And we quote verbatim from the response given by the leader of the National Front: "That depends on what area you're talking about. . . . Jews have lots of power in the press, just as Bretons have in the navy and Corsicans in the customs service; this to me is incontrovertible." And all the good souls of the left and right, along with the bought media, called him a "hate-monger." So the two things got mixed up together. What difference did the actual sequence of events make? Carpentras equals National Front! Pierre Joxe was not about to miss an opportunity to sling some mud: surely some of it would stick. . . . The expulsion machine was fired up. . . . The slander machine was set in motion.

Le Quotidien de Paris echoed the charge that the event was being deliberately manipulated to make the National Front appear responsible. Like *National-Hebdo*, this newspaper frequently alluded to the demonization of Le Pen. It was also obsessed with ascertaining the precise degree to which Félix Germont's body had been impaled. The paper seized on what it took to be a certain hesitation in the language used by the prosecutor in Nîmes, who spoke of a "staged scene involving the insertion of a pointed object into the crease in the buttocks of an exhumed cadaver" while acknowledging that there had

---

*During 1992 demonstrations against Ceaucescu in this Romanian city, a mass killing supposedly took place, but the death toll was later revealed to be grossly exaggerated.

indeed been "an intent to impale the body of Félix Germont." But "sources close to the investigation" had told *Le Quotidien* that "the tip of the umbrella had just barely been inserted near the anus." For the extreme-right-wing press, this "discrepancy" stood as incontrovertible proof that a hoax had taken place, since the impalement had been widely reported in the mainstream press, and the sexual overtones of the act, suggesting perversity of a psychopathic order, had indeed had a profound and lasting impact on public opinion. In light of all this, the paper concluded that "the impalement so graphically described by [former socialist Prime Minister] Laurent Fabius on [the public television channel] FR3 is a myth—a myth deliberately concocted by certain political leaders in order to foster an understandable public reaction of horrified revulsion."[13]

Thereafter, some people began to look at what had happened in Carpentras in a very different light, with the paradoxical result that the massive national reaction seemed to justify the very anti-Semitism that it was supposed to combat. What if the unanimous revulsion, uniting people normally separated by political and ideological differences, were merely the product of a vast hoax deliberately contrived to discredit a political adversary? And had not Jews themselves used the event, as they used the Shoah, to justify their presence in French society? If so, then would not the attempt by Jewish leaders to promote a greater presence for the Jewish community in French public life have had the unintended consequence of justifying the French community's exclusion of a subculture whose manners and customs, described by the press in ethnographic detail that emphasized their strangeness, set them apart from other Frenchmen? In a time of danger and uncertainty, when the ideology of cultural difference has been used as yet another device for excluding those who are different, communitarization might have numerous unintended consequences, or so it was argued.

The most comprehensive statement of this skeptical view appeared in an article by Paul Yonnet, and the attention that it attracted highlighted a subtle but worrisome shift in the interpretation of Carpentras. In many respects, Yonnet's article seemed to accept the view that the event had been deliberately manipulated: it used some of the same formulations as the skeptics, such as "brainwashing machinery," "slander machine," "exclusion mechanism," and so on, all of which had appeared in such journals as *National-Hebdo*, *Le Choc du mois*, and *Le Figaro–Magazine*. But as political scientist Nonna Mayer has pointed out, these doubts were raised "even before the time [of the crime] was definitively established after an investigation that took several weeks. The original estimate that the attack had taken place on the night of May 9–10 seemed plausible at the time." Furthermore, "the violation of Félix Germont's corpse was confirmed by crime-scene photographs and by the original police report. It was not until the corpse was re-exhumed [on May 15] and autopsied that the degree of penetration could be determined." Hence, "contrary to what Yonnet insinuates, the public was not deliberately deceived about the nature of the crime. . . . To judge only by the established facts as we know them today, there was no 'Carpentras affair' comparable to the Timişoara hoax in Romania or the coverage of the Gulf War."[14]

The primary target of Yonnet's "Machine Carpentras" article was the antiracist movement, which even before the cemetery was desecrated had been "trying to build itself up a worthy adversary, a danger sufficient to put people into a real tizzy." In so doing, Yonnet argued, the movement's leaders were "gambling with the interests of Jewish Frenchmen and taking the risk of provoking a kind of 'soft' anti-Semitism in reaction"[15]—because National Front voters would not abandon Le Pen over this kind of issue. According to the article, the obsession with Vichy's responsibility in the deportation of Jews during the war was being used to justify a misleading "continuity" and to "indict Le Pen . . . on the basis of a historical anachronism." Yonnet further alleged that the political elite, including both socialist and Gaullist leaders with the crucial support of CRIF President Jean Kahn, had thus "fabricated the perfect demonized enemy. . . . The antiracist movement needed a worthy adversary regardless of the cost. . . . The Carpentras machine was intended to purge French politics of Le Pen as if by magic and to purge French society of the issues that Le Pen has raised."[16] Ultimately, then, the culprits were the antiracists, for it was they who had constructed the events of Carpentras in such a way as to serve the needs of their own strategy. Socialist leaders, with support from the media, had manipulated the date of the crime, according to Yonnet, in order to make it coincide with Le Pen's television appearance. They had also allowed people to believe that the body had been impaled in order to "purge" Le Pen. As in a detective novel, it was enough to show who profited from the crime to conclude that the Jews must have been behind it. Not only were top political leaders encouraging Jews to think of themselves as a "community," but many in the Jewish rank-and-file were themselves clamoring for more community, as Yonnet demonstrated by examining the programs of any number of Jewish organizations. This had ended up provoking a reaction that had played into the hands of the National Front, he argued. The Carpentras events were then deliberately manipulated in order to thwart the rise of Le Pen. For Yonnet, then, the communitarization of the Jews played a fundamental role: it allegedly greased the wheels of "the machine for manufacturing a Lepenist vote."

The deliberate self-communitarization of the Jews, Yonnet maintained, was nothing more than "Pétainism in reverse." Jews were voluntarily ostracizing themselves, refusing to marry non-Jews, deliberately segregating themselves in order to protect their purity, and rejecting "French people belonging to no community other than the French, seen as fundamentally deprived, as individuals without a community, as Frenchmen without community standing or, indeed, in a stateless status of some sort." For Yonnet, such communitarization implied a kind of " 'racist' antiracism," to which the response was "xenophobic 'antiracist' racism" concerned with avoiding a "dissolution of national identity." In his view, people who insisted on "bolstering the integrity of their little ethnic and religious community, or even their ethnic, religious, and biological, hence racial, community," were "horses of another color" from "those who fear a weakening of the integrity of the 'greater French community.' " The former run with the antiracists, the latter with the National Front. "But at night they all eat the same oats from the same troughs. . . convinced as they are of the horror of racial mixing." Ultimately, they enlisted "much of the press and the political world in their dirty little war."[17]

Very clearly, then, Yonnet attacked Jewish identity politics (which he analyzed solely on the basis of articles that appeared in the press) for provoking a reaction that drove many voters into the arms of Le Pen. Antiracism had brought on "antiracist racism," and from there it was but a short step to the National Front, which politicians had then sought to derail by manipulating the events at Carpentras. But Yonnet offers no evidence to support this reasoning, which amounts to little more than a series of accusations justified by a kind of prosecutorial logic. Crucial questions are begged: To what degree have French Jews embraced the politics of communitarization? How can we gauge the depth of the movement? Yonnet's whole case stands or falls with the answers. More generally, Yonnet presents anti-Semitism as an almost normal reaction to Jewish identity politics. But haven't the primary manifestations of anti-Semitism in France been directed at assimilated Jews, such as Alfred Dreyfus and Léon Blum, state Jews who, to be sure, never renounced their faith but deliberately remained aloof from any involvement in the Jewish community or religious practice?

Yonnet is at pains to place Jewish identity politics in the same basket as the National Front's xenophobic reaction so as to condemn both, much as other writers have tried to draw a parallel between racism and antiracism. Yonnet's argument, utterly devoid of compassion for the fears of French Jews and showing no sign of comprehending their reactions, however extreme they may appear, leaves a bitter taste in the reader's mouth, as does his discussion of the "arrival of Sephardic Jews from North Africa," whom he sees purely and simply as inveterate racists obsessed with biological purity. One's irritation is only compounded by the fact that, despite Yonnet's hostility to the National Front, his views have been most warmly received on that end of the political spectrum. For example, François Brigneau, explicitly citing Yonnet's article, tried to make a case that the conspiracy against Le Pen had resulted in a judicial error: "As the work of distinguished humanists who frequently invoke the Dreyfus Affair, this conclusion is as ridiculous as it is deplorable."[18] Le Figaro–Magazine observed, "The National Front is glad to have this unexpected support."[19] To be sure, the Front's support has grown increasingly diverse. On May 14, 1990, for example, Jean-Marie Domenach wrote, "There is an antiracism that moves in phase with racism, which is both a repercussion of racism and a stimulus to it. I am speaking of antiracism that is exploited for political ends, given that politicians are always looking for an enemy to form coalitions against." Later that year, in October, Domenach fully embraced Yonnet's argument. "There was indeed a hoax," he wrote. "By whom and for whom? It was a disgusting use of a corpse for propaganda purposes, as was done on a larger scale in Timişoara." For a "detailed analysis," Domenach urged his readers to refer to the article by Yonnet. He then concluded on this note: "No one can yet tell the truth, no one yet dares to tell the truth, about Carpentras. But we must at least try to discover the truth. In the very name of truth, because the heirs of the Dreyfusards cannot allow even the best of causes to rest on a bed of lies."[20] Against this line of argument, Nonna Mayer has observed that the "routinization of anti-Semitism, distortion of logic, and denial of history are tactics of the extreme right. The 'machine' is in reverse and backing straight up to the National Front."[21] Indeed, when a Molotov cocktail was tossed at the synagogue in Villepinte on December 31, 1992, *Minute* and *Présent* called this a hoax as well; in 1993, *Présent* printed several full-page "exposés" of the Carpentras "hoax," which it blamed on politicians who exploited for "antiracist" purposes an anti-Semitic act whose perpetrators had never been caught. Finally, in June 1995, when Roger Hanin's film *Train d'enfer* was shown on television between the first and second rounds of the presidential elections, Jean-Marie Le Pen accused the networks of deliberately running the film in an attempt to discredit him. "Five years after the Carpentras hoax, the public has again been totally manipulated. . . . The networks have adopted the tactics of Dr. Goebbels."

The crime has thus far resisted every effort to explain it; meanwhile, in a strange way, it has reoriented the debate about the place and role of Jews in contemporary France. As *Le Figaro* has pointed out, Yonnet's ideas have been dismissed out of hand by certain intellectuals because "the Jewish question remains taboo. It is forbidden territory unless it is approached in a certain way and with a certain frame of mind already approved in advance. Isn't it about time that the perverse effects of these infernal mechanisms were dissected?"[22] Yonnet's characterization of supposed Jewish identity politics as "Pétainism in reverse" actually did give rise to vigorous debate in the national press, a debate that surprisingly found the left-wing newspaper *Libération* opposing the left-wing weekly *Le Nouvel Observateur*, which wrote: "As to the questions concerning the Jewish community and its being tempted by identity politics and exclusionary practices, and concerning the resurgence within that community of a less tolerant brand of Judaism, Yonnet is not the only one to raise them. A certain 'clumsiness' in his style does not negate the entirety of his argument."[23]

So, once again, we are back to the reified "Jewish community," when all the evidence shows that community to be extremely diverse in its behavior and more likely to embrace assimilation than to be tempted by particularism. Leaving aside Yonnet's offensively one-sided arguments about Carpentras, what stands out in his piece is the total denial of Jewish memory, which for him is just another manifestation of identity politics. Even though he is careful to point out that his analysis concerns only "a fraction of the French Jewish community," the reader learns nothing about the rest. The concern with preserving a distinctive Jewish culture is dismissed out of hand simply because it happens to come at a time when many leaders would like the "Jewish community" to be a stronger political presence as well as in a period of markedly more frequent anti-Semitic attacks aimed precisely at sites associated with Jewish memory—and no one can say that "manipulation" was in any way involved in the vast majority of these incidents. Do these events mark the return of Abbé Grégoire or the posthumous triumph of Maurice Barrès? To be sure, both the assimilationist republican and the nationalist worried about the cultural homogeneity of France were critical of the survival of private allegiances within the public sphere, or within a society conceived as destined to remain uniformly Catholic. Today, we are told that such allegiances cannot be allowed to haunt the memory of the living without provoking, as an almost legitimate reaction, a Lepenist-type movement around the issue of immigration. Indeed, in the first round of the 1995 presidential elections, Jean-Marie Le Pen came in first in Carpentras, Avignon, Cavaillon, Isle-sur-la-Sorgue, Apt, Tarascon, Bollène, and Lunel, all places symbolic in one way or another of French Judaism. The warm reception accorded to Yonnet's iconoclastic reinterpretation of Carpentras ultimately proves that, for Jews at any rate, it is no small feat to negotiate the arduous path between citizenship and community, assimilation and identity.

Conclusion

Contemporary history continues to be shaped by memory, by the incessant reconstruction of the nation's past to which France seems increasingly prone. Although Jews have been implicated in France's past for many centuries, their role in creating this national mood of introspection has been modest at best. At a time when memory has become a national obsession, the relative amnesia of French Jews has been a source of misunderstanding, with significant political consequences. This became quite clear in the five years between 1989 and 1994, which witnessed the celebration not only of the bicentennial of the French Revolution but also of the centennial of the Dreyfus Affair and the fiftieth anniversary of both the rise and fall of Vichy—all important milestones marking events that had a profound effect on the destiny of French Jews. Of the most significant historical commemorations of the late twentieth century, only the seventy-fifth anniversary of World War I has been exempt from debate about the role of the Jews. During that war, of course, a temporary reconciliation was achieved among what Maurice Barrès called the "great families of France." In that brief period of national unity, the role of the Jews was not an issue; their integration was taken for granted, and nothing distinguished them from other soldiers at the front. But if one takes a closer look at even that war, one finds that within the French army anti-Semitism may well have persisted just below the surface.[1]

The celebration of the Revolution's bicentennial gave rise to an intense debate about what the Revolution had meant. Anti-Jacobin historians won an almost total victory, and various forms of resistance to the authoritarian revolutionary state were treated with newfound respect. The French found themselves regretting the execution of Louis XVI and shedding tears over the fate of Marie-Antoinette. Many denounced the Revolution for its centralizing, homogenizing tendencies. In the debate that pitted revisionist historians such as François Furet and Mona Ozouf against the disciples of Albert Soboul, the place of the Jews in the revolutionary period had little or no importance. Recent historical scholarship has ignored the question, even though the emancipation of the Jews gave rise to considerable political and philosophical debate at the time.[2] Meanwhile, other academics with no particular expertise in this area but holding opposing views about Jewish identity took it upon themselves to launch a polemic that intersected with contemporary debates about broader issues. For one group of scholars, the French Revolution was totally evil because it led to complete eradication of a distinctive Jewish identity. Just as other scholars once again touted the Vendéan resistance and rejected the homogenizing aims of the Revolution, these champions of Jewish identity forcefully insisted that the French model of emancipation, which left no room for particularism of any sort, also "precluded" any Jewish presence. Because of the Revolution, "the Jew in his historical dimension was denied. He became a citizen." By contrast, another group of scholars argued that the Revolution had allowed Jews at long last to live "free and happy" lives. It liberated them to develop their own identity within the French national community.[3] As we have seen, the way in which Abbé Grégoire conceived of the "regeneration" of the Jewish citizens of the future was more than a little dubious, for he hoped that the Jews would shed their beliefs and "superstitions" and language so that they might at last be "incorporated" into the nation and thus disappear as Jews.

Some Jewish intellectuals fasten on this reductive dimension of Gré-goire's thought and also cite Clermont-Tonnerre's hostility to the persistence within French society of any form of Jewish "nation." In so doing, they reject the universalist dimension of French political thought because of its hostility to any variety of multiculturalism, and go on to justify the purely instrumentalist view of the republican state that is common today in certain Orthodox circles. This debate is obviously related to the larger critique of Jacobinism that has informed much recent historiography.

Similarly, in the commemoration of the Dreyfus Affair it sometimes seems as though the Jewish aspect has once again been relegated to the shadows. Various commentators have maintained that anti-Semitism was at most a contributing rather than an essential factor in both the inception and evolution of the Affair. In this view there is implicit criticism of those who hold that the fate of the Jews in this period was inextricably intertwined with the history of the Republic and that Dreyfus, a state Jew who was more deeply involved with Jewish culture than many commentators care to admit, stands as a symbol of this historical nexus.[4] Looking beyond this relatively muted academic debate, we find a number of public incidents that show how murky the public understanding of Dreyfus the man remains, as opposed to knowledge of the course of various trials during the Affair or the actions of the principal protagonists. In short, the Affair, for which no official commemoration was planned, is still a source of controversy whose repercussions indirectly influence the image of Jews in France today. The Affair symbolizes the marriage of France and its Jews, and what is peculiar about it is the way it takes Jews, who are such a familiar fixture of the public sphere, and particularizes them, thus setting them apart. In the collective memory of France, everything is supposed to have returned to normal once Dreyfus was found innocent. One tends to forget about the sense of Jewish identity that emerged at the time, because such feelings of identity are seen as having no place in a Republic that has reinstated its emancipatory values. It is as if the tradition of Grégoire left no room for any kind of group allegiance. Hence, even though the Affair symbolizes the temporary exclusion of a group from the body of the nation, it is ultimately remembered as a key moment in the civic integration of the Jews.

The celebration of the fiftieth anniversary of Pétain's defeat, which came in the same year as the Dreyfus centennial, again attested to the strength of what has been called the "Vichy syndrome." France still has not come to terms with this dark period in its history. Here the fate of the Jews haunts the national memory. The widely publicized trials of Klaus Barbie and Paul Touvier emphasized the responsibility of Vichy itself in the deportation, although for technical legal reasons Touvier could be tried only as an agent of the Nazis, which in a strange way tended to exonerate the very Vichy regime that he had served so faithfully. The trials of erstwhile Vichy civil servants such as Maurice Papon, who went on to enjoy a successful career in the Fifth Republic, have also placed the Jews once again in the public spotlight. The Jews were excluded from occupied France, whether out of simple indifference or overt collaborationist zeal. Take the case of Lucien Febvre, the great historian and professor at the Collège de France. In the spring of 1941, he wanted to recommence publication of the journal *Annales*, which he and another great historian, Marc Bloch, had jointly edited. Under the anti-Jewish laws, Bloch was not allowed to teach, nor could his name appear on the masthead, but as co-owner of the celebrated journal he was in a position to block publication. In a letter to Bloch, Febvre wrote, "The *Annales* are a French journal. And their death will be yet another death for my country."[5] The most celebrated artists of the time were only too glad to display the fruits of their talent to the occupiers, and the majority of judges were only too willing to enforce the most wicked of laws.[6] Political leaders and bureaucrats, steeped in republican values, nevertheless embraced the government's authoritarian logic without much difficulty. As in the time of the Dreyfus Affair, countless republican officials forgot the ideals of 1789 they had learned in republican classrooms, and without so much as a moment's hesitation enlisted in the service of the counterrevolution. Not only Bousquet and Papon but also Pierre Laval and Marcel Déat had been good republicans before the war and then became collaborators during the Occupation, just as their predecessors—good republicans like General Mercier, Félix Faure, and Jules Méline—had refused to listen to talk of Dreyfus's innocence. But Vichy rejected the idea of Jewish integration and turned its back on both Grégoire's dream of civic emancipation and the post-Dreyfus belief in a final, healing assimilation. From the time of the Revolution to the end of the Affair, the cohesiveness of the national community had increased, albeit by fits and starts; the integration of all citizens diminished the likelihood of any fragmentation along community lines. With Vichy, however, the hope of integration ended. A reviled community was recreated by government fiat, the better to destroy it.

In October 1940, the so-called Statute on Jews systematically eliminated Jews from the civil service, abruptly ending emancipation via the state. Ultimately, Jews were eliminated from public life altogether.[7] Hence it has been argued with considerable justice that the bicycle racetrack known as the Vel' d'Hiv' (Vélodrome d'Hiver), where so many Jews were taken after being rounded up by French police in July 1942, "is less than ideal as a symbolic site for commemorating indigenous French anti-Semitism, of which a much better symbol would be the promulgation of the first Statute on Jews on October 3, 1940, a measure enacted without pressure from the Germans and in fact more discriminatory than the anti-Jewish ordinances established by the Nazis in the Occupied Zone a few days earlier."[8] It was the Republic's replacement, the new "Etat français," which at one stroke banished a whole group of its citizens from public life, going so far as to deprive some of them of their nationality as well as their rights as citizens. In the blink of an eye, the French model of emancipation—a republican tradition stemming directly from the universalist values of 1789—was smashed to pieces. At long last, the counterrevolution had triumphed, the counterrevolution that throughout the nineteenth century and the first part of the twentieth had worked so hard to overthrow the Republic. Vichy's triumph, under the Nazi boot, was also the triumph of de Maistre, Drumont, Barrès, and Maurras. Vichy severed the bond between the nation and the state and destroyed the noble ideal of public service. It also marked the triumph of a segment of civil society that had always opposed the meritocratic republican state, in which talent, not religion, was the only prerequisite for advancement. Finally, Vichy marked a return to the Ancien Régime, in the sense that every citizen was required to be a member of some community. Excluded from public service, Jews were obliged to join Jewish organizations such as the Union Générale des Juifs de France, which was charged with representing them as an ethnic—indeed, a racial—group before Vichy authorities, thus depriving them of still more of their rights as citizens. The banishing of Jews from public life, coupled with the obligation that they embrace a collective identity, left an indelible mark on Jewish memory. Yet, when the nightmare was finally over, Jews for a long time tried to forget their difference and become fully integrated citizens of the Republic: "In the immediate postwar period, Jewish memory of the genocide was in abeyance. . . . The model established by the Revolution lived on." It took almost a generation for "the community to begin searching for its own history within the national history and to attempt to construct its own memory."[9]

It is therefore Vichy rather than the Dreyfus Affair that haunts the collective consciousness of France, occasionally leading to surprising slips. When questioned about his connections with Vichy, for example, President Mitterrand replied: "You ask me about 'anti-Jewish laws.' Not that this mitigates or excuses them in any way, but the laws in question applied to foreign Jews, about whom I was totally ignorant."[10] The president's indifference to the fate of foreign Jews is surprising enough, but, more than that, his statement shows that he had only a tenuous grasp of the legal status of French Jews during the war. It was a little like Raymond Barre's famous statement after the bombing of the Copernic synagogue, in which he explicitly distinguished between Jewish victims and "innocent French people" injured by the blast. Mitterrand's statement similarly drove a wedge between French Jews and their fellow citizens. Coming as it did after Copernic and Carpentras, and after statements by de Gaulle, Pompidou, and Giscard d'Estaing that were widely interpreted as anti-Semitic, Mitterrand's remark implied that Jews might feel some sort of double allegiance that would set them apart from other Frenchmen. And it was made at a time when the government tended to look to the "Jewish community" for advice about relations with the state of Israel, and when the public tended to view Jews as constituting a distinctive community with a will of its own entitling it to participate as a collective entity in a dialogue with the powers that be. Thus Mitterrand's slip, like the many that preceded it, reinforced the tendency to look to the Jews as a community, of which we have already noted numerous signs.

If, for a time, the Dreyfus Affair posed a challenge to Grégoire's emancipatory ideal, and if Vichy marked both the banishment of Jews from public life and the imposition of the idea of a "Jewish community," then Carpentras must be seen as a symbolic moment, a moment in which that community voluntarily or involuntarily elected to turn inward and thus became a reality that Jewish citizens, like it or not, would have to deal with. Philo-Semitic communitarization replaced anti-Semitic communitarization. Though profoundly different, both of these modes of communitarization were incompatible with the idea of integration through citizenship alone. Carpentras marked a major milestone in the long road traveled since 1791, a renunciation not only of the ideals championed by Grégoire but also of the enthusiasm for universalist principles that grew out of the Dreyfus Affair. The philo-Semitic mobilization that was France's response to the anti-Semitic outrages committed at Carpentras was organized around a communitarian paradigm, whereas the Dreyfusards who had fought for the captain's release had pinned their hopes on the universalism of the Enlightenment.

Yet, shortly before the Carpentras incident, the president of the Republic had stood alongside the mortal remains of Abbé Grégoire and René Cassin when the two men were solemnly laid to rest in the Pantheon. By thus bestowing its supreme honor on these two individuals, the Republic embraced the emancipatory ideals of the former and identified itself with the work of the latter, a state Jew who, by persuading the United Nations to adopt the Universal Declaration of Human Rights, had spread the universalist ideals of 1789 to the entire world. The pantheonization of a state Jew alongside the abbé who had been the apostle of republican assimilation marked the Republic's definitive recognition of the remarkable qualities of its state Jews, one of whom now numbered among the few officially designated "great men" of France. Cassin was laid to rest in the very monument that symbolized the unity of France in a ceremony that provoked the wrath of the extreme right, who were outraged at this public reaffirmation of Grégoire's hoped-for alliance between the Republic and its Jewish citizens. A better symbol of the continued vigor of republican ideals could not be imagined: a state Jew, a proponent of universalism, solemnly laid to rest in the Pantheon beside Abbé Grégoire, the foremost proponent of the emancipatory ideal of the Enlightenment. Just as that ideal seemed on the verge of total collapse, France chose to commemorate it with an impressive ceremony. Paradoxically, this belated consecration came at the precise moment when the Republic was preparing to renounce the ideals of 1789, now seen as excessively assimilationist, and in the name of respect for differences was moving away from what it now understood to be a too uncompromising insistence on "regeneration." This homage to an all-but-vanished past thus coincided with the culmination of a process of voluntary or involuntary communitarization which, in the name of respecting identity, had severed the bond of citizenship.

AFTERWORD: 1999

In November 1998, the leading French polling organization, SOFRES, published the results of a poll that indicated a marked shift in the French public's attitudes toward Jews. Pessimists had regarded such a shift as highly improbable at a time when extremist views were once again being expressed in France. Just one year after the Church issued a formal declaration of repentance at Drancy, the site of France's most notorious deportation camp, and only a few months after former Vichy official Maurice Papon was tried on charges of crimes against humanity—a trial that many people considered point-less or, worse, likely to exasperate moderates and rekindle dangerous passions—the SOFRES poll refuted the notion that the French were inclined to minimize the importance of Vichy and impatient at being repeatedly forced to recall that vexed period in the nation's history. Except for those who declared their allegiance to the National Front, virtually everyone responding to the survey agreed that President Jacques Chirac's July 1995 statement concerning France's responsi-bility in the extermination of the Jews was either a "good" or a "very good" idea. These opinions were expressed by 86 percent of the respondents who claimed allegiance to the parties of the left, and by 85 percent of those who claimed allegiance to the parties of the right. Eighty-four percent of regularly practicing Catholics shared these views, as did 83 percent of those professing to be "without religion." The bishops' declaration of repentance at Drancy also garnered broad support: 86 percent of those polled agreed that the bishops were right to issue a statement that amounted to a plea that the Church be forgiven for its behavior under Vichy. Once again, these views transcended party affiliation, for they were shared by 72 percent of the respondents who identified with the left and by 70 percent of those who identified with the right. In other words, Frenchmen of every political stripe save those identifying with the National Front believed that Vichy, one of the darkest moments in France's history, deserved a place in the nation's collective memory.

Furthermore, 74 percent of those polled agreed that it is reasonable even at this late date to prosecute people implicated in crimes against humanity during World War II. Eighty percent of respondents who identified with the left felt this way, as did 70 percent of those who identified with the right. Seventy-two percent of practicing Catholics agreed, as did 79 percent of those who considered themselves nonreligious. These figures tell us a great deal about the political and moral conscience of people in France today. Nevertheless, this impressive expression of conscience, which reflects an almost universally shared ethical position, should not be allowed to hide a shift whose consequences have yet to be fully appreciated. To be sure, 81 percent of the French believe that the extermination of the Jews by the Germans was "one of the most important events of World War II" (though one may wish to challenge the notion, implicit in the question, that the Holocaust can be compared to other "important" events). And only 2 percent of respondents agree that it was only a "minor detail," as National Front leader Jean-Marie Le Pen has alleged.[1]

Of course, a poll provides only a fleeting image of public opinion, and no firm conclusions can be drawn. Nevertheless, it is clear that the recognition of France's responsibility has gone hand in hand with a willingness, dismaying in the current climate, to equate the Shoah with other historical events. This tendency has been supported by a broad range of research purporting to broaden the definition of genocide even if that means denying the uniqueness of the Shoah. It is this paradox that I propose to discuss here: although it is true that almost everyone in France now accepts responsibility for the country's dark past, it may also be true that the Shoah is gradually losing its exceptional status, as is, to an even greater extent, the destiny of French Jewry.

There is no denying that France today attaches fundamental importance to the deportation of Jews during World War II, and that, after long years of silence, of repression of the "dark years," the "Vichy syndrome" has become increasingly difficult to ignore. What is more, officials at the highest levels of government have entered into fruitful dialogue with representatives of Jewish groups. Indeed, the hundredth anniversary of the Dreyfus Affair provided a golden opportunity for such dialogue. The government honored the persecuted captain for his courage. It staged an official ceremony on the parade ground of the Ecole Militaire, the very site where Dreyfus was stripped of his rank, in another famous ceremony. It commemorated every stage of the Affair, which some commentators characterized as a forerunner of what happened to the Jews under Vichy (this interpretation of events is too simplistic to be accepted at face value, however). It acknowledged the responsibility of the general staff of the armed forces. And it called attention to the incredible upsurge of anti-Semitism in the final years of the nineteenth century. But, at the same time, it consistently highlighted the courage of Zola and the commitment of men such as Clemenceau, Jaurès, and other republican political leaders to the Dreyfusard cause. The government pointed out that it was republican courts that ultimately rehabilitated the captain. And it sought to identify anti-Semitic activities exclusively with the Republic's nationalist and religious opponents. The Affair was set in the context of a "Franco-French" cultural war, a war that pitted one France against another. The almost universal initial condemnation of Dreyfus was ignored, as was the Republic's persistent indifference to the captain's fate. In the imagery of commemoration, it was republican France that came to the rescue of the good captain in the name of human rights. The fact that Dreyfus was a Jew was all but ignored. The message was that republican France was and is prepared to defend all of her citizens. A manly, courageous, and loyal officer, Dreyfus was ultimately welcomed back into the French army, where, in spite of everything he had endured, he helped defend his country against a foreign aggressor. Both he and his son fought in many World War I battles against Germany. As a result, Jews once again became citizens of France on a par with all other citizens, and so (it was thought at the time) they would remain. "Fanatics of the Republic" once again gave themselves body and soul to the nation. As quickly as possible, France laid to rest the nightmare of the Affair. So ran the message of the official commemoration of the Affair: this was the "sacred union" that President Jacques Chirac was celebrating when he dedicated the Dreyfus memorial on the rue du Cherche-Midi, the location ultimately chosen for a statue of the captain that had repeatedly been moved about because for a long time the memories it symbolized were dangerously explosive.

This proclamation of Dreyfus's innocence and acknowledgment of the republican government's role in his conviction, as well as of the failure of republican politicians to live up to their own ethical standards at the time of the Affair, was overshadowed by awareness of another government's responsibility for what took place at Drancy.[2] Indeed, the obvious involvement of the state in the Dreyfus Affair, as well as the almost universal approval of the president's willingness to acknowledge that involvement, helped to lay the groundwork for the more difficult task of acknowledging Vichy's tragic role in the deportation of French and foreign Jews, something that the French had for a long time found it almost unbearable to contemplate. The first breach in the wall of silence was opened up by the work of American historians such as Robert Paxton, who was the first to focus specifically on the actions of Vichy as distinct from those of the Nazi occupiers. When Paxton and other historians emphasized the importance of French nationalism and anti-Semitism in these events, their conclusions initially received a rather chilly reception in France, even from many historians. It took time for memory to mature. Slowly, the last witnesses to these events vanished from the scene. A new view of the Vichy years began to evolve, despite Georges Pompidou's express wish that France forget a period when "the French didn't love one another," despite François Mitterrand's subtle hairsplitting and unfortunate lapses of memory concerning anti-Semitic statutes supposedly forced on Vichy and applicable only to foreign Jews, and despite the shocking revelations in September 1994 concerning Mitterrand's long friendship with René Bousquet. Bousquet, who was secretary general of police under Vichy, was responsible for agreements with the Nazis that facilitated the arrest of many Jews, and the late President Mitterrand maintained a friendship with him, without apparent misgivings, for many years. There were also belated revelations about Mitterrand's murky activities during the Occupation. And Mitterrand made a point each year of dispatching flowers to adorn the grave of Marshal Pétain, the head of state under Vichy. Hence it came as a relief when President Chirac and Prime Minister Lionel Jospin at long last made clear, powerful, and healing statements about French government activities during World War II. In July 1995, President Chirac noted that French laws excluding Jews from public life, and French police involvement in arresting and incarcerating Jews in camps at Drancy, Les Milles, and Gurs (where they awaited deportation), meant that "France, the home of enlightenment, committed unforgivable crimes. Going back on its word, it handed people under its protection over to their executioners. . . . [To the Jews deported from France] we owe a debt that can never be repaid."[3] Two years later, Prime Minister Jospin made a virtually identical statement at a ceremony on the site of the Vel' d'Hiv', where Jews rounded up by French police were held in July 1942. For Jospin, "the collective crime," the "unpayable debt" of France, "the home of enlightenment," which "handed people under its protection over to their executioners," remained unforgivable. He acknowledged that "these arrests were decided, planned, and carried out by Frenchmen. Government officials, bureaucrats, policemen, and gendarmes all took part. Not a single German soldier was necessary for this felony to be carried out. This crime must leave an indelible mark on our collective conscience. . . . With this day we honor our 'duty to remember.' I believe in this duty. I see it as a republican obligation. Memory is a republican obligation. It is one of the cornerstones of our national identity. Without memory there is no nation. . . . Just as there are in France *lieux de mémoire*, or places to remember, may the trial of [former Vichy official Maurice Papon] be for society a 'time to remember.' . . . The atrocious images of the Shoah must forever remain in our consciousness. 'Remember! Never forget!' May these time-honored prescriptions be an inspiration to us."

These two statements stood in sharp contrast to Mitterrand's reluctance to own up to the past. As late as September 1994, Mitterrand declared that he would "not make excuses in France's name. In my view, France is not responsible." Though it is true that political rivals Chirac and Jospin both acquitted the Republic and placed blame exclusively at the door of Vichy, they nevertheless laid the groundwork for further admissions of guilt. On October 1, 1997, for instance, the Church confessed its "shame for its sins" and conceded that anti-Judaism was indeed "the fertile ground" in which "the poisonous plant of Jew-hatred flourished." It admitted that the teaching of what Jules Isaac once called "contempt" for the Jews had led it to remain silent under Vichy and fail to express outrage when anti-Jewish laws excluded Jews from public life. The Church also acknowledged that it had by and large collaborated with the Vichy regime, notwithstanding the protests of a few bishops following the dramatic roundup of Jews in 1942. Its silence had "cleared the way for a lethal chain of events." Furthermore, "there is no denying the indirect if not direct role of common anti-Jewish sentiments culpably perpetuated within the Christian community in the historical process that led to the Shoah. . . . Today we confess that this silence was a sin. We also acknowledge that the Church of France failed in its mission of educating consciences. . . . This is a fact that we recognize today. This failure on the part of the Church of France and its responsibility to the Jewish people are part of its history. We confess this sin. We beg God's forgiveness and ask the Jewish people to hear these words of repentance. This act of memory commits us to heightened vigilance on behalf of humanity now and in the future."[4] This expression of repentance was far more radical than when the Vatican a short time later, in March 1998, acknowledged a sense of responsibility for the deportation of the Jews. Nevertheless, it drew an angry reaction from Jean-Marie Le Pen's National Front as well as from some Catholic quarters: "We do not accept this capitulation by the bishops," wrote the Catholic newspaper *Présent* on October 2. The writer accused the Church of surrendering to pressure from Jews and Freemasons and denounced "this generation of bishops, [which] is the most tragic face of the country's misfortune." Similarly, the Lepenist newspaper *National-Hebdo* voiced the opinion that the Church had thrown in its lot with the Revolution, the Masonic Republic, and capitalism: "The confession at Drancy has proved this beyond a shadow of a doubt. From now on the bishops will be performing in the role of priests before the Jews. This is one sign. The fact that the man behind all this was Cardinal Lustiger, the archbishop of Paris, is another."

Indeed, further acts of contrition in October 1997 suggested that French society had, virtually as a whole, taken upon itself repentance for its treatment of the Jews. For example, an important police union asked "forgiveness" for the "active collaboration of a not insignificant number of national police officers in the deportation of Jews from France." Groups of doctors and other professionals similarly asked for forgiveness, attesting to the importance of the history of the Occupation in France today. In all these statements, Drancy served as a symbol of France's role in the Shoah. The rehabilitation of Dreyfus and the acknowledgment of Vichy's guilt also pointed toward a desire to restore the Jews' place in the history of France. In the late 1990s, the historical contribution of Jews to French society has become a common theme and looms large in the national consciousness. During the bicentennial commemoration of the French Revolution, for example, the role of Abbé Grégoire in the emancipation of the Jews was featured in several events. The 190th anniversary of the Great Sanhedrin was commemorated at the Hôtel de Ville in Paris. An impressive Musée d'Art et d'Histoire du Judaïsme was dedicated. Paul Touvier and Maurice Papon were tried for crimes against humanity. July 16 was established as the date when the deportation of the Jews would henceforth be officially commemorated. This choice of date—the anniversary of the roundup of Jews by French police—was symbolic, for it emphasizes the role of the Vichy regime. And last but not least, commissions have been set up to look into the confiscation of Jewish property during World War II. In each of these instances, the government either took the initiative or associated itself with someone else's initiative. The highest authorities in the land were behind the Zakhor, which has made the duty to remember an essential ingredient of French national identity. In each case, the Jews have been restored to a central place in the history of French society.

On March 2, 1997, for example, the gathering of the Great Sanhedrin was commemorated for the first time. Jewish leaders invited to the Elysée listened to the following declaration by President Jacques Chirac:

> In welcoming you to the Elysée Palace, I wanted to call attention to the part that the Republic as a whole is taking in this anniversary. The purpose of our gathering tonight is to express gratitude, the gratitude of our nation for all that the Jewish community has contributed and is contributing to it. . . . The occasion is also a time for dialogue and exchange at a time when France, facing a difficult turning point in its history, needs to think about its identity. The history of your community, of its successful commitment to serving France and the Republic while adhering to its own values and its own faith, is an example upon which we would do well to meditate together. . . . That is why the Jews of France would identify with the Republic. That is why they would draw upon themselves the hatred and violence of those nostalgic for the old order. . . . First there was the Dreyfus Affair. . . . The worst was yet to come. Nazism. The Occupation. The dark years. Betraying the values, the genius, and the mission of France, the French State, the government of Vichy, made itself an accomplice of the unspeakable. A year and a half ago, I insisted on formally acknowledging the responsibility of the French State in the arrest, deportation, and death of thousands upon thousands of Jews. We must pursue the duty of memory to its conclusion. We must ensure that the role of Vichy and its representatives is fully brought to light. . . . The Jews of France have shown us that it is possible to remain true

to one's faith, traditions, and culture and to pass one's principles and identities on to one's children while remaining loyal to the values of the Republic and passionately loving one's country. . . . The France that we love is not and never will be a mosaic of juxtaposed communities. It is an open nation, generous but, when it comes to fundamental values, unyielding. Among those values is the ideal of integration.

In the text of the president's speech, the word *Juif* was consistently capitalized. Given the conventions of the French language, this implied that he was thinking of *les Juifs* as a distinct people or nationality, whose collective identity was not simply a matter of religion (thus echoing, but on a positive note, de Gaulle's harsh characterization of the Jews as "an elite people, sure of themselves and domineering"). His portrait of Jewish history depicted the moment when they became citizens of the Republic as a crucial moment. For him, it was the identification of Jews with the Republic that triggered the violent reactions against them, from the Dreyfus Affair to Vichy, which he once again condemned. Remarkable as this speech was, it was nevertheless almost contradictory in its apparent though unavowed wish to reconcile two different approaches to Jewish citizenship. On the one hand, the president extolled republican integration as the enduring foundation of French identity and rejected any notion of France as a "mosaic of juxtaposed communities." On the other hand, he congratulated "the Jewish community of France" for its fundamental contribution to the nation and rejoiced in its fidelity to its religion and cultural identity. What remained unclear, however, was the extent to which the community of citizens was willing to permit the continued existence of particular communities keen to defend their own identities. To what extent would the powerful return of memory, as well as the emphasis placed on the "duty to remember," result in a variety of possibly incompatible memories? The rebirth of a Jewish identity in contemporary France points up just such ambiguities. Jews would no longer be satisfied with a citizenship defined in universalistic terms, since such a definition had not protected them from the Dreyfus Affair or Vichy, nor had it saved them from a hostile "recommunitarization" which had been difficult for them both individually and collectively and had led to radical exclusion from the nation during the Occupation. As a result, they were now consciously seeking a new equilibrium between citizenship and communal roots. Given the weight of this past, is it even possible today to seek a return to a traditional French model of integration, which, from the French Revolution and Abbé Grégoire to the convocation of the Great Sanhedrin by Napoleon, had assumed that, even though the "Jewish community" would survive as a formal entity, all differences of culture and identity would be submerged in the nation? Is it possible to advocate a vision of society that is simultaneously Jacobin and Girondin? If one tries to "imagine" today's France, is it possible by some miracle to erase all differences, make the national memory compatible with the memories of particular groups, and meld the public space of the citizen with the various communities of faith, culture, and tradition?[5] Is it possible both to recognize the Jewish people and to extol the virtues of integration into the one and only national community?

France stands today at a crossroads in its history. It hesitates between "Girondinization" and perpetuation of its traditional Jacobin vision—or, in other words, between acceptance of social, cultural, geographical, and linguistic pluralism and preservation of a public sphere consisting of a unified body of citizens defined in terms of a single unitary principle. The expression of repentance not only toward Jews but also toward Protestants (for the Saint Bartholomew's Day massacre) and Muslims (for the Algerian War) is ultimately part of a vast process of pluralization. Other aspects of this process include administrative decentralization, the recognition of peripheral languages, and the granting of a large degree of autonomy to Corsica. Yet the past treatment of the Jews remains distinct, because its consequences were so terrible and because the Jews have played such a central role in the history of France. The memory of all this, which has lately asserted itself repeatedly, has therefore been particularly distressing. It was not without irony that the president's praise of the Jewish "community" was offered in commemoration of a meeting of the Great Sanhedrin convoked by Napoleon at a particularly difficult time in French Jewish history, when Jews were called upon to give up their traditions and integrate into the nation (in every way, including by intermarriage) or else face severe sanctions. Napoleon would hardly have understood the language of Jacques Chirac. He would have heard only the praise of integration and would have vehemently rejected any attempt to recognize the traditional values of any community, but especially of the Jewish community, whose disappearance he openly desired.

Another sign of public recognition came on November 30, 1998, when President Chirac formally dedicated the largest museum of Jewish history and art in Europe. Financed by the state and the city of Paris, the new Musée d'Art et d'Histoire du Judaïsme is located in the Hôtel de Saint-Aignan, one of the handsomest seventeenth-century edifices in the Marais quarter of Paris. The carefully renovated building houses not only a collection from an earlier museum on the rue des Saules but also the important Strauss-Rothschild collection (transferred from Cluny), as well as materials on loan from the Pompidou Museum, private collections, and other sources. Lavishly funded by the government, the new museum does an impressive job of re-creating the political and cultural history of the Jews of France through the display of countless religious objects and historic documents. Located in the heart of historic Paris, it stands as unmistakable evidence of the Jewish presence in France since the Middle Ages, a presence at last acknowledged and documented by the state. Nevertheless, visitors to the museum cannot help noticing how little attention is paid to the Shoah, which is touched on only indirectly by the exhibits in just one room. This is a legitimate choice on the part of the curators, given the vast extent of French Jewish history, yet it means that virtually nothing is said about the role of Vichy at a time when memories of Vichy have become a national preoccupation. It is as if French Jews had decided to close the book on this chapter of the "past that will not pass" and to pursue instead the goal of integration while preserving an identity based essentially on religion, seen as compatible with full recognition of the Jewish role in French history. As if the overwhelming reality of Vichy, apparent in countless books, films, oral histories of survivors, debates among historians, public trials, and so on, had to be contained for the sake of harmonious integration. As if this taming of the past makes it possible to confine the memory of the deportation to the Memorial to the Unknown Jewish Martyr that had stood since 1953 at a nearby location in the Marais, once home to so many Jewish immigrants (indeed, that Shoah memorial was the first in the world, predating even Yad Vashem).[6] As if Renan's warning had at last been heeded; that nations cannot survive unless their citizens are willing to forget the massacres that once divided them. As if the admonition to "remember" issued by both the president and the prime minister has transformed Vichy and Drancy into national rather than Jewish memories, in a sense liberating Jews to embrace a "republican Judaism" that each day seems a little more real in the wake of these official pronouncements.[7] And, finally, as if the public, national memory of the Shoah is matched by ever more vivid private memories but at the same time perhaps places increased constraints on any public expression of communal memories.[8]

Nevertheless, forgetting about this past in the short term is next to impossible. Indications of this impossibility are apparent in France almost daily. For example, on December 1, 1998, an incident occurred that revealed the depth of the prejudice that still exists in French society. Alain Terrail, an attorney holding an important position with a high appellate court, published an article in the newsletter of an association of magistrates whose members are generally identified as right-wing. In this article he attacked Albert Lévy, a deputy prosecutor in Toulon, whose mayor is a member of the National Front. For months Lévy had been the target of vehement attacks by city officials. Various local proceedings had been initiated against him, and Lévy had been served with injunctions ordering him to desist from open criticism of the mayor's policies. There had even been a move to have him committed to a mental institution, as if one would have to be crazy to resist a takeover by the National Front. In any case, Terrail concluded his article with the following observation: "There is no need to create a scandal over the Lévy affair or denounce it as a witch-hunt. . . . Lévy has gone to the oven so often . . . that he has finally burned himself." These words triggered a vast outcry, for they suggested to many people that the ideas of the extreme right were now affecting people in high public positions. The minister of justice initiated an investigation, and the organization of magistrates in whose newsletter Terrail had published his article voluntarily disbanded. Clearly, Terrail had borrowed a page from Le Pen's notebook.* To everyone's surprise, Vichy and the Shoah had injected themselves into the pages of a professional journal. They came up again when Daniel Cohn-Bendit, a candidate representing the French Green Party in upcoming European Parliament elections, visited a nuclear-waste treatment plant in the French town of La Hague. He was greeted by a violent demonstration of angry workers faced with unemployment in the wake of a German decision to abandon nuclear energy. "What will the Germans use to fuel their ovens?" the workers demanded to know. Clearly, this is a past that will not pass.[9] In fact, France finds itself in the thick of struggles over racism and anti-Semitism in Western Europe, and many polls suggest that anti-Semitic sentiment continues to run high in substantial segments of the population. The Drumont tradition, which led directly to Vichy, has not disappeared, and its legacy can be seen today in various sectors of the extreme right.[10]

In this respect, the Shoah changed nothing. True, anti-Semitism has disappeared from the left-wing press, but it frequently manifests itself in organs of the extreme right as well as in less predictable places. At the time of the official commemoration of the Dreyfus Affair, for example, the newspapers were full of reassuring articles, yet *La Vie* published the results of a poll that paints a vivid portrait of the status of Jews in today's France: 45 percent of those surveyed believe that anti-Semitism, racism, and xenophobia have increased in France since the Dreyfus Affair (among eighteen-to-twenty-four-year-olds, 57 percent were of this opinion), and 68 percent believe that "the lessons of the Dreyfus Affair are still applicable today" (among those identifying with the left, 81 percent held this view). In January 1995, an IPSOS–*Tribune Juive* poll reported that only 60 percent of those surveyed believed that a Jew could be elected president of France,

*Le Pen had achieved notoriety for his outrageous pun on the name of erstwhile Minister Charles Durafour: *four* in French means "oven," and Le Pen had alluded to Durafour-*crématoire*, or "crematory oven," evoking memories of Auschwitz. —TRANS.

and 49 percent believed that "hostility toward people of Jewish descent" is "fairly to very common." Fifty-eight percent of the French think that French Jews feel closer to Jews of other nationalities than to other French people, a result that suggests that the goal of integration, which was pursued in one way or another by the Revolution, Napoleon, and the Third Republic, remains elusive. This is an important finding, and its implications are all the more far-reaching given that the average French person believes that there are 3.6 million Jews in France (19 percent believe that the number is between two and five million, and 18 percent believe that it is more than five million, whereas the actual number is approximately 650,000). To people who believe that the Jews of France are this numerous and this closely allied with one another, they must seem quite a powerful force. One-third of the French believe that the number of Jews in the world is fifty million, yet another exaggeration expressing the Jews' supposed power. This huge, ill-defined population of Jews is seen as constituting a sort of "Jewish international" indifferent to the national interests of any country. Fantasies such as these are reminiscent of *The Protocols of the Elders of Zion.* They foster doubts about the loyalties of French Jews, and thus contribute to an unconscious belief in the likelihood of Jewish treason, a belief that has manifested itself repeatedly in episodes ranging from the Dreyfus Affair to the shipment of missiles that vanished from Cherbourg.[11]

Yet the same polls also tell us that 96 percent of those surveyed indicate that they were "somewhat to greatly shocked" by the vandalization of Jewish cemeteries, and that 91 percent were "somewhat to greatly shocked" by denials of the Holocaust. Despite this, Holocaust denial has found its ablest proponents in France. Florent Rassinier was the first to deny that the Holocaust had taken place, in his book *Mensonge d'Ulysse*, published in 1948 and translated into German, Spanish, Italian, and English. He continued to attack the Shoah and the gas chambers until his death in July 1967, and at various points his views received a surprisingly tolerant hearing. His successor has been the no-less-radical Robert Faurisson, who holds a doctorate in literature and a university professorship. In 1975, he wrote a letter to the editor of *Le Monde*: "May I ask you once again when your newspaper is going to stop harping on the most humongous fraud ever perpetrated in modern times, the alleged 'Hitlerian gas chambers'?"[12] In December 1980, he again asserted, "The alleged Hitlerian gas chambers and the alleged genocide of the Jews are both aspects of the same historical falsehood, which has paved the way for a gigantic political and financial fraud." In 1986, Henri Roques, speaking at the Université de Nantes, made similar assertions in a thesis that provoked such a scandal that the minister of education was obliged to intervene to prevent his being awarded a degree. Many academics have sung the same tune, most notably at the Université de Lyon. Others agree with Jean-Marie Le Pen that the concentration camps were merely a "minor detail" of World War II. The revisionist cause has also been sensationalized by spectacular trials and media coverage, and Le Pen's National Front has garnered as much as 15 percent of the vote in election after election. In recent years, admired public figures such as Abbé Pierre, the ardent champion of the poor, have embraced certain revisionist views. It is strange to find revisionist opinions being touted across the political spectrum. Before being taken up by the extreme right, these views were endorsed by politicians of the socialist, communist, and Trotskyist left. One of these, Rassinier, was even elected as a deputy for a short time. Such diverse political affinities have cleared the way for others to express less extreme views that still tend to discredit Jewish memories of the Shoah. For instance, Jean-Marie Domenach, the former editor of the journal *Esprit*, vigorously attacked those who in his eyes were reaping the "dividends" of Auschwitz. This climate of opinion has certainly colored scholarly debate in general, as well as polemics around the differences and similarities between communist and fascist regimes, the uniqueness of the Shoah as compared with other instances of genocide, and so on.[13] What links all these views is the denial of the uniqueness of the Jewish destiny and, beyond that, of the legitimacy of singling out Jewish martyrs for special reverence. To be sure, there have been similar debates in other countries, as the polemic that erupted in Germany around the historian Ernst Nolte's interpretation of fascism attests. But the centrality of Jews in the history of France has lent a particular coloration to the debate there and probably

made it a more sensitive issue. Can one go so far as to suggest that
the refusal to draw a continuous line from the Dreyfus Affair to Vichy
(a refusal that in some respects is justified), or at least to recognize
the similarity of the logic at work in both episodes (with calls for murder of the Jews during the Affair ultimately being carried out under
Vichy), has led to a denial of the crucial place of the Shoah in World
War II and beyond, as well as to a virtual denial of the role of anti-
Semitism in the Dreyfus Affair itself? Surely this is too simplistic,
and many who would support the latter assertion have not taken a position on the former. A more cautious formulation may nevertheless
be reasonable: is it possible to discern, behind both events, the same
impalpable logic, the same refusal to recognize the central importance of Jew-hatred not only in French history from Dreyfus to Vichy
but in European history from the Enlightenment to the Shoah?

At the beginning of this afterword, I stressed that the Shoah is now
an important, even a familiar, fact in French public debate. This shift
did not come about in response to the theses of the revisionists,
which, though widely reported, have in the end had little impact. It
has accompanied a certain shift in attitudes toward Jews themselves,
who have also become in a sense a familiar presence, though a presence increasingly understood as one form of cultural expression
among others. If anything unites the French, it is opposition to
American-style multiculturalism, which is seen as a threat to the Jacobin social contract. Yet in recent years there has been increased
tolerance of particularistic memories and identities, provided that
these carry no claim to possession of the truth and are reduced to the
status of folklore. European-style regionalism has lent an undeniable
impetus to this tendency. Thus French Judaism, which, though still
rejected by some, is now recognized by both church and state, is supposed to relinquish its central place in the nation's history and imagination to become merely one legitimate form of identity. If right-wing
extremism does not revive old demons, will this not spell the end of
Franco-Judaism in its traditional form? This transformation has been
abetted by French Jews themselves, many of whom have been
tempted to turn their attention away from the public sphere and toward civil society, dedicating themselves to the task of organizing a

community represented by its own official institutions and shaped by a revival of religion and tradition. Signs of this turning inward of the Jewish community are everywhere: in major community events and holidays, and in the return to picturesque traditional practices and strict religious observance. As in the past, this has led to a widening of the gap between Jews and non-Jews and to an instrumental politics directed at purely pragmatic ends. At the same time, Jews have moved away from a universalist conception of citizenship rooted in the public sphere, a conception once fervently supported by state Jews and other adepts of "republican Franco-Judaism."[14] Is this the direction in which things are ultimately headed?

The increasing democratization and gradual Americanization of French society, which with each passing day shows itself more and more prepared to embrace social and ideological pluralism, may thus have devastating implications for the destiny of French Jews. Jews were fully reintegrated into the nation after the Dreyfus Affair, and again during the Fourth Republic, which succeeded Vichy. This reintegration was sponsored, moreover, by a government that continues to beat its breast over the errors of its past. No longer can anti-Semitism prosper by accusing Jews of dominating the "Jewish Republic." Yet, at the same time, French Jews seem to be suffering from a loss of their due historical weight. At a time when the example of Israel demonstrates that Jews can be full-fledged participants in their own history, French Jews have gradually been disassociating themselves from a state that itself seems to be losing momentum as it renounces its Jacobin arrogance of old. As a result, Jews may come to occupy a less central place in the French imagination even as France becomes increasingly integrated into Europe, within whose confines Jews will increasingly figure as one of many "ethnic," religious, linguistic, or regional minorities. The turn to civil society and the Jewish community that has occurred in the wake of Carpentras very likely spells an end to the glamorous destiny that many state Jews enjoyed before, during, and after the Dreyfus Affair. Then their fate was bound up with the universalism and rationalism of the republican state, which brought important benefits, but also dramatic risks that turned sour under Vichy. Henceforth they may be simply members of a minority that is often compared symbolically to the Armenians or to the Muslim minority in France. At the end of the twentieth century, signs of a fragmentation of extremist protest can be perceived for the first time in a society that is both open and secular, and in which Jews no longer hold leading roles. It is as if the Jews of France, who have so often been urged to remember the past and to remain faithful to their traditions, have begun to retrace the path that led them from Biblical times to the dawn of modern history.[15] As if, even as they have become a primary focus of historians studying events from Dreyfus to Vichy, French Jews themselves felt compelled to turn their backs on a history that is no longer within their grasp.

NOTES

1. A JACOBIN REGENERATOR

1. Yosef Yerushalmi, *From Spanish Court to Italian Ghetto* (Seattle: University of Washington Press, 1980).

2. Ibid.

3. See Michael Marrus, *The Politics of Assimilation: The French Jewish Community at the Time of the Dreyfus Affair* (Oxford: Clarendon Press, 1971); and Paula Hyman, *From Dreyfus to Vichy: The Remaking of French Jewry, 1906–1939* (New York: Columbia University Press, 1979).

4. See Pierre Birnbaum, *Un Mythe politique: "La République juive," de Léon Blum à Pierre Mendès France* (Paris: Fayard, 1988), p. 322, trans. by Miriam Kochan as *Anti-semitism in France: A Political History from Léon Blum to the Present* (Oxford: Blackwell, 1992).

5. P. Grunebaum-Ballin, *L'Abbé Grégoire et les Juifs* (Paris: Société des Etudes Juives, 1931), p. 18.

6. Henry Torrès, *Le Procès des pogromes* (Paris: Editions de France, 1928), pp. 49, 53.

7. Théodore Reinach, *Histoire des israélites depuis l'époque de leur dispersion jusqu'à nos jours* (Paris: Hachette, 1885). Reinach did, however, note that "Grégoire was naïvely convinced that the Jews had always benefited from the maternal solicitude of the Church, an idea that dominated all his thinking." Théodore Reinach's brother Joseph denounced the accusations of ritual murder that were leveled against the Jews, particularly in his examination of the motives behind the case of Raphaël Lévy, which erupted in September 1669.

In two different places he noted that Grégoire also rejected these accusations (see Joseph Reinach, *Essais de politique et d'histoire* [1899], pp. 301, 331). By contrast, Joseph Salvador, in his important book, *Paris, Rome et Jérusalem* (Paris, 1860), does not mention the role that Grégoire played during the French Revolution.

8. S. Poserner, *Adolphe Crémieux, 1796–1880*, vol. 1 (Paris: Félix Alcan, 1934), pp. 119–20. See also Daniel Amson, *Adolphe Crémieux: L'Oublié de la gloire* (Paris: Editions du Seuil, 1988), pp. 88–90.

9. See Frances Malino, "The Right to Be Equal: Zalkind Hourwitz and the Revolution of 1789," in Frances Malino and David Sorkin, *From East to West: Jews in a Changing Europe, 1750–1870* (Boston: Basil Blackwell, 1990).

10. Reprinted by Flammarion in 1989 with a lengthy preface by Rita Hermon-Belot. The most substantial recent study of Abbé Grégoire and the Jews is still Paul Catrice, "L'Abbé Grégoire, 'ami de tous les hommes,' et la régénération des Juifs," in *Mélanges de science religieuse* 36 (1979). On the emancipation of the Jews during the French Revolution, see Bernhard Blumenkranz and Albert Soboul, eds., *Les Juifs dans la Révolution française* (Toulouse: Privat, 1976), especially the long contribution by François Delpech. See also Delpech's *Sur les Juifs* (Lyons: Presses Universitaires de Lyon, 1983); and David Feurwerker, *L'Emancipation des Juifs en France, de l'Ancien Régime à la fin du Second Empire* (Paris: Albin Michel, 1976).

11. Abbé Grégoire, *Observations nouvelles sur les Juifs et spécialement sur ceux d'Allemagne* (1808), p. 124.

12. Quoted in Martine Lemalet, "L'Emancipation des Juifs de Lorraine à travers l'oeuvre de Berr Isaac Berr, 1788–1806," in Bernhard Blumenkranz, ed., *Juifs en France au XVIIIe siècle* (Commission Française des Archives Israélites, 1994), pp. 167–68.

13. Grégoire, *Essai sur la régénération physique, morale et politique des Juifs*, p. 141.

14. See Michel de Certeau, Dominique Julia, and Jacques Revel, *Une Politique de langue: La Révolution française et les patois* (Paris: Gallimard, 1975), chap. 8.

15. As such, he favored unification of the territory and was opposed to federalism in any form. See Suzanne Citron, *Le Mythe national: L'Histoire de la France en question* (Paris: Editions Ouvrières, 1987), pp. 154–55.

16. Edouard Drumont, *La France juive* (Paris: Marpon et Flammarion, 1886), p. 280.

17. For a different interpretation, see Pierre Pierrard, *Juifs et catholiques français* (Paris: Fayard, 1970), especially the introduction, entitled "From Abbé Grégoire to Drumont."

18. Bernard Plongeron, *Théologie et politique au siècle des Lumières* (Geneva: Droz, 1973); and Bernard Plongeron, "Abbé Grégoire," in *Dictionnaire d'histoire et de géographie ecclésiastiques* (1988). See also Catrice, "L'Abbé Grégoire," pp. 157 ff. On Grégoire's Jansenism, see Ruth Necheles, *The Abbé*

Grégoire, 1787–1831 (Westport, Conn.: Greenwood, 1971), chap. 1. See also Timothy Tackett, *Religion, Revolution, and Regional Culture in Eighteenth-Century France: The Ecclesiastical Oath of 1791* (Princeton: Princeton University Press, 1981).

19. Grégoire, *Essai*, p. 126. Jacob Katz, in *Hors du ghetto* (Paris, Hachette, 1984), argues that Gregoire championed the Jews because, for him, the hope of conversion and the humanistic ideas of the Enlightenment merged into one.

20. Abbé Grégoire, *Histoire des sectes religieuses* (Paris, 1828), vol. 3, pp. 427–28. As recently as 1962, Paul Grunebaum-Ballin made fun of commentators who in his view mistakenly saw Grégoire as wanting to convert the Jews (see "Grégoire convertisseur? ou La Croyance au retour d'Israël," *Revue des études juives,* July–Dec. 1962). By contrast, Necheles, *Abbe Grégoire*, p. 44, points out that "the Jews never fully understood that Grégoire's ultimate hope was to convert them." On this debate, see the important article by Catrice, "L'Abbé Grégoire," pp. 166–69. See also Jacques Lévy, "Henri Grégoire: Lumière et ombre," *Sens,* June 1978.

21. Bernard Plongeron, *Conscience religieuse en révolution* (Paris: Picard, 1969), p. 175.

22. On the Constitutional Church, see Paul Christophe, *1789: Les Prêtres dans la Révolution* (Paris: Editions Ouvrières, 1986), pp. 176 ff.; and Pierre Pierrard, *L'Eglise et la Révolution, 1789–1889* (Paris: Nouvelle Cité, 1988), pp. 98 ff. The Constitutional Church included priests who swore an oath of allegiance to the Revolution.

23. Concerning Grégoire's efforts on behalf of the blacks of Haiti and Santo Domingo, see Grunebaum-Ballin, *L'Abbé Grégoire*, who argues on p. 267 that Grégoire hoped to see "the eventual triumph of Christian law and the human law of brotherly love throughout the inhabited world." See also Necheles, *Abbé Grégoire*, chaps. 3 and 4.

24. Bertrand Badie and Pierre Birnbaum, *Sociologie de l'Etat* (Paris: Pluriel, 1982), trans. by Arthur Goldhammer as *The Sociology of the State* (Chicago: University of Chicago Press, 1983).

25. Jean Leca, "Individualisme et citoyenneté," in Pierre Birnbaum and Jean Leca, *Sur l'individualisme* (Paris: Presses de la Fondation Nationale des Sciences Politiques, 1986), pp. 176–77.

26. Grégoire, *Essai*, p. 130.

27. Quoted in Pierrard, *L'Eglise*, p. 45.

28. See Philippe Sagnac, "Les Juifs et la Révolution française," *Revue d'histoire moderne et contemporaine,* Jan.–March 1899.

29. Frances Malino, *The Sephardic Jews of Bordeaux: Assimilation and Emancipation in Revolutionary and Napolenoic France* (Birmingham, Ala.: University of Alabama Press, 1978).

30. Feuerwerker, *L'Emancipation*, pp. 429 ff.

31. Grégoire, *Essai*, p. 131.

32. Robert Anchel, *Napoléon et les Juifs* (Paris: Presses Universitaires de France, 1928), p. 35.

33. Grégoire, *Essai*, p. 151. Rita Hermon-Belot rightly notes, "Grégoire was a long way from wishing to see the state secularized" (see her preface to the *Essai*, p. 32).

34. Ibid., p. 169.

35. Thiery, *Dissertation sur cette question: Est-il des moyens de rendre les Juifs plus heureux et plus utiles en France* (Paris: Editions d'Histoire Sociale, 1968), vol. 2, p. 84.

36. W. C. Dohm, *De la réforme des Juifs* (Paris: Stock, 1984), p. 83. This edition includes a very substantial preface by Dominique Bourel.

37. Ibid., p. 83.

38. Mirabeau, *Sur Moses Mendelssohn: Sur la réforme politique des Juifs* (Paris: Editions d'Histoire Sociale, 1968), p. 84.

39. Quoted in Sagnac, "Les Juifs et la Révolution française," p. 212.

40. Grégoire, *Essai*, pp. 109–10.

41. Ibid., p. 139.

42. Abbé Grégoire, "Motion en faveur des Juifs," in *L'Assemblée nationale constituante* (Paris: Editions d'Histoire Sociale, 1968), vol. 7, p. 41.

43. Pierrard, *L'Eglise*, p. 44.

44. Ibid., p. 114.

45. *Adresse présentée à l'Assemblée nationale,* Aug. 31, 1789, by the deputies of the Jews settled in Metz, in the three bishoprics, and in Alsace and Lorraine (Paris: Editions d'Histoire Sociale, 1968), vol. 5, p. 11.

46. See Malino, *Sephardic Jews of Bordeaux,* pp. 24, 46 ff.

47. "Adresse présentée à l'Assemblée nationale, le 26 août 1789, par les Juifs résidant à Paris," in *Adresses, mémoires et pétitions des Juifs* (Paris: Editions d'Histoire Sociale, 1968), vol. 6, p. 6. See Shmuel Trigano, *La République et les Juifs* (Paris: Presses d'Aujourd'hui, 1982), p. 51.

48. Moses Mendelssohn, *Jérusalem* (Paris: Presses d'Aujourd'hui, 1982), p. 186. Translation of the German original, *Jerusalem* (Berlin: 1783). See also Alexander Altmann, *Moses Mendelssohn: A Biographical Study* (London: Littman Library of Jewish Civilization, 1973).

49. Mendelssohn, *Jérusalem,* p. 180.

50. Quoted by Dominique Bourel in introduction to ibid., p. 44.

51. Dohm, *De la réforme des Juifs,* p. 88.

52. Ibid., p. 43.

53. Ibid., p. 89.

54. See Guy Chaussinand-Nogaret, *Mirabeau* (Paris: Editions du Seuil, 1982), pp. 102, 291.

55. Arthur Herzberg, *The French Enlightenment and the Jews* (New York: Columbia University Press, 1968), p. 363. A similar view can be found in W. Rabi, *Anatomie du judaïsme français* (Paris: Editions de Minuit, 1962). Shmuel

Trigano is even more critical: "The Jew as positive being was proscribed. . . . The triumph of the Revolution required the transformation of the Jew." (*La République et les Juifs*, pp. 25, 70.) A similar argument can be found in Eric Smilévitch, "Halaka et Code civil: Questions sur le grand Sanhédrin," *Pardès* 3 (1986).

56. Simon Dubnov, *Histoire moderne du peuple juif* (Paris: Payot, 1933), vol. 1, p. 135.

57. James Darmesteter, *Coup d'oeil sur l'histoire du peuple juif* (Paris, 1881), p. 17.

58. Ibid., p. 19. "I am only infinitesimally Jewish; I am a student of the Bible," Darmesteter said. See Marrus, *The Politics of Assimilation*.

59. See, for example, Dominique Schnapper, *Juifs et Israélites* (Paris: Gallimard, 1980), trans. by Arthur Goldhammer as *Jewish Identities in France: An Analysis of Contemporary French Jewry* (Chicago: University of Chicago Press, 1983).

60. Albert Hirschman, *Exit, Voice, and Loyalty* (Cambridge, Mass.: Harvard University Press, 1970).

61. *Le Matin*, Oct. 31, 1902.

62. Doris Bensimon, *Socio-démographie des Juifs de France et d'Algérie* (Paris: Presses Orientalistes de France, 1976).

63. Emile Poulat, *Liberté, laïcité: La Guerre des deux France et le principe de la modernité* (Paris: Le Cerf, 1987).

2. RESPONDING TO THE REVOLUTION

1. See Michael Marrus, *The Politics of Assimilation: A Study of the French Jewish Community at the Time of the Dreyfus Affair* (Oxford: Clarendon Press, 1971) and Paula Hyman, *From Dreyfus to Vichy: The Remaking of French Jewry, 1906–1939* (New York: Columbia University Press, 1979).

2. Pierre-André Taguieff, *La Force du préjugé* (Paris: La Découverte, 1988); Anne-Marie Durantin-Crabol, *Visages de la nouvelle droite* (Paris: Presses de la Fondation Nationale des Sciences Politiques, 1989).

3. Eugen Weber, *Peasants into Frenchmen* (Stanford: Stanford University Press, 1976).

4. Phyllis Cohen Albert, "Ethnicité et solidarité chez les Juifs de France," *Pardès* 3 (1986): 29–53.

5. Michael Graetz, *Les Juifs en France au XIXe siècle: De la Révolution à l'Alliance israélite universelle* (Paris: Editions du Seuil, 1989), p. 25.

6. Ibid., p. 55.

7. Aron Rodrigue, *De l'instruction à l'émancipation: Les Enseignants de l'Alliance israélite universelle et les Juifs d'Orient* (Paris: Calmann-Lévy, 1989).

8. Graetz, *Les Juifs*, p. 11.

9. On this broad subject, see David Feuerwerker, *L'Emancipation des Juifs en France, de l'Ancien Régime à la fin du Second Empire* (Paris: Albin Michel,

1976); Bernhard Blumenkranz and Albert Soboul, eds., *Les Juifs et la Révolution française* (Toulouse: Privat, 1976); Gérard Nahon, "Séfarades et ashkénases en France: La Conquête et l'émancipation, 1789–1791," in M. Yardeni, ed., *Les Juifs et la Révolution française* (Paris: Robert Laffont, 1989); Mireille Hadas-Lebel and Evelyne Oliel-Grausz, *Les Juifs et la Révolution française: Histoire et mentalités* (Louvain-Paris: E. Peters, 1992).

10. Werner Sombart, *The Jews and Modern Capitalism* (Glencoe, N.Y.: Free Press, 1951).

11. See Paul Butel, *Les Négociants bordelais: L'Europe et les îles au XVIIIe siècle* (Paris: Aubier, 1974); Frances Malino, "The Right to Be Equal: Zalkind Hourwitz and the Revolution of 1789," in Frances Malino and David Sorkin, *From East to West: Jews in a Changing Europe, 1750–1870* (Oxford: Blackwell, 1990); Frances Malino and Jean-Pierre Poussou, "Un Peuple sans droits," in Yves Lequin, ed., *La Mosaïque France* (Paris: Hachette, 1988).

12. Pierre Guillaume, *La Population de Bordeaux au XIXe siècle* (Paris: Armand Colin, 1972).

13. Malino, "Right to Be Equal."

14. Graetz, *Les Juifs,* chaps. 4 and 5.

15. Hyppolite Castille, *Les Frères Pereire,* G 21088 BN, 1861.

16. "Situation générale des individus qui professent la religion israélite," quoted in Jean Cavignac, "Les Israélites bordelais au XIXe siècle," unpublished thesis, University of Bordeaux III, 1986, pp. 641–42. Cavignac emphasizes the need to distinguish between the more prominent Jews and poorer Jews, who were largely excluded from the local process of assimilation. See also Jean Cavignac, *Dictionnaire du judaïsme bordelais aux XVIIIe et XIXe siècles* (Bordeaux: Archives Départementales de la Gironde, 1987).

17. Malino, "Right to Be Equal," p. 44.

18. Patrick Girard, *Les Juifs de France de 1789 à 1860* (Paris: Calmann-Lévy, 1976), p. 132.

19. Michael Hechter, "A Theory of Group Solidarity," in Michael Hechter, *Microfoundation of Macrosociology* (Philadelphia: Temple University Press, 1983), p. 19.

20. Alessandro Pizzorno, "Sur la rationalité des choix démocratiques," in Pierre Birnbaum and Jean Leca, *Sur l'individualisme* (Paris: Presses de la Fondation Nationale des Sciences Politiques, 1986), p. 19. Translated by John Gaffney as *Individualism: Theories and Methods* (Oxford: Clarendon Press, 1990).

21. Albert Hirschman, *Exit, Voice, and Loyalty* (Cambridge, Mass.: Harvard University Press, 1970).

22. Yosef Yerushalmi, "Un Champ à Anathoth: Vers une histoire de l'espoir juif," in *Mémoire et histoire* (Paris: Denoël, 1986), p. 94.

23. Graetz, *Les Juifs,* p. 429.

24. Freddy Raphael and Robert Weil, *Juifs d'Alsace* (Toulouse: Privat, 1977).

25. André Néher, *L'Existence juive* (Paris: Albin Michel, 1962), p. 260.

26. Raphael and Weil, *Juifs d'Alsace*, p. 404. See also H. Tribout de Morembert, "Les Juifs de Metz et de Lorraine, 1791–1795," in Blumenkranz and Soboul, eds., *Les Juifs et la Révolution française.*

27. Paula Hyman, *The Emancipation of the Jews of Alsace* (New Haven: Yale University Press, 1991).

28. Samuel Popkin, *The Rational Peasant* (Los Angeles: University of California Press, 1979).

29. Bernhard Blumenkranz, *Les Juifs en France: Ecrits dispersés* (Paris: Franco-Judaica, 1989), p. 58.

30. Pierre Birnbaum, *Les Fous de la République: Histoire des Juifs d'Etat, de Gambetta à Vichy* (Paris: Editions du Seuil, 1994), trans. by Jane M. Todd as *The Jews of the Republic: A Political History of State Jews in France from Gambetta to Vichy* (Stanford, Calif.: Stanford University Press, 1996).

31. Catherine Nicault, *La France et le sionisme, 1897–1948: Une Rencontre manquée?* (Paris: Calmann-Lévy, 1992).

32. Vicky Caron, *Between France and Germany: The Jews of Alsace-Lorraine, 1871–1918* (Stanford: Stanford University Press, 1988), chaps. 1–4.

33. "Adresse présentée à l'Assemblée nationale le 31 août 1789 par les députés réunis des Juifs établis à Metz, dans les trois évêchés, en Alsace et en Lorraine," in *La Révolution française et l'émancipation des Juifs* (Paris: Editions d'Histoire Sociale, 1968), vol. 5, pp. 5, 11. See also the letter from Berr Isaac Berr, who represented the Jews of Nancy, to Abbé Grégoire dated April 22, 1790, in which Berr asks that, in the event that the Assembly does not grant Jews the right to become active citizens, they be allowed to "remain in their particular community and to maintain for themselves and at their own expense rabbis and other leaders for the purpose of upholding the civil as well as the religious order" (ibid., vol. 8). Later, however, Jacob Berr wrote, "Old Berr Isaac Berr asked to maintain the legal existence of our communities and syndics. In other words, he wanted us to remain estranged from the rest of society. Is it not clear, then, that he wished to isolate us from a generous nation that wanted to clasp us to its bosom?" (Quoted in Martine Lemalet, "L'Emancipation des Juifs de Lorraine à travers l'oeuvre de Berr Isaac Berr, 1788–1806," in Bernhard Blumenkranz, ed., *Juifs en France au XVIIIe siècle* [Commission Française des Archives Israélites, 1994], p. 165.)

34. Mirabeau, *Sur Moses Mendelssohn: Sur la réforme politique des Juifs* (Editions d'Histoire Sociale, 1968), p. 65.

35. "Pétition des Juifs établis en France adressée à l'Assemblée nationale," *La Révolution française et l'émancipation des Juifs*, vol. 5, p. 82.

36. This petition to the National Assembly, which was dated December 21, 1789, was signed by representatives of the leading Jewish families, including the Gradises, Rabas, Dacostas, and Rodriguèses. See *La Révolution française et l'émancipation des Juifs*, vol. 5.

37. The Jews of Avignon likewise hastened "to abdicate their separate existence

so as to rise to the rank of citizens alongside other citizens of France" ("Observations pour les Juifs d'Avignon à la Convention nationale," in *La Révolution française et l'émancipation des Juifs,* vol. 5).

38. See "Adresse présentée à l'Assemblée nationale le 26 août 1789, par les Juifs résidant à Paris," in *La Révolution française et l'émancipation des Juifs,* vol. 5.

39. See Robert Anchel, *Napoléon et les Juifs* (Paris: Presses Universitaires de France, 1928); and Simon Schwarzfuchs, *Napoleon, the Jews, and the Sanhedrin* (London: Routledge and Kegan Paul, 1979).

3. From Court Jews to State Jews

1. Werner Sombart, *The Jews and Modern Capitalism* (New Brunswick, N.J.: Transaction Books, 1982).

2. For recent critiques of Sombart, see Paul Mendès-Flohr, "Werner Sombart and Modern Capitalism: An Analysis of Its Ideological Premises," *Leo Year Book,* no. 21, 1976; and Werner Mosse, "Judaism, Jews, and Capitalism: Weber, Sombart, and Beyond," *Leo Year Book,* no. 24, 1979. See also Gary Abraham, *Max Weber and the Jewish Question* (Urbana, Ill.: University of Illinois Press, 1992).

3. Sombart, *Jews and Modern Capitalism,* p. 49.

4. Hannah Arendt, *The Origins of Totalitarianism* (New York: Harcourt Brace and World, 1951), vol. 1, *Antisemitism,* p. 14. The classic work on court Jews is Selma Stern, *The Court Jew* (New Brunswick, N.J.: Transaction Books, 1985).

5. See Ernest Hamburger, *Juden im Offentlichen Leben Deutschlands* (Tübingen: J.C.B. Mohr, 1968); Werner Mosse, *Juden im Wilhelminischen Deutschland 1890–1914* (Tübingen: J.C.B. Mohr, 1976); and "From the Wilhelminian Era to the Third Reich," *Leo Year Book,* no. 31, 1986.

6. See Pierre Birnbaum, *Les Fous de la République: Histoire des Juifs d'état, de Gambetta à Vichy* (Paris: Editions du Seuil, 1994), trans. by Jane M. Todd as *The Jews of the Republic: A Political History of State Jews in France from Gambetta to Vichy* (Stanford, Calif.: Stanford University Press, 1996). See also Perrine Simon, "Contribution à l'étude de la bourgeoisie juive à Paris entre 1870 et 1914," unpublished thesis, Institut d'Etudes Politiques, 1982.

7. Hyppolite Castille, *Les Frères Pereire,* p. 40, NG 21088, Bibliothèque Nationale, 1961. See also Frédéric Barbier, *Finance et politique: La Dynastie des Fould, XVIIIe–XXe siècle* (Paris: Armand Colin, 1991).

8. Michael Graetz, *Les Juifs en France au XIXe siècle: De la Révolution à l'Alliance israélite universelle et les Juifs d'Orient* (Paris: Calmann-Lévy, 1989), chap. 4.

9. See Richard Rohl, "L'Industrialisation française: Une Remise en cause," *Revue d'histoire économique et sociale,* 1964, no. 3, p. 415. See also R. Cameron, *La France et le devenir économique de l'Europe, 1800–1971* (Paris: Editions du Seuil, 1971), pp. 188 ff.

10. Jean-Charles Asselain, *Histoire économique de la France*, vol. 1, *De l'Ancien Régime à la Première Guerre mondiale* (Paris: Editions du Seuil, 1984), chap. 4.

11. Jean Bouvier, *Les Rothschild* (Paris: Club Français du Livre, 1960), pp. 76–95, 101.

12. Ibid., p. 102.

13. See Bertrand Gille, *Histoire de la maison Rothschild* (Geneva: Droz, 1965); and Bouvier, *Les Rothschild*, pp. 145 ff. On the conflict between the Rothschilds and the Pereires, see Bertrand Gille, *La Banque de France au XIXe siècle* (Geneva: Droz, 1970); and Jean Bouvier, *Un Siècle de banque française* (Paris: Hachette, 1973), pp. 207 ff.

14. Jules Mirès, *A mes juges* (Paris, 1861), pp. 87–93.

15. Fritz Stern, *Gold and Iron: Bismarck, Bleichroder, and the Building of the German Empire* (New York: Vintage, 1979).

16. Alain Plessis, *Régents et gouverneurs de la Banque de France sous le Second Empire* (Geneva: Droz, 1985), pp. 44, 265. Among the two hundred shareholders in the Banque de France, there were no Jews except for the d'Eichtals and Foulds, who had converted, and the jeweler Halphen. The leading figures included the Dollfuses, J. Périer, H. Germain, Lemercier de Nerville, the de Germinys, and the Laffittes, along with Berthier, the Prince de Wagram Sauvaire de Barthélemy, Pillet-Witt, Ackermann, the Vicomte d'Argout, and any other representatives of the bourgeoisie and aristocracy.

17. Adeline Daumard, *Les Bourgeois et la bourgeoisie en France* (Paris: Aubier, 1987), p. 102.

18. Bouvier, *Les Rothschild*, p. 11.

19. Herbert Lüthy, *La Banque protestante en France* (Geneva: SEVPEN, 1965); and J. Néré, "La Haute Banque protestante de 1870 à 1885," in *Les Protestants dans les débuts de la IIIe République* (Paris: Editions Protesantes, 1978).

20. Plessis, *Régents et gouverneurs*, p. 268.

21. See Guy Palmade, *Capitalisme et capitalistes français au XIX siècle* (Paris: Armand Colin, 1961).

22. With the exception of the remarkable Javal dynasty; see Emmanuel Chadeau, *L'Economie du risque: Les Entrepreneurs, 1850–1980* (Paris, 1988).

23. Jean-Noël Jeanneney, *François de Wendel en République: L'Argent et le pouvoir, 1914–1940* (Paris: Editions du Seuil, 1976).

24. Palmade, *Capitalisme et capitalistes français*, pp. 178–82.

25. Louis Bergeron, "Vers un renouvellement des entreprises et des hommes," in Yves Lequin, ed., *Histoire des français: XIXe–XXe siècles*, vol. 2 (Paris: Armand Colin, 1983), p. 281. See also François Job, *Les Juifs de Nancy* (Nancy: Presses Universitaires de Nancy, 1991), p. 101.

26. Louis Bergeron, *Les Capitalistes en France (1780–1914)* (Paris: Gallimard, 1978).

27. Louis Girard, Antoine Prost, and Remi Gossez, *Les Conseillers généraux en 1870: Etude statistique d'un personnel politique* (Paris: Armand Colin, 1967).

28. Jean Lhomme, *La Grande Bourgeoisie au pouvoir, 1830–1880* (Paris: Presses Universitaires de France, 1960).

29. See J.-P. Poussou, "A l'école des autres," and Yves Lequin," La Trace de l'Ancien Régime," both in Yves Lequin, *La Mosaïque France* (Paris: Larousse, 1988).

30. See Cameron, *La France et le devenir économique*, p. 188.

31. See Vicky Caron, *Between France and Germany: The Jews of Alsace-Lorraine, 1871–1918* (Stanford: Stanford University Press, 1988), chaps. 1–4.

32. Jean-Pierre Chaline, *Les Bourgeois de Rouen: Une Elite urbaine au XIXe siècle* (Paris: Presses de la Fondation Nationale des Sciences Politiques, 1982). On the eve of World War I, the largest silk-and-ribbon supplier in Paris was Brach, Blum, et Compagnie. See Louis Bergeron, "Les Voies du grand commerce," in Lequin, *La Mosaïque France*, p. 253.

33. Jean Lambert-Dansette, *Quelques Familles du patronat textile de Lille-Armentières (1789–1914)* (Lille: Presses Universitaires de Lille, 1954).

34. Claude Fohlen, *L'Industrie textile au temps du Second Empire* (Paris: Plon, 1954), p. 436.

35. See Michael Burns, *Dreyfus, a Family Affair: From the French Revolution to the Holocaust* (New York: HarperCollins, 1991).

36. See Paula Hyman, *From Dreyfus to Vichy: The Remaking of French Jewry, 1906–1939* (New York: Columbia University Press, 1979), pp. 119, 136. The same was true in Lorraine—for example, in Lunéville. See Françoise Job, *Les Juifs de Lunéville aux XVIIIe et XIXe siècles* (Nancy: Presses Universitaires de Nancy, 1989).

37. See Adeline Daumard, ed., *Les Fortunes françaises au XIXe siècle* (Paris: Mouton, 1973).

38. Adeline Daumard, *La Bourgeoisie parisienne de 1815 à 1848* (Paris: SEVPEN, 1963).

39. See Louis Girard, *La Politique des travaux publics sous le Second Empire* (Paris: Armand Colin, 1952); François Caron, *Histoire de l'exploitation d'un grand réseau: La Compagnie du chemin de fer du Nord, 1846–1937* (Paris: Mouton, 1973).

40. According to David Landes, there was in fact no real clash between the traditional view of banking, symbolized by the Rothschilds, and the view of the Pereires; see his "Vieille Banque et banque nouvelle: La Révolution financière du XIXe siècle," *Revue d'histoire moderne et contemporaine*, July–Sept. 1956.

41. When René Girault wanted to create a portrait of the businessman of 1914, he chose to contrast Henri Germain—the creator of the Crédit Lyonnais, who played a crucial role in industrialization, and whom Girault regarded "as the leading financial mind of his generation"—with Alphonse de Rothschild, who in Girault's view "was still the leading gambler." See his "Pour un portrait nouveau de l'homme d'affaires français vers 1914," *Revue d'histoire moderne et contemporaine*, no. 16, July–Sept. 1969, p. 343.

42. Pierre Birnbaum, *Le Peuple et les gros: Histoire d'un mythe* (Paris: Hachette, 1995).

43. Georges Dairnwaell (known as Satan), *Histoire édifiante et curieuse de Rothschild Ier, roi des Juifs* (Paris, 1846). See also Georges de Pascal, *La Juiverie* (Paris, 1887); Jacques de Biez, *Les Rothschild et le péril juif* (Paris, 1891); Jules Guesde, "A mort, Rothschild," in Jules Guesde, *Etat, politique et morale de classe* (Paris: Girard, 1901), pp. 444–47.

44. Karl Marx, *Oeuvres politiques* (Paris: Pléiade ed.), vol. 1, p. 358. Heinrich Heine had this to say about Fould's election in Tarbes: "His ascent to the rank of deputy gives me genuine pleasure for the simple reason that it gives the ultimate sanction to the principle that Jews have the same rights as other citizens. . . . Age-old intolerance will vanish when Jews with no merit other than their money can become deputies, the highest civic honor in France, as easily as their Christian brothers, and in this respect the nomination of Mr. Achille Fould represents the triumph of civic equality" (p. 1315).

45. The literature on the subject contains numerous works of high quality. See Robert Byrnes, *Antisemitism in Modern France* (New Brunswick, N.J.: Rutgers University Press, 1950); Stephen Wilson, *Ideology and Experience: Antisemitism in France at the Time of the Dreyfus Affair* (London: Associated Press, 1982); Paul Kingston, *Antisemitism in France during the 1930s: Organizations, Personalities, and Propaganda* (Hull, Eng.: University of Hull Press, 1983); Frederick Busi, *The Pope of Antisemitism: The Career and Legacy of Edouard Drumont* (New York: University Press of America, 1986); Jeanne Verdès-Leroux, *Scandales financiers et antisémitisme catholique: Le Krach de l'Union générale* (Paris: Le Centurion, 1969); Pierre Sorlin, *"La Croix" et les Juifs* (Paris: Grasset, 1967); Marc Angenau, *Ce qu'on disait des Juifs en 1889* (Paris: Presses Universitaires de Vincennes, 1987); and Michel Winock, *Edouard Drumont et Cie: Antisémitisme et fascisme en France* (Paris: Editions du Seuil, 1982).

46. Sorlin, *"La Croix,"* p. 105.

47. See Pierre Birnbaum, "Anti-Semitism and Anti-Capitalism in Modern France," in Frances Malino and Bernard Wasserstein, eds., *The Jews in Modern France* (Waltham, Mass.: Brandeis University Press, 1985).

48. David Feuerwerker, *L'Emancipation des Juifs en France, de l'Ancien Régime à la fin du Second Empire* (Paris: Albin Michel, 1976); Gérard Nahon, "Séfarades et ashkénases en France: La Conquête de l'émancipation (1789–1791)," in M. Yardeni, ed., *Les Juifs et la Révolution français* (Paris: Robert Laffont, 1989).

49. Michel Roblin, *Les Juifs de Paris: Démographie, économie, culture* (Paris: Picard, 1952); Doris Bensimon-Donath, *Socio-démographie des Juifs de France et d'Algérie* (Paris: ALC, 1976), pp. 9–22; Michael Marrus, *The Politics of Assimilation: A Study of the French Jewish Community at the Time of the Dreyfus Affair* (Oxford: Clarendon Press, 1971), pp. 45 ff.; Béatrice Philippe, *Les Juifs à Paris à la Belle Epoque* (Paris: Albin Michel, 1992).

50. See Caron, *Between France and Germany,* chap. 4. The author shows, for example (see p. 85), that in Hagenau between 1873 and 1898 30 percent of the 309 Jews who emigrated went to France and 56 percent went to the United States, especially to New York and New Orleans.

51. Hyman, *From Dreyfus to Vichy;* Nancy Green, *Les Travailleurs immigrés juifs à la Belle Epoque* (Paris: Fayard, 1986); Jonathan Boyarin, *Polish Jews in Paris: The Ethnography of Memory* (Bloomington: Indiana University Press, 1991).

52. Christine Piette, *Les Juifs de Paris, 1808–1840: La Marche vers l'assimilation* (Quebec: Presses Universitaires de Laval, 1983).

53. The two quotes are taken from Hyman, *From Dreyfus to Vichy,* pp. 179–80.

54. *Archives israélites,* May 1, 1913. As Nancy Green points out, "The individualistic ethic of 'every man for himself' caused the established community to rise up against the immigrant threat" (*Les Travailleurs,* p. 86).

55. See Birnbaum, *The Jews of the Republic.*

56. Herbert Lottman, *La Dynastie Rothschild* (Paris: Editions du Seuil, 1995).

57. When Camille Sée was named secretary to the minister of the interior in 1870, he was actually granted sweeping powers. Adolphe Crémieux became minister of the interior in charge of law enforcement under the provisional government and later served as minister of justice. Other Jewish ministers of the interior included David Raynal (1893–94), L. L. Klotz (1913), Abraham Schrameck (1925), Georges Mandel (1940), and, under the Fourth Republic, Jules Moch (1953). Alexandre Israël served as undersecretary of state in the Ministry of the Interior in 1932. Pierre Massé was undersecretary of state in the Ministry of War in 1917; E. Ignace served that same year as undersecretary of state in the Justice Ministry. Both took firm measures to keep up morale among soldiers at the front. Some state Jews played key roles in the struggle against the extreme right: Abraham Schrameck and Georges Mandel vigorously defended the Republic against the Action Française and the extremist *ligues.* Others fought the anarchists: Raynal, for example, directed the arrests of anarchists ordered by the prefect Lépine. Jules Moch, whose government service dates back all the way to 1937, did not hesitate to use force to put down Communist-led strikes in 1953. André Hesse was appointed minister of colonies in 1925, a post in which Georges Mandel also served in 1939. This ministry was of great symbolic importance because of its key role in Jules Ferry's republican strategy.

58. André Hesse and Moch later used the same position to implement a policy of state-inspired industrialization "from above."

59. Joseph Reinach was a leader of the Opportunists; Léon Blum, Salomon Grümbach, and Jules Moch were important figures in the Socialist Party. Alfred Naquet was a notable presence in anarchist circles.

4. THE LOVE OF LEARNING

1. Raymond Aron, *Essais sur la condition juive contemporaine* (Paris: Editions de Fallois, 1989), pp. 260–61.
2. Nicolas Baverez, *Raymond Aron* (Paris: Flammarion, 1993). Baverez adds that Aron "continued to take a passionate interest in Captain Dreyfus's tragic fate, the study of which was both the starting point and the ending point of his historical thinking."
3. Raymond Aron, *Mémoires* (Paris: Julliard, 1983), pp. 17–19.
4. Raymond Aron, "L'Essence du totalitarisme selon Hannah Arendt," *Commentaire,* special issue on Raymond Aron, Feb. 1985, pp. 416–17.
5. Aron, *Mémoires,* p. 708.
6. Aron, *Essais,* p. 31.
7. On Raymond Aron and Judaism, see Jean-Louis Missika, "Juif par le regard de l'autre?," *Commentaire,* Feb. 1985; Aline Benain, "L'Itinéraire juif de Raymond Aron: Hasard, déchirement et dialectique de l'appartenance," *Pardès,* vol. 2, 1991. Ariane Chebel d'Appollonia, "Morale et politique chez Raymond Aron," unpublished doctoral thesis, Institut d'Etudes Politiques de Paris, 1993.
8. Aron, *Essais,* p. 272.
9. Alain Touraine, *Un Désir d'histoire* (Paris: Stock, 1977), p. 76.
10. Not all Jewish sociologists were affected this way. For example, Georges Friedmann, the great labor sociologist, wrote that his "encounter with Israel was in fact [his] first encounter with Judaism." His participation in the Resistance legitimized his "roots in French soil," and Vichy had little impact on his republican loyalties. He described a prewar trip to Poland in these terms: "The Jews, with their long cloaks, beards, and curly sideburns, their rituals around food, and their religious taboos, seemed so different from 'us' assimilated French Jews, or 'lost' Jews. Memories of what my father had told me about the Dreyfus Affair coincided in my mind and sensibility with the sight of crowds of Jews in Warsaw and Lodz" (Georges Friedmann, *Fin du peuple juif?* [Paris: Gallimard, 1965] p. 8).
11. Robert Nye, *The Origins of Crowd Psychology: Gustave Le Bon and the Crisis of Mass Democracy in the Third Republic* (London: Sage, 1975), pp. 93–94. As Yvon Thiec points out, "Durkheim's theory of social cohesion, which reflected his concern with unifying French society, contrasts sharply with the dualistic elite/masses vision of Le Bon" (Yvon Thiec, "Gustave Le Bon, prophète de l'irrationalisme de masse," *Revue française de sociologie,* July–Sept. 1981, p. 422).
12. Ian Lubek, "Histoire de psychologies sociales perdues: Le Cas de Gabriel Tarde," *Revue française de sociologie,* July–Sept. 1981, p. 377.
13. Jean Milet, *Gabriel Tarde et la philosophie de l'Histoire* (Paris: Vrin, 1970). Gabriel Tarde's son, Guillaume de Tarde, denies that his father was silent

about Dreyfus. Instead, he states, the elder man "took a position on the Affair that was primarily based on law and secondarily on emotion and politics per se. He was a Dreyfusard, which earned him ostracism from a number of quarters." (Quoted in ibid., p. 41.)

14. Quoted in Marcel Fournier, *Marcel Mauss* (Paris: Fayard, 1994), p. 167.

15. Emile Durkheim, "Antisémitisme et crise sociale," in E. Durkheim, *Textes*, vol. 2 (Paris: Editions de Minuit, 1975), pp. 252–53.

16. Ibid., pp. 253–54.

17. The quotations that follow are taken from Emile Durkheim, "Lettres d'Emile Durkheim à Henri Hubert," published with an introduction by Philippe Besnard in *Revue française de sociologie*, July–Sept. 1987.

18. Emile Durkheim, "Lettres à Célestin Bouglé," in Durkheim, *Textes*, vol. 2, pp. 417, 426. He also says (p. 429), "In Paris I have of course been running all over the place collecting information about the Affair."

19. "Lettres de Durkheim," *Revue française de sociologie*, Jan.–March 1979, p. 120.

20. Durkheim, "Lettres d'Emile Durkheim à Henri Hubert," p. 501.

21. See Pierre Birnbaum, *Les Fous de la République: Histoire des Juifs d'Etat, de Gambetta à Vichy* (Paris: Editions du Seuil, 1994), chap. 1, trans. by Jane M. Todd as *The Jews of the Republic: A Political History of State Jews in France from Gambetta to Vichy* (Stanford, Calif.: Stanford University Press, 1996).

22. "Gambetta was his idol," according to G. Davy, "Emile Durkheim," *Revue de métaphysique et de morale*, no. 26, 1919, p. 189.

23. Quoted in Fournier, *Marcel Mauss*, p. 167. On the relationship between Mauss and Lucien Herr in this period, see Marcel Fournier, "Portraits de Lucien Herr par Marcel Mauss," *Etudes durkheimiennes*, Winter 1994, vol. 6.

24. Fournier, *Marcel Mauss*, p. 170.

25. Ibid., p. 166.

26. Unpublished letter from Emile Durkheim to Marcel Mauss, March 19, 1898. I wish to thank Philippe Besnard for informing me of its contents.

27. Fournier, *Marcel Mauss*, p. 170.

28. Ibid., p. 204.

29. Ibid., p. 216.

30. Jean-Claude Chamboredon, "Sociologie de la sociologie et intérêts sociaux des sociologues," *Actes de la recherche en sciences sociales*, March 1975, p. 14. Halbwachs, still a student, "was caught up in the great political movement stemming from the Dreyfus Affair." See Victor Karady's introduction to Maurice Halbwachs, *Classes sociales et morphologie* (Paris: Editions de Minuit, 1972). See also John Craig, "Maurice Halbwachs à Strasbourg," *Revue française de sociologie*, Jan.–March 1979, p. 289.

31. Christophe Charle, "Le Beau Mariage d'Emile Durkheim," *Actes de la recherche en sciences sociales*, Nov. 1984, p. 48. On the connections between Durkheim and Lucien Lévy-Bruhl, see Dominique Merllié, "Lévy-Bruhl et

Durkheim: Notes biographiques en marge d'une correspondance," *Revue philosophique,* Oct.–Dec. 1989.

32. Private collection, Lévy-Bruhl family.

33. Lucien Lévy-Bruhl, preface to *Carnets de Schwartzkoppen* (Paris: Editions Rieder, 1930), p. 28.

34. See chapter 10 below.

35. See Pierre Birnbaum, "Les Juifs entre intégration et résistance," in Pierre Birnbaum, ed., *La France de l'affaire Dreyfus* (Paris: Gallimard, 1994), pp. 506, 525, 533.

36. See Christophe Charle and Eva Telkes, *Les Professeurs au Collège de France* (Paris: Centre National de Recherche Scientifique, 1988).

37. Letter received by Célestin Bouglé, *Revue française de sociologie,* Jan.–March 1979, p. 41.

38. See Terry Clark, *Prophets and Patrons: The French University and the Emergence of the Social Sciences* (Cambridge, Mass.: Harvard University Press, 1972), pp. 172 ff.; Yash Nandan, "Le Maître, les doctrines, les membres et le magnum opus: Une Etude critique et analytique de l'école durkheimienne et de *L'Année sociologique,*" unpublished doctoral thesis, Faculté des Lettres, University of Paris, 1974.

39. Philippe Besnard, "La Formation de l'équipe de *L'Année sociologique,*" *Revue française de sociologie,* Jan.–March 1979, p. 18.

40. Durkheim, "Lettres à Célestin Bouglé," p. 417.

41. See Jean-François Sirinelli, *Intellectuels et passions françaises* (Paris: Fayard, 1990), p. 25.

42. This lecture was published as a pamphlet, *La Tradition française* (Paris, 1899), quote on pp. 24–27.

43. Carol Iancu, "L'Affaire Dreyfus à Montpellier," in Carol Iancu, ed., *Les Juifs à Montpellier et dans le Languedoc* (Montpellier: Université Paul-Valéry, 1988), pp. 306–12. Bouglé remained committed for a long time. In February 1909, for example, he gave another lecture in Montpellier, this time before the Jeunesse Laïque et Républicaine. See *La Dépêche,* no. 146, February 17, 1909, Archives Départementales (hereafter AD) 54. On local letters of protest, see also no. 286, AD 39.

44. Célestin Bouglé, *Pour la démocratie française* (Paris: Cornély, 1900), pp. 30–32.

45. Durkheim, "Lettres à Célestin Bouglé," p. 425.

46. Bouglé, *Pour la démocratie française,* p. 56.

47. Ibid., p. 94.

48. Vincent Duclert, *L'Affaire Dreyfus* (Paris: La Découverte, 1994), p. 76.

49. Christophe Charle, *Naissance des "intellectuels," 1800–1900* (Paris: Editions de Minuit, 1990), pp. 196–97, 215. On this milieu, see also Paula Hyman, *From Dreyfus to Vichy: The Remaking of French Jewry, 1906–1939* (New York: Columbia University Press, 1979), chap. 2.

50. See Vincent Duclert, "Les Revues dreyfusardes: L'Emergence d'une société intellectuelle," *Revue des revues*, no. 17, 1994.

51. Hubert Bourgin, *De Jaurès à Léon Blum: L'Ecole normale et la politique* (Paris: Fayard, 1938), pp. 221, 233.

52. Giuliana Gemelli, "Communauté intellectuelle et stratégies institutionnelles: Henri Berr et la fondation du Centre international de synthèse," *Revue de synthèse*, April–June 1987, p. 228. For a study of the *Revue de synthèse* and its relations with sociologists like Durkheim and Durkheimian economists such as Simiand, see Martin Fugler, "Analyse ou Synthèse: *La Revue de synthèse historique* et l'histoire, 1900–1910," unpublished master's thesis, Université de Sciences Sociales de Strasbourg, 1985.

53. Henri Berr, *Peut-on refaire l'unité morale de la France?*, Henri Berr archives, HBR, 2 A 13, pp. 4–11. This document was published by Armand Colin in 1901. There are few copies extant; one can be consulted at the Institut Mémoires de l'Edition Contemporaine.

54. Thanks to Madame Jacqueline Pluet-Despatin for this information. See also her contribution, and those of Peter Schöttler and Christophe Prochasson, to a colloquium on "Henri Berr et la culture de son temps" organized by the Institut Mémoires de l'Edition Contemporaine, October 1994. Prochasson emphasizes the close connection between the Durkheimians and the *Revue de synthèse*, whose contributors included not only Mauss and Hubert but also Bouglé and Durkheim, who by 1914 had published four book reviews in the journal.

55. Xavier Léon, letter to his mother, quoted in Christophe Prochasson, "Philosophie au XXe siècle: Xavier Léon et l'invention du 'système R2M' (1891–1902)," *Revue de métaphysique et de morale*, nos. 1–2, 1993, p. 127.

56. Jean-Louis Fabiani, *Les Philosophes de la République* (Paris: Editions de Minuit, 1988), pp. 37, 155.

57. A. Darlu, "De M. Brunetière et de l'individualisme," *Revue de métaphysique et de morale*, nos. 3–4, 1998. He expressed the hope that Brunetière would "learn to put the interests of conscience ahead of the greater interests of society" (p. 400).

58. Quoted in Prochasson, "Philosophie au XXe siècle," p. 130.

59. Perrine Simon-Nahum, "Xavier Léon/Elie Halévy: Correspondance, 1891–1898," *Revue de métaphysique et de morale*, nos. 1–2, 1993, p. 8.

60. Quoted by Michèle Bo Bramsen, "Contribution à une biographie intellectuelle d'Elie Halévy," unpublished thesis, Fondation Nationale des Sciences Politiques, Paris, 1971, p. 72.

61. Ibid., pp. 79, 83, 85, 86.

62. Jean-Pierre Halévy, preface to Daniel Halévy, *Regards sur l'affaire Dreyfus* (Paris: Editions de Fallois, 1994), p. 11.

63. Ibid., pp. 32, 35. See also Marcel Proust, *Correspondance avec Daniel Halévy* (Paris: Editions de Fallois, 1992).

64. Halévy, *Regards,* p. 62. See also Alain Silvera, *Daniel Halévy and His Times* (Ithaca, N.Y.: Cornell University Press, 1966), p. 91.

65. Here one might compare the fates of Durkheim and Bergson; see Louis Greenberg, "Bergson and Durkheim as Sons and Assimilators: The Early Years," *French Historical Studies* 4 (1976). Or of Durkheim and Julien Benda, who were different in every respect; see Louis-Albert Revah, *Julien Benda* (Paris: Plon, 1991), p. 25.

66. Quoted in Fournier, *Marcel Mauss,* p. 168.

67. Durkheim, "Lettres à Célestin Bouglé," pp. 423, 428. On Bouglé, see William Logue, "Sociologie et politique: Le Libéralisme de Célestin Bouglé," *Revue française de sociologie,* Jan.–March 1979; and, in the same issue, Paul Vogt, "Un Durkheimien ambivalent: Célestin Bouglé, 1870–1940."

68. On the local context, see Elisabeth Cazenave, "L'Affaire Dreyfus et l'opinion bordelaise: Essai de méthodologie," *Annales du Midi,* Jan. 1972. On these incidents, see my introduction to Emile Durkheim, *Le Socialisme* (Paris: Presses Universitaires de France, 1972).

69. Steven Lukes, *Emile Durkheim: His Life and Work* (London: Allen Lane, 1973), pp. 347, 349, 358.

70. The letter of protest signed by Durkheim is apparently not very well known. AD Gironde, 1 M 431.

71. Ibid.

72. Ibid.

73. This letter is presented in *Etudes durkheimiennes,* no. 7, June 1982.

74. Brunetière was a complex writer, however. Shortly before joining the anti-Dreyfusard camp, he attacked both racism and anti-Semitism and was positive on the subject of American democracy. See Antoine Compagnon, "Zola à Columbia," in Philippe Hamon and Jean-Pierre Leduc-Adine, eds., *Mimesis et Semiosis: Littérature et représentation* (Paris: Nathan, 1992).

75. Letter from Emile Durkheim to Célestin Bouglé, April 3, 1898, *Revue française de sociologie,* April–June 1976, p. 169.

76. Emile Durkheim, "Lettre à Henri Hubert," *Revue française de sociologie,* July–Sept. 1987, p. 492. On the context, see Antoine Compagnon, *La IIIe République des lettres* (Paris: Editions du Seuil, 1983), p. 69.

77. See François-André Isambert, "La Naissance de l'individu," in P. Besnard, M. Borlandi, and P. Vogt, eds., *Division du travail et lien social* (Paris: Presses Universitaires de France, 1994). See also François-André Isambert, "Durkheim et l'individu," in W. S. Pickering and W. Watts-Miller, eds., *Individualisme et droits de l'homme selon la tradition durkheimienne,* Occasional Papers, no. 1 (Oxford: British Centre for Durkheimian Studies, 1993).

78. Emile Durkheim, "L'Individualisme et les intellectuels," in Emile Durkheim, *La Science sociale et l'action* (Paris: Presses Universitaires de France, 1970).

79. Emile Durkheim, "L'Etat," in Durkheim, *Textes,* vol. 3, pp. 172–78. See

Pierre Birnbaum, "La Conception durkheimienne de l'Etat: L'Apolitisme des fonctionnaires," *Revue française de sociologie,* April–June 1976.

80. Emile Durkheim, *Leçons de sociologie physique des moeurs et du droit* (Paris: Presses Universitaires de France, 1950), p. 3.

81. Ibid., pp. 96, 111, 113.

82. Durkheim, "L'Individualisme et les intellectuels," pp. 270, 275. In light of this, it is hard to understand how Marco Diani could have written, "In the teaching of both Barrès and Durkheim, the desire for justice is replaced by the desire for social solidarity." And it is particularly odd, given Durkheim's emphasis on respect for the individual, that Diani could also claim that both writers "aimed at all cost to create a new discipline capable of uniting the moral forces in society. These new disciplines, which implied total subordination of the individual to society, obviously foreshadowed the fascist movement of the early twentieth century." (Marco Diani, "Metamorphosis of Nationalism: Durkheim, Barrès, and the Dreyfus Affair," *Jerusalem Journal of International Relations* 4 [1991]: 91.) Durkheim's patriotism, which was defined in almost Kantian terms at the time of the Affair, has little in common with the Catholic, anti-Semitic nationalism of Barrès. At the opposite extreme, Mark Cladis interprets Durkheim's response to Brunetière as a defense of moral individualism, and he links Durkheim to John Rawls. See his *Communitarian Defense of Liberalism: Emile Durkheim and Contemporary Social Theory* (Stanford: Stanford University Press, 1993), chap. 1, and p. 271. By contrast, Wille Watts-Miller sees Durkheim as a "liberal communitarian" because he conceived of the social system in terms at once holistic and individualistic. Watts-Miller places Durkheim close to Charles Taylor, Rawls's adversary. See Willie Watts-Miller, "Durkheim: Liberal Communitarian," in Pickering and Watts-Miller, eds., *Individualisme et droits humains.* One could extend the debate by presenting Durkheim both as a precursor of Rawls (on account of his concern with keeping social and cultural commitments out of the public sphere, hence a consistent communitarian who stresses the way in which the "self" is woven into the very fabric of society) and as a moderate who ultimately acknowledged his Judaism and publicly defended persecuted Jews. Obviously, these comments call for systematic elaboration.

83. Durkheim, "L'Individualisme et les intellectuels," pp. 267–75.

84. See Yves Déloye, *Ecole et citoyenneté: L'Individualisme républicain de Jules Ferry à Vichy* (Paris: Presses de la Fondation Nationale des Sciences Politiques, 1994).

85. Emile Durkheim, "L'Elite intellectuelle et la démocratie," in Durkheim, *La Science sociale et l'action,* p. 281.

86. Robert Bellah, "Morale, religion et société dans l'oeuvre durkheimienne," *Archives des sciences sociales et des religions,* Jan.–March 1990. According to Bellah, Durkheim was "a high priest and theologian of the civil religion of the Third Republic" (p. 10).

87. See Pierre Birnbaum, ed., *La France de l'affaire Dreyfus* (Paris: Gallimard, 1994).

88. See René Lacroze, "Emile Durkheim à Bordeaux," *Annales de l'Université de Paris,* Jan.–March 1960.

89. Pierre Lasserre, *La Doctrine officielle de l'université* (Paris: Mercure de France, 1912), p. 243.

90. Dom Besse, *Les Religions laïques* (Paris: Nouvelle Librairie Nationale, 1913), p. 240. On these attacks, see Claire-Françoise Bompaire-Evesque, *Un Débat sur l'université au temps de la IIIe République: La Lutte contre la nouvelle Sorbonne* (Paris: Aux Amateurs de Livres, 1988).

91. Emile Durkheim, "Rapport sur la situation des Russes du département de la Seine," presented by Noureddine Elkarati, *Genèses,* Dec. 1990.

92. Letter from Emile Durkheim to Marcel Mauss, Feb. 5, 1916. I thank Philippe Besnard for kindly allowing me to quote an excerpt from this unpublished letter.

93. Letter from Emile Durkheim to Fournière, Oct. 28, 1902, *Revue française de sociologie,* Jan.–March 1979, p. 119.

94. Eugen Weber, *The Nationalist Revival: 1905–1914* (Stanford: Stanford University Press, 1950).

95. Albert Thibaudet, *Les Idées politiques de la France* (Paris: Stock, 1932), p. 159.

96. W. Rabi, "Ecrivains juifs face à l'affaire Dreyfus: Etude des comportements," in Géraldi Leroy, ed., *Les Ecrivains et l'affaire Dreyfus* (Paris: Presses Universitaires de France, 1983), p. 24.

97. See Jean-Claude Filloux, "Il ne faut pas oublier que je suis fils de rabbin," *Revue française de sociologie* April–June 1976; J. Prades, *Persistance et métamorphose du sacré* (Paris: Presses Universitaires de France, 1987); Eugen Schonfeld and Stjepan Mestrovic, "Durkheim's Concept of Justice and Its Relationship to Social Solidarity," *Sociological Analysis,* Summer 1989. The latter two authors state (p. 113), "Despite the fact that Durkheim deliberately rejected Judaism and the role of the rabbi, he was still a prophet. . . . One can cautiously relate his conception of justice to his Jewish upbringing."

98. Jean-Claude Chamboredon, "Emile Durkheim: Le Social, objet de science—du moral au politique?," *Critique,* July 1984, pp. 495, 513. It may come as a surprise to find that in this fundamental article Chamboredon makes fun of the application to Durkheim of the concept of an "epistemological break," which others have applied to Marx: "Here is yet another difficulty for the concept of an 'epistemological break' " (pp. 523–24). This is a rather clumsy joke about a rabbi's son.

99. Ibid., p. 497. Chamboredon adds: "Here one would have to look carefully at the chronology of the Dreyfus Affair (before it entered its more public phase) and of Durkheim's work on suicide" (p. 531). Note, however, that the first issue of *L'Année sociologique,* published in 1898, made no allusion to the deep crisis that France was then experiencing.

100. Philippe Besnard, *L'Anomie* (Paris: Presses Universitaires de France, 1987), p. 123.

101. Emile Durkheim, *Les Formes élémentaires de la vie religieuse* (Paris: Alcan, 1925), pp. 547, 607.

102. Durkheim, "Antisémitisme et crise sociale," p. 253. In a somewhat unfair comment on this sentence, Alain Policar, in "Destin du franco-judaïsme ou les illusions de l'universalisme abstrait," *Les Temps modernes,* Nov. 1993, p. 61, writes, "We cannot fail to be dumbfounded by such depths of naïveté."

103. On August 12, 1916, Durkheim, on vacation in Cabourg, wrote to Marcel Mauss: "Already met here thirty-six Jews (or Jewesses) I know, not to mention all the unknown Semites I hear around me. But not a single Indo-European I know. What a reversal of natural proportions." In another letter to Mauss, on the 16th, he writes: "The beach is full of Jews. I know more than thirty Semites of every sex in Cabourg, and not one Indo-European." I thank Philippe Besnard for making these unpublished letters available.

104. These two excerpts come from Fournier, *Marcel Mauss,* p. 39.

105. *Archives israélites,* Nov. 22, 1917. For W. S. Pickering, *Durkheim's Sociology of Religion* (London: Routledge and Kegan Paul, 1984), Durkheim "was concerned with the Jewish question throughout his life" (p. 17). Oddly, Pickering (p. 18) draws a parallel between Durkheim and Disraeli, whose values were very different and who did not hesitate to convert. For a more systematic summary of the author's more recent views, see W. S. Pickering, "The Enigma of Durkheim's Jewishness," in W. S. Pickering and H. Martin, *Debating Durkheim* (London: Routledge and Kegan Paul, 1994), especially pp. 22–23, 34–37.

106. *L'Univers israélite,* Nov. 30, 1917. Of Lucien Lévy-Bruhl's death, the same issue remarked: "Though French first and foremost, he never ceased to feel Jewish. He was a citizen of a world in which there is nothing contradictory about those two things."

107. Perrine Simon-Nahum, *La Cité investie: La "Science du judaïsme" française et la République* (Paris: Le Cerf, 1991), pp. 272, 279.

108. Georges Davy, "Centenaire de la naissance d'Emile Durkheim," *Annales de l'Université de Paris,* Jan.–March 1960, p. 16. In another work, still speaking about Durkheim, Davy writes, "Morality needs a prophet, and one whom every man can hear" (*L'Homme, le fait social et le fait politique* [Paris: Mouton, 1973], p. 19).

109. R. Maublanc, *Europe* 23 (1930): 297.

110. Jean-Claude Filloux, *Durkheim et le socialisme* (Geneva: Droz, 1977). Filloux points out, for example, that Durkheim's father's first name was Moïse (Moses).

111. From the obituary in *L'Univers israélite,* which adds, "He was a citizen of a world in which there is nothing contradictory about those two things."

112. Aron, *Essais sur la condition juive contemporaine,* p. 64. The second quotation

is in Chepel d'Apollonia, "Morale et polique chez Raymond Aron," vol. 1, p. 254.

5. THE DRUMONT PARADIGM

1. *La Libre Parole*, June 19, 1910.
2. Ibid., Feb. 16, 1901.
3. Edouard Drumont, *La Fin d'un monde* (Paris: Savine, 1889), p. iv. See also Edouard Drumont, *La France juive* (Paris: Flammarion, 1886), vol. 1, p. 175; and Edouard Drumont, *Mon Vieux Paris* (Paris: Flammarion, 1893), pp. 193 ff. See also, by the same author, *La Dernière Bataille* (Paris: Dentu, 1890), p. 544.
4. *La Libre Parole*, Nov. 3, 1906.
5. Ibid., April 20, 1914.
6. For a recent summary, see Gérard de Puymène, *Chauvin, le soldat-laboureur: Contribution à l'étude des nationalismes* (Paris: Gallimard, 1993). See also Jean-Paul Honoré, "Le Discours politique dans l'affaire Dreyfus," unpublished doctoral thesis, University of Paris III, 1982; Janine Ponty-Lavieville, "La France devant l'affaire Dreyfus: Contribution à une histoire sociale d'opinion publique, 1898–1899," unpublished doctoral thesis, Ecole Pratique des Hautes Etudes, 1971.
7. Zeev Sternhell, *Maurice Barrès et le nationalisme français* (Brussels: Complexe, 1985), pp. 19, 42.
8. Drumont, *La France juive*, vol. 1, p. 471; vol. 2, p. 27.
9. Edouard Drumont, *Les Juifs contre la France: Une nouvelle Pologne* (Paris: Librairie Antisémite, 1899), pp. 9, 68, 96.
10. Edouard Drumont, *Les Tréteaux du succès: Figures de bronze et statues de neige* (Paris: Flammarion, 1900), p. iii. See also Edouard Drumont, *Le Testament d'un antisémite* (Paris: Dentu, 1891), p. 417.
11. Pierre Birnbaum, *Un Mythe politique: "La République juive," de Léon Blum à Pierre Mendès France* (Paris: Fayard, 1988), trans. by Miriam Kochan as *Antisemitism in France: A Political History from Léon Blum to the Present* (Cambridge: Blackwell, 1992).
12. The curious re-emergence of this Drumont-invented theme is discussed in Paul Zawadski, "Antisémitisme en Pologne à l'heure de la transition vers le postcommunisme," unpublished manuscript.
13. Krzysztof Wolicki, "Une Pologne toute catholique?," *Le Débat*, Sept.–Oct. 1991.
14. Steven Kaplan, *Adieu 89* (Paris: Fayard, 1993), pp. 219 ff.
15. Drumont, *Les Tréteaux*, p. 53.
16. Drumont, *La France juive*, vol. 2, p. 427; see also vol. 1, p. 286.
17. Edouard Drumont, *Vieux Portraits, vieux cadres* (Paris: Flammarion, 1903), p. 5.

18. Edouard Drumont, *Le Secret de Fourmies* (Paris: Savine, 1892), pp. 9–10.

19. Ibid., pp. 7, 76.

20. Edouard Drumont, *La France juive devant l'opinion* (Paris: Flammarion, 1886), pp. 202–3.

21. Drumont, *La Dernière Bataille*, pp. 16, 50. Similarly, in *La Fin d'un monde*, Drumont begins one chapter with the phrase "we sociologists" (p. 263). In *La Libre Parole*, July 13, 1908, Drumont wrote, "Yes, my dear sociologists, that is the law: conquered races are absorbed by conquering ones." In the list of contributors to the collection taken up for Colonel Henry's widow, one identified himself as "a sociologist who, seeing what the Jews have done to France in one short year, is glad to make this gift as proof of his unspeakable disgust" (Pierre Quillard, *Le Monument Henry* [Paris: Stock, 1899], p. 499).

22. Drumont, *La Fin d'un monde*, pp. xvii–xviii.

23. Jan Goldstein, "The Wandering Jew and the Problem of Psychiatric Anti-Semitism in Fin-de-Siècle France," *Journal of Contemporary History* 20 (1985): 540, 546.

24. Jan Goldstein, "The Use of Male Hysteria: Medical and Literary Discourse in Nineteenth-Century France," *Representations*, Spring 1991, p. 154.

25. Drumont, *La Dernière Bataille*, pp. 142, 183, 515. In *La Libre Parole*, Dec. 13, 1903, he wrote: "Race is the most solid basis for psychological induction."

26. Drumont, *La Dernière Bataille*, pp. 163, 184, 506, 508.

27. Ibid., p. 136. At about the same time, one of Drumont's followers argued that "the Jew, having gotten hold of the wallet, now wants the brains as well" (André de Boisandré, *Petit Catéchisme antijuif* [Paris: Librairie Antisémite, 1904], p. 3).

28. Drumont, *La Dernière Bataille*, p. 286.

29. Edouard Drumont, *De l'or, de la boue, du sang* (Paris: Flammarion, 1896), pp. 77–79.

30. *La Libre Parole*, Sept. 26, 1905.

31. See Zeev Sternhell, *La Droite révolutionnaire, 1885–1914: Les Origines françaises du fascisme* (Paris: Editions du Seuil, 1978), chap. 3; and Daniel Pick, *Faces of Degeneration* (Cambridge: Cambridge University Press, 1989).

32. *La Libre Parole*, June 24, 1907. At the same time, Maurice Barrès wrote: "The brains of foreigners are not made the same way as our brains" (quoted in Sternhell, *Maurice Barrès*, p. 251).

33. Drumont, *La Fin d'un monde*, p. xvii.

34. Drumont, *La France juive*, vol. 1, pp. 105, 108; vol. 2, p. 442.

35. *La Libre Parole*, June 19, 1904.

36. Ibid., Sept. 17, 1904.

37. Ibid., July 22, 1908. See also the June 18, 1904, issue.

38. Drumont, *La France juive*, vol. 1, p. 293.

39. Drumont, *Le Testament d'un antisémite*, pp. 138, 171–72.

40. *La Libre Parole*, Dec. 31, 1898.

41. Drumont, *La France juive devant l'opinion,* p. 170.

42. *La Libre Parole,* March 12, 1892.

43. Drumont, *La France juive,* vol. 1, p. 286.

44. *La Libre Parole,* July 13, 1908. See also, for example, Drumont, *La France juive,* vol. 1, p. 104; and Drumont, *La Dernière Bataille,* p. 204.

45. *La Libre Parole,* Jan. 1, 1904.

46. Ibid., May 11, 1894.

47. Drumont, *La Fin d'un monde,* p. iii.

48. Drumont, *De l'or, de la boue, du sang,* p. 169.

49. *La Libre Parole,* Jan. 21, 1908.

50. Drumont, *La Dernière Bataille,* pp. 192–93.

51. See Stephen Wilson, *Ideology and Experience: Antisemitism in France at the Time of the Dreyfus Affair* (London: Associated University Press, 1982), chap. 13.

52. *La Libre Parole,* Sept. 5, 1908.

53. Interview with Drumont published by François Bournand in *Les Juifs, nos contemporains* (Paris: A. Pierret, 1898), p. 35.

54. *La Libre Parole,* Jan. 1, 1904.

55. Ibid., May 3, 1902.

56. See Pierre Birnbaum, *"La France aux Français": Histoire des haines nationalistes* (Paris: Editions du Seuil, 1993).

57. Eugen Weber, *France, Fin de Siècle* (Cambridge, Mass.: Harvard University Press, 1986) p. 50.

58. Frederick Busi, "The First Dreyfus Affair," *Judaism,* Winter 1978; and Frederick Busi, *The Pope of Antisemitism: The Career and Legacy of Edouard-Adolphe Drumont* (Lanham, Md.: University Press of America, 1986).

59. Drumont, *La France juive,* vol. 1, pp. 446–47.

60. Ibid., pp. 422–23.

61. Jeanne Verdès-Leroux, *Scandale financier et antisémitisme catholique: Le Krach de l'Union générale* (Paris: Le Centurion, 1969), p. 147; Pierre Pierrard, *Juifs et catholiques* (Paris: Fayard, 1970); Pierre Sorlin, *"La Croix" et les Juifs* (Paris: Grasset, 1967).

62. Pierre Birnbaum, *Les Fous de la République: Histoire des Juifs d'Etat, de Gambetta à Vichy* (Paris: Editions du Seuil, 1994), pp. 162 ff., trans. by Jane M. Todd as *The Jews of the Republic: A Political History of State Jews in France from Gambetta to Vichy* (Stanford, Calif.: Stanford University Press, 1996), pp. 119 ff.

63. *La Libre Parole,* May 26, 1892.

64. Busi, *Pope of Antisemitism,* pp. 18, 35.

65. Drumont was not the only writer to claim that Jewish officers were guilty of treason. Even before the eruption of the Affair, the subject was broached by Georges Corneilhan in *Juifs et Opportunistes* (1899). Conversely, on January 15, 1889, a man by the name of Dreyfus was arrested in Strasbourg for

spying on behalf of France. See Marc Angenot, *"Un Juif trahira"*: *Le Thème de l'espionnage militaire dans la propagande antisémitique, 1864–1894* (Montreal: CIADEST, 1994), p. 94.

66. Birnbaum, *Les Fous de la République,* chap. 11.

6. THE ERA OF LEAGUES

1. Eugen Weber, *The Nationalist Revival in France, 1905–1914* (Berkeley: University of California Press, 1968).

2. In 1893, Garnier founded the Union Nationale, a nationalist Catholic political organization which was quite active in the anti-Semitic movement. The Union maintained close ties with the anti-Semitic leagues led by Drumont and Guérin.

3. See Stephen Wilson, "Catholic Populism in France at the Time of the Dreyfus Affair: The Union Nationale," *Journal of Contemporary History* 10, no. 4 (1975).

4. Sylvie Fayet-Scribe, *Associations féminines et catholicisme* (Paris: Editions Ouvrières, 1990).

5. On the Marquis de Morès and his anti-Semitic gangs, see Robert Byrnes, *Antisemitism in Modern France* (New Brunswick, N.J.: Rutgers University Press, 1950); and Pierre Pierrard, *Juifs et catholiques français* (Paris: Fayard, 1970), p. 138.

6. See Bertrand Joly, "The *Jeunesse Antisémite et Nationaliste, 1894–1904,*" in Robert Tombs, ed., *Nationhood and Nationalism in France: From Boulangism to the Great War, 1889–1918* (London: HarperCollins, 1991). See also the very rich archives in Archives Nationales, F 7 12459.

7. See Stephen Wilson, *Ideology and Experience: Antisemitism in France at the Time of the Dreyfus Affair* (London: Associated University Press, 1982), pp. 197–99; and AN F 7 12459.

8. On anti-Masonic organizations before 1914, see the *Bulletin de la Société Augustin Barruel,* no. 8, 1981.

9. Bernard Ménager, "Nationalists and Bonapartists," in Tombs, ed., *Nationhood and Nationalism.*

10. William Irvine, *The Boulanger Affair Reconsidered: Royalism, Boulangism, and the Origins of the Radical Right in France* (New York: Oxford University Press, 1989), chap. 6.

11. William Serman, "The Nationalists of Meurthe-et-Moselle, 1888–1912," in Tombs, ed., *Nationhood and Nationalism,* p. 130.

12. See especially Eugen Weber, *Action Française* (Stanford, Calif.: Stanford University Press, 1962). See also Pierrard, *Juifs et catholiques,* pp. 170 ff.; Stephen Wilson, "L'Action française et le mouvement nationaliste français entre les années 1890 et 1900," in *Etudes maurrassiennes* 4 (1980); and Victor Nguyen, *Aux origines de l'Action française* (Paris: Fayard, 1991).

13. See the rich archives on Action Française in this period: APP 1341, 1342, 1343.

14. O. L. Arnal, *Ambivalent Alliance: The Catholic Church and the Action Française* (Pittsburgh: University of Pittsburgh Press, 1985). For a more general view, see Gérard Cholvy and Yves-Marie Hilaire, *Histoire religieuse de la France contemporaine*, vol. 2 (Toulouse: Privat, 1986), chaps. 3 and 4. The authors examine the "extremist temptation" of many Catholics as well as the opposition of some, from the Sillon to the liberals to the "intransigent" position. For Eugen Weber quotation, see p. 65 of his book, *Action Française*.

15. See Zeev Sternhell, *La Droite révolutionnaire, 1885–1914: Les Origines françaises du fascisme* (Paris: Editions du Seuil, 1978), chap. 2.

16. Here I am largely following Jean-Pierre Rioux, *Nationalisme et conservatisme: La Ligue de la patrie française, 1899–1904* (Paris: Beauchesne, 1977). See also Sternhell, *La Droite révolutionnaire*.

17. See D. R. Watson, "The Nationalist Movement in Paris, 1900–1906," in David Shapiro, ed., *The Right in France, 1890–1919* (London: Chatto and Windus, 1962).

18. See the fine book by Zeev Sternhell, *Maurice Barrès et le nationalisme français* (Brussels: Complexe, 1985).

19. These riots are described in Wilson, *Ideology and Experience*, chap. 3.

20. See Geneviève Dermenjian, *Juifs et Européens d'Algérie: L'Antisémitisme oranais, 1892–1905* (Jerusalem: Institut Ben-Zvi, 1983); and Yves Déloye, "Citoyenneté et sens civique dans l'Algérie coloniale: L'Emancipation politique de la minorité juive au XXe siècle," unpublished master's thesis, University of Paris I, 1987.

21. Pierrard, *Juifs et catholiques,* pp. 92 ff.

22. Serman, "Nationalists of Meurthe-et-Moselle," pp. 127–30.

23. Pierrard, *Juifs et catholiques,* pp. 102 ff.; Wilson, *Ideology and Experience,* chap. 4.

24. See Michael Burns, "Qui Ça Dreyfus?: The Affair in Rural France," *Historical Reflections* 5 (1978); and Michael Burns, *Rural Society and French Politics: Boulangism and the Dreyfus Affair, 1886–1900* (Princeton: Princeton University Press, 1984). On this fundamental debate, see Edward Berenson, "Politics and the French Peasantry: The Debate Continues," *Social History*, May 1987; and especially the fine article by Nancy Fitch, "Mass Culture, Mass Parliamentary Politics and Modern Anti-Semitism: The Dreyfus Affair in Rural France," *American Historical Review*, Feb. 1992. On the role of anti-Semitic propaganda and its use in various art forms, see Norman Kleeblatt, *The Dreyfus Affair: Art, Truth, and Justice* (Berkeley: University of California Press, 1987); and Paula Hyman, "The Dreyfus Affair: The Visual and the Historical," *Journal of Modern History*, March 1989.

25. According to Weber: "There was a nationalist party: beaten in 1902 and decimated in 1906, it ceased to matter. For a time its survivors disappeared from

view. Then a double threat led to a reaction in their favor, or at any rate in favor of the ideas they stood for" (*Nationalist Revival*, p. 268). See also David
Sumler, "Domestic Influences on the Nationalist Revival in France, 1909–
1914," *French Historical Studies*, Autumn 1970.

26. Pierre Guiral, "Le Nationalisme à Marseille et en Provence de 1900 à 1914,"
    in *Opinion publique et politique extérieure* (Rome: Collection de l'Ecole
    Française de Rome, 1981), p. 345. For a recent overview, see Paul Mazgay,
    "The Origins of the French Radical Right: A Historiographical Essay,"
    French Historical Studies, Autumn 1987.

27. See Pierrard, *Juifs et catholiques;* and Jean-Marie Mayeur, "Les Catholiques
    dreyfusards," *Revue historique*, April–June 1979.

7. THE HIDDEN FACE OF THE REPUBLICAN STATE

1. Bertrand Badie and Pierre Birnbaum, *Sociologie de l'Etat* (Paris: Pluriel,
   1982), trans. by Arthur Goldhammer as *The Sociology of the State* (Chicago:
   University of Chicago Press, 1983).

2. See Christophe Charle, *Les Elites de la République* (Paris: Fayard, 1987); and
   Vincent Wright, "L'Epuration du Conseil d'Etat en juillet 1879," *Revue d'histoire moderne et contemporaine*, Oct.–Dec. 1972.

3. See Pierre Birnbaum, *Les Fous de la République: Histoire des Juifs d'Etat, de
   Gambetta à Vichy* (Paris: Editions du Seuil, 1994), trans. by Jane M. Todd as
   *The Jews of the Republic: A Political History of State Jews in France from
   Gambetta to Vichy* (Stanford, Calif.: Stanford University Press, 1996).

4. AN F 19 5447.

5. AN F 19 5613.

6. Quoted in Jean-Pierre Royer, "La Magistrature déchirée," in Pierre Birnbaum,
   ed., *La France de l'affaire Dreyfus* (Paris: Gallimard, 1994).

7. *La Libre Parole*, Sept. 29, 1894.

8. AN F1 B I. 358.

9. Edouard Drumont, *La France juive* (Paris: Flammarion, 1886), vol. 1, p. 421.
   See also *La Libre Parole*, Feb. 16, 1895.

10. *Le Pays*, April 18, 1885. See the very complete police dossier, dossier Levail-
    lant, B A 1155.

11. *La Cocarde*, Feb. 6, 1888.

12. *La Libre Parole*, March 29, 1893.

13. Isaïe Levaillant, *Ma Justification* (Paris: Alcan-Lévy, 1895), pp. 1, 37.

14. *L'Autorité*, Feb. 12, 1895.

15. *L'Intransigeant*, Feb. 12, 1895.

16. *Journal de Paris*, May 21, 1895, AN F 19 5634.

17. *L'Univers israélite*, April 30, 1897.

18. Ibid., June 23, 1899.

19. On this episode and Levaillant's role in it, see Pierre Birnbaum, "La Citoyen-

neté en péril: Les Juifs entre l'intégration et al résistance," in Birnbaum, ed., *La France de l'affaire Dreyfus.*

20. *L'Univers israélite*, March 13, 1903.
21. *La Libre Parole*, Aug. 7, 1899.
22. AN F1 B I 526.
23. AN F1 B I 297.
24. AN F1 B I 530.
25. AN BB 6 II 1230.
26. AN BB 6 II 824.
27. AN BB 6 II 789.
28. For details, see Royer, "La Magistrature déchirée." I am following his analysis closely.
29. *La Libre Parole*, Feb. 10, 1906.
30. *L'Intransigeant*, Nov. 8, 1903. See also the Dec. 19, 1902, issue.
31. AN BB 6 II 1230.
32. *La Libre Parole*, April 20, 1907.
33. Jean-Pierre Machelon, *La République contre les libertés?* (Paris: Presses de la Fondation Nationale des Sciences Politiques, 1976).

8. MILITARY PASSION THWARTED

1. See Robert Gauthier, ed., *Dreyfusards!* (Paris: Gallimard, 1965), p. 47.
2. *La Libre Parole*, May 23, 1892.
3. Ibid., Jan. 12, 1898.
4. Ernest Crémieu Foa, *La Campagne antisémite: Les Duels, les responsabilités* (Paris: Alcan-Lévy, 1892). Later, the anti-Semitic author Raphaël Viau provided a lengthy reconsideration of these end-of-the-century duels in *Vingt Ans d'antisémitisme* (Paris: Fasquelle, 1910). In 1935, Jean Drault, a faithful friend of Drumont, fondly remembered these duels in *Drumont* (Paris: Société Française d'Editions Littéraires et Techniques, 1935). On these various types of duels, see Simon Arbellot, *La Fin du boulevard* (Paris: Flammarion, 1965); and Robert Nye, *Masculinity and Male Codes of Honor in Modern France* (Oxford: Oxford University Press, 1993).
5. *Archives israélites*, June 30 and Sept. 15, 1892; *L'Univers israélite*, July 1 and 21, 1892.
6. Archives of the Central Consistory, minutes, no. 5, June 22, 1892.
7. See *Archives israélites*, Sept. 1, 1892.
8. *L'Univers israélite*, July 21 and Dec. 1, 1892.
9. See David Cohen, *La Promotion des Juifs en France à l'époque du second Empire*, vol. 2 (Paris: Librairie Honoré Champion, 1980); William Serman, *Les Officiers français dans la nation, 1848–1914* (Paris: Aubier, 1982); Pierre Birnbaum, *Les Fous de la République: Histoire des Juifs d'Etat, de Gambetta à Vichy* (Paris: Editions du Seuil, 1994), trans. by Jane M. Todd as *The Jews of*

the Republic: A Political History of State Jews in France from Gambetta to Vichy (Stanford, Calif.: Stanford University Press, 1996).

10. *Archives israélites,* Feb. 15, 1894; *L'Univers israélite,* Oct. 6, 1894, Sept. 30, 1898, Oct. 21, 1898, Sept. 29, 1899, and Oct. 6, 1899.

11. Jean-Marie Bredin, *L'Affaire* (Paris: Presses-Pocket, 1983), pp. 30 ff.; Michael Burns, *Dreyfus, a Family Affair: From the French Revolution to the Holocaust* (New York: HarperCollins, 1991).

12. The information on the three officers named Dreyfus is taken from their personnel files, Service Historique des Armées, Vincennes.

13. *L'Univers israélite,* July 15, 1927.

14. Ibid., Jan. 16, 1894, Jan. 16, 1895, and Sept. 9, 1898; *Archives israélites,* Nov. 1, 1894.

15. *L'Univers israélite,* Nov. 16, 1893, May 16, 1895, and Jan. 14, 1898.

16. Ibid., June 16, 1893.

17. *Archives israélites,* Jan. 17, 1895.

18. *La Croix,* Nov. 9, 1894. *La Croix* regularly attacked Jewish officers. See, e.g., the issues for Dec. 12, 1886, April 10, 1897, and April 14, 1894. In the issue for Dec. 12, 1886, shortly after the publication of Drumont's book *La France juive,* one can read this: "There are forty of their race at the Ecole Polytechnique."

19. J.-M. Villefrance, *La Patrie* (Paris, 1899), p. 69.

20. *L'Univers israélite,* Feb. 16, 1900. Note, too, that early in 1895 a nephew of Captain Dreyfus who had been preparing to enter Polytechnique chose to cut short his studies instead (ibid., Feb. 1, 1895).

21. The statistics, as well as General Dennery's observation, can be found in Philippe Landau, "Les Officiers juifs et l'Affaire," *Archives juives,* Sept. 1994, p. 12.

22. *L'Univers israélite,* Nov. 11, 1904; *Archives israélites,* Nov. 16, 1904.

23. Service Historique des Armées 1 KT 50.

24. On this incident, see Birnbaum, *The Jews of the Republic,* pp. 327 ff.

25. See Serman, *Les Officiers,* p. 108.

26. Service Historique des Armées, Vincennes, 3rd series, 582, dossier Bloch.

27. *La Libre Parole,* Nov. 17, 1898.

28. Private archives of Emile Mayer. I wish to thank Henri Shapira for allowing me to consult them.

29. See Jérôme Helie, "L'Arche sainte fracturée," in Pierre Birnbaum, ed., *La France de l'affaire Dreyfus* (Paris: Gallimard, 1994).

30. Pierre Quillard, *Le Monument Henry* (Paris: Stock, 1899), pp. 6–7; Stephen Wilson, "Le Monument Henry: La Structure de l'antisémitisme en France, 1898–1800," *Annales,* no. 2, March–April 1977.

31. See Philippe Landau, "Les Juifs de France et la Grande Guerre, 1914–1941: Patrie, République, mémoire," unpublished doctoral thesis, University of Paris VII, 1992.

32. See *La Libre Parole,* July 16, 1902, Feb. 1, 1905, and Sept. 29, 1907.

33. *Archives israélites,* Aug. 17, 1905.
34. *La Libre Parole,* 1905 almanac.

9. JEWS, ITALIANS, AND ARABS

1. Quoted in Michelle Perrot, *Les Ouvriers en grève: France 1871–1890,* vol. 1 (Paris: Mouton, 1974), p. 178.
2. Michelle Perrot, "Les Rapports entre des ouvriers français et des ouvriers étrangers (1871–1892)," *Bulletin de la Société d'histoire moderne* 12 (1960): 12.
3. On violence against Italian immigrants, see Pierre Milza, "L'Emigration italienne en France de 1870 à 1914"; Jean-Charles Bonnet, "Les Italiens dans l'agglomération lyonnaise à l'aube de la Belle Epoque"; and Teodosio Vertone, "Antécédents et causes des événements d'Aigues-Mortes," all in Jean-Baptiste Duroselle and Enrico Serra, eds., *L'emigrazione italiana in Francia prima del 1914* (Milan: Franco Angeli, 1978). See also Abel Chatelain, *Les Migrants temporaires en France de 1800 à 1914,* vol. 1 (Lille: Publications de l'Université de Lille, 1976), pp. 869 ff.; Yves Lequin, *Les Ouvriers de la région lyonnaise, 1848–1914,* vol. 2 (Lyons: Presses Universitaires de Lyon, 1977), pp. 90 ff.; Yves Lequin, ed., *La Mosaïque France* (Paris: Larousse, 1988), p. 389; Serge Bonnet and Roger Humbert, *La Ligne rouge des hauts fourneaux* (Paris: Denoël, 1981), chap. 14; Gérard Noiriel, *Le Creuset français* (Paris: Editions du Seuil, 1988), pp. 258 ff.; Pierre Milza, *Voyage en Italie* (Paris: Plon, 1993), chap. 4.
4. The number of Jewish immigrants from Eastern Europe who entered France between 1881 and 1914 has been estimated at 30,000, versus 1,974,000 who entered the United States and 120,000 who entered Great Britain. See Paula Hyman, *From Dreyfus to Vichy: The Remaking of French Jewry, 1906–1939* (New York: Columbia University Press, 1979). Although the number of Jewish immigrants in France rose in the 1920s, there were relatively few at the time of the Dreyfus Affair. Note, by comparison, that more than 200,000 Italian workers entered France between 1870 and 1891. On the expulsion of Jewish immigrants and the concomitant rise of anti-Semitism, see Nancy Green, *Les Travailleurs immigrés juifs à la Belle Epoque* (Paris: Fayard, 1986), pp. 66 ff.; and Béatrice Philippe, *Les Juifs à Paris à la Belle Epoque* (Paris: Albin Michel, 1992), chaps. 1 and 2.
5. Commission Nationale Consultative des Droits de l'Homme, *1993: La Lutte contre le racisme et la xénophobie* (Paris: La Documentation Française, 1994), and *1994: La Lutte contre le racisme et la xénophobie* (Paris: La Documentation Française, 1994), p. 21.
6. Emile Témine, "Espagnols et Italiens en France," in Pierre Milza and Denis Peschanski, eds., *Exils et migrations: Italiens et Espagnols en France, 1938–1946* (Paris: L'Harmattan, 1994), p. 27.

7. See chapter 12 below.
8. See Commission Nationale, *1994*, pp. 51 ff.
9. Nonna Mayer, "Racisme et antisémitisme dans l'opinion publique française," in Pierre-André Taguieff, ed., *Face au racisme*, vol. 2 (Paris: La Découverte, 1991), p. 71.
10. See chapter 12 below.

10. On Secularism

1. More than six thousand people took part in this demonstration. See *Libération*, Jan. 17, 1994; *Le Monde*, Jan. 18, 1994; and *Le Canard enchaîné*, Jan. 19, 1994.
2. *Le Monde*, Nov. 18, 1993.
3. CRIF, Political Study Committee review of the press, Nov. 23, 1993.
4. Erik Cohen, *L'Etude et l'éducation juive en France* (Paris: Le Cerf, 1991), pp. 25–27.
5. *Le Monde*, June 30, 1994.
6. *Libération*, Feb. 10, 1995.
7. *Le Monde*, Nov. 17, 1989; *Libération*, Nov. 17, 1989; *L'Est républicain*, Nov. 17, 1989. The last-named paper featured a headline that read: "Aix, the Poison of Anti-Semitism."
8. See Emile Poulat, *Liberté, laïcité: La Guerre des deux France et la principe de la modernité* (Paris: Le Cerf, 1987), pp. 255 ff.
9. Adolphe Crémieux, *Victor Hugo contre Falloux* (Paris: Brochure, 1994), pp. 59, 67. This publication contains the text of the debate on the Falloux Law.
10. *L'Univers israélite*, Sept. 1850 and Jan. 1851.
11. *Archives israélites*, Nov. 1850.
12. Ibid., Feb. and Dec. 1851.
13. Perrine Simon-Nahum, *La Cité investie: La "Science du judaïsme" française et la République* (Paris: Le Cerf, 1991).
14. Jules Ferry, *Discours et opinions de Jules Ferry*, vol. 4 (Paris: Armand Colin, 1896), p. 127.
15. See Pierre Birnbaum, *Les Fous de la République: Histoire politique des Juifs d'Etat, de Gambetta à Vichy* (Paris: Editions du Seuil, 1994), chap. 9, trans. by Jane M. Todd as *The Jews of the Republic: A Political History of State Jews in France from Gambetta to Vichy* (Stanford, Calif.: Stanford University Press, 1996).
16. See Phyllis Cohen Albert, "Israelite and Jew: How Did Nineteenth-Century French Jews Understand Assimilation?," in Jonathan Frankel and Steven Zipperstein, eds., *Assimilation and Community: The Jews in Nineteenth-Century Europe* (Cambridge: Cambridge University Press, 1992); and Phyllis Cohen Albert, "L'Intégration et la persistance de l'ethnicité chez les Juifs dans la

France moderne," in Pierre Birnbaum, ed., *Histoire politique des Juifs de France* (Paris: Presses de la Fondation Nationale des Sciences Politiques, 1990). Paula Hyman describes "the resistance" of the Jews of Alsace in the nineteenth century to univeralist assimilation in *The Emancipation of the Jews of Alsace: Acculturation and Tradition in the Nineteenth Century* (New Haven: Yale University Press, 1991). See also Martine Cohen, "De l'émancipation à l'intégration: Les Transformations du judaïsme français au XIXe siècle," *Archives des sciences sociales des religions,* July–Sept. 1994.

17. See Yves Déloye, *Ecole et citoyenneté: L'Individualisme républicain de Jules Ferry à Vichy* (Paris: Presses de la Fondation Nationale des Sciences Politiques, 1994).

18. *Archives israélites,* Sept. 25, 1871, p. 429.

19. Ibid., Jan. 5 and April 13, 1905.

20. *L'Univers israélite,* July 14, 1905.

21. Ibid., June 30, 1905. See also June 16, 1905.

22. Ibid., Dec. 30, 1904, and Jan. 12, 1906. See also Dec. 2, 1904, July 28, 1905, and Aug. 25, 1905. Jay Berkovitz cites statements made by Jewish dignitaries opposed to separation in *The Shaping of Jewish Identity in Nineteenth-Century France* (Detroit: Wayne State University Press, 1989), pp. 238 ff.

23. *L'Univers israélite,* Feb. 6, 1906.

24. Ibid., March 24, 1905.

25. *Archives israélites,* March 16, 1905. See also July 6, 1905, in which Prague expresses the hope that these future difficulties will make it possible to combat the "decay" in French Jews' "spirit of responsibility."

26. Ibid., Oct. 27, 1904.

27. *Le Monde,* Nov. 11, 1989.

28. Ibid., Feb. 23, 1994.

29. Ibid., April 3, 1995.

30. Ibid., April 17, 1995.

31. Ibid., Nov. 11, 1989, and Nov. 1, 1993.

32. Ibid., Nov. 19, 1993.

33. See the chapter entitled "From Mao to Moses" in Judith Friedlander, *Vilna on the Seine: Jewish Intellectuals in France since 1968* (New Haven: Yale University Press, 1990).

34. Cohen, *L'Etude et l'éducation juive,* p. 31.

35. Zosa Szajkowski, *Jewish Education in France, 1789–1939* (New York: Columbia University Press, 1980).

36. See Laurence Podselver, "La Tradition réinventée: Les Hassidim de Loubavitch en France," *Revue des études juives,* July–Dec. 1992, p. 448.

37. *La Croix,* April 13, 1989.

38. *Le Monde,* Nov. 18, 1993.

39. See Stéphane Arfi and Jérôme Guilbert, "Les Rabbins et la politique," paper

located in the library of the Institut d'Etudes Politiques of Paris, 1989. See also a more concise report on this research, "Les Rabbins et la politique: Autorités sacerdotales et représentations," *Pardès* 14 (1991).

40. *La Tribune juive*, Dec. 2, 1993, compares the situation of the imam today today to that of the rabbi at the end of the nineteenth century.

41. See Jean-Marc Chouraqui, "De l'émancipation des Juifs à l'émancipation du judaisme: Le Regard des rabbins français du XIXe siècle," in Birnbaum, ed., *Histoire politique.*

42. *Le Monde*, Oct. 21, 1989.

43. Renée David, "Juifs et musulmans à l'école laïque: Deux Poids, deux mesures?," *Panoramiques*, no. 7, 4th quarter of 1992. The entire issue is devoted to the theme of "Religious Jews: From the Religious to the Cultural?"

44. *Le Monde*, Oct. 25, 1989.

45. Ibid., Feb. 23, 1990.

46. *Le Nouvel Observateur*, Nov. 2, 1989. Somewhat later, the historian Jacques Le Goff observed, "They mentioned Munich. If I were to allow myself to speak as loosely as they do, I might speak of a Maginot Line of secularism. And everybody knows what Maginot Lines are worth." ("Derrière le foulard, l'Histoire," *Le Débat*, Jan.–Feb. 1990, p. 28.)

47. *Libération*, Dec. 13, 1989. Elisabeth Badinter made a similar statement: "There is a sweeping religious offensive under way in France and elsewhere, and most notably a fundamentalist offensive. Among Jewish children, for example, the number who wear skullcaps to public schools is growing, a fact that I deplore." (*Le Nouvel Observateur*, Nov. 9, 1989.)

48. *Le Nouvel Observateur*, Nov. 2, 1989. See also David Beriss, "Scarves, Schools and Segregation: The Foulard Affair," *French Politics and Society,* Winter 1990.

49. Dominique Schnapper and Chantal Benayoun, "Citoyenneté républicaine et spécificité juive," *Les Nouveaux Cahiers*, Summer 1989, p. 8. See also Dominique Schnapper, "Les Juifs et la nation," in Birnbaum, ed., *Histoire politique.*

50. "Le Double Schisme," *Les Nouveaux Cahiers*, no. 111, Winter 1992–93. See also the reactions published in no. 114, Autumn 1993.

51. "La Communauté juive est-elle menacée de l'intérieur?," *Les Nouveaux Cahiers*, no. 112, Spring 1993.

52. Martine Cohen, "Les Juifs de France: Affirmations identitaires en évolution du modèle d'intégration," *Le Débat*, May–Aug. 1993; Renée David, "Le Renouveau juif laïque en France," *Les Nouveaux Cahiers*, no. 114, Autumn 1993.

53. *Le Nouvel Observateur*, June 9, 1994.

54. *Le Monde*, June 16, 1994.

55. CRIF, Political Study Committee, review of the press, May 20, 1994.

56. *Le Monde*, June 26, 1994.

57. Ibid., Nov. 22, 1994.

58. *Le Figaro*, March 20, 1995.

11. IDENTITY AND PUBLIC SPACE

1. See, for example, Will Kymlicka, *Liberalism, Community, and Culture* (Oxford: Clarendon, 1991); and Stephen Mulhall and Adam Swift, *Liberals and Communitarians* (Oxford: Basil Blackwell, 1992).

2. John Rawls, *Political Liberalism* (New York: Columbia University Press, 1993).

3. See Charles Taylor, ed., *Multiculturalism and the Politics of Recognition* (Princeton: Princeton University Press, 1992); and Amy Gutmann, "The Challenge of Multiculturalism in Political Ethics," *Philosophy and Public Affairs* 22 (1993).

4. Bertrand Badie and Pierre Birnbaum, *Sociologie de l'Etat* (Paris: Pluriel, 1982), trans. by Arthur Goldhammer as *The Sociology of the State* (Chicago: University of Chicago Press, 1989); Rogers Brubaker, *Citizenship and Nationhood in France and Germany* (Cambridge, Mass.: Harvard University Press, 1992).

5. Pierre Birnbaum, "Du multiculturalisme au nationalisme," in *La Pensée politique* (Paris: Gallimard/Seuil, 1995).

6. Robert Paxton's *Vichy France: Old Guard and New Order, 1940–1944* (New York: Alfred A. Knopf, 1972), published in French translation in 1973, was the first book to emphasize the responsibility of the Vichy government in the arrest and deporation of Jews. It provoked a vigorous debate in France, with some reactions verging on the xenophobic. Henry Rousso, *Le Syndrome de Vichy* (Paris: Editions du Seuil, 1987), trans. into English by Arthur Goldhammer as *The Vichy Syndrome* (Cambridge, Mass.: Harvard University Press, 1992), revealed the durability of the Vichy syndrome.

7. On these events, see Henry Weinberg, *The Myth of the Jew in France, 1967–1982* (Oakville, Ont.: Mosaic Press, 1987); and Maurice Szafran, *Les Juifs dans la politique française* (Paris: Flammarion, 1990).

8. Jacques Rondin, *Le Sacre des notables* (Paris: Fayard, 1985); Vivien Schmidt, *Democratizing France: The Political and Administrative History of Decentralization* (Cambridge: Cambridge University Press, 1990).

9. See *Le Monde,* March 2, 5, 10, and 16, 1994; *L'Express,* March 17, 1994; *La Tribune juive,* March 24, 1994.

10. Dominique Schnapper and Sylvie Strudel, "Le 'Vote juif' en France," *Revue française de science politique,* Dec. 1983.

11. Laurence Podselver, "Le Retour juif à Sarcelles," *Hommes et migrations,* Nov. 1994.

12. *Le Monde,* April 10, 1990.

13. Sylvie Strudel, "Les Juifs et la politique: Une Etude de cas, Sarcelles ville-loupe," unpublished doctoral thesis, Institut d'Etudes Politiques de Paris, 1991, vol. 2, p. 487.

14. *Le Monde,* April 17, 1995.

15. *Libération,* April 6, 1995.

16. CRIF, Political Study Committee, review of the press, April 7, 1995.

17. See Pascal Perrineau, "Le Front national: 1972–1992," in Michel Winock, ed., *Histoire de l'extrême droite en France* (Paris: Editions du Seuil, 1993).

18. Pierre Birnbaum, *"La France aux Français": Histoire des haines nationalistes* (Paris: Editions du Seuil, 1993).

19. Pierre-André Taguieff, *La Force du préjugé: Essai sur le racisme et ses doubles* (Paris: La Découverte, 1988).

20. F. Dazi and R. Leveau, "L'Intégration par le politique: Le Vote des Beurs," *Etudes,* Sept. 1988.

21. Chantal Benayoun, "Identité et citoyenneté: Juifs, Arabes et Pieds-noirs face aux événements du Golfe," *Revue française de science politique,* April 1993; Chantal Benayoun, "L'Esprit du temps: Les Définitions identitaires chez les Juifs et les Arabes en France," *Revue européenne des migrations internationales* 3 (1993).

22. Commission Nationale Consultative des Droits de l'Homme, *1995: La Lutte centre le racisme et la xénophobie* (Paris: La Documentation Française, 1995), p. 33.

23. Haut Conseil à l'Intégration, *Conditions juridiques et culturelles de l'intégration* (Paris: La Documentation Française, 1992), p. 63. For a recent discussion of this question, see John McKesson, "Concept and Realities in a Multiethnic France," *French Politics and Society,* Spring 1994.

24. Dominique Schnapper, *L'Europe des immigrés* (Paris: François Bourin, 1992), pp. 157–66.

12. Carpentras

1. See *Le Monde, Libération,* and *L'Humanité,* May 12, 1990; *Libération,* May 15, 1990; *La Lettre de la nation,* May 15, 1990.

2. *Le Monde,* May 13–14, 1990, May 15, 1990; *La Croix,* May 15, 1990; *L'Humanité,* May 12, 1990; *Témoignage chrétien,* May 27, 1990; *Le Figaro–Magazine,* May 19, 1990.

3. *Libération,* May 17, 1990; *La Croix,* May 17, 1990.

4. *Le Monde,* May 13–14, 1994. Annie Kriegel had this to say about the phenomenon of communitarization: the Jewish community is "fragile, nervous, haunted. Alas, it is not difficult to perusade it to allow itself to be overprotected, instrumentalized, infantilized, ghettoized, and, worst of all, denationalized, relegated to a separate category which sets it apart from the national community to which it belongs. How insistently the media focused on the three or four Israeli flags in the Bastille parade, flags that had no business being there! How pharisaically they reported the two thousand requests for information concerning emigration to Israel received by the Agence Juive (the same thing happened after Copernic)." (*Le Figaro,* May 19, 1990.)

5. *La Croix*, May 15, 1990; *Libération*, May 14, 1990; *Le Quotidien de Paris*, May 14, 1990; *Le Figaro*, May 14, 1990; *Témoignage chrétien*, May 21, 1990.

6. *Le Quotidien de Paris*, May 15, 1990.

7. *Le Monde*, May 16, 1990.

8. *Libération*, May 14, 1990.

9. This list was compiled from the press archives of the Institut d'Etudes Politiques in Paris. I also used the *Rapport sur l'antisémitisme en France, 1993*, Commission de Recherche et de Documentation sur l'Antisémitisme, 1994.

10. Vandalism in Jewish cemeteries is a regular occurrence in France. See Simon Epstein, *L'Antisémitisme français aujourd'hui et demain* (Paris: Belfond, 1984).

11. *Le Monde*, Nov. 22, 1994.

12. *Le Point*, May 14 and 21, 1990; *Le Figaro*, May 14, 1990; *La Croix*, May 12, 1990; *Le Monde*, May 13 and 18, 1990; *Libération*, May 12 and 17, 1990; *Guardian*, May 19, 1990.

13. *Le Figaro–Magazine*, May 19, 1990. *Le Figaro* also frequently expressed the idea that Carpentras was being used to demonize Le Pen. See the May 15, 1990, issue of the paper, for example. Writing in *Témoignage chrétien* on May 27, 1990, Georges Montaron made the same point: "It would be a mistake to blame this deleterious climate solely on Jean-Marie Le Pen and the National Front." The other quotes are from *Aspects de la France*, May 17, 1990, and *Le Choc du mois*, July–Aug. 1990. In the same issue, one can also read this: "The crowd knew who had committed the ignoble crime. . . . Obviously he should have been stopped on his way out of the TV studio at Antenne 2 and asked to show his fingernails before he had time to clean them. And then a search should have been made of his house before he had time to go to the store and buy a new pedestal for his deck umbrella." See also *Le Quotidien de Paris*, May 15; June 7, 8, and 10; and July 17, 1990. After the big Carpentras demonstration, Raoul Girardet characterized the march as "trumped up" (*factice*): "All this looks like an old trick of the left's, now that it has no principles to defend . . . and nothing more to say, so it has to go around inventing demons [sic] so that it can pose as Saint George and slay them" (*Le Quotidien de Paris*, May 16, 1990). The statement by the Nîmes prosecutor was published in *Le Monde*, June 9, 1990.

14. Nonna Mayer, "L'Affaire Carpentras," *L'Histoire*, Oct. 1991, p. 14.

15. Paul Yonnet, "La Machine Carpentras," *Le Débat*, Sept.–Oct. 1990, p. 21. See also the interview with Yonnet in *Le Point*, Nov. 5, 1990, in which he says, "even if the hypothesis that the whole thing was set up is false, what happened at Carpentras was instinctively reframed by journalists and politicians."

16. Yonnet, "La Machine Carpentras," pp. 21, 23, 25, 26. Yonnet nevertheless rejects the idea that there was a "conspiracy." The point of his article, he says, is to understand how "a social mechanism was constructed, how it created itself in a comprehensible fashion so that all it took was a spark to set off a con-

flagration that was entirely controlled and propagated by the politicians and the media" (*Libération*, Nov. 27, 1990).

17. Yonnet, "La Machine Carpentras," pp. 30–32.

18. *Minute*, Nov. 29, 1990. *Le Point* also devoted a generous amount of space to Yonnet's argument. See the Nov. 5, 1990, issue of the magazine. By contrast, Maurice Szafran rightly noted that Yonnet "cannot tolerate the idea that Jewish Frenchmen are demanding their share of memory, that they have not yet fully digested the Pétainist episode, and that they still want to know more about Auschwitz" (*L'Evénement du jeudi*, Dec. 6, 1990).

19. *Le Figaro–Magazine*, Nov. 17, 1990.

20. *La Quotidien de Paris*, May 14, 1990; *Le Monde*, Oct. 31, 1990.

21. Nonna Mayer, "Carpentras, machine arrière," *Commentaire*, Nov. 1990, p. 80. See also Nonna Mayer, "Carpentras and the Media," *Patterns of Prejudice* 1 (1991). Léon Poliakov argues, in *Patterns of Prejudice* 2 (1991), p. 58, that the comparison of Jewish behavior with the Lepenist movement is "grotesque," See also Nelly Hansson, "France: The Carpentras Syndrome and Beyond," *Patterns of Prejudice* 1 (1991). According to the *Rapport sur l'antisémitisme*, 1993, p. 33, Paul Yonnet allegedly participated in the 1993 Salon du Livre d'Assas at the Université d'Assas, where he appeared along with Jean Madiran and François Brigneau.

22. Jean Bothorel, "Machineries infernales," *Le Figaro*, Dec. 4, 1990.

23. See *Libération*, Nov. 9 and 27, 1990; *Le Nouvel Observateur*, May 23, 1991. In his response, Alexandre Adler wrote: "And it is this French Jewish community, as assimilated and cautious as any community ever was, that is being accused of extremism and particularism!" (*Le Nouvel Observateur*, June 26, 1991.)

CONCLUSION

1. See Philippe Landau, "Les Juifs de France et la Grande Guerre, 1914–1941: Patrie, République, mémoire," unpublished doctoral thesis, University of Paris VII, 1992.

2. In the voluminous *Dictionnaire critique de la Révolution française*, ed. François Furet and Mona Ozouf (Paris: Flammarion, 1988), trans. into English by Arthur Goldhammer as *The Critical Dictionary of the French Revolution* (Cambridge, Mass.: Harvard University Press, 1990), there is no entry dealing with the historical and philosophical debate about the emancipation of the Jews. The name of Abbé Grégoire is mentioned several times but never in connection with his role in granting citizenship to Jews. Nor is there any article on Jewish emancipation in another massive encyclopedia of the Revolution edited by a member of the opposing school, Michel Vovelle: *Révolution et République: L'Exception francaise* (Paris: Kimé, 1994).

3. See Shmuel Trigano, *La République et les Juifs* (Paris: Presses d'Aujourd'hui, 1982), p. 44. Théo Klein takes a similar position, condemning the "cultural

homogenization" imposed by the Jacobins, in Gérard Belloin, ed., *Entendez-vous dans vos mémoires* (Paris: La Découverte, 1988), pp. 82–83. For a different view, see Robert Badinter, *Libres et égaux* (Paris: Fayard, 1989).

4. On certain aspects of this discussion, see Laurent Gervereau and Christophe Prochassin, *L'Affaire Dreyfus, 1894–1910* (Paris: Musée d'Histoire Contemporaine, BDIC, 1994).

5. See Philippe Burrin, *La France à l'heure allemande* (Paris: Editions du Seuil, 1995), p. 325. Burrin soberly characterizes this as "a monumental but unsurprising gaffe." Note, however, that Renée Poznanski explains the survival of the majority of French Jews as "the effect of 150 years of emancipation, whose surface manifestations a government suppress but whose deep roots it cannot, even with massive support, eradicate, especially when it attempts to do so in the shadow of an occupying force" (*Etre juif en France pendant la Seconde Guerre mondiale* [Paris: Hachette, 1994], p. 708).

6. "Juger sous Vichy," *Le Genre humain*, no. 28, Nov. 1994.

7. See "L'Encadrement juridique de l'antisémitisme sous le régime de Vichy," colloquium held at the Faculté de Droit et de Sciences Politiques of the Université de Dijon, Dec. 1994.

8. Eric Conan and Henry Rousso, *Vichy: Un Passé qui ne passe pas* (Paris: Fayard, 1994), p. 65.

9. Annette Wieviorka, *Déportation et génocide: Entre la mémoire et l'oubli* (Paris: Pluriel, 1995), p. 436. Note that, after Paul Touvier was found guilty and sentenced to life in prison, *Le Monde* (April 23, 1995) wrote; "The Jewish community is all but unanimous in rejecting anything that might resemble an erasure of the past. . . . On the matter of memory, the Jewish community finds the president's hot-and-cold attitude irritating. It was glad that he went to Izieu to commemorate the deportation of forty-four Jewish children on orders from Klaus Barbie. But it was outraged when he advocated 'forgetting about' men like Paul Touvier, René Bousquet, and Maurice Papon. . . . The Jewish community is puzzled." This article is yet another instance of communitarization from above.

10. *Le Monde,* Sept. 14, 1994.

AFTERWORD

1. SOFRES, "Sondage pour le CRIF," Nov. 1998. See also *Le Monde*, Nov. 27, 1998.

2. Marc Olivier Baruch, *Servir l'Etat français: L'Administration en France de 1940 à 1944* (Paris: Fayard, 1997).

3. *Le Monde,* July 17, 1997.

4. Ibid., Oct. 2, 1997.

5. Pierre Birnbaum, *La France imaginée: Déclin des rêves unitaires* (Paris: Fayard, 1998).

6. Annette Wieviorka, "Un Lieu de mémoire: Le Mémorial au martyr Juif in-connu," *Pardès* 2 (1985). On p. 87, the author notes, "This monument has given rise to a ritual whose genealogy is not Jewish but secular and republi-can."

7. Phyllis Cohen Albert, "L'Intégration et la persistance de l'ethnicité chez les Juifs dans la France moderne," in Pierre Birnbaum, ed., *Histoire politique des Juifs de France* (Paris: Presses de la Fondation Nationale des Sciences Poli-tiques, 1990).

8. See Anita Shapira, "The Holocaust: Private Memories, Public Memories," *Jewish Social Studies,* Winter 1998.

9. Eric Conan and Henry Rousso, *Vichy, un passé qui ne passe pas* (Paris: Fayard, 1994); Henry Rousso, *La Hantise du passé: Entretien avec Philippe Petit* (Paris: Editions Textuel, 1998).

10. See, for example, Pascal Perrineau, *Le Symptôme Le Pen* (Paris: Fayard, 1998).

11. *La Vie,* Feb. 24, 1994; *La Tribune juive,* Feb. 16, 1995.

12. Quoted in Florent Brayard, *Comment l'idée vint à M. Rassinier: Naissance du révisionnisme* (Paris: Fayard, 1996), p. 443, which sets forth the debate on this issue in French society. See also Nadine Fresco, *Fabrication d'un antisémite* (Paris: Editions du Seuil, 1999).

13. See the reactions to the publication of Stéphane Courtois, *Le Livre noir du communisme* (Paris: Editions du Seuil, 1997).

14. Chantal Benayoun, *Les Juifs et la politique* (Paris: Centre National de Recherche Scientifique, 1984); Annette Benveniste, *Le Bosphore à la Roquette: La Communauté judéo-espagnole à Paris* (Paris: L'Harmattan, 1989); Sylvie Strudel, *Votes juifs* (Paris: Presses de la Fondation Nationale des Sci-ences Politiques, 1996); Laurence Podslever, "La Séparation, la redondance et l'identité: Les Hassidim de Lubavitch à Paris," *Pardès* 7 (1988); Laurence Podslever, "Les Lubavitch et la question de l'Etat: Défiance traditionnelle et pragmatisme messianique," in Birnbaum, ed., *Histoire politique des Juifs de France;* Pierre Birnbaum, "Grégoire, Dreyfus, Drancy et Copernic: Les Juifs au coeur de l'histoire de France," in Pierre Nora, ed., *Les Lieux de mémoire: Les France, I* (Paris: Gallimard); Véronique Poirier, *Ashkénazes et Séfarades: Une Etude comparée de leurs relations en France et en Israël (1950–1990)* (Paris: Le Cerf, 1998); Jean-Jacques Becker and Annette Wieviorka, eds., *Les Juifs de France de la Révolution française à nos jours* (Paris: Liana Levi, 1998); "Carrefours français," *Les Cahiers du Judaïsme,* no. 3, 1998.

15. Yosef Yerushalmi, *Zakhor, Jewish History and Jewish Memory* (Seattle: Uni-versity of Washington Press, 1982). See the observations of David Myers, "Of Marranos and Memory: Yosef Hayim Yerushalmi and the Writing of Jewish History," in E. Carlebach, J. Elfron, and D. Myers, eds., *Jewish History and Jewish Memory: Essays in Honor of Yosef Hayim Yerushalmi* (Waltham, Mass.: Brandeis University Press, 1998), pp. 11 ff.

INDEX